SWEET TASTE OF LIBERTY

SWEET TASTE OF LIBERTY

A TRUE STORY OF SLAVERY AND RESTITUTION IN AMERICA

W. CALEB MCDANIEL

OXFORD
UNIVERSITY PRESS

OXFORD

UNIVERSITY PRESS

Oxford University Press is a department of the University of Oxford.
It furthers the University's objective of excellence in research, scholarship,
and education by publishing worldwide. Oxford is a registered trade mark of
Oxford University Press in the UK and certain other countries.

Published in the United States of America by Oxford University Press
198 Madison Avenue, New York, NY 10016, United States of America.

Library of Congress Cataloging-in-Publication Data
Names: McDaniel, W. Caleb (William Caleb), 1979– author.
Title: Sweet taste of liberty : a true story of slavery and restitution in
America / W. Caleb McDaniel.
Description: New York, NY : Oxford University Press, [2019] | Includes
biblioographical references and index.
Identifiers: LCCN 2018047090 | ISBN 9780190846992 (hardcover : alk. paper)
Subjects: LCSH: Wood, Henrietta, approximately 1818/20–1912. |
Slaves—Kentucky—Biography. | Women slaves—Kentucky—Biography. |
Freedmen—Ohio—Cincinnati--Biography. | Wood, Henrietta, approximately
1818/20–1912—Trials, litigation, etc. | Trials
(Kidnapping)—Ohio—Cincinnati. | African
Americans—Reparations—History—19th century.
Classification: LCC E444.W815 M35 2019 | DDC 306.3/62092
[B]—dc23 LC record available at https://lccn.loc.gov/2018047090

1 3 5 7 9 8 6 4 2

Printed by Sheridan Books, Inc.
United States of America

In Memory of Winona Adkins (1944–2018)
Great-great-granddaughter of Henrietta Wood

[She] saw her life like a great tree in leaf with the things suffered, things enjoyed, things done and undone. Dawn and doom was in the branches.

—Zora Neale Hurston
Their Eyes Were Watching God

CONTENTS

CONTENTS

SWEET TASTE OF LIBERTY

THE WORLD OF
HENRIETTA WOOD

- - - Gerard Brandon's
       Flight to Texas

MICHIGAN

Chicago

IOWA

ILLINOIS

INDIANA   OHIO

Area of Detail
Cincinnati

KANSAS TERRITORY

MISSOURI

Louisville
                 Lexington

Ohio River

KENTUCKY

Arkansas River

Mississippi River

TENNESSEE

Nashville

INDIAN TERRITORY

Little Rock

ARKANSAS

MISSISSIPPI   ALABAMA

TEXAS

LOUISIANA

Natchez

Sabinetown   Alexandria

Brandon's
Camp

Brazos River

New Orleans

Gulf of Mexico

0   100   200

Miles

N
W   E
S

Map 1

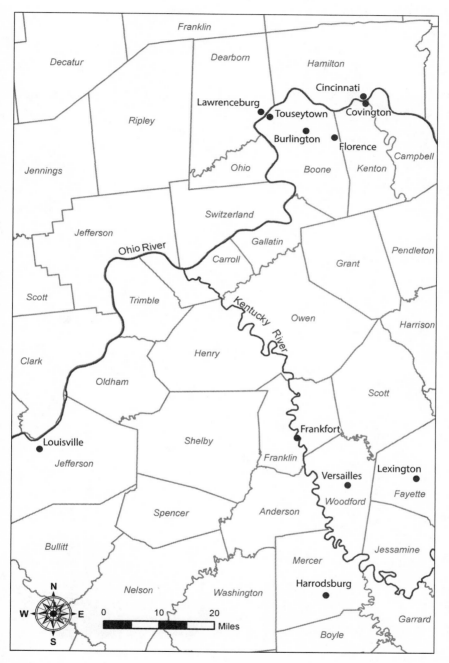

Map 2

PROLOGUE

Zebulon Ward of Arkansas liked to say that he was the last American ever to pay for a slave.

It would have been a "doubtful honor" even if it were true, as one newspaper said about Ward in 1887. Ward's story, however, was dubious itself, and the true story brought him no honor at all. Eight years before the Civil War began, he had kidnapped a free woman and sold her as a slave. After the war, she had sued him for an enormous amount of money, arguing that she deserved reparations for her enslavement. But Ward preferred to tell his own version of the facts, making himself out to be "The Last Slave Buyer." Many who heard his story would never learn the truth.[1]

Tall and broad-shouldered, with a cropped, gray beard, Ward was well known by the 1880s as a man with a knack for spinning yarns, perhaps "the most unique raconteur south of the Mason and Dixon." Some said he looked like Ulysses S. Grant and had even impersonated the ex-president at a party both men attended. True or not, that was the kind of story he loved to tell, and Ward's stories often made their way into the press. "Portions of his history are like a romance," wrote one reporter in 1888.[2]

By then Ward was one of the richest men in the South, having made his fortune leasing state prisons in the region. He claimed to have served in two wars, and some called him "Colonel." He may have been most famous, though, as a horseracing enthusiast, a "man of the turf." Before settling in Arkansas, Zeb Ward had raised Thoroughbreds in his native state, Kentucky, and at one race held in 1863, his horse had been the only one to hear the starter's signal: the filly won while the other horses stayed at the starting line. Delighted by his luck, Zeb had pocketed the stakes—along with another anecdote for his repertoire.[3]

He found a perfect stage for his stories in 1887, during a long stay at New York's St. James Hotel. Located on Broadway and Twenty-sixth Street, the hotel had a popular bar for actors, socialites, and turfmen such as E. Berry Wall, the dandyish "King of the Dudes" who claimed to have introduced the cocktail and the tuxedo to Americans. As a raconteur himself, Ward felt right at home, and reporters found him at the hotel in a "reminiscent mood." Most evenings, admirers crowded around to hear his stories, told with an "old-school eloquence" that drew listeners in. And no story impressed them more than the one about how he allegedly became "the last man in this country to pay for a negro slave."[4]

The story was brief, according to Ward, and it had the feel of an anecdote he must have told before. This time, though, a reporter in the audience wrote it down.

> Colonel Zeb Ward, of Little Rock, Ark., who has been warden of three state penitentiaries, declares that he was the last man to pay for a negro slave in this country, and that was the result of a suit brought against him a few years ago by a woman slave whom he wished to set free, but who remained with him during a long dispute in the courts regarding her ownership. She sued for remuneration for six years' service after the emancipation act, and gained a verdict. Colonel Ward says that in making out the draft for the amount found he worded it: "To pay for the last negro that will ever be paid for in this country."[5]

That account soon traveled far beyond New York. Within days, it had been reprinted in cities across the country: Cleveland, Chicago, New Orleans, San Francisco. Then the story kept spreading, even though it was mostly false.[6]

At least one person could have corrected the record, however: the woman who remained nameless in Ward's popular account. Unbeknownst to him, she was living in Chicago in 1887, along with a son who had just begun attending law school there. And had anyone told *her* what Ward said in New York, she would have told them a very different story.

Her name was Henrietta Wood. Her story began in Kentucky. She was born there, enslaved by a man named Tousey, and then sold twice in her youth before being taken to New Orleans. Eventually, she was brought north to Cincinnati, Ohio, where Wood's mistress at the time declared that she was free. That happened in April of 1848. But in 1853, as she was settling into freedom, Wood was kidnapped in a carriage, taken back to Kentucky, and reenslaved by a stranger—Zebulon Ward.

Ward sold Wood to a slave trader who took her to Mississippi, and a cotton planter who bought her there later moved her to Texas—facts that Ward did not mention in his story at the St. James. Far from wishing to free her, he had captured and sold a woman who was already free. He thereby doomed her not to "six years' service," as his version had it, but to more than a decade of reenslavement in the Deep South. As a result, Wood's son would be born into slavery, too, in 1856. Neither of them would be freed until after the Civil War.

Even then, freedom proved to be a fragile thing. Twice enslaved and twice freed, Wood knew how easily a doom could follow dawn. Later, as she was looking back upon her eventful life, she would even describe her few years in antebellum Ohio as a "sweet taste of liberty," as if freedom could only be sampled in sips. By 1869, a few years after she had tasted liberty again, Wood only had about $25 to her name. But she used that money to return from the South to Cincinnati, the city she had called home sixteen years before, and the next year, she filed a lawsuit against Ward for what he had done. Her suit demanded $20,000 in damages and lost wages.[7]

The case was ultimately heard by a federal court in Ohio, showing just how much had changed because of the Civil War. Before the war, a Supreme Court chief justice had famously declared that people of African descent could not be citizens or file suit in a federal court. The Civil Rights Act of 1866 and the Fourteenth Amendment to the Constitution, adopted in 1868, rejected that view and extended national citizenship to former slaves such as Wood. Then, in 1878, after almost a decade of litigation in the twilight of Reconstruction, Henrietta Wood won her case against Zebulon Ward—to his great embarrassment and the amazement of all. The amount she won was $2,500—far below what her lawsuit had asked, and even lower than what a man like Ward could have paid, but still much more than other former slaves had received.[8]

It remains the largest known sum ever awarded by a US court in restitution for slavery.

Wood's suit never would have happened, much less ended the way that it did, without her determination to tell her own story. She started telling it in the earliest hours after her abduction. She told it to the lawyers who filed her postwar suit. And she also gave long interviews to two Ohio reporters, which make it possible even now to piece together her story. One was published in 1879 in the *Ripley Bee*, a small paper in a town with a long Underground Railroad history. The other appeared three years earlier in the *Cincinnati Commercial*, thanks to a staff reporter named Lafcadio Hearn.[9]

The encounter with Hearn was especially fortunate and fateful. An immigrant born to a Greek mother and a British father, Hearn left Ohio not long after his interview with Wood, eventually moving to Japan and becoming a celebrated writer there under the name Koizumi Yakumo. He got his start as a bohemian and a journalist in Cincinnati, where he earned a reputation, as Hearn himself put it, for writing about "the Odd, the Queer, the Strange, the Exotic." Hearn's taste for strange tales led him to slaughterhouses and séances, as well as to dingy tanyards and waterfront bars. He was also noted, however, for collecting tales from African Americans living along the river, most of them in a poor neighborhood where few reporters went. That was how he met Wood in 1876.[10]

Hearn described Wood to his readers as a "powerful woman, probably at least six feet in height," tall enough to look Zeb Ward in the eye. One of the stories she related told of the time when Ward's wife tried to whip her. "Guess not," Wood replied, "it takes men to whip me." The power of her memory was what most amazed Hearn, a man with indistinct memories of his own troubled childhood and a distinct interest in stories about American slavery. Before joining the *Commercial*, Hearn had scandalized his white friends by marrying a woman of color, another former slave. Her name was Alethea Foley, also known as "Mattie," and although she and Hearn soon split up, she later told another reporter how they met. Foley was working as a cook in the boardinghouse where Hearn stayed, and he often "found his way to the kitchen and spent hours talking to Alethea of the misery of her youth in slavery."[11]

Wood also decided to entrust her story to Hearn, a story that made claims about what she was due. "Doubtless there are many ex-slaves in this and other cities whose experiences have been not less bitter or less eventful," Hearn said, introducing "Story of a Slave" in the *Commercial*, "but these seldom care to speak of their life before freedom, or can remember the incidents of such a life so fully." Hearn concluded with a brief summary of her suit against Ward, noting that she "did not forget who had wronged her."[12]

Hearn was right: Henrietta Wood did not forget. But her interviews do not contain everything that she remembered. Unlike Ward or Hearn, she could not read or write, and she did not have the kinds of public platforms they enjoyed. She relied on a few white men to put her story to paper, and much was undoubtedly lost in that translation. Although Hearn assured his readers that he presented Wood's story "just as it was told," he also admitted to leaving out some parts that he deemed "too horrible for publication." He removed "some vernacular peculiarities" as well. And there were other facts of her life—such as the origins of her surname—that she never shared or he did not record. Minor errors marred the interviews, too. Hearn heard the name of Wood's first owner as "Moses Tauser." Three years later, the *Bee* reporter heard the last name as "Touci." Moses Tousey was the man's actual name.[13]

There were also things that Wood herself did not know for certain. "I can't quite tell my age," she told Hearn in 1876, but she guessed that she was "about fifty eight or fifty nine years old," meaning she was born around 1818. Another record from late in her life put her birth in 1820. She told Hearn she was "about fourteen" the first time she was sold, and that was in 1834, the year Tousey died.[14]

Both interviews nevertheless contain a wealth of details about Wood's life, many of which can be filled out with other sources, too. And although the restitution that she eventually won was rare, her experiences in slavery were far more representative. If the stories of enslaved women were less well known in the nineteenth century than stories such as Ward's, the reason had little to do with what women were able or willing to recall. It had more to do with what others at the time were willing to hear.[15]

Unlike the story that Ward told at the St. James, neither of Wood's interviews was ever widely reprinted. For decades they were forgotten, except among collectors of the writings of Lafcadio Hearn, all of whom were more interested in him than in her. Although her legal victory was widely reported in 1878 and 1879, the general public had already forgotten Wood a few years later, when Ward trotted his version out for barflies on Broadway. No one knew her on the street; no image of her exists. Ward's story did not even give Wood's name, and no one who published his version supplied it.[16]

It is no surprise, then, that she quickly fell into obscurity. Only two decades after slavery had ended, most Americans preferred to hear "last slave" stories such as Ward's, stories that emphasized progress and expiated guilt by relegating slavery to the nation's fading past. Wood's pursuit of damages argued for a less popular view: that the past might make continuing claims on the present. As the *New York Times* noted in 1878 when it reported the decision, her victory raised larger questions about slavery's aftermath: "Who will recompense the millions of men and women for the years of liberty of which they have been defrauded? Who will make good to the thousands of kidnapped freemen the agony, distress, and bondage of a lifetime?" The suit was about more than Henrietta Wood alone. It was about what former slaves were owed for their enslavement, as well as about the real differences that restitution could make. Where had men such as Ward gotten all their wealth? Where, for that matter, had the country gotten its riches? And what could the amount that Wood won do for families like hers? What did freedom mean without restitution for slavery?[17]

By 1887, however, such questions did not interest very many white Americans. Most, even in the North, believed that ex-slaves were owed nothing more than emancipation. It had taken a costly civil war to abolish slavery, and even some Americans who supported abolition believed that those who had been freed owed the nation in return. The idea of reparations had few friends—and powerful enemies. When a national organization of former slaves arose in the 1890s to advocate reparations, led by a woman named Callie House, it withered under a combination of public indifference and aggressive harassment by federal officials. Meanwhile, white southerners devised new ways to exploit freed people, such as the convict leasing regimes that Zebulon Ward helped pioneer.[18]

When Wood's life ended in 1912, the dream of reparations for slavery therefore seemed as unlikely as ever. It seemed no more likely in 1951, when Arthur H. Simms, the son she bore in Mississippi, died at the age of ninety-five, having practiced law in Chicago for more than fifty years. But Simms's life as a lawyer was made possible in part by the money that his mother had managed to win, an amount worth more than $60,000 today. As a woman who had been enslaved only a few years before her suit, she confronted odds that were longer by far than any that Ward ever faced, and her victory was not even assured by the time she was interviewed. Her conversation with Hearn took place before the case concluded. And in her last recorded words to the *Ripley Bee*, Wood said she was still waiting for Ward to "pass over them checks."[19]

Nonetheless, a check did eventually come, establishing for both Wood and Ward unique places in history. Contrary to what Ward later would claim at the St. James Hotel, he was not the last American to pay for a slave. He was among the very few, and perhaps the very last, to pay a former slave for having enslaved her. The true story, the one that Ward did not want to tell, was that of a black woman who survived enslavement twice—and then made a powerful white man pay.

PART I

THE WORST SLAVE
OF THEM ALL

CHAPTER ONE

THE CROSSING

The blinds had been drawn and buttoned over all of the carriage windows. In hindsight, that should have been the very first sign of trouble. "Still, I never suspected," Henrietta Wood told Lafcadio Hearn more than two decades later, after she had finally returned to Cincinnati. Otherwise, she might not have left behind in her room the papers that proved she was free.[1]

Rebecca Boyd, her employer at the time, was the one who suggested the carriage ride to Covington, Kentucky, on the southern side of the Ohio River. "Henrietta," Wood recalled her saying, the memory of that day still vivid in her mind, "I want you to come over the river with me; I have some friends to see, and we can get back in time for supper."[2]

Before that Sunday in April 1853, Wood had been working for Boyd for only about three months. She cleaned the rooms in the boardinghouse that Boyd ran on Fourth Street in Cincinnati. And every day she wondered whether she would be paid for her work. Boyd's husband, a dentist, had an easier time yanking teeth from patients than Wood had pulling a wage from his wife—the worst employer Henrietta had known in the five years since she was freed. Boyd kept saying that she would pay, but Wood had not seen a cent.[3]

Wood might have believed that Sunday would be different. Another employee later recalled hearing Boyd say she was crossing the river to see about some money she was owed. Maybe she finally intended to settle her accounts. Or maybe Rebecca Boyd made the trip seem like an olive branch. She knew that Wood was a woman used to being on her feet all day. Surely, then, she might enjoy a leisurely carriage ride? A respite from the woodstoves and buckets, the chamber pots and slop jars, that had occupied most of her waking hours for the past twenty years?[4]

Boyd sent for the hack. Wood got in. The driver steered them west on Fourth before turning left and heading south in the slanting afternoon light. Dust swirled in the carriage's wake as it clattered along the cobblestones to the bases of Walnut and Vine, where a swath of unpaved ground sloped down toward the river. There, a steam-powered ferry was waiting to carry them and other passengers across a quarter mile of water, and the driver directed the curtained carriage right onto its deck. The ferry took only a few minutes to cross the Ohio River.[5]

Even then, Wood did not suspect the extent of the danger ahead. In those days people moved regularly between Cincinnati and Covington, twin cities whose daily commerce required crossing the river. John Gilbert, the black man driving the carriage, returned to Cincinnati later that night, and Wood must have assumed that she would, too. But when the carriage drove straight through town and out into the gloaming, she may have begun to fear the truth: she would not be back for supper.[6]

The carriage had moved well into the country when the driver finally pulled on his reins. Boyd opened the door and got out to speak with three men on the road. Wood told Hearn that she recognized one of them as a man named Frank Rust, whom she had seen at the boardinghouse; the bumps on his face gave him away. Another she later identified as Willoughby Scott. Wood remembered watching from her seat as one of those men—or perhaps Zebulon Ward, the third man there—walked up to Boyd and shouted in mock anger.[7]

"What are you doing with my nigger?"

Boyd laughed and joked back with a sarcastic reply.

"Oh, she's free."

More laughter pealed as Wood saw a roll of cash changing hands in the shadows. Then she heard an order to get out of the hack. The conversation that evening would haunt her for years, enabling her to recount it for Hearn.

"Now, don't run, or I'll shoot you," one of the men said.

"I've got nothing to run for," Wood replied.

"She talks mighty big, don't she," sneered one of the men. Another walked up and fixed her with a stare.

"Don't you know me?" he asked.

The others laughed again. Boyd returned to her seat alone. Then the driver turned the carriage back toward the river.[8]

That night, after the men had forced her to walk into Covington, Wood found herself trapped in a fourth-story room. In her interview with the *Ripley Bee* in 1879, she remembered that a white man stood guard at her door. Downstairs, she had seen men tying up their horses and drinking at a bar. Upstairs, the kidnappers frisked her and rifled through her pockets, failing to find what they wanted.[9]

"Where's your papers?" they demanded. She told them. They left. Later, though, one returned to taunt her with more questions.[10]

"Don't you want to see Josephine White?"[11]

Wood said no, but the name must have struck her like a slap in the face: the sudden, stinging realization that Josephine was behind this. White's mother, Jane Cirode, had helped Wood to secure the freedom papers that the men wished to find; Josephine and her husband, Robert, had always wanted Jane to sell Henrietta instead. A theory began to form in her mind as the daylight ebbed from her room. A landlady also came to her door with a meal of crackers and tea. But Wood did not feel like eating, so the woman retreated downstairs, muttering under her breath that the whole thing was a shame.[12]

"I lay awake all night," Wood later recalled, "and I prayed that the good Lord would stand by me and deliver me out of my trouble."[13]

At sunrise, Wood rose and went to the window for "one last look at old Cincinnati, where I had had a sweet taste of liberty." She could see the Ohio River below, the water running high. It would be a busy day on the landing. Steamboats were preparing to leave for Pittsburgh, St. Louis, and Louisville, a city she knew well from her days before freedom. A boatload of cotton was arriving from New Orleans, another place she had lived during her first enslavement. Carriages swarmed around the ferry dock, ready to take boarders to houses like those where she had worked for years—most recently Mrs. Boyd's, but also the one on Broadway and Fifth, run by a Mrs. Wilcox, and of course Mrs. Cirode's. Wood recalled spying a fiddler on board a passing lumber raft. Another figure danced. Then a sharp knock on the door brought her back into the room.[14]

"God damn you," shouted the knocker. "Are you never going to get up?"[15]

Wood left the room and followed the man down the stairs. There were now only two men from the night before: Rust and Scott. They put her into a buggy again, steering it onto the turnpike running south toward Lexington. Soon they arrived in Florence, a tiny crossroads town where travelers often rested after the steep climb from the river. The group checked in for the night at one of the village's roadside inns, and Wood was forced to the floor in the same room as her captors.[16]

Wood managed some sleep, but only "a little," as she recalled. When dawn came the men roused her while preparing to leave for a short trip to nearby Burlington, where they planned to collect some slaves they had bought before going on to Lexington. She was to remain locked in their room until they returned. The kidnappers repeated a warning not to talk as they left: "You'd better know nothing about Cincinnati," which meant, as she later put it, "'Nigger, I'll whip you if you do.'" In so many ways, she found herself back where she began.[17]

When her captors had gone, Henrietta was left to ponder their next moves—and hers. She had passed her childhood right there in Boone County, Kentucky, not far from Florence and Burlington, though the Covington turnpike had not been built when she last lived nearby. She had spent no time in Florence, and now she was headed to Lexington, another unfamiliar town. More familiar, though, was what the men likely planned to do. She figured that they would put her with some slaves "they were collecting for the Southern market," forcing them all onto a steamboat bound for New Orleans, or marching them overland in a long line, each person shackled to another. She knew from having been there what awaited in New Orleans: a levee full of markets where human beings were sold. In the end, she would probably be taken to the cotton fields.[18]

At that point in her life, Wood had not yet been on the front lines of the cotton states, which by then produced two thirds of the world's supply of the crop. But she had lived in Louisiana, and she knew that the shores of the Mississippi River were lined with booming plantations. She had seen the cotton bales that were carried on steamboats down the Mississippi and shipped to foreign ports such as Liverpool and Le Havre. Cotton had reorganized the rhythms of national and global markets that stretched far beyond her lines of sight.[19]

Long before she ever saw a cotton plant, Wood also knew about the crop's human toll. Most enslaved people who had lived in Kentucky or Virginia did. Nearly one million slaves had already been moved against their will from states in the Upper South to the cotton fields of what was then the nation's southwestern frontier. The massive forced migration resembled a second Middle Passage, ripping apart and scattering countless black families. Hundreds of miles away from the places they were born, slaves who arrived in the Southwest were forced to stoop over plants they had never grown before, pushed to plant and weed and pick from every sunrise to every sunset.[20]

Those who were sent built new communities, formed new family ties. They tried to wring what concessions they could from those who wielded the whips and hoarded the region's guns. Some fought back or ran away when they learned they were being sold "down the river." Others kept on fighting when they arrived. And still others destroyed themselves in final acts of defiance or grief. At various points on the bottom of the Mississippi were the bodies of those who had jumped overboard and drowned themselves on the way to the cotton states. They picked a death of their choosing instead of what awaited them there.[21]

Henrietta Wood now confronted a similar mix of options, though her power to choose among them was terribly constrained. One option was to try to regain her freedom, to fight her abduction even to the death. A different kind of struggle was already familiar: the daily fight to live as freely as she could within slavery. The taste of liberty lingered; Cincinnati was nearby. But if she had any hopes of returning across the river, she knew that she would have to defy her captors' threats. She would have to tell her story.

The first chance arrived when a young white man entered her room in Florence, interrupting her racing thoughts. The man (Wood recalled guessing that he was the innkeeper's son) informed her about the captors' orders not to let her out, not even for meals downstairs. Although he was accustomed to boarding slave traders and their captives, these instructions had raised his suspicions.

"Now, I want you to tell me the truth," the man said. "Where did they get you?"[22]

Years later, Wood gave the man's name as "Williams," probably the Jonathan Williams listed in records from about that time as a Pennsylvania-born innkeeper, the owner of one slave. Whoever he was, Williams urged her to confide in him.[23]

She hesitated, even though the man seemed sincere. "I didn't want to tell him," Wood later confessed, "because I was afraid."[24]

His question—*Where did they get you?*—also had so many answers. Which "where," after all? Which "they"? She could say that the men had "gotten" her in Covington from Boyd. Before that, Jane Cirode had "gotten" her from Cirode's husband when he left New Orleans. He had "gotten" her from a man named Henry Forsyth in Louisville, Kentucky, who had "gotten" her from a man named Omer Tousey of Indiana. And he "got" her by inheritance from the estate of his father, Moses, who owned Wood's mother, a woman named Daphne. She had been stolen at birth, in a sense, not in a curtained carriage or by a special ruse, but by laws that systematically robbed black women's wombs. Where did they "get" her? She could say it was from Daphne or from Daphne's mother, or from her mother, or hers. From a long train of usurpations that had crossed the Atlantic Ocean long before she crossed the Ohio. The "getting" of her had begun far away and long ago, before she was even born.[25]

"You need not fear," Wood remembered Williams saying. "They'll not be back before eleven o'clock, and I'll not betray you."[26]

Wood remained unsure, she recalled. But at last, she "took courage," perhaps a deep breath. Then she "told him all."[27]

CHAPTER TWO

TOUSEYTOWN

The first place Henrietta Wood could remember was Moses Tousey's northern Kentucky farm, which lay on the southern banks of the Ohio River. Tousey was one of the earliest white settlers of Boone County, having arrived there from western New York in about 1804 with his brothers, Thomas and Zerah. The trio of Yankees built adjoining farms by the mouth of Second Creek—"right opposite Lawrenceburg," Indiana, as Wood later recalled. This was the place she said she was born, either in 1818 or in 1820.[1]

Locals knew the tiny hamlet along the river as "Touseytown." It boasted a distillery, a mill, and a warehouse where tobacco could be inspected, as well as a flatboat that could ferry goods and people to Indiana. Even then, the hamlet was not much compared with nearby settlements such as Louisville, Cincinnati, or even Lawrenceburg. But Touseytown wore the trappings of wealth at a time when northern Kentucky remained a rural frontier, part of the Far West of the young United States. The Touseys belonged to a wave of white migrants who had rushed into Kentucky after 1790, tripling the state's population by 1800 and doubling it again by 1820. Most had come with pioneer dreams of wresting farms from wilderness, then passing them on to their children, and the Tousey brothers had done better than most.[2]

Land ownership in Kentucky was concentrated in the hands of an elite, forcing many settlers to rent, but the Tousey brothers had acquired land of their own. Most white families in the area farmed corn, some tobacco, often relying on wealthier neighbors for the infrastructure that helped bring crops to market—ferries, distilleries, mills. The Touseys were part of that wealthier class. In 1825, when a "tremendous" fire in Touseytown, visible from Indiana, destroyed the distillery and "Horse Mill" on Zerah Tousey's farm, a Lawrenceburg newspaper expressed concern. "The loss of the mill will be severely felt," it reported, because "the whole neighborhood" relied on it for grinding.[3]

In truth, the neighbors may have felt the loss more than the Touseys, who had another form of property that set them apart from many: all three of the brothers owned slaves, and slaves gave white families the power to rebound from disasters. The forced labor of enslaved people could help to build or rebuild a farm. It could be rented out to poorer farmers, too, earning income for a slaveholder while broadening support for human bondage among those who could not afford slaves of their own. In short, owning slaves gave a white family a means of securing and growing its wealth. A slave could be used as collateral for a loan. A slave, like real estate, could be bequeathed to heirs. A slave could always be sold for cash, in good times or in bad.[4]

Tousey possessed "only a few blacks," Wood later told Hearn. According to census records, the three he enslaved in 1820 had increased to eleven a decade later. By the time Wood reached adolescence, at least two dozen enslaved people, owned by various Touseys, lived and worked in Touseytown, and the rise in their numbers reflected a more general trend. Kentucky's black population grew at an even faster rate than its white population between 1790 and 1820. By 1830, nearly a quarter of the people living in the state were enslaved. Compared with the more populated areas of central Kentucky, relatively few slaves lived along the northern borders of Boone County. But among the "few blacks" in Touseytown were people who were very important to Henrietta: the people she first loved and was loved by in return.[5]

She remembered her father, for instance, as a man called William or Bill. She remembered and preserved the name of her mother: Daphne. Henrietta had siblings, too, and many decades later, she could still tell stories about her Touseytown relations, like the time when a brother named Joshua fell and hit his chin on a coffee pot. The pot left a scar on Joshua's face, and as Wood recalled, she would often "feel sorry" for the gash that "disfigured him when a baby."[6]

As for Henrietta, she may have been not much older than a baby herself when Joshua fell, perhaps too young to fully understand what it meant to be enslaved. She was no more than seven years old when fire destroyed the mill. Other formerly enslaved people often recalled not knowing yet, at that early age, that they could be bought and sold. Only slowly did they realize why their parents could not ensure a future together as a family, much less an inheritance like the ones that white settlers hoped to bequeath to their sons. By law, Henrietta, Joshua, Bill, and Daphne belonged to a Tousey, just like the horse that walked around the mill, grinding the neighborhood's corn into meal.[7]

The enslaved people of Touseytown also felt a sense of belonging to each other, no doubt: they cherished the ties that bind parents to child, brother to sister, friends to friends. But Wood was born with a price on her head that she could not yet see. And by the time she reached twenty years of age, two different white men would fix that price and pay to make her theirs.[8]

Before 1830, enslaved people came to Kentucky in one of three ways. Some were forced to move by white settlers from states such as Virginia, where nearly three hundred thousand slaves lived in 1790. Wood's parents were probably among those brought by migrants who moved west after the American Revolution. Other people became slaves in Kentucky simply by being born. Since the seventeenth century, American slaveholders had adopted the rule that any children born to an enslaved woman belonged to their mother's owner. Kentucky made the rule state law in 1798, continuing a Virginia code: "the descendants of the females" of slaves were unfree. Because Daphne was enslaved, Henrietta was born into bondage, too.[9]

White Kentuckians chose to perpetuate slavery in their state even at a moment when slavery was beginning to end in some parts of the country. Only a few years before the Touseys left New York, the legislature there passed an act of gradual emancipation, freeing slaves born after July 4, 1799, once they reached a certain age. As they traveled to Kentucky, the Touseys probably also passed through Pennsylvania, where legislators had enacted a similar law in 1780, citing the contradictions between slavery and the ideals of the American Revolution. By following the Ohio River, the Touseys eventually entered the Northwest Territory, which included what became the states of Ohio, Indiana, and Illinois. In 1787, Congress had banned slavery entirely from this territory, and the ban was ratified by the state constitutions of Ohio in 1802 and Indiana in 1816.[10]

In each of these states, those who favored emancipation succeeded only through struggle against powerful opposition. In none of these states were free black persons legally regarded as first-class citizens, the equals of their white neighbors. Instead, they were treated as a despised community and held down by discriminatory laws. In Ohio, for example, white conservatives feared that the abolition of slavery in their state would attract unwanted runaway slaves and free black immigrants to the state. So in 1804, the legislature passed a series of "Black Laws" that prohibited African Americans from attending public schools, voting, serving on juries, or testifying against whites. Similar laws were soon adopted by legislatures in other northern states, especially as free black communities grew. In every state where slavery had begun to die, white supremacy lived on.[11]

Still, in many states there was a clear if halting movement in the direction of emancipation. Kentucky—and the Touseys—went in the opposite direction. Some of the early migrants to the Bluegrass State did resist attempts to make Kentucky a slave state at its founding. They left behind pockets of moderate antislavery views that could explain later why Williams's family in Florence, or that innkeeper in Covington, believed that Wood's abduction in 1853 was wrong. But early emancipationists were ultimately outvoted. Kentucky's first state constitutional convention, in 1792, decided to legalize slavery. Seven years later, a second state constitution reaffirmed the decision.[12]

As a child, therefore, Henrietta could stand enslaved on the banks of the Ohio and look across the river at a state where slavery was illegal. It was a distance crossed regularly by the Touseytown ferry. But in practice, the border between slavery and freedom was still as fluid as the river itself. Many white settlers in Indiana were related to slaveholders in Kentucky. Not all agreed with the ban on slavery in the

Northwest; some had lobbied for its repeal. Others held black inden-
tured servants in years-long contracts approximating slavery, and many
more depended on trade with white Kentuckians, shared their racial
prejudices, and assisted in capturing runaway slaves. (In 1826, when an
enslaved couple ran away from Boone County to Indiana, hoping to be
married in freedom, a Lawrenceburg paper printed a mocking article
about their capture and the "sound drubbing" they got when returned
to Kentucky.) Although the proximity of Kentucky slaves to a zone of
legal freedom encouraged some to escape, the same proximity endangered the freedom of black people in Indiana, who were constantly at
risk of being enslaved. One white Indianan reported in 1821 that "we
hear many sad stories of kidnapping."[13]

Kidnapping was the third way that enslaved people arrived in the
Bluegrass State, and Wood may have known some victims of these ab-
ductions as a child, decades before she became one herself. In 1812, for
example, a man called Sampson was kidnapped in Lawrenceburg,
taken across the river, and purchased by Zerah Tousey. Sampson toiled
for Zerah for the next seventeen years, and given Touseytown's small
size, Henrietta and her family most likely knew him.[14]

Perhaps they also knew that in 1829, Sampson somehow returned to
Lawrenceburg, where he soon appeared in public records as a free
"man of colour." That same year, Sampson filed lawsuits in the Dearborn
County Circuit Court against Tousey and an Indianan named William
Record. Sampson told the court that Tousey and Record had conspired
to kidnap and imprison him in Indiana in 1812. They then "carried him
into the state of Kentucky," where Record fraudulently "sold and con-
veyed" him to Tousey "as a slave or servant." Sampson sued the men
for $1,500, and in April 1830, an Indiana jury ruled in his favor, though
it ordered only Record to pay Sampson $83—a tiny fraction of what
the lawsuit asked.[15]

By then, Sampson had launched a separate lawsuit against Zerah
Tousey for $1,000. It eventually reached the Indiana Supreme Court.
At the time, some Indiana jurists were increasingly sympathetic to the
plight of men and women who were illegally enslaved. In 1820, a ruling
by the state Supreme Court had upheld Indiana's 1816 ban on slavery

and affirmed that any people still enslaved in the state must be freed. But in 1831, the year Zerah Tousey died, Sampson's case was suddenly dropped from the high court's docket, before any arguments were heard.[16]

News of Sampson's case may well have traveled across the river to Touseytown. Though Wood never said so, it is conceivable that she or her relatives heard something about his ordeal. Either way, Sampson's story underscored the dangers that free people of color faced if they lived along the borders of slave states. His partial success in court did suggest, even then, the possibility of holding a former enslaver to account. But it also provided a precedent that few others could follow—certainly not an enslaved person legally brought to Kentucky, or born within its borders. And in the end, after almost two years of litigation, even Sampson was probably left with no more than $83 to show for seventeen years as a slave.[17]

When Sampson left Touseytown, Henrietta was only nine or maybe eleven years old—about the age when many enslaved children first became conscious of their legal status as property. Some, remembering their childhoods as adults, spoke of a slowly dawning realization about the way the white world saw them, a terrible knowledge that might be learned from various rites of passage: the first time they were made to join in the labor of enslaved adults; the first time that someone they knew ran away; the first time they witnessed a whipping; or the first time they heard an owner threaten them or a loved one with sale. For Henrietta Wood, one such time may have been in 1831, when Moses Tousey published a notice in a Lawrenceburg newspaper. The ad announced that he planned to "expose at public sale" all his furniture, livestock, and "moveable property," including all his "Negroes."[18]

No record shows whether Tousey found any buyers, or if the people he hoped to sell ever learned of his plans. At least for the moment, Henrietta remained in Touseytown—long enough, perhaps, for her mother, Daphne, to teach important lessons about her daughter's true value, and about the world in which she would soon have to survive alone. Like other parents of enslaved children, she would have taught

Wood that she should never see herself as a thing. Nonetheless, Daphne also had to warn her daughter that a master would see her as a chattel, one whose body could bear even more property for him. Perhaps it was in Touseytown, too, that Wood first heard of slave traders who tempted masters with "cash for negroes," and then carried souls off, God knew where, never to be seen again.[19]

Whatever the case, Daphne did not have much time left to tell her daughter all the things she wanted to say. Touseytown started a slow decline after Wood was born. Most of the Tousey brothers' children drifted to Indiana, or larger towns in Kentucky, and each departure made it more likely that their fathers' property would also one day be dispersed. Meanwhile, new settlers in the area gravitated to the Lawrenceburg side of the river. The rise of steamboats after 1819 began to make ferries such as Touseytown's obsolete. The fire that destroyed the hamlet's distillery and mill occurred in 1825, followed not long after by other disasters for Moses. In 1831, his wife, Ann, left him. In 1833, his house caught fire. In 1834, he died.[20]

In her interview with Lafcadio Hearn, Wood later recalled that Moses Tousey's children returned to the farm after his death "to see after things," a return that proved disastrous to her own family. Tousey's son Omer (whose name Wood remembered, or Hearn mistook, as "Homer") was a rising politician across the river. Moses's daughter had also settled in Indiana, where her son would grow up to become governor of the state. Neither one wished to put down roots again in Boone County; neither was compelled by law to free their father's slaves. Instead, Wood recalled, they made "a division of the property," including the people whom Tousey had enslaved. Then, as she told Hearn, "we were all sold."[21]

At about that same time, as required by law, Tousey's executors also made an inventory of all his worldly goods. The list, completed in October 1834, began with nine enslaved people. At the top were the two names that Wood later gave as those of her parents: "1 Negro Man Bill," valued at $150, and "1 Negro Woman Daphney," valued at $50 less. Seven other people, including a "Negro Boy Joshua," were immediately followed by fifty head of hogs and pigs. Together, the total value of the slaves Tousey owned was appraised at $2,000, more than all the rest of his movable property combined.[22]

No "Henrietta" appeared, however, on the inventory of Tousey's estate. As a teenager, she was more marketable than her older parents or the younger people on the list. So by the time Moses Tousey's list of property was made, his heirs must already have determined her fate.

"I was taken together with brothers and one sister, to Louisville," she recalled, "and sold there to a Mr. Henry Forsyth, for $700." She would remain in the memory of those left behind as daughter to Daphne, sister to Joshua, the sibling whose scar she had pitied as a child. But as far as she knew in 1834, Henrietta would never see any of them again. And as for the siblings brought with her from Touseytown to Louisville, none were purchased by Forsyth. Four decades later she could still report to Hearn that "I never saw them since."[23]

CHAPTER THREE

DOWNRIVER

After she was sold to Henry Forsyth, Henrietta Wood spent more than two years working at his home in Louisville. Much later, when she was interviewed by Lafcadio Hearn, she lingered on those years for only thirty-four words. Perhaps Wood said more than Hearn decided to report. Or perhaps the brevity suggested how painful those days had been. At no more than sixteen years of age, Henrietta was cut off from family and sold to a "pretty mean man," who forced her to do "cooking, washing, scrubbing." Henry Forsyth "treated me roughly," Wood tersely recalled. He "often flogged me," she said.[1]

She did not say, or Hearn did not record, all the things that rough treatment entailed. Another formerly enslaved woman recalled the fifteenth year of age as "a sad epoch in the life of a slave girl." It was a time when many leering white men began to "whisper foul words" to the young black girls whose bodies they owned and could violate without fear of legal prosecution. Being treated "roughly" could have signified many kinds of physical, verbal, or sexual assault, in addition to the whippings that she did name, and whatever Forsyth did, Henrietta suffered it all without her family's support.[2]

She also had to adjust to surroundings that were starkly different from what she knew before. By 1830, Louisville was Kentucky's largest city. Its population exceeded that of Boone County as a whole. More than a hundred steamboats stopped regularly at its landing, and their passengers could stay at well-appointed hotels. Compared with Moses Tousey's farm, the city must have seemed a bewildering new world, a whirl of "activity and motion," as one visitor described it. Though it stood by the same river that ran beside Touseytown, Louisville more closely resembled "a seaport," with "stores filled with the commodities and manufactures of every clime."[3]

Henry Forsyth kept one of those stores near the river at the corner of Third Street and Water, only a few blocks away from his home. In her brief recollections to Hearn about that time, Wood called it a "naval supply store," perhaps because Forsyth sold bookings on steamboats such as the *Industry* and the *Orleans*. Sometimes Forsyth also sold shares in new steamboats constructed at boatyards nearby. His main business, however, was as a wholesale and commission merchant, one of dozens in the city. He made his profits by trading in the vast array of goods that arrived by steamboat from up and down the river. Customers at his waterfront store could buy Brazilian coffee and Monongahela whiskey, Turks Island salt or Alabama cotton, and by 1833, Forsyth was a man on the make—the owner of two slaves and a total estate worth at least $20,000.[4]

Only a few years later, Forsyth would be worth more than five times that amount. By 1837, he had owned as many as nine slaves and held important civic positions as a stock commissioner and a director of the Bank of Kentucky. He rubbed shoulders with men such as George Keats, brother of the English poet and owner of a fancy house near Forsyth's. Not long after buying Wood, Forsyth also helped found the company that was chartered to build the original Galt House hotel.[5]

It was a dramatic rise to prominence by a man who was born in Ireland at about the time the Touseys left New York, and it paralleled the rise of Louisville itself. By 1835, the once small village on the nation's western frontier boasted a wholesale business of $29 million a year. A city booster confidently declared that "Louisville is as clearly marked out by nature, as the great heart of western commerce, as New Orleans is, as the great mart of the South." In Louisville, members of wealthy white families could take piano lessons or bet on Thoroughbred horses at the city's Oakland Race Course, a forerunner of Churchill Downs. Those wealthy enough to do so also assigned domestic work to hired servants or slaves, making the freedom not to launder or prepare meals a marker of race and class. Awash in new wealth, white Kentuckians consigned young women like Henrietta Wood to the hot and tedious work of chambermaids and cooks.[6]

But then came a sudden crash, for Forsyth and for Louisville. It started with the Panic of 1837, a national financial crisis. As lenders rushed to call in debts during the panic, many merchants lost their wealth. Forsyth was among the businessmen who suffered, especially as a director of the Bank of Kentucky. For two years, Forsyth and the bank battled creditors and debtors alike in a cascade of complicated suits. Forsyth was reduced to a clerk by the time it had subsided; maybe a renter, too. He would later bounce back to solvency, but the Irishman disappeared from the county's property rolls for a time, along with all the people whom he once enslaved.[7]

Most likely all of those people—eight in all on the eve of the panic—had been sold away or seized from Forsyth as he struggled to stay afloat. In her later interview with Hearn, Wood reported only what Forsyth had done to her. "He sold me to a Frenchman" named William Cirode, she said, a fellow merchant who paid "either $700 or $800." The exact price the Frenchman paid may have been lost to memory, but Wood did not forget her new owner's name, for Cirode's story would be entangled with hers for many years to come. It was William's wife, Jane, who would later help Wood gain her first taste of freedom. And it was their daughter, Josephine, whose desire to see Henrietta sold would later set in motion the crime that took that freedom away.[8]

Like Forsyth, William Cirode was an immigrant to the United States. Born Louis-Guillaume-Marie Cirode in France, he arrived in Lexington, Kentucky, from Nantes in 1816, at age twenty-four, adopting an anglicized version of his name. The unusual surname was still often mangled by Americans as "Cerrode" or even "Corode," but Cirode's new home did retain some reminders of France. A French jeweler, Antoine Dumesnil, also settled in Lexington at about that time, and both men belonged to a growing diaspora of émigrés from Napoleonic France and Saint-Domingue, the French sugar colony where enslaved revolutionaries had overthrown the white planter class and established the new Republic of Haiti in 1804. Although most French refugees settled in large port cities, a significant number made their way to the western backcountry.[9]

Meanwhile, in the East, French immigrants forged alliances with friends in high places. One society of émigrés lobbied the federal government to give its stockholders public land in the South where they could settle, and in 1818, they succeeded. Congress granted the group four townships on lands recently seized from the Creek and Chickasaw nations by the United States. Cirode and Dumesnil were shareholders in the society and were granted 120-acre and 240-acre plots, respectively, near Mobile, Alabama.[10]

Both men may have considered a move to the Deep South. But—like most of the grantees—Cirode never claimed his land. By 1818, he had good reasons to remain in Kentucky. In August, he married Jane White, an English-born woman ten years his junior, and his brother Yves had followed him to Kentucky. William had also begun to prosper as a "skin dresser," opening a tanyard in Lexington near "the Catholic burying ground." The business did well, perhaps by using French innovations in tanning, and by 1823, the operation had expanded to include a tanyard in Frankfort. Cirode sold "leather, shoes, boots," as one advertisement he placed in a newspaper put it. Another promised local farmers that he could make "coarse Shoes for their negroes," fitted to the specified length of their feet.[11]

By his own account, Cirode's "industrious" habits had paid off: "I have the satisfaction to know that my exertions have been rewarded by an increase of property," he wrote to a local newspaper in 1824. But Lexington remained a rough-and-tumble town in those years, and the Frenchman made enemies, too. In the same letter to the *Kentucky Gazette,* Cirode revealed that one Thursday night in August 1824, a group of "ruffians" had burst into the terrified tanner's home, dragged him into the street, and given him a vicious and humiliating beating.[12]

Cirode could not see his assailants, who had not been brave enough, he later said, to attack him "in day light." He called them "irresponsible bravo's, fellows without character or property," who had probably been hired by his "enemies." Since the start of a nationwide recession that began in 1819, there had been periodic violence between Lexington's workingmen and property holders; perhaps those conflicts were to blame. Or perhaps Cirode's profession had rankled some of his neighbors. Townsfolk in the West often complained of the noxious chemicals that ran off from tanyards into local streams, not to mention the stench from rotting flesh that had been scraped from raw skins. Then again, the Frenchman may have been a victim of xenophobia, or even of random crime.[13]

Cirode, at least, saw nothing random about the attack. In his letter to the *Gazette*, he offered a $50 reward for anyone with information about his attackers, describing himself as a "friendless foreigner" who spoke "the language of this country badly" and kept mostly to his "tan yard and family." Expecting little help from the authorities, Cirode felt surrounded by enemies, and soon he was looking to leave. By 1828, the Frenchman had sold both of his tanyards and moved his family, now with four children, west, to a booming Louisville.[14]

The river city proved to be a more welcoming place. Cirode set himself up as a merchant on Fifth Street near the Ohio River, trading in finished hides and other goods. He joined the Mechanics' Saving Institution of Louisville, an organization to which Forsyth also belonged. By 1830, Cirode had purchased valuable real estate in Louisville, and he also owned seven slaves. In late 1837 or early 1838, he would add to their number by purchasing Henrietta Wood.[15]

By then, two decades after arriving from France, Cirode had lived, like Forsyth, a version of the American dream. He had gone from doing dirty manual work to respectability as a merchant. Yet Cirode remained restless, and by the time he purchased Wood he was already making plans to move again, this time even farther away, to the city of New Orleans. Maybe there, in that cosmopolitan city, with its large Francophone community, his nationality and native tongue would finally be assets instead of liabilities.

For Wood, the idea of going to New Orleans could only have prompted the opposite feelings: sadness, panic, dread. She was approaching her twentieth year when Forsyth sold her to Cirode, and over the course of her life, New Orleans had grown to become the third-largest city in the United States. It was also home to one of the largest slave markets in the world. Since 1815, a stampede of white American settlers had rushed into the nation's Southwest, occupying land in Louisiana, Mississippi, and Alabama. Their numbers had far outpaced the wave of migration that had brought the Touseys, Forsyth, and Cirode to Kentucky. The result was an unprecedented demand for slaves by cotton and sugar planters in the Lower South, and professional slave traders in the Upper South moved quickly to meet that demand. In the meantime, stories about what happened to slaves after they were taken to New Orleans made their way back on river steamboats to the Upper South. Many slaves remembered masters who threatened them with sale down the river. As one formerly enslaved Kentuckian would recall, a trip to New Orleans was regarded like a trip to "Hell, few ever returning who went there."[16]

A descent to New Orleans must have seemed a hellish prospect to Wood, too, not least because it would lower her odds of ever seeing her family again. As long as she still lived along the Ohio River in Louisville, Henrietta may have had reasonable hopes of reuniting with Daphne, Joshua, or Bill. Some of her siblings, she knew, had also been sold in the city, and whatever remained of Touseytown was only a short distance away. She might even have contemplated how she could return. In 1836, an eighteen-year-old enslaved woman named Easter did escape from Forsyth, who advertised a reward for her capture in the local press. Henrietta may well have known Easter before then, and if so, the flight may have led her to ponder the risks and potential rewards of making a run of her own.[17]

But then Cirode purchased Wood and forced her to move with him downriver, hundreds of miles away from every place and person she knew. "He took me at once on the steamboat 'William French' to New Orleans," Wood later recalled, referring to a 265-ton boat that made its first trip down the Mississippi in the spring of 1838. He opened a store in New Orleans, Wood explained to Hearn, and for the next six or seven years, she would work as a cook and housekeeper for the Cirodes there.[18]

Henrietta Wood stepped off the *William French* at a time when the slave population of New Orleans itself was in decline. Most slaves who arrived in the city were soon resold to the owners of surrounding plantations. In fact, many never made it past the first few blocks by the river, where numerous slave traders operated slave pens and showrooms.[19]

Enslaved women who did housework in the city proved the one exception to the steady drain of urban slaves to the countryside, but black domestic servants were not immune to sale. New Orleans had a thriving market for domestic help sought by wealthy families, and more black women were arriving all the time. As the labor needs or financial means of white households changed, the slaves who worked as cooks, cleaners, or nurses were frequently sold from one owner to another, usually for about the price that Wood remembered Cirode paying for her. By 1850, one in five of the slaves living in the city was sold every year. The chance that urban laborers might be sold several times during their lives was high.[20]

Wood's six- or seven-year tenure in the Cirodes' house was therefore relatively long and not at all inevitable. The Frenchman had no qualms about selling a human being. In 1828, while still in Lexington, he had advertised for sale a "likely Negro woman with two fine Children and another expected in the Christmas holydays." He touted her as "an excellent cook, washer and ironer" who could also work in the fields. A decade later, at about the time he bought Wood, Cirode also purchased another woman, named Caroline, from a Louisville merchant. After two years, Cirode resold Caroline to a buyer in New Orleans, pocketing $100 in profit from the sale.[21]

The Cirodes' decision to keep Wood may indicate her special skill at the labor she performed. Housework in those days was a demanding job with few devices to help. Every day, enslaved women hauled water, tended fires, lifted and leaned on heavy irons. Their presence in the intimate spaces of a white family's home only increased the pressure to satisfy an exacting master and mistress—to prepare a meal to their specifications, or brush a carpet to their liking, but without crossing any social lines that separated master and slave. That made the work mentally exhausting as well. Wood's experience as a cook and cleaner may have helped her through many years in the service of the Cirodes, though she shared very little in her interviews about her years in New Orleans.

She later told Hearn that "the Frenchman and his wife were fair kind of folks," and she remembered being "pretty well treated" by them.[22]

As with Tousey and Forsyth, however, a sudden change in Cirode's fortunes or ambitions would have convinced him to sell Wood. Success in New Orleans was never guaranteed. On the contrary, Cirode had chosen to make his move at a perilous moment in the city's economic history. In the 1830s, the regional cotton boom had led to a commercial boom in the city, as merchants flocked to New Orleans to supply surrounding planters. But the Panic of 1837 that overturned Forsyth's fortunes struck New Orleans even harder. Hundreds of firms closed in the very years when Cirode was trying to establish his new store, which traded in "Wholesale and retail Western produce." At any moment, Cirode's fortunes could have taken a dive.[23]

At first, he prospered instead. Cirode started his career downriver with no less than $10,000 in capital to invest in his store on Poydras Street. The store specialized in pork, hides, tanner's oil, and whiskey from up the river, and according to later court records, Cirode quickly earned a reputation as "a prudent and safe man in business" who paid his bills in cash. By 1843, William and Jane were doing well enough to move into a two-story brick house on Dauphin, near DuMaine. Henrietta may have lived in a room of her own upstairs, or in a building behind the house.[24]

Cirode's success in the city must have vindicated his hope that here, at last, he would be a "friendless foreigner" no more. By 1840 he had transferred the management of any remaining Louisville business to former associates there. His adult children moved down the river, too. Cirode's daughter Josephine married Robert White, a Kentuckian, in September 1840, and the newlyweds moved to Mobile, Alabama, where Daniel Cirode, her brother, already lived. Daniel and his new brother-in-law established their own mercantile firm in Mobile, supported by gifts from William Cirode of at least $6,000. Meanwhile, the elder Cirode began to believe he could settle down for good. On September 17, 1840, he appeared before a court in Louisville (perhaps while in Kentucky for Josephine's marriage) and successfully applied to become a citizen of the United States.[25]

But trouble found Cirode again in the spring of 1842, when the Mobile firm of Daniel Cirode and Robert White suddenly verged on collapse. William rushed to Alabama as soon as he heard the news. For months, he had been advancing goods, money, and slaves to his son and son-in-law, along with generous helpings of advice. He urged them to buy and sell in cash. Whenever the older man was away, Daniel and Robert had apparently discounted his advice, running up dangerous lines of credit. Now, unable to pay their debts, they risked losing all—including the capital that he had invested in their store.[26]

Moving quickly, Cirode filed a lawsuit in a Mobile court to seize the remaining stock of the firm. The trouble worsened when several New Orleans merchants who had accounts with the Mobile firm accused him of being a silent partner and therefore complicit in the collapse. Some said the elder Cirode had misled them about how well he knew his sons' insolvency, and then fraudulently seized their stock as if he were just any investor—instead of a heavily interested member of the family. Some believed that he should pay their remaining debts. On January 14, 1843, Jane Cirode opened the door of her home on Dauphin and found a sheriff there. He held in his hands a summons to the Orleans Parish Commercial Court, and it said her husband had been sued for nearly $1,800—the first of several lawsuits to come.[27]

Right or wrong, or some of both, the mounting accusations destroyed the Frenchman's reputation for prudence. Before long the old sense of embattlement that Cirode had felt in Lexington began to rear its head: the fear that in America he would always be surrounded by shadowy enemies who were eager to see him fail. Cirode fought plaintiffs in court for the rest of that year and part of the next. His lawyers tried to depict him as a long-suffering father whose trust had been abused by ungrateful sons. But too many former associates who had known him on Poydras Street could testify that he had vouched for the Mobile firm, even after he must have known that it was failing.

As verdicts against him accumulated, so did judgments adding up to thousands of dollars. In one suit, Cirode appealed his case all the way to the Supreme Court of Louisiana, where he lost again. The Frenchman could see no recourse but to run, and Cirode's name began to appear on the lists of passengers for ships running between Cuba and the northern United States. In March 1844, he applied for a passport in Philadelphia, and shortly thereafter, he abandoned his family and returned in disgrace to France, apparently never to return.[28]

Wood did not know all the details about Cirode's troubles, but she did know the impact that they had on his family—and on her: "somehow or other they quarreled at last," she later explained to Hearn, "and the old man sold the store, left his wife and went back to France." Yet "before he left," Wood recalled, he "gave his wife some blacks." Jane decided to move "up the river again to Louisville," most likely in 1844, and she took several of her husband's slaves with her, Henrietta among them. It was a move that would soon result in unexpected joy for Wood.[29]

Not that her joy was Jane Cirode's concern. Abandoned by her husband, Jane Cirode needed to find some way to make money for herself and the two younger children still in her care. Wood later recalled that soon after arriving in Louisville, Jane Cirode moved to Cincinnati, but before going, she decided to "hire out" the enslaved people she had brought with her from Louisiana. Wood was one of the slaves she decided to leave behind in Kentucky.[30]

At the time, Louisville had a thriving market for the labor of hired-out slaves—people who worked in exchange for a fee paid to their owner. The city had continued to grow in Wood's absence, and slaves could now be found in a variety of jobs: as stevedores and draymen along the docks, as waitresses and waiters in restaurants, as laborers in factories as well as homes. By 1844, Jane Cirode could select from several agents in the city who offered to help slaveholders locate hirers, handle all terms, and forward the "wages" they earned. One advertisement from June 1844, at about the time Wood returned, mentioned a "likely negro woman" available for rent "for the balance of the year." Another from 1845 advertised "for hire, a negro woman, who is an excellent servant and a good cook and washer." Even after accounting for fees to hiring agents, the typical rates promised Cirode a reliable revenue stream of about $100 a year per hired slave.[31]

The arrangement made Louisville the first place Henrietta had ever lived where her owner was not living, too, and her initial experiences of being hired out—first to a man named Lyons, then in the home of Charles Mynn Thruston, a lawyer—may have offered other advantages. Enslaved people who were rented out often had more freedom than other slaves to move about the city. (One newspaper at the time complained of the "corrupting tendency" of slave hirelings who believed they could "act without restraint.") Wood may even have had some freedom to negotiate her hiring. Although slaves were sometimes hired out directly by owners or their agents, Louisville also had a traditional hiring day. Every January 2, thousands of servants, free and enslaved, gathered at the corner of Fourth and Market to be questioned and selected by employers for the coming year. Cirode may well have elected to allow Wood to arrange her own hire there.[32]

If so, she could have spoken persuasively about her skills and experience, having already spent a decade doing domestic work. Perhaps she could even influence whether her hirer changed at the end of a year. Even in the best of circumstances, of course, she remained legally enslaved. She did not earn even the paltry wages paid to immigrant or poor white women for domestic work. By law, she remained an asset belonging to someone else. Still, Wood later told Hearn that she "had been pretty well treated in Louisville," referring to this second period in the city, and being hired out likely had much to do with that retrospective view. But so did another memory from those Louisville years—one even more pleasing, and even more remarkable, than her unexpected return.[33]

It happened toward the beginning, while Henrietta Wood was hired out to "lawyer Thurston," the *Ripley Bee*'s misspelling of Charles Thruston's name. Speaking many years later to the reporter, Wood recounted her memory of "a tall, brown-complexioned man," a neighbor who "used to come to our house to see a house maid who lived where I did." One night, the two women sat by the fire after work, talking about their pasts and also about the man, when the maid turned to Wood with a question later recounted in the *Bee*.[34]

"Henrietta," she said, "did you have a brother, Joshua?"

Wood remembered being flabbergasted by the question, and even more astounded at what came next.

"I believe," the maid continued, "this Josh who comes to see me is your brother."

The next day, the tall man came to call again, and the maid questioned him further about her suspicion, asking whether he had a sister named Henrietta.

Once, yes, he did. Now, he "guessed she was dead."

Asked about his parents' names, he replied, according to Wood, that "his father was always called Bill Touci and his mother's name was Daphne Touci." The reporter from the *Bee* recorded "Tousey" as "Touci," but those were the names of Wood's parents, too. Like many enslaved people, they had apparently become known by the surname of a family who had owned them.

At first, the coincidence must have seemed too good to be true. Henrietta had her memories of a brother named Josh, the one she had left behind a decade before in Touseytown. But it was still hard to believe that this tall man could possibly be the "Negro Boy Joshua" who had once appeared on the inventory of Tousey's estate.

"I was so glad" at the thought, Wood told the *Bee* in 1879, that "I didn't know what to do."

At last, she resolved to question the man for herself, pretending at first "like we was no akin" and trying to find out as much as she could about his past before revealing hers. She would hold in reserve the clue that would be "proof positive that he was my brother"—the scar that she had pitied on Josh's face as a child.

The meeting quickly confirmed Henrietta's dearest hopes. Joshua seemed to know so much about their people, though he did not recognize the sister who had been away for a decade or more, maturing from a girl into a grown woman. She stuck to her plans at first by pretending not to know him. Gradually, though, Wood grew "so happy," as she recalled, that she could not contain herself—or conceal who she was any longer. Finally, she asked Joshua to show his chin.

He did, and there it was: the scar that the coffee pot had made years before. Though "covered with whiskers" now, the disfigurement seemed to her "the prettiest spot" on his face, leaving her unable to speak at first. "I threw my arms around his neck, which liked to scared him to death," she said. "But when I told him he was my brother, he gave me hug for hug." They shared in a joy that most people who were separated by sale longed for intensely, but seldom received.

Immediately the siblings began to tell all that they knew about their relations, though the reminiscence would prove more somber than the reunion. After Moses Tousey died, Joshua had apparently also been taken away and sold "by young master Touci," presumably Omer Tousey. Now, Wood remembered, neither of them could say "where either father or mother, sister or brother were." Some of their kin they could fondly discuss "for we knew they were in their graves." Others, they feared, had disappeared into "the cotton fields of Mississippi; others again among the cane in Louisiana," and thinking of them brought the stabbing pain of never knowing where a missing loved one was. Sister and brother both bore scars that were not easily seen.[35]

"I tell you," she later told the reporter from the *Bee*, "when we get to heaven, won't we have a talk?"[36]

For the moment, however, Henrietta was full of awe and emotion. She had gone to the city known to slaves as a kind of "Hell," a place of no return. Then she had returned to discover a foretaste of heaven on earth. Who knew what else the future might hold?

CHAPTER FOUR

WARD'S RETURN

A story was later told about Zebulon Ward, probably told first by Zebulon himself. One day, it was said, he was on the road to a town in central Kentucky and came across a stranger with a wagon full of barrel staves. Knowing little about the product or its price, Ward bought the whole load right on the spot. Then, spurring his horse, he raced into town and sold the "hoop-poles" for a profit, before the original owner and his wagon could arrive. A Louisville paper recounted the tale after Ward had died, calling it the perfect illustration of his "bold speculative nature" and the reason why he had "made and lost half a dozen fortunes" by age forty-five. And although the paper did not mention it, the same speculative nature also helps to explain how and why his life came to intrude on Wood's.[1]

Ward's life had started in Harrison County, not more than four years after Wood was born and only a few counties away. His grandfather Zebulon Headington had come to Kentucky from Maryland in about 1795, part of the same wave of migrants that soon brought the Touseys from New York to Boone County. Like them, Headington came west hoping to plant a farm and build an estate he could leave behind to descendants like his grandson and namesake.

The older Zeb succeeded in the first of those goals, acquiring several slaves and ninety acres on the banks of Indian Creek. In the end, however, the younger Zeb would not be born to wealth. Ward's father, Andrew, was a poor man who married Headington's daughter Elizabeth in 1803. Nine years later, having failed to acquire a farm of his own, he left to fight in the War of 1812. His wife and six children stayed in Headington's house. When Andrew returned from the war, a gunshot wound had cost him the full use of his left arm, but he reenlisted anyway in 1814, perhaps to escape growing tensions at home. By the time he returned for good in 1819, Elizabeth had begun to speak of divorce. In 1822, when she bore Zebulon Ward, the couple's ninth child and youngest of four sons, he entered a family already in danger of breaking up.[2]

The Wards tried to reconcile at first, circling each other in a small cabin on Headington's land. Andrew apparently began to drink, perhaps to dull the pain from his wartime wounds—or the shame from his dependence on his father-in-law. In 1830, he did secure a meager veteran's pension. But in 1834, while on a trip to Lexington to collect his annual payment, he passed out drunk in a grocery store. When he awoke his pension certificate and a wallet full of cash were gone. Andrew petitioned the War Department for a replacement, alleging that his certificate had been stolen "by a negro." Another affidavit in the case made clear that Ward's drinking was to blame.[3]

Meanwhile, the Wards' marriage buckled under its strains. In 1835, when Zebulon was thirteen years old, his father filed for divorce. Andrew alleged that his wife had left him repeatedly between 1821 and 1828, sometimes for weeks or months at a time. Now she had finally abandoned him for good. He blamed the separation on Elizabeth's "peevishness" and "irritability." Ward's own petition hinted at other causes, however, including his failure to provide. Andrew had no land or slaves; he had been unable to keep his only horse. All he owned, by his own account, were "Such articles as the urgency of the moment or necessity of the day Called for," and in 1837 he lost his pension certificate for the second time. Several years later, he died, leaving no inheritance worthy of the name.[4]

Zeb Ward's grandfather died in 1841, and although the older man did leave a small estate that his grandchildren later divided, Andrew Ward's sons were mostly left to fend for themselves. His firstborn, James, headed south. Andrew Harrison Ward (also known as Harry) decided to study law, starting his education at Transylvania University in Lexington. When lack of funds forced Harry to pause his studies in 1837, just as the panic struck, he left law school to work as a purser on steamboats, first on the Tombigbee River and then on the Mississippi. At about the same time, he was joined "on The River" by his younger brother, Zebulon, then a boy of about fifteen years of age.[5]

Ward's life and Wood's had not intersected by then, unless somehow by chance. But on the same day when William Cirode took Henrietta aboard the *William French* in Louisville and steamed toward New Orleans, a teenaged Zeb may well have been on the Mississippi, too. He was just beginning to chase his own dreams of striking it rich.

Steamboats first appeared on American rivers not long before Ward's father went off to war: the boats and their powerful engines were barely older than Zebulon himself. By the time he joined his older brother Harry in the late 1830s, there were hundreds of steamboats on the nation's western waterways, with many ways for young white men to get on board. Cabin boys might be as young as nine or ten. Most boys, though, aspired to find a position on a steamboat's uppermost deck. Up there, where the captain gave orders and the pilot steered, a lucky boy might become an apprentice to the clerk, the vessel's third officer and the man chiefly responsible for the business side of a boat's operations. From him, a boy could gain a hands-on education: how to figure, how to measure, how to keep accounts. Then, if he played his cards right, an apprentice clerk might graduate to a full clerkship, with a salary as high as $900 a year.[6]

In the meantime, the riverboats held out other attractions to an adolescent boy. The men who made up steamboat crews were known to enjoy strong drink. Alcohol fueled a rowdy culture of coarse talk, gambling, fisticuffs, and cards. Often the rough fun spilled onto shore at river towns such as Natchez, Mississippi, where dockside taverns and brothels in the infamous Under-the-Hill district catered to gamblers and boatmen. Harry Ward later recalled the steamboats being filled with mountebanks, phrenologists, and card sharks—the sort of men who passed their hours by betting whose shot could hit a target on the banks and might just as easily turn their guns on each other. River work, in the words of another observer, was "a young man's job, full of violence and change."[7]

That was the world in which Zeb Ward formed some of his first ideas about what it meant to be a man, imbibing a masculinity that was equal parts malevolence and mirth. It was not an egalitarian world by any means. A steep hierarchy divided white officers from white crew members, all of whom possessed more power and prospects than the slaves and free black men who also worked on steamboats as firemen, barbers, draymen, and stevedores. But the steamboats were democratic enough to give Zebulon an escape from a past that might have been confining had he stayed at home. On the river his father's troubles made little difference, and a man could make his own myths and money grabs, away from many of the social rules that governed life onshore. Years later, after Ward had returned to Kentucky and run its state penitentiary for a time, a prisoner would recall him as "one of the strangest men I ever knew, physically handsome, socially magnetic, but utterly devoid of heart"—and always ready to gamble. On Sundays, he said, Ward "often declared that any man could worship according to the dictates of his conscience;—sing, pray, preach, play marbles, euchre, or quoits." It was the worldview of a steamboat man.[8]

The steamboats had also taught Ward more than cards and marbles. On the river he learned the risks and rewards of financial speculation. A steamboat was easy enough to launch, but to turn a profit it had to distinguish itself in a crowded field. Captains competed to show that their vessels could chug from New Orleans to points up the river faster than anyone else's, even when loaded with passengers and cargo. When determining prices for freight and passage, clerks sometimes had to gamble as much as the sharpsters in the staterooms. Offering a discount to customers on one part of the river might enable a steamboat to fill up fast and beat its competitors to a destination where higher rates could be charged. A skillful captain and crew could reap a windfall from such schemes. But if a steamboat reached a levee after valuable cargo had already left, or just as the going rates fell, a trip could just as quickly fail.[9]

Other dangers also loomed along the river. Low-draft steamboats could easily hit an underwater tree, or snag, and sink, and their engines were prone to explosions that sent cargo and passengers flying, especially since captains were under pressure to keep their steamers at a high boil. One English traveler who took a trip from Louisville to New Orleans on the *William French*, not long after Wood's journey with Cirode on the same boat, noticed with horror that the captain had taken on a load of gunpowder bound for Memphis and stored it near the engines. "The carelessness respecting human life in this country is surprising," he said in a private letter, before giving his final impression of those he met on board: "the making of money appears to be their chief pursuit."[10]

That pursuit appealed to Zebulon Ward. His brother Harry left the river to finish his legal education in Lexington, where he was admitted to the bar in 1844, but Zeb remained on steamboats for several more years. In 1874, he was still remembered by a leading newspaper in Louisiana as a former "freight clerk on our Cincinnati and New Orleans steamers." Later family stories, probably drawing on Ward's own recollections, said that in about his twenty-first year he moved to Nashville, where he next found work on the steamboats of the Cumberland River.[11]

Eventually, though, Zebulon left the steamboats behind—if not the thrills for which they were so notorious. One family story claimed that ill health caused him to move from Nashville to Cuba for convalescence; another claimed that he went to the island to chase a new business venture. Still another story, unconfirmed by any official records, had Ward returning from Cuba to enlist in the US Army in 1846 and fight in the war against Mexico that began that year, "serving in the field with distinguished credit to himself." That may have been why, in later life, he styled himself as a colonel.[12]

Any one of those tales remained difficult for later tellers to prove, but together they portrayed a restless man, a striver. A final story only confirmed the portrait. Not long after the US–Mexican War ended, Ward evidently caught the California gold fever and joined the rush of young Forty-Niners to the mining camps of the Golden State. On May 11, 1850, he boarded the steamship *Alabama* in New Orleans for a journey that took him to Chagres, Panama. There he embarked with other rushers on an overland trek to the western side of the isthmus. Then he traveled by boat to San Francisco and spent a brief time panning for gold around Sacramento.[13]

By the end of the year, however, Ward was either running out of luck or running out of patience with the nomadic life. In October he boarded a boat headed back to Panama. Ward then returned to Kentucky and obtained a marriage certificate to wed Mary E. Worthen of Harrison County in Cynthiana, near his childhood home, on January 9, 1851. Zebulon and Mary settled in Covington, Kentucky, opposite Cincinnati, and their first child, a son, was born the following February. As 1853 began, the family's taxable property had already grown to include a horse, a slave, and $75 worth of gold and other valuables—all that remained, perhaps, from Ward's California dreams, but still more than his father had achieved.[14]

It finally appeared as if Ward was ready to settle down and take up the responsibilities of a husband, a father, and a citizen. In January 1853, he was even appointed by the Kenton County sheriff as his deputy in Covington. And it was also in Covington, not long after taking his new job as a deputy sheriff, that Ward would first hear about Henrietta Wood—along with a gamble that sparkled like a new flash in his pan.[15]

CHAPTER FIVE

CINCINNATI

Louisville was not the same city for Wood once she learned that her brother was in it. Though it would always be the place where she had been flogged by Henry Forsyth and sold to William Cirode, now it would also be where the reunion with Joshua had occurred. Her interviews would not contain any more information about him. Nonetheless, her work in Louisville may have allowed her to keep in touch with Josh, as well as with the maid who had helped to reintroduce them while Wood was working for Thruston.

Wood did not remain long in Thruston's home. Her next job was cooking and cleaning rooms at the Louisville Hotel, described in advertisements at the time as a "handsome structure" on Main. William Bishop, the manager of the hotel, sent Jane Cirode $75 a year for her work, Wood recalled, and she stayed there for a few years. But then came another move—and another surprise.[1]

"My mistress came down to Louisville," she later told Lafcadio Hearn, "and took me back with her to Cincinnati."[2]

That turn in the story may have surprised Hearn, too. By 1876, many people in the United States envisioned the Ohio River before the Civil War as a yawning chasm between slavery and freedom, one that slaves had only ever crossed at great personal risk and with help from station-masters on the fabled Underground Railroad. Harriet Beecher Stowe's *Uncle Tom's Cabin*, the nineteenth century's best-selling novel, depicted the Ohio as a latter-day Jordan River, a border to a Promised Land that slaves could only pass over in dramatic fashion—in skiffs under cover of night, for example, or by fleeing across floes of ice, bloodhounds at their heels. Wood recalled a far less eventful passage to the North. Sometime before 1848, Jane Cirode simply took her from Kentucky to Ohio, where she would live for the first time in a free state and eventually get her first taste of what it was like to be legally free.[3]

She arrived in Cincinnati at a time of explosive growth for the city. The population had more than doubled since 1840 and would reach 115,000 residents by decade's end. Nearly half were immigrants from Ireland and Germany, and Cincinnati's boom reflected its growing reputation as a place with plentiful jobs and commercial opportunities. Dubbed by some the "Queen City of the West" for its size and busy landing, it was known to others by the nickname of "Porkopolis." Every year, hundreds of thousands of pigs were unloaded from steamboats and herded up Main Street to be slaughtered and processed into meat at one of the city's numerous packing plants, leaving the streets and canals littered with gristle, offal, dung, and blood. The filthy conditions bred disease, as in the cholera outbreak of 1849, and the situation was not helped by the loose pigs that roamed the streets, feasting on brackish water and trash. One visitor noted that "all Cincinnati is redolent of swine."[4]

Yet Cincinnati also had the tang of liberty in the air. The Queen City was the first place where Wood could be sure she would never see people being sold, though that did not mean she never saw reminders or residues of slavery. Ohio had made slavery illegal in its constitution of 1802, but its proximity and economic ties to Kentucky had encouraged its citizens to compromise with the slaveholders on their border. The majority of Ohioans believed that when enslaved people ran away to Ohio, their owners had the right to track them down.[5]

Most white Ohioans also believed that people of African descent did not deserve the same respect or rights as Americans who were marked by law and custom as "white." In August 1829, a white mob had rampaged through a black neighborhood in the Fourth Ward, destroying houses and causing more than half of the city's black population at the time to flee north to Canada or to other states. And for decades, Ohio politicians had reassured their southern neighbors that Ohio's own laws did not threaten the ability of slaveholders to bring enslaved people with them when traveling across the river for short periods.

Before 1840, it was not unheard of for enslaved people to be hired out in Cincinnati by owners in Kentucky.[6]

Arrangements like that had diminished by the time Wood arrived, though their fate remained uncertain. In 1841, Justice Ebenezer Lane of the Ohio Supreme Court suggested in one of his rulings that even a slave brought temporarily into the state by an owner was *automatically* free, but later that year, another white mob tore through a black neighborhood in Cincinnati, fueled by city newspapers that routinely depicted "negroes" as a nuisance population. In the years immediately following the 1841 riot, some in the Queen City still considered Lane's ruling a nonbinding opinion.[7]

Cincinnati was thus far from a paradise for a free black woman; it was a city riven with conflict over slavery. In fact, it may have been unclear to Wood whether she was free at all. Jane Cirode's views on the matter remained, at first, unclear. One thing, though, quickly became apparent: Cirode had brought Wood to Cincinnati expecting that the woman she had long enslaved would still be working for her.

Since arriving in Ohio a few years earlier, Jane Cirode had opened a boardinghouse on the north side of Sixth Street, midway between Sycamore and Main. Cirode needed to pay her bills, and taking in boarders was one of the few respectable urban enterprises that a woman of her age and marital status could initiate on her own. Wood recalled that when she arrived in Cincinnati, she went to work in the boardinghouse, cooking and washing as she had done in the Louisville Hotel.[8]

There was no evidence that Cirode intended to free her right away. In fact, Cirode's decision to bring Wood to Cincinnati may have been prompted by an inability to keep hiring her out in Kentucky. In 1876, Wood recalled that she was "very ill" at the time of her move: "my mistress had to pay out a deal of money" to a doctor in the city "for attending me." The unnamed illness may have kept Wood from continuing to work for Bishop.[9]

On the other hand, Cirode's decision to bring Wood to Ohio may have had more to do with the aftermath of her husband's flight to

France. William Cirode's adversaries had not given up on recovering the money from their lawsuits against him, which made the Frenchman responsible for paying thousands of dollars to various plaintiffs. As soon as those plaintiffs realized that William had absconded, they and their agents had started looking for any property he still owned that could be seized by courts and sold.

That search began in the summer of 1844, when the sheriff of Orleans Parish attempted to find Cirode and force him to satisfy one of the first verdicts against him. He discovered that the Frenchman had fled New Orleans and that none of his property was anywhere to be found—with one exception. In 1843, Cirode had purchased an enslaved woman named Margaret, along with her nine-year-old daughter. Cirode and his wife had apparently left her behind, perhaps hired out to someone in the city. Finding no other assets of Cirode's to collect, the sheriff, according to court records, "seized and took in my possession the slave Margaret," making no note of what happened to her child. That August, Margaret was sold at public auction in New Orleans.[10]

Margaret's sale satisfied only a tiny part of what Cirode owed to only one of the men who sued him: Samuel Bell. Other plaintiffs were looking for the Frenchman's property, too. William's return to France and Jane's return to Kentucky had temporarily stymied his pursuers, but before long, the creditors tracked the family back to Louisville. There, they found that the Frenchman still owned land—and some slaves.

Cirode had sensed that this would happen even before he left. He knew that collectors would come, and he had tried to take steps to protect at least some of his wealth, even if that meant playing fast and loose with the law. On January 25, 1844, only three days after losing an appeal at the Supreme Court of Louisiana, Cirode approached William Weathered, a friend in New Orleans, and told him he wished to set aside some of his real estate in Louisville as an inheritance for his daughter, Josephine White. He asked Weathered to hold some land in trust for her.

Weathered agreed to sign some papers, drawn up by Cirode, which stated that Cirode had mortgaged his land to Weathered to repay a

$5,000 debt he had supposedly incurred before his Mobile troubles began. That would have allowed Weathered to claim that he had a clearer right to Cirode's property than any New Orleans collectors. In reality, though, Cirode had never been indebted to Weathered. The mortgage was a ruse designed to keep his actual creditors at bay.[11]

Eventually the fraud was discovered by another plaintiff, James Johnston. In 1845, Johnston filed a suit against Cirode's former associates in Louisville, and he argued that the mortgage to Weathered was void. He won the case in January 1846, and most of the Frenchman's remaining real estate in Louisville was seized and sold by court decree.[12]

In the course of his suit, however, Johnston raised another question: where were William Cirode's slaves? Johnston's petition to the Chancery Court in Louisville alleged that before leaving New Orleans, Cirode "ran off all of his negroes" from the city. Johnston now demanded that the Frenchman or his agents appear before the court to tell what became of them.[13]

Another plaintiff, Pierre Roy, repeated the question in a lawsuit in Louisville only a few years later. By then, Roy, a former associate of Cirode's, had been forced to pay off some of the Frenchman's many debts, and he wanted to be reimbursed from whatever remained of Cirode's estate. Toward the end of 1849, Roy succeeded in locating one more lot of land in Kentucky that Cirode still owned, and he also learned that a "negro man William" had been hired out for $100 a year by an agent of Jane Cirode. When Roy won his suit, in 1850, both the enslaved man named William and the town lot belonging to Cirode were sold at public auction outside a courthouse in Louisville.[14]

By then, Jane Cirode had likely already learned that her husband's creditors were closing in. And if an agent or a friend in Louisville did tip her off, then Cirode would have had a mixture of motives for her sudden decision to bring Wood with her to Cincinnati. She may have preferred, all things considered, to continue hiring Wood out in Kentucky, collecting a steady annual check. But that would leave Wood vulnerable to seizure by a court, and such a loss would deprive Cirode of profits from her labor. Like many slaveholders who lived near the borders of other states, however, Cirode had a third option: she could remove

Wood into a new jurisdiction, one that Kentucky courts could not easily reach.[15]

Putting Wood to work in the boardinghouse also saved Cirode the costs of hiring someone else to clean rooms and cook for her business—a low-profit venture even in the best of cases. The boardinghouse was one of nearly two hundred in the city, many operated by women and most offering rooms and meals for several dollars per week, with laundering available for an added fee. Landladies competed to show that their houses were better kept than the others, taking in hired help when they could, and in Cirode's house, Wood did the sort of work that could attract and keep customers—without being paid herself.[16]

Wood later recalled to Hearn that she worked at the boardinghouse for months before Cirode said anything about her freedom. Although one of Ohio's so-called Black Laws required that any black newcomer to the state be registered with a court as free before they could be employed, the law was unevenly enforced, and Cirode probably remained among those inclined to ignore Lane's 1841 ruling on automatic emancipation. Perhaps she even held the promise of an eventual manumission over Wood's head to secure her help.[17]

Cirode was running a risk, though, by bringing Wood to the city. Henrietta's duties required her to go into the streets, at the very least to draw water or to empty chamber pots. Eventually she might learn from someone there, or perhaps from a meddling guest, that there were legal grounds for her to claim her freedom—if she had not already divined that fact. Those concerns, more than any other, likely moved Jane Cirode to act in the end. Even so, she waited until the spring of 1848, after Wood had been in the city for about a year, before she finally visited the Hamilton County Courthouse and registered Wood's presence in Cincinnati—an act that also made Henrietta verifiably free.

The courthouse stood at the corner of Main Street and Court, only a few blocks north of Cirode's boardinghouse. When completed in 1819, the building had still been on the outskirts of town, but the city's sprawl had long since surrounded the courthouse with slaughterhouses and factories. Now it was considered by many to be an aging eyesore, a boxy, boring structure with a wooden spire and a cupola colonized by pigeons. Wood remembered it as the scene of a turning point in her life: the definitive moment when she ceased to be, legally speaking, Jane Cirode's slave. "My mistress gave me my freedom," she later recalled, "and my papers were recorded."[18]

On paper, Henrietta Wood was now one of Cincinnati's more than three thousand free people of color, one of the largest such communities in the nation. After the mob attacks of 1841, the community's leaders had worked hard to build institutions for self-defense and mutual aid in the city: churches, charities, and even some networks with white sympathizers. Even before the mob attacks, a small number of white antislavery activists in the city had also begun working together with black men and women: denouncing slavery, assisting runaway slaves from across the river, and protesting the state's Black Laws until their partial repeal in 1849. Wood may well have come into contact with some of those organizations or activists, and with other free black women and men.[19]

Yet her daily life also went on, at first, as it had before. She would quickly learn that free black women had few choices for jobs in Porkopolis. Almost every black woman in the city—probably nine out of ten—labored at the same work that she had done for years: washing, ironing, and cleaning.[20]

Wood, too, continued to do the same job for Cirode. And even though she was free, she did not get good wages. As she later told Hearn, her former mistress only "gave me a little money from time to time"—nothing she could depend on to build a livelihood of her own, or to move very far away.[21]

That lack of mobility may have been precisely what Cirode intended. Her own feelings about Wood's legal freedom never would be clear. She may have acknowledged her freedom grudgingly, and only on the condition that Wood remain in her employ. Perhaps she even intended to send Wood back to Kentucky once her husband's creditors had given up their search for his slaves. In any case, the white woman seemed reluctant to give up her habit of command. Jane was accustomed to telling Henrietta where she would go and what she would do, and she had given her some cash from time to time. Even after all of Wood's unpaid toil, Cirode could still believe that it was Wood who owed something to her. Such may have been the depth of her assumptions about the right to rule.

Whatever Cirode's reasoning, it frustrated Wood. She understood her freedom to include, at a minimum, that she be paid for her work. The conflicts between the two women must have ranged across other terrain as well, conflicts repeated in many households where work once done by enslaved black women was suddenly performed by women who had been freed. Both before and after slavery, black women and white women frequently disagreed over tasks and expectations. But as soon as the work of a chambermaid or cook was paid instead of compelled, black women had more bargaining power than before. A laundress who knew she would be paid by the piece or the pound might complete her work more quickly than she had done while enslaved, expecting that her employer would provide more tasks to fill her time— and her pockets. At the same time, freed women still often expected to receive customary privileges that were sometimes granted even to the enslaved, such as a room of their own, or time off on Sundays, or the supplies to do the work—all of which their employers might refuse or count as wages. Wood worked for at least two more years without ever receiving what she believed to be fair pay, until she decided to gauge the measure of her freedom from Cirode. As Wood later put it, "I left her at last."[22]

The leaving must have been a thrilling step for Wood, however limited her options for better employment. She began by looking for work within the same neighborhood, and she was hired for several domestic positions in succession, mainly at boardinghouses and family homes that fell between Sixth Street on the north, Fifth Street on the south, and Sycamore and Broadway to the west and east. She also began to collect, for the first time in her life, some "little things" that she could truly say were *hers*.[23]

At some point, she even acquired a small trunk in which to keep the few possessions that she could afford. Her most precious possession, though, was a copy of her "freedom papers" that she had received when they were recorded. Though long in coming, those papers, which she also stored in her trunk, afforded her an autonomy she had never had before. And they only became more precious after she struck out on her own, because one day, while Wood was "working around," she witnessed the Hamilton County Courthouse going up in flames.[24]

The fire broke out on a Monday in July 1849. It began, according to later reports, when sparks from a nearby slaughterhouse ignited the building's cupola in the heat of the afternoon. Before long, another witness recalled, the wooden roof was engulfed by "wrapping, warping, writhing, enclosing flames." The fire sent billows of smoke and ash into the summer sky. Scores of birds fled their nests in the crumbling rafters. The "dome, spire and steeple and roof soon fell with a tremendous crash" into the heart of the structure. Then the blaze burned on, blackening all the walls.[25]

Few white residents of the city were sorry to see the building go. (One prominent antislavery lawyer noted in his diary that afternoon that he "never saw the firemen so slow in getting out their Engines— Every body glad that the old Nuisance abated.") A new, more modern building later arose in its place. For Wood, however, the burning of the courthouse must have been a chilling sight. Inside that smoldering wreck was the proof that she was free.[26]

Wood later recalled hearing that "the big book" in which free papers like hers were recorded had been saved from the fire and moved to Columbus—a consoling rumor, though probably untrue. Returning home that night after witnessing the blaze, she may have sought a little reassurance in the copy of her papers that she still possessed, maybe buried them just a bit deeper in her trunk.

One year then passed, then another, and another. Henrietta drifted farther south of Cirode's place, looking for work. At last she took a job in a boardinghouse run by Rebecca Boyd, a dentist's wife whose place she found on Fourth Street, nearer the river. Boyd had a much rougher and more transient clientele: "steamboatmen," Wood recalled. In other ways, though, her new boss proved to be much like Cirode. She "never paid me a cent," Wood later told Hearn, "although she promised to do so all the time."[27]

Still, Wood had those papers. She had the power to leave. And so she did not suspect the worst when Boyd came to her in April 1853, four years after the courthouse had burned, and suggested they take a nice Sunday ride in a carriage before supper—across the Ohio River, with all the curtains drawn.

CHAPTER SIX

THE PLAN

As night fell, three men met the carriage on a road outside Covington. That brought the number involved in Wood's abduction to five: Rebecca Boyd, John Gilbert, Franklin Rust, Willoughby Scott, and Zebulon Ward. But two other people had helped set the events of that night in motion: William Cirode's daughter, Josephine, and her husband, Robert White.

After the troubles in Mobile that chased Cirode to France, the Whites had followed Josephine's mother, Jane, back to Kentucky. By 1849, they had settled in Covington, where Robert opened another store selling "Family Groceries, Pure Old Wines, and Liquors." For several years he paid for an advertisement on the front page of the *Covington Journal*, suggesting some degree of success.[1]

As 1853 began, however, White was facing disaster again. He had lasted longer in Kentucky than he did in Alabama, perhaps by being more careful this time with credit, as his father-in-law had once urged; White's ad promised that he would "sell only for cash." Nevertheless, in April 1853, the same month Wood was kidnapped, White sold his entire stock at auction. By July, he was out of business and rumored to have assigned and stored his remaining property away—a means of avoiding creditors. This time, though, his father-in-law could not bail him out.[2]

Or could he? At some point that spring, the Whites remembered one of the slave women Jane Cirode had brought back to Kentucky almost ten years earlier. Robert and Josephine both knew that William Cirode had left Henrietta with his wife, and Josephine had "always wanted her mother to sell me," as Wood later recalled.[3]

By 1853, selling a woman like Wood could bring a significant sum. In the few years prior there had been a boom in the growth of professional slave-trading firms in Kentucky. Franklin Rust—the man with the bumpy face whom she identified as one of her captors—was well known as a "negro trader." He lived outside of Covington. And Washington "Wash" Bolton was the Kentucky agent for one of the largest slave-trading businesses in the nation. Founded in Memphis in 1847, within ten years Bolton, Dickens, and Company would run "through transactions amounting in the aggregate to several millions of dollars," according to a later lawsuit involving the firm's dissolution. Wash Bolton had been with the company since 1850, and he often paid agents to travel through Kentucky, buying up slaves for sale down the river. A person sold for $400 in 1830 might be worth four times as much in 1853.[4]

The Whites would have known, of course, that Cirode had taken Wood to Ohio, and indeed may even have seen her there on visits across the river. They may have believed that they were still entitled to the capital that Wood once represented. William Cirode had clearly meant to leave some of his property behind for his daughter, and after the Frenchman's fraudulent mortgage with Weathered was exposed, Josephine may have coveted his slaves all the more. They were the only form of inheritance that she had left.

Once Wood was living as a free woman in Cincinnati, however, selling her was not a simple proposition. Before she could be sold, she would have to be abducted. Before she could be abducted, she would have to be found. The Whites wanted the money from a sale, but they did not want the dirty work that would have to be done. So sometime in the spring of 1853, they evidently decided to bring someone else into their confidence: the deputy sheriff of Kenton County, Zebulon Ward.

Robert was the one who apparently spoke to Zeb about the subject, perhaps while the officer stopped in for a dram or a chat at his store. He evidently made the deputy sheriff a proposal. If given $300 for Wood up front, an amount far below the price she would fetch once captured, White would sell his supposed rights to the woman to Ward.[5]

What White suggested was risky, no doubt. After all, Wood might not be easily found. Or she might be taken, but die or escape before she could be sold. If Ward agreed to the deal, he would have to account for possible resistance to her capture. And if he did pay $300 up front, his bet would be in the pot from the start.

Yet Ward never was afraid to roll the dice. Whether the job could be done was a fair question. Gold in the hills and gold in his pocket were two different things, Ward knew. But if the thing could be done, it would have appealed enormously, for it became more like the questions Ward knew best. Could he buy the hoop poles cheap and then sell them dear? Could his steamboat give a low rate and then speed up the river, where even higher rates might be found? Could he arrange the capture of Wood and sell her for a profit? In the end, Ward decided that he could. He told White they had a deal.

According to later testimony by Ward himself, the deal was struck in March 1853, when he paid Robert White $300. Exactly what White had told him is difficult to know. Ward claimed to have believed that Wood had belonged to White "for many years" and had gone without his consent to Ohio. It would not have been unusual for a deputy sheriff along the border to help in the recovery of a runaway slave.[6]

It would have been unusual, though, for the sheriff first to pay the owner, and the amount that Ward remembered paying further undercut his later claim that he was just enforcing the law. Slaveholders who wished to recover runaway slaves often paid a bounty to have them tracked down. So if Wood was a runaway, it would have made more sense for White to pay the deputy than the other way around. Then the Whites could profit by selling her themselves, for a much higher price than the one Ward paid.[7]

Three hundred dollars made more sense if White owed a debt to Zebulon Ward, or the other way around. Then the amount Ward paid could have been a way of settling accounts, with the value of the slave taking care of the balance. But even such a scenario strains the imagination. Wood was not an asset ready to hand. She had no value for either man unless she could be captured.

Ward and White were doubtless aware that capturing and selling Wood were acts of questionable legality at best, even in Kentucky, but the Whites may have believed they could make a case in court that she should never have been freed by Jane Cirode. (In fact, that claim would later be advanced by Ward, revealing that he probably knew more about the family's history than he sometimes let on.) Or, if he knew that his title to Wood was not clear, White might have been trying to cut his losses by shifting risks onto the buyer—Ward. Perhaps Ward even paid the $300 for nothing more than tips about her whereabouts, along with a plausible story for buyers down the line. Finally, simply to consider all the possibilities, perhaps Ward did not pay Robert White at all. The only evidence that he did remains his own word. The deputy sheriff might only have heard White telling stories about a woman freed by his mother-in-law—and then decided to act on his own.

Whatever occurred, Ward next had to formulate a plan to capture the woman he probably paid for—a plan that revolved around two practical questions. First, who could help him find and abduct Wood from Ohio? Then, once she was safely across the river and in his grasp, who would be willing to buy her—hopefully for a price above the one that Ward had paid?

The buyer was the lesser of Ward's concerns. Slave traders advertised widely in the papers. Many would buy with few questions asked, and all of them knew how to make a slave disappear to a distant state. By 1853, a black woman sold in Covington or Lexington could be loaded on a ferry or a train to Louisville and placed that same day on a steamboat bound for Natchez or St. Louis or New Orleans.[8]

Ward knew from his own years on the river what would happen then. Most captains or clerks would view an enslaved passenger as familiar cargo. A bystander would scarcely raise an eyebrow at any particular woman, not when thousands were shackled to decks every year. As one steamboat captain at the time said, the "transportation of slaves was part of the regular business of steamboats on the Ohio River." One formerly enslaved man later recalled that the appearance of "a drove of southern slaves on a southern steamboat" was "an occurrence so common, that no one, not even the passengers, appear to notice it, though they clank their chains at every step." If Ward could sell the woman from Cincinnati down the river, then the chances were good he would never hear of her again.[9]

That plan presumed that Ward could capture her first, but slave traders in Kentucky knew how to do that, too. One of the most notorious was a man named Lewis Robards. His slave pen in Lexington doubled as a well-known "rendezvous for a gang of kidnappers and nigger thieves," according to testimony in a lawsuit involving him, and the gang often crossed the river to do its work. Once, for example, the gang used an ax to break open the door of a free black family's cabin in Portsmouth, Ohio. The brigands assaulted a man in the house and then seized a five-year-old girl named Martha. She and six of her siblings were taken away to be sold.[10]

In another 1850 incident, which ended up in court, Robards was found to have paid a man $600 to kidnap Arian Belle, a free black woman in Mason County, and her four-year-old child under cover of night. Robards succeeded in selling the woman for $850 to a Louisiana planter and even had her boarded on a steamboat bound for the Mississippi River, before some white neighbors of Belle's intervened and stopped the sale.[11]

No one could say for sure how many kidnappings had occurred at the hands of Robards's gang. Men such as these had good reason to keep their movements cloaked. Occasionally, though, the mask fell off, disclosing a shadowy underworld. The man Robards paid to kidnap Belle, for example, was James Macmillan, an agent who usually worked for Robards buying slaves and sometimes worked for Wash Bolton, too. Receipts in Robards's account books confirm at least one transaction between the trader and Willoughby Scott, one of the men Wood identified as a kidnapper; on March 25, 1853, Scott sold Robards a fourteen-year-old boy named Armstead, a thirteen-year-old girl named Roxanna, and an eleven-year-old named Sarah Ann. Franklin Rust was also a usual suspect in such affairs. A few slave-catching networks in the border states even included free black men who aided kidnappers for pay and some security for themselves; John Gilbert, the black driver of the carriage that brought Wood across the river, may have been one of them.[12]

Technically, predators such as these and officers such as Ward were on opposite sides of the law, but kidnapping gangs often worked with sheriffs, too. Lawmen could help by giving the gangs legal cover, spinning stories about how the people they were capturing were fugitive slaves. Sheriffs in slave states also had every incentive to tolerate kidnappers instead of working against them.[13]

Ward thus had many reasons to anticipate success. There were men who would buy—and gangs who would catch—Henrietta Wood. But there were also some potential snags he would have to steer around. And first among those obstacles was a movement of radical abolitionists on the other side of the river, who by 1853 had a reputation for thwarting plans like his.

Organized opposition to slavery had existed among some white reformers in the United States since the eighteenth century. The Pennsylvania Abolition Society, founded in 1775 and rooted in an older tradition of Quaker opposition to slavery, had pursued a careful strategy of lobbying for gradual emancipation, as had postrevolutionary manumission societies in other states. Though these groups often relied on the actions of free and enslaved African Americans to initiate litigation attacking slavery, most elite white philanthropists stopped short of including black abolitionists as equal partners in the struggle.[14]

The early 1830s marked a watershed in the history of American abolitionism. In 1832 in Boston, a group of abolitionists, white and black, joined together in a society calling for immediate emancipation of all slaves, using grassroots tactics that were far more radical than those used by earlier antislavery groups. The formation of the Boston group was followed in 1833 by a national organization, the American Anti-Slavery Society, which would eventually comprise about three hundred thousand members across the free states, including formerly enslaved activists such as Frederick Douglass. The new society made some of its most significant converts in the northeastern region of Ohio known as the Western Reserve, and in 1835, abolitionists there had formed the Ohio Anti-Slavery Society.[15]

Abolitionists met with more resistance along the Ohio River. Cincinnati in particular had a reputation as the most culturally southern city in the northern United States, and abolitionists were far less welcome there than in the Western Reserve. In August 1837, Cincinnati constables even assisted some Kentucky "desperadoes" in entering the home of a black man to capture a woman inside. That same year, another band of white men seized Eliza Jane Johnson, a black woman living in nearby Ripley, Ohio, who was alleged to have run away. The men flogged Johnson and took her without warrant to Kentucky, where a county judge ruled that she was not the runaway that the men had intended to capture. He kept her jailed anyway and said that she could be sold in two months.[16]

Though abolitionists publicized such outrages, many locals reacted only with shrugs. By custom, the white citizens of Ohio had usually made clear that they would not disturb the rights of enslavers to their south. Ohio politicians often lauded the absence of slavery in their own state, yet most were willing to look the other way when Kentuckians entered Ohio to capture black men and women. The constant potential for serious conflict over runaway slaves in the region made accommodation seem necessary, and many feared that more liberal antislavery laws would attract an unwanted wave of black people into Ohio. In 1839, the Ohio state legislature even passed a law that penalized helping escaped slaves.[17]

These developments left free black men and women themselves to form the front lines of resistance to slavery in southern Ohio. In addition to attending state and national conventions of free black activists, including one held in Cincinnati in 1852, African Americans led the way in organizing the networks that became known as the Underground Railroad. Many put their own lives on the line to assist runaway slaves in Cincinnati and to fight "slave catchers." John Hatfield, for example, spent the 1840s running a barbershop and bathhouse only a few blocks away from the neighborhood where Wood found work after obtaining her freedom. He described himself as a "mulatto" born in Pennsylvania and often harbored runaway slaves in his home. Black settlements in the city's hinterlands performed the same work of taking in black people who made it across the river and helping them get to relative safety farther north.[18]

Slowly, free black activists also started to win some sympathy from white allies and abolitionists in the Old Northwest. Some Ohio state leaders even began to adopt their rhetoric. In 1842, one former senator in Ohio warned that kidnappings of black Northerners were a potential "cause of war." Then, a few years later, an Ohio attorney bemoaned the existence of "a horde of pirates" on both sides of the Ohio River who "make man-catching a trade," denouncing them as "enemies of the human race."[19]

Sympathetic white lawyers were especially important to the free black community in southern Ohio, and among the most sympathetic was Salmon P. Chase. In 1837, Chase was one of the first to argue in court that any enslaved person who set foot on Ohio soil with the consent of an owner was automatically freed—the position that Judge Ebenezer Lane eventually affirmed in 1841. Using such arguments, white lawyers could sometimes secure writs of habeas corpus to try to stop would-be enslavers before they returned to Kentucky with their captives. Chase's views were far from universally shared, but antislavery lawyers knew which judges were the most likely to be persuaded, and activists such as Hatfield knew which lawyers were most like Chase.[20]

All of this was enough to cause deep concern among slaveholders who lived just across the river. They worried that the organized work of abolitionists to change Ohio laws and protect fugitives would lead to the slow but steady disappearance of slaves who lived close to free state borders. Some Kentuckians even channeled their ire over abolitionist meddling into armed vigilante groups whose members swore to defend slavery in the state.[21]

One such group, the Kenton County Association, formed in Covington in November 1841, stating that "its object shall be the security of our Servants, and the recovery of such as may abscond from their masters or owners." Members of the association agreed to patrol the county to keep an eye out for "suspicious persons" and to ensure that all laws respecting slaves and free black people were being followed. In 1847, association members even traveled to Cass County, Michigan, hoping to capture and bring back a number of free black families whom they claimed were runaway slaves. The expedition included Frank Rust as a hired gun.[22]

The raiders returned home to Kenton County empty-handed after local antislavery Quakers managed to block the slave-catchers in court, but the episode hardly quelled white Kentuckians' concerns. And it did not prevent further conflicts along the Ohio between "river pirates" and their opponents. Although black families in Cass County may have breathed a temporary sigh of relief, others were not so fortunate, including a man named George Jackson, whose sad story was related in the *Cincinnati Gazette* on May 11, 1850.

Jackson had lived in Cincinnati "for several years." He kept a bar in the National Theater. But a white man who lived in Tennessee claimed that Jackson was his slave. At about half past one on May 10, a Friday afternoon, Jackson was walking near the corner of Walnut and Fifth Streets, not far from Jane Cirode's boardinghouse on Sixth, when several men accosted him. Jackson was "dragged down Walnut street to the river," reported the *Gazette* the next day, while a concerned crowd followed the men. The crowd had barely advanced a block when one of the men holding Jackson "brandished a bowie knife, and the other drew a pistol."[23]

"He's my nigger and I'll have him," barked a third man to the crowd.

Unbowed, the crowd continued to follow the men to Columbia Street. According to the *Gazette*, members of the mob even threw "stones and brickbats" at the kidnappers, wounding one. Jackson, meanwhile, continued to scream for help. The scuffle so delayed his captors that when they arrived at the water's edge, the steam ferry to Covington was already pulling away.

"Hold up!" shouted one of the abductors to the ferry captain, yelling that if he did not, "he was no Kentuckian." They reached the wharf with Jackson still in tow, just as the ferry's bow "had been pushed off." But then, said the *Gazette*, the men "were able to force the negro on the stern." A few more stones from the crowd fell harmlessly into the water, and the ferry steamed silently across the Ohio.[24]

The Quakers in Michigan and the crowd that tried to help Jackson showed the progress that abolitionists had made over the previous decade. They had aroused significant concern over the operations of "river pirates" in the region. Both episodes also showed what Ward might contend with while trying to capture Wood. That April, a little more than a week after Wood was abducted, the *Covington Journal* would claim that "within a month past, perhaps not less than forty slaves have run away from the northern border of Kentucky" to Cincinnati, "where every obstacle is thrown in the way of a re-capture of fugitives."[25]

In truth, though, by 1853 the dangers facing runaway slaves and free black residents in Cincinnati were greater than the obstacles that confronted their enemies. In September 1850, Congress had approved a new federal Fugitive Slave Law that had passed with the strong support of border-state politicians. The new law stipulated that when an alleged fugitive was captured in a free state, a special federal commissioner—not a local or state judge—would decide whether the person in question was a slave. And the thinnest evidence would now suffice to prove ownership of a person. A simple affidavit by the purported owner, or a runaway advertisement that matched the physical description of the person captured, could be enough to satisfy a commissioner that a black man or black woman was a slave.[26]

The law did not stop runaway slaves from escaping into the North. By some estimates, such escapes from Kentucky even grew in the decade after the law was passed. Still, free black Americans across the North immediately grasped the danger in these draconian new rules. The 1850 federal law denied any due process rights to people accused of being slaves and allowed federal marshals to deputize any white citizen to assist in making arrests. A black woman captured and brought before a commissioner could not produce freedom papers in her defense, testify on her own behalf, or argue that her captor had mistaken her for someone else. The federal commissioners in a case were even paid more money—$10 instead of $5—if they decided in favor of the captor than if they released the alleged fugitive.[27]

Some free black Northerners resolved to resist the law's enforcement; others decided to leave the country rather than risk enslavement. One resident of Salem, Ohio, in the northeastern part of the state, reported in the fall of 1850 that many "fugitives" living there had already fled "to Canada, in consequence of the infamous slave bill." John Hatfield wrote that the "oppressive laws" eventually convinced him to leave Cincinnati for Canada, too.[28]

For Ward, meanwhile, the Fugitive Slave Law of 1850 offered a useful backup plan if anything went awry while kidnapping Wood. If abolitionists in Ohio tried to interfere, or a lawyer such as Salmon Chase caught wind of what was happening, Ward could claim that she was in fact a runaway slave. With a quick appearance before a federal commissioner and some prima facie evidence of his rights to Wood, Ward could be on his way.[29]

On the other hand, Ward knew that the Fugitive Slave Law had also sparked defiance among abolitionists. Stowe's serialized novel *Uncle Tom's Cabin* was inspired by opposition to the law and her own observations of life in Cincinnati. The completed novel appeared, to wide acclaim, in 1852—a year before Zeb struck his deal with Robert White. By then, several high-profile incidents in other states had also indicated what concerted resistance to the Fugitive Slave Law could do. In February 1851, an interracial group of abolitionists in Boston succeeded in disrupting a hearing involving a runaway slave named Shadrach Minkins. He escaped to Canada. Later that same year, abolitionists in New York muscled their way into a city jail and freed a runaway, only a few weeks after a gun battle in Christiana, Pennsylvania, between local abolitionists and a posse of slave catchers.[30]

In this climate of heightened conflict, it would hardly have been wise for Ward to storm into Cincinnati. Better to move more discreetly. Send Frank Rust into the city to scout out Wood's location. Make a side deal with someone she knew, perhaps an employer who could bring Wood into her confidence. Put her in a carriage with the windows blacked out, so that no pious meddler could see she was inside. Then lure her across the river before a hue and cry could be raised.

So, at least, Ward may have thought, but there was always one contingency he could not control. He could not predict in advance how Wood might react. Only a few years before, in May 1848, Rust had purchased a family of enslaved people—a man, wife, and child—from a farmer in Kentucky. Rust brought all three to a pen in Covington, intending to "start with them the next day down the river," as an article in the *Cincinnati Enquirer* noted. But in the morning, the jailer entered their cell to find a horrifying scene: the bodies of all three people "weltering in their blood—*their throats having been cut!*"[31]

A story to explain the bloodshed quickly emerged in the press. It was said that the distraught father, fearing he would be separated from his family, had murdered his wife and child with a common penknife and then tried to cut his own throat, leaving him barely alive and unable to speak. Whatever actually happened, the slaughter left abolitionists and their enemies to do the talking about the case. Antislavery newspapers north of the river claimed that the man and his wife evidently considered the slavery for which they were bound "a hell, to be gladly escaped from by death."[32]

Antiabolitionists, on the other hand, made the counterclaim that the enslaved man Rust had purchased in 1848 requested his own sale but then came to regret his own choice. All that mattered to Rust, in the end, was that the human beings he had purchased were worth much less to him dead than alive. In 1853, Ward would have wanted to avoid a similar loss.[33]

That was why, on that Sunday in April of 1853, after Wood stepped out of Rebecca Boyd's hack and into the custody of Rust, Ward, and Scott, the abductors would watch her carefully throughout the coming night. A guard would be placed at the door—"one of the poor white trash," Wood later recalled, "you could find every place in the South them days, who were ready to hunt a runaway nigger or do any other dirty work the slave owners might bid them."[34]

Her skirt pockets were carefully searched—not just for freedom papers, but also for any instruments that she might turn into weapons. The men did everything they could to prevent her death or escape. Still, there was more than one way for Wood to ruin Ward's plans. His gang was well prepared if she tried to run or to cut her throat. They were less prepared for what would happen when she decided to speak.

CHAPTER SEVEN

THE FLIGHT

As Henrietta Wood finished telling her story, the innkeeper who had appeared at her door in Florence wanted to know more.

"Who do you know in Cincinnati?" Williams asked.[1]

It was the second morning of her captivity, and the men who had warned her not to talk still had not returned from their side trip to Burlington. From outside her second-story room came the sounds of traffic on the turnpike below. Besides Williams, a group of women—maybe his mother and sisters, she thought—had gathered to listen to Wood's sad tale. They "were all standing round talking and feeling sorry for me," she later recalled. "The family all said they knew I'd been stole." Now they wanted to know whom she had met during her years of freedom.[2]

Twenty-three years later, Lafcadio Hearn apparently asked the same question in his interview with Wood. She replied then with a partial list of the people she had worked for after leaving Jane Cirode. One was "Mrs. Tuttle," probably the French-born Sarah A. Tuttle, who kept a boardinghouse on the corner of Sycamore and Fifth. Another employer she remembered as "Preacher Swampson," though Hearn may simply have misspelled the name of the Reverend Leroy Swormstedt, a Methodist minister who lived on Broadway between Fifth and Sixth. Finally, Wood had also worked for a "Mrs. Wilcox," likely a free black woman who maintained a boardinghouse.[3]

Looking back, that work may have been especially meaningful, because the Wilcox family held an elite position within the city's free black community. Samuel T. Wilcox was a former steamboat steward who by 1850 had used real estate investments to accumulate $25,000 in capital. That year, he opened a grocery store on the corner of Broadway and Fifth, where his shelves boasted a cornucopia of fruits, vegetables, cigars, fine wines, and other high-end goods. In one year alone, Wilcox recorded $140,000 in sales, making him one of the nation's most successful black entrepreneurs, even as he carefully concealed his race from suppliers up the river.[4]

Wilcox's store sat on the northern edge of a First Ward neighborhood where many of Cincinnati's African Americans then lived, and Wood placed the boardinghouse where she worked for a Mrs. Wilcox on the same corner. Probably Mrs. Wilcox was Samuel Wilcox's wife, or at least a close relation, and in her example Wood may have seen what freedom might ultimately make possible for her. In addition, by working for a prominent free black family, she would have learned more about her own legal rights, as well as strategies used by other free black persons to defend their community against frequent attacks.[5]

In Florence, however, time was of the essence, and the question from Williams—*who do you know?*—was still in the air. Wood likely knew that Wilcox was not the best contact to mention to a white stranger in Kentucky, even one who seemed surprisingly willing to help. Instead, she mentioned her former owner, Cirode, who could at least verify that Wood had been freed. She also mentioned the Tuttles. Then she threw out a name that Williams seemed to know: Leonard Armstrong.

"Do you know Leonard Armstrong, really?" Wood remembered Williams asking. "Well I know Leonard, too."[6]

The name hung suspended between them, like a rope bridge swinging above a windy gorge. Finally, Wood recalled, the innkeeper risked a step in her direction.

"I'll go over to Cincinnati," Williams said, "and if you are free they shall not take you any farther than Lexington."[7]

Just then, the sound of a buggy on the road interrupted their talk. The captors had suddenly returned, earlier than expected, and Williams shut the door behind him as he left. "Immediately after," Wood explained to Hearn, she heard the horn announcing that the stagecoach to Lexington would be leaving soon, and a "shout came up the stairs for me to come down." Williams appeared at her bedroom again to repeat his promise. "I'll see you in Lexington," he said, "and if I can't do you any good, have no fears. I'll do you no harm."[8]

Outside Wood saw Scott again, but Rust had not returned. A new trader, Washington Bolton, had replaced him. The sun was high when they opened the door of the already crowded coach. Wood recalled being squeezed into the compartment. Then the driver, seated on top, turned toward Lexington, deep in the heart of Kentucky. The stage made its way across miles of macadamized road, bouncing through ruts and potholes and stopping once so the horses could rest. Henrietta remained silent throughout the entire trip.[9]

It was already dark by the time the coach arrived in Lexington. Wood remembered it pulling up beside "a large building, having a yard around it, with a high fence." She and the other passengers were guided inside, and she saw a crowd of "colored persons" standing around in the dimness. She heard an iron gate clanging shut behind her. Then, as she later put it, "my heart sank within me" as she realized where she was. She had arrived in the "slave pen" of the trader Lewis Robards.[10]

Of all the Kentucky slave traders whose business was booming in the early 1850s, Robards was the most established. An active buyer since 1848, he had first set up shop at the Phoenix Hotel in Lexington, where he announced that he would purchase any "merchantable negroes" at "the HIGHEST CASH PRICE." Then Robards expanded. He leased a building on Broadway that was previously used by William Pullum, another Lexington trader, and he also acquired a second building—an old theater on Short Street. He then rebuilt the theater into what he called "the largest and best constructed...jail in the West."[11]

By 1853, that jail was widely known as a place where Kentuckians could buy slaves or pay to have them temporarily confined. Robards sold to local buyers and to interstate traders who collected large groups of people and took them to markets farther south, and he employed agents who traveled through the countryside purchasing slaves for him. One such agent, Rodes Woods, described the boss's typical orders in a deposition for a trial. He was supposed to "buy any negroes I could" so they could "be sold as quickly as possible for cash."[12]

In the morning light, Henrietta could see more of the complex where such sales took place. During the night, she had been confined in the common "pen" where Robards kept most of the slaves he would sell. Now she saw that adjoining the pen was a two-story brick house where Robards himself lived, along with a woman of color who was known locally as his wife but was probably his slave. Her name, "Beck Robards," would stick with Wood throughout the decades to come.[13]

That first day in Lexington, Wood was moved quickly into Robards's house. The reason, she guessed, was that "buyers were permitted to go in and out of the slave pen," and there was a danger that someone aware of her abduction might spot her outside. But Robards might also have had other plans for Wood. It was well known that the house was where he imprisoned his "choice stock" of women, as some called them—"fancy girls" who were groomed by Beck and then marketed to male customers. One visitor who saw the inside of the house in 1854, only one year after Wood arrived, described its finely appointed rooms where "handsome," light-skinned women sat "at their needle work awaiting a purchaser." It was said that when potential buyers arrived, Robards or Beck made the women stand, turn around, and expose themselves to their clients' gapes and gropes.[14]

Whether Wood was subjected to such sexual abuse, she either did not say or Hearn did not record. Over the following days, however, she took in her surroundings, including a sixty-foot-long saleroom known as "the show." The word evoked the prison's earlier life as a working theater, and Wood first glimpsed the inside by peering through a small hole in a wall. Later, in the *Ripley Bee*, she would describe the scene. Within were "50 or 60 inmates of all ages and colors of both sexes." Enslaved women and girls were clad in calico dresses of blue or red with white spots. Enslaved men had "dark blue pants, blue blouse coats and broad lay-down collars." She saw shoppers making these people dance, "feeling their limbs" and shoving their fingers into their mouths, "looking at their teeth just as you would a horse's." Some of the inmates she observed were busily walking around, anxiously checking their appearance. A spot of dirt or uncombed hair might well bring a whipping.[15]

Henrietta eventually withdrew her eye from the wall, fearing that she too would soon be in the show. All her hopes now were pinned on the promise that Williams had made.

For two weeks at least, no news came. Wood spent most days inside, where she was forced to assist in the marketing of human beings for sale, sewing shirts worn by the men in the show. She ate her meals in the kitchen, always under the eye of Beck. Then one morning, as she was taking her breakfast, Wood looked up and saw Williams in the yard, furtively scanning faces. She recalled that he turned, looked through a window, and saw her sitting there.[16]

Williams quickly looked away and hurried out of the yard, but Wood could not suppress a small, reflexive grin. Surely the innkeeper had come because he knew she had told him the truth. Maybe he even had some proof to show that she was free. Beck, however, noticed the flash of recognition. She immediately ran to find Robards, and Wood remembered hearing her tell him what had happened: "Henrietta smiled at a stranger."[17]

Minutes later, Robards had forced her into another buggy, a bonnet wrapped around her face. She was taken to the house of a woman named Fogle. "She wants you to do some sewing," Wood remembered Robards claiming, as though he could hide the real reason for the flight. The trader had already guessed that the stranger would be back. Inside Fogle's house, Wood sat down to receive her instructions, but the women had not even picked up their needles before the buggy reappeared. "An overseer named Woods" now drove the hack, she recalled—perhaps the man, Rodes Woods, whom Robards employed both as a doctor and purchasing agent. He ordered her to get her things and "jump in." Wood had no things to get except for the bonnet on her head, and "nothing to do but obey." "So I got in," she told the *Bee* in 1879, "and he drove me to a place thirty miles from there that day."[18]

The buggy headed southwest onto another pike, carrying her deeper into the countryside, farther away from freedom. Outside, the spring pastures were riotous with life: May flowers; timothy grass; tall, muscular Thoroughbreds. Wood remembered a rural world she had not seen since childhood passing by as she rode: "the birds chattering among the trees, the crow was cawing, the squirrel was running through the woods." Horses let out to graze "came galloping up to the fence to take a look at me," she recalled, "then with head and tail up, trotted nimbly by our side till a partition fence in the meadow brought them to a stand still." To Wood, they appeared to be "mocking" her enslavement and reveling in their freedom.[19]

"I seemed to be," she remembered feeling, "the worst slave of them all."[20]

PART II

FORKS OF THE ROAD

CHAPTER EIGHT

RAISING A MUSS

The farther south the carriage went, the more discouraged she became. Soon they crossed the Kentucky River and continued to Harrodsburg, where Wood was left for the night. The next day, as night fell again, Robards himself came to get her. The trader was "mad, and told me roughly to get into the buggy," she recalled, and she was "afraid that when he got me out in the woods, he would kill me."[1]

What Robards said in the buggy did not calm her fears, as she told Lafcadio Hearn. "On the way back," Wood remembered, "he asked me if I knew the young man that I had smiled at in the show." She replied that she had seen him in Florence but claimed not to know his name.

"Well," Robards spat, "that man's raising a muss about you. But he ain't raising a muss to get you free. He's just raising a muss to hurt Frank Rust."

Wood recalled the trader cursing as he continued.

"God damn you," he said, "he wouldn't care if you never got your freedom."[2]

She had plenty of time to worry about that as the buggy bounced back to Lexington. The carriage arrived in the middle of the night, and Robards put her back inside his jail. Then, in the morning, he told her that she had to go to the courthouse, warning her "to keep your mouth shut, except just to answer what questions you are asked."[3]

Wood remembered deciding to do as Robards demanded. In Florence, she had defied an order to keep quiet, but in the trader's jail "they thought nothing" of hauling black men and women away "and flogging them to death." As before, however, the fear of what would happen if she told her story wrestled with the hope that Williams could help. She was going, after all, to court.[4]

People on both sides of the Ohio had been "raising a muss" about Wood ever since her abduction, more than she could have known at the time. On June 3, 1853, the *Cincinnati Gazette* reported that the case had "created much excitement among the colored population of our city." Women and men in Cincinnati's free black community—people she had worked with and lived alongside—were probably the first to notice Henrietta's disappearance, and at some point, the authorities were alerted. Rebecca Boyd and John Gilbert—the "colored man" who had driven her across the river—were brought before a magistrate and charged with "kidnapping a colored woman," and the news spread quickly across abolitionist networks. On June 24, Frederick Douglass himself noticed the arrest of Boyd and Gilbert in his Rochester, New York, newspaper, reporting that "the case excites a good deal of interest."[5]

John Jolliffe, an abolitionist lawyer, had also quickly been engaged to prosecute the accused. The son of Virginia Quakers, Jolliffe was a short, earnest man who had practiced law in Cincinnati since 1841, and by 1853 he was one of a few local lawyers well known as an ally to people of color. He often worked pro bono to defend runaway slaves or help with manumissions and even wrote two abolitionist novels based on his legal work. The first, published in 1856, features a character named Aaron, who is born free in Ohio but kidnapped and enslaved as a child. Aaron escapes to Ohio as an adult, but then, like Wood, is abducted again and taken by ferry across the Ohio River, while citizens of the free state look on, indifferent. In real life, Jolliffe was determined not to be one of the bystanders depicted in his fiction.[6]

Gilbert and Boyd were brought before a magistrate again on June 6, 1853, and by then Jolliffe and two other lawyers had collected evidence of a crime. At the June 6 hearing, for instance, Jolliffe presented testimony from Ellen Hamilton, who worked for Boyd as a cook. Though described by a journalist as a "white girl," she may have been the "Ellen Hamilton" listed in the 1850 Census as a black woman in Ward 9, the wife of a cook. Either way, Hamilton had seen Boyd with Wood in a carriage driven by Gilbert. She testified that "the curtains of the carriage were ordered to be buttoned down all around." When Boyd and Gilbert returned several hours later, they "did not bring Henrietta," and Boyd told the cook that some "men took her away from us" in Kentucky, claiming that Wood had gone with the men of her own accord. Hamilton had since heard that "Henrietta sent word" of where she was, perhaps a sign that Williams had already been in the city, asking about Wood and sharing what he knew.[7]

Hamilton's testimony was damning enough, but Jolliffe's team had another witness, a woman named Sarah Spears, possibly a Virginia-born "mulatto" woman who appeared in the 1850 Census. Spears probably worked for Boyd as well, and she said "that Mrs. B told her all about going to Kentucky and losing Henrietta." She identified "Russ" as one of the men who "came up to the carriage." She also said that later, a man named Scott "had forced his way into the room occupied by Henrietta for the purpose of finding the free papers." He enlisted the others at the boardinghouse to search for Wood's documents. Eventually they were found in her trunk, and Spears handed them over to Scott outside. Those papers had clearly shown that Wood had been "manumitted by Jane M. Cirode of Ky. on the 15th of April, 1848."[8]

With the evidence of Spears and Hamilton, Jolliffe had enough for an indictment, and the magistrate ruled that both defendants should be held on bail. As the *Cincinnati Gazette* reported, the facts at least proved Wood had been taken by the defendants in a carriage. Even the *Enquirer*, an antiabolitionist newspaper, found that conclusion to be "strongly corroborated by other witnesses." Both papers agreed that Wood's disappearance was "of so suspicious a nature" as to make it almost certain that she was taken illegally and expressed surprise that the defense had "not brought more testimony" to the contrary.[9]

Meanwhile, on the other side of the river, Williams had also been busy. Wood later learned that after she was rushed away to Harrodsburg, he had returned to the trader's pen. This time he brought the sheriff, Waller Rodes, with him. Williams and Rodes searched the jail without finding Wood. Undaunted, the innkeeper found the driver who had taken her there from Florence. Sheriff Rodes then ordered Robards to bring her back from Harrodsburg. And at about that same time, possibly only a few days after Jolliffe won an indictment in Ohio, a lawsuit was filed in Kentucky in the Fayette County Circuit Court. "Lewis Robards" was entered as the lone defendant; the plaintiff was "Henrietta Wood."[10]

In 1879, Wood summarized that litigation for the *Ripley Bee*. "Some kind of suit" was started in her name in Lexington, she said. Unfortunately, a courthouse fire in 1864 would destroy all of the papers created during the case, a loss that would prove significant later. A court order book from 1853 did survive, however, and it shows that an equity suit had been filed in Fayette County on Wood's behalf—a lawsuit asserting that she should be freed.[11]

The courts of antebellum Kentucky, like those in other southern states, did recognize that a free person might be illegally held as a slave, and people of color sometimes did manage to win "freedom suits." Most belonged to one of two types. The first were cases in which plaintiffs alleged that they had been legally freed in Kentucky by an owner in a will or by some other act of manumission, only to be held in slavery by another party. The second were cases in which plaintiffs claimed to have been freed outside of Kentucky, only to be brought to the state and re-enslaved.[12]

One example of the first, heard by the Kentucky Court of Appeals in 1836, even resembled Wood's story. Like hers, it involved a white woman who had freed a slave after separating from her husband. Cloe Pen had come to Kentucky in 1806, bringing an enslaved woman with her. That woman had given birth to Aleck, whom Pen freed in her will in 1813. Aleck lived as a free man in Kentucky for five years until a white man, Samuel Tevis, enslaved him. Tevis contended that Aleck had belonged to Pen's now-deceased husband and not to Pen, who therefore had no legal right to free him. Tevis also said that he had paid money to the representatives of the husband's estate to buy Aleck, ostensibly with plans to free him someday. But Tevis never had liberated

Aleck. So in 1832, the enslaved man sued for his freedom in a Shelby County court. The court initially dismissed Aleck's case, claiming it had no jurisdiction to set him free. The Court of Appeals then reversed that decision, noting that the extraordinary crime of depriving a free man of freedom made a victim like Aleck "eminently entitled to the extraordinary assistance of a Court of Equity." "Actual slavery is altogether unlike any trespass on a freeman, as a freeman," said the court, which ultimately declared Aleck free.[13]

In 1840, the state Court of Appeals heard a similar suit. A man in Louisville, William White, had freed several slaves upon his death. White's heirs had ignored his wishes, claiming that he had not been of sound mind, and one heir had destroyed the only copy of his will. The people White had freed filed a suit against the heirs, who were trying to keep them enslaved. The plaintiffs not only won the case, but because the defendants had held the slaves "for their own unjust profit," a judge also ruled that the former slaves were entitled to $500 each in restitution. In another, much earlier freedom suit, *Thompson v. Wilmot*, a kidnapped free person of color in Kentucky was awarded $691.25.[14]

By the time of Wood's abduction, some plaintiffs had also been successful in the second type of freedom suit, involving enslaved people who claimed to have been freed outside of the state. Kentucky courts had often ruled that people who were formally freed by an owner somewhere else remained free in Kentucky. The trickier cases, from the perspective of Kentucky judges, were those where an enslaved person had passed into a state where slavery was illegal, had then returned to Kentucky, and then made a claim to freedom solely on the grounds of having been in a free state. Even in those freedom suits, though, some plaintiffs had won, provided that they had lived in the free state for an extended period of time and established "domicile" there.[15]

Those precedents meant that Wood had at least some hope for success in 1853. After all, the testimony collected by Jolliffe in Cincinnati showed that Wood had been living there as a free woman since at least April 15, 1848. But the discovery of evidence in Cincinnati did not mean that it would reach a court in Lexington, where Jolliffe had no influence at all. In addition, even successful freedom suits in Kentucky had to overcome significant obstacles. The tolerance of such suits by Kentucky courts had never arisen from any deep-seated hostility toward slavery as a whole; on the contrary, the idea of *wrongful* enslavement reinforced the idea that most cases of slavery were right. That was why state laws placed heavy burdens of proof on slaves who claimed to be free. In Kentucky, a person of color was presumed a slave until proven otherwise.[16]

Winning restitution in successful freedom suits had also become more difficult by 1853. Although Aleck had received some financial damages after winning his 1836 suit against Tevis, the Kentucky Court of Appeals had made clear that Tevis would not have been liable had he shown he was ignorant of Aleck's free status. The Kentucky General Assembly passed a law in 1840 codifying that principle: white defendants in freedom suits would be exempted from paying damages if they had bought or enslaved a person in good faith. Not surprisingly, most later white defendants claimed the exemption. Restitution was seldom paid.[17]

Kentucky plaintiffs who claimed they had once lived in a free state also faced challenges unique to such suits. No state law *required* Kentucky courts to decide such cases in favor of the plaintiffs, or even to abide by the "once freed, always free" rule. Most judges believed that local courts had the authority to decide a person's status on the basis of its own state's laws. The US Supreme Court affirmed that principle in *Strader v. Graham* (1851), a case that originated in Kentucky. In essence, that ruling confirmed that when Kentucky courts did grant freedom to plaintiffs who had lived in a free state, no controlling federal law or procedure forced them to do so.[18]

Kentucky courts did still have some interest in getting along with northern neighbors by honoring manumissions in Ohio and other bordering states. They hoped that northern courts would reciprocate by honoring the laws that permitted slavery to their south. But the rights of slaveholders also weighed heavily in the rulings of Kentucky judges, who could easily find reasons to tilt the scales in favor of slavery.[19]

Wood's chances of winning a freedom suit were therefore far from assured. Nonetheless, state law did make it a crime to "remove, or attempt to remove, from this Commonwealth, any person of color having a suit pending for freedom." For the time being, that law theoretically protected her from being sold away until her case closed. The freedom suit that someone had filed in her name thus had an immediate effect: it forced Robards to go to Harrodsburg and bring her back to Lexington, where, the morning after they had returned, the trader came and told her she would have to appear in court.[20]

Lexington's courthouse, a red-brick building with a large clock tower on top, stood near the center of town in a square that was bordered on the south by Main, on the north by Short Street, and on the west by Cheapside, a block where townsfolk and farmers often came to shop for goods—and slaves. Robards's jail on Short Street was only a few blocks away, and on court days Cheapside often echoed with the sounds of slaves being hawked to the highest bidder. Though the courthouse looked much like the one in Ohio that Wood had once watched burn, this one had a slave market in its shadow.[21]

That morning, Wood was taken through Cheapside to the courthouse, where Lewis Robards had often appeared as a defendant before. The trader was frequently sued for unscrupulous practices or debts, and he was used to making excuses in his defense. Henrietta, on the other hand, stood for the first time inside the courthouse walls, trying to answer only the questions she was asked—her name, where she worked, and how long she had been with Mrs. Boyd.[22]

"I don't remember exactly what they said," she later confessed to Hearn, and any record of the hearing would be destroyed forever in 1864, when the case file for Wood's freedom suit was incinerated inside another courthouse building. She did recall that a lawyer challenged one answer she gave, but that she was "afraid to say anything back." Then, after the hearing ended, she was taken back into the square, back through Cheapside, back down Short Street, and back to Robards's jail.[23]

Before long, she recalled hearing the voice of a lawyer inside the pen, saying they could not hold her. Then she heard the voice of Washington Bolton, the trader whom she remembered first appearing in Florence.

"I bought that woman and gave $700 for her," Bolton fired back at the lawyer, "and I didn't ask nobody to sell me a free nigger." He swore he would return to Covington and get his money back.[24]

Wood recalled Bolton as "a regular blood thirsty butcher of a man." She was sure that he would get the refund he desired. From whom was less clear. Wood thought she heard the trader say he would recover the money from "White," which she took as another sign of Josephine White's complicity. Bolton may have referred, though, to a sometime partner in trade named White, or a merchant in Covington also called White, or a stage driver from Covington by the same name.[25]

Or perhaps Hearn or Wood heard the name wrong, and Bolton never mentioned getting his money from a White at all. In fact, it is far more likely that he wanted to see Ward.

CHAPTER NINE

WOOD V. WARD

On June 20, 1853, no more than two weeks after the case of *Wood v. Robards* began, Zebulon Ward or his lawyer walked into the same courthouse where Wood had recently stood and declared that he would be the new defendant in the suit. "By consent" of both parties, the case against Robards was dropped, and the freedom suit became *Wood v. Ward*.[1]

Ward did not admit to wrong by taking Robards's place. His appearance as defendant nonetheless proved that he must have paid something to someone for the rights to sell Wood. Why else enter the case? Most likely Zeb had paid Robert White $300, as he always claimed, then tried to recoup his money quickly by selling Wood to Washington Bolton in Covington. That would explain why she remembered Bolton appearing in Florence to take her to Lexington. Then the suit began and Bolton came to get his money back, leaving Ward at least $300 in the hole. Now, if Wood lost her freedom suit in Fayette County, he could potentially sell her again. But if she won, it would mean hundreds of dollars gone to waste for Ward, not to mention exposure in some shady business.

In short, Ward knew that he had a stake in the outcome of the case. He would also have to walk a fine line to win. The deputy sheriff needed to admit that he had paid $300 for Wood—a curious amount that was far below the usual asking price for a woman her age—but also that he had done nothing illegal. His line of defense in the case would ultimately attempt both things, and he summarized it in a subsequent suit where the events surrounding Wood's capture were at issue again. First, he said he had known nothing of her emancipation when he paid

Robert White. Second, even if Jane Cirode had emancipated her, Ward claimed she had done so illegally. In his telling of the story, he had bought a runaway slave.[2]

It was a story crafted to make Ward appear the victim in the case. And it would also be a difficult story for Wood to disprove—especially without the copy of the freedom papers that her captors had confiscated. Ward may well have expected a quick and easy win.

Quick, however, the suit was not. "It took a long time," as Wood later recalled, and that was partly because Ward's story would be challenged in court. The lawyer who had come to confront Bolton at Robards's jail—a man she referred to in 1879 as "Mr. Kinkead"—was going to try to prove that she should be freed.[3]

"Lawyer Kinkead," as Wood called him in her interview with Hearn, was George B. Kinkead, one of the most respected attorneys in Kentucky. In 1830, he had graduated second in his class at Lexington's Transylvania University, home of one of the most distinguished law schools in the South. He had since served as an attorney for the commonwealth and as Kentucky's secretary of state, and soon he would accept a professorship at the newly reorganized law school of his alma mater. In 1853, Kinkead ran a thriving private practice in Lexington, where he counted among his clients a fellow lawyer and former Illinois congressman named Abraham Lincoln.[4]

How Kinkead learned about Wood's case never became clear. Williams may have sought out the lawyer's help after following Wood to Lexington. Or Kinkead could have learned of the suit in the normal course of his business. In fact, when the June term began, one of Kinkead's brothers-in-law, Henry C. Pindell, was serving temporarily as judge of the Fayette County Circuit Court. Kinkead and Pindell, both lawyers, had married two sisters, and their wives' third sister had married William S. Bodley, a lawyer and former judge who lived in Louisville. In this extended legal family, very little that occurred at the courthouse remained a secret for long.[5]

The case also may have been one of unusual interest to Kinkead, who was known as a vocal critic of slavery—albeit a conservative one.

A devout Presbyterian, he had once said in public that "the bond and the free" shared a "common Father." He was on record arguing that slavery was an unfortunate evil, foisted on his generation by the crimes of earlier Americans. In 1850, Kinkead had even shared those views in a controversial speech delivered in Frankfort, the capital. In that speech, after noting that slavery had "retreated from the North toward the South," Kinkead predicted that "even in Kentucky, at no distant day, the relation of master and slave shall cease." In the meantime, slaves and former slaves deserved "the deepest commiseration and pity."[6]

That pity went only so far: Kinkead was no John Jolliffe. First, despite his belief that slavery would eventually disappear, Kinkead owned seven slaves in 1850. Second, he was as critical of abolitionists such as the ones in the American Anti-Slavery Society as he was of slavery itself; he described them as "fanatics" and enemies of the Union. And third, Kinkead was a colonizationist. He hoped that individual owners, one at a time, would voluntarily manumit their slaves, and that former owners or the federal government would then sponsor the transportation of free black persons to colonies in Africa or elsewhere.[7]

This was not an original idea. The American Colonization Society, which was founded in 1816, had established a colony for freed Americans in Liberia. It had enjoyed the support of prominent Americans for decades, though free black northerners had resisted the society from the start. Its plan for the gradual emancipation and expatriation of slaves was so respectful of slaveholders' rights and so consistent with white supremacy that leading supporters included slaveholders such as Kentucky politician Henry Clay. The plan had numerous supporters in the free states, too, including Kinkead's client and Clay's admirer, Lincoln.[8]

Colonizationism was also enjoying a resurgence in the early 1850s, partly in response to the rising sectional tensions caused by the Fugitive Slave Law. Many conservative border state residents on both sides of the river saw the law as only a partial solution to the flight of runaway slaves and the political instability they caused. The more lasting solution, colonizationists believed, was to engineer a whiter population. The surge of support for colonization after 1850 reflected an abiding belief among most white Americans that people of African descent simply were not fit for freedom in the United States.[9]

Certainly that was Kinkead's view. Like other colonizationists, he combined his reservations about slavery with even greater anxieties about whether free black people could ever become citizens. In his 1850 Frankfort speech, which was given to raise funds for the Kentucky Colonization Society, Kinkead argued that a free black person was "a cancer on our social, and an anomaly in our political life"—"a curse to himself and the white man." Once emancipated, a former slave's only hope, according to Kinkead, was to leave the country, because "even when clothed with liberty, he is among us but not of us, his condition the strongest term of reproach."[10]

Such were the ideas of the man who would serve as Henrietta Wood's attorney—a man whose vision of the nation's future had no room for her. Still, it is doubtful that she could have found more sympathetic counsel in Lexington. And Kinkead's beliefs did align with her interests in one important way: colonizationists insisted on the absolute right of slaveholders to free their slaves. The individual power of manumission was crucial to their plans. Kinkead had argued in 1850, for example, that he wished "to leave with the master, the sole determination of his duty in the station he may be placed, without any force save the sweet force of religion and of reason." Sometimes, that position could lead a lawyer with colonizationist views to defend slave owners. In 1847, for example, Lincoln had defended a Kentuckian seeking to recover slaves in Illinois on the grounds that his client had only brought the slaves to that free state temporarily and did not intend to free them. In Wood's case, however, if it could be shown that some previous owner *had* intended to free her, Kinkead may have felt compelled to argue for her liberty.[11]

In fact, by the end of the summer of 1853, Kinkead was convinced that she did have a case. At some point, probably from an interview with her, he learned that she had once been hired out in Louisville to Charles Mynn Thruston, a fellow colonizationist attorney. Kinkead either knew Thruston or knew someone who did. So he reached out to Bodley, his brother-in-law in Louisville, and asked him to approach the now elderly man. Then, on September 14, 1853, Kinkead wrote to thank Bodley for his efforts.[12]

"My Dear Judge," he began, "I received your letter this morning. I think from the testimony of Thruston I will be able to get proof to sustain Henrietta's claim to freedom."[13]

After Zebulon Ward became the defendant in *Wood v. Ward*, the suit had lain dormant for two months as the parties prepared their cases. The start of the September term for the Fayette County Circuit Court brought a sudden flurry of action. On September 15, 1853, the day after Kinkead wrote his hopeful letter to Bodley, Ward filed some sealed depositions with the court clerk. And on the same day, Kinkead made a motion demanding that his client be removed from Robards's jail, where she had been confined all summer long.

Kinkead had been concerned about Robards's custody of Wood from the beginning. The trader was already infamous in town for selling people south under suspicious circumstances. An experienced lawyer would have known that his client's safety was at risk as long as she remained in his hands. That was why Kinkead had appeared at Robards's jail shortly after her first trip to the courthouse. "I heard lawyer Kinkead come in," she recalled, and he said "they could not hold me." Nonetheless they kept her where she was.[14]

That finally changed in September. Wood recalled the court ordering Robards to "turn me over," and the court's order book corroborates her account. She did not move far. Ward had her locked up in another "slave pen," this one owned by the trader William Pullum. It stood nearby on Broadway and had once been leased by Robards, too.[15]

The new prison was, unsurprisingly, not an improvement. The cells measured seven feet tall and eight feet square, barely enough space for Henrietta to stretch her body out or lay herself down. Rats often scurried across the wet stone floors. Shards of light entered only from small, grated windows near the ceiling of her cell, which was guarded by a ponderous door with iron bars. Over the coming months, as Kinkead argued her case in court, she would remain inside this prison, recalling later that "the sun never shined on me all that time—never once."[16]

Meanwhile, Wood remembered, she "had to wash and iron, and cook" in the jail. Court records suggest that Ward may even have collected rent from her work. In June 1853, when the Fayette County Circuit Court agreed to substitute Ward as the defendant in her suit, it also ordered that "the same preference is given said Ward in hiring the Plaintiff, as by order of the County Judge was given to Boulton, Dickinson & Co." The clerk misspelled the name of Wash Bolton's firm, but the meaning of the order was clear: Wood's owners—first Bolton, then Ward—were given the legal power to make her work for their profit until her case was decided. In the eyes of Fayette County, she remained a slave until and unless she could prove otherwise.[17]

Thus she worked and waited. The days and weeks blurred together in the jail's dimness. But one day, she later told Hearn, Ward himself came to see her. It may have been the first time she had set eyes on him since the night of the carriage ride—as well as the first time she heard what he planned to argue in court. He asked if she thought that Jane Cirode had a legal right to free her.[18]

"I knew nothing about mistress's rights," Wood replied.

"Well," Wood remembered Ward saying in response, "she hadn't, and I bought you from your mistress' children."

Before he left, Ward demanded to see her hand, and she held it out for inspection, grasping right away what he wanted to know. "I knew the rascal must have seen my papers in Mrs. Boyd's house," Wood explained to Hearn, "because in my papers was written some scars on my right hand by which I might be known," as well as "a birth mark." Later, according to Wood, he "pretended in the Courthouse that I was a runaway slave from Louisville, and that he remembered I had belonged to him by seeing the scars on my hand."[19]

Whether or not Ward did try that approach in court, the memory was significant for Wood mostly because of what it said about him. Ward was a man who would bend the facts to suit the case if he had to. And now she was sure he knew, despite what he sometimes claimed, that her freedom papers had been stolen away.

Wood remained confined in one of Pullum's cells throughout the fall of 1853, as her case was continued to another term. She stayed there through the winter, too, trying to fan a flickering hope that Kinkead would win her case. But at some point during that time, another visitor came to see Wood, breaking the tedium of her days.

"While I was there," she told the *Bee*, "my mother came to see me."[20]

The plot twist would have been implausible in one of John Jolliffe's novels, much less in real life—especially since Henrietta had already been able to reunite with Joshua, her brother. But in 1850, the federal census for Kentucky did list a black woman, living just across the Fayette County line, who was born in Virginia in 1780, a date that made her old enough to be Wood's mother. The census taker also wrote down the woman's name. "Daphne Tousey," age "70," sex "F," color "B."[21]

The first name—Daphne—matched the one that Henrietta always gave as her mother's. The last name fit with what her brother had said in Louisville. Now, the elderly woman appeared in the census as free, living just north of Lexington, with a white woman for whom she probably worked.[22]

No record reveals how Daphne had become free, or how she might have learned that her long-lost daughter was in the jail. Wood's interviews did not shed light on either question. Neither Henrietta nor Joshua had known where their parents were at their reunion ten years earlier, though it is possible that one or both of them knew by 1853. If Joshua still lived and worked near Charles Thruston's house, perhaps Kinkead's efforts to contact the lawyer had somehow alerted Wood's brother to her imprisonment, enabling him to then inform their mother—if in fact they had previously reunited, too.

On the other hand, Wood's case may have attracted the notice of the local black community, Daphne included, just as it had caused excitement in Cincinnati. Wood later told the *Ripley Bee* that when her mother came to visit, she said she always "supposed I had fallen into the trader's hands." Perhaps she still made a habit, even in old age, of passing by the slave jails to look for the child who had been sold away long before.[23]

In any case, in her interview with the *Ripley Bee*, Wood depicted this meeting as more melancholy than the one with her brother. She recalled that her mother "told me that my father was dead...," a phrase that trails off in the paper, as if Wood said more than the reporter chose to record. Doubtless, Daphne and Henrietta shared other news about their loved ones and their memories of Touseytown, and each recollection helped to cement the stories that Wood later shared.[24]

Henrietta did not tell her mother about Cincinnati, however. She had her reasons, maybe concerned that speaking of those years would make her current plight even harder for Daphne to bear. Possibly she herself had begun to lose hope of regaining her freedom. Either way, "I never told her how I came there," Wood recalled of the conversation with her mother in the jail, and "she didn't know I had ever been free." There is no record of their meeting ever again.[25]

CHAPTER TEN

THE KEEPER

By the end of 1853, Henrietta Wood had been imprisoned for most of the year, and her legal prospects were worsening on both sides of the river. In Cincinnati, the criminal case against Rebecca Boyd and John Gilbert was postponed to November because some witnesses could not be found. Not until December was the case actually tried in the city's criminal court—Judge Jacob Flinn presiding.[1]

The defendants could hardly have hoped for a more favorable judge. Flinn was a proslavery Democrat, and in August, he had ruled against John Jolliffe himself in a case involving three people suing for their freedom. Flinn's ruling in that case had outraged abolitionists, who claimed that the judge had been drunk on the bench; on September 1, a public meeting that Jolliffe attended called for Judge Flinn to be impeached. The next day, while Jolliffe was out shopping with his family, Flinn approached the Quaker lawyer from behind and struck him with a blow that knocked him out. When Jolliffe regained consciousness, the judge was kicking and cursing him as a "damned abolitionist."[2]

By the time Wood's kidnappers came before Flinn's court three months later, the judge had been fined for the assault and Jolliffe had recovered. Still, recent events did not bode well for the prosecution team, which, for obvious reasons, no longer included Jolliffe. The indictment against Boyd, Gilbert, and Frank Rust (who at some point had been charged, too) alleged that they had "by fraud and violence, seized upon Henrietta Wood" and taken her out of Ohio, "under the pretence that she was a slave." Those actions, prosecutors argued, violated an 1831 state law that penalized the kidnapping of free people of color. But Flinn ruled that the antikidnapping statute had been "rendered inoperative and void" by a decision of the US Supreme Court in 1842. After Flinn's ruling, the defendants were acquitted by a jury. Eight months after Wood's abduction, three of her captors were cleared in a trial that lasted less than a day.[3]

Kinkead was not faring much better in Kentucky. In September, Wood's lawyer had been optimistic that Charles Mynn Thruston would help him prove that she was free. But Thruston died on January 7, 1854, and the deposition he left behind disappointed Kinkead. The Louisville lawyer seemed to recall a deed of trust made out by William Cirode allowing his wife to use his slaves but making clear that they belonged to her son and would return "to her children after her death." Whether such a deed would have given the Cirode children some legal grounds for contesting Wood's manumission was unclear. Nonetheless, the deed, as described, certainly played into Ward's narrative about the case. Kinkead complained in a February letter about Thruston's deposition that it didn't "suit" him: "I want to show that the wife had the power to emancipate."[4]

Kinkead appealed to his brother-in-law in Louisville to look for the rumored deed in the county court there, hoping that it would prove things were not as Thruston remembered. No document ever turned up to challenge Thruston's testimony. Then, two days after Kinkead wrote his letter, Ward won a motion before the Fayette County Circuit Court to take new depositions and "to recross interrogate Mrs. Cirode," who still lived in Ohio.[5]

Everything seemed to be going Zebulon's way, and not just in court, for while Wood remained in Pullum's jail, Ward had also begun to nurse a new ambition that promised to make him rich, and in the new year he intended to get what he wanted. He wanted to be the next keeper of Kentucky's state prison.

Founded in 1798 and surrounded by an imposing stone wall, the state penitentiary of Kentucky stood across the street from the governor's mansion in Frankfort. Two crenellated towers on either side of the gate loomed over the town like a medieval castle. Inside, though, the prison looked more like a factory. Since 1825, it had been run on the Auburn

Plan, so named because it originated at a prison in Auburn, New York. Under this plan, prisoners were kept in isolation at night but put to hard labor together during the day. In Kentucky, they manufactured goods for sale outside the walls, and the keeper of the prison, instead of receiving a salary, was allowed to control the convicts' work and then keep as much as half of the profits from whatever they made. That was why the position of keeper was known, in the words of one newspaper, as "the most lucrative one in the State of Kentucky." Joel Scott, the first keeper under the 1825 plan, cleared profits of more than $80,000 during his term. His successor earned $200,000 in just ten years.[6]

Those were sums that a former steamboat clerk could appreciate, but the job was not easy to get. The position was filled by a vote in the General Assembly, and Ward had only been back in Kentucky for a few years. Though his job as a deputy sheriff did require him to transport convicts from Covington down to Frankfort, he had no prior experience as a prison manager, unlike the current keeper, Newton Craig. Craig had held the post since 1844 and had also won praise for his efforts to balance the work of convicts with moral improvement. Every Sunday morning, Craig assembled the prisoners and forced them to hear a sermon, sometimes delivered by Craig himself.[7]

Yet Craig's belief in his reformatory abilities also contained the seeds of his eventual fall from grace—and of Ward's sudden rise. Craig's troubles began near the beginning of his term, when a pair of abolitionists were sentenced to the penitentiary for helping an enslaved Kentuckian named Lewis Hayden and his family escape to the North. Calvin Fairbank was a radical antislavery minister from Ohio with ties to Oberlin College. Delia Webster, his accomplice, was a schoolteacher, born in Vermont, who had moved to Lexington in 1843. Neither showed any remorse at trial. Craig, a proslavery Christian, nevertheless dedicated himself to their reform. In his memoirs, Fairbank recalled that Craig spent many a sermon railing against abolitionists or defending slavery as divinely ordained, and soon the keeper began to see what he thought were fruits of repentance.[8]

Delia Webster struck up a friendship with the keeper, and Craig helped to arrange for her pardon after only two months. Following her release, Craig also employed Webster as a governess for his children and loaned her money to buy a farm in Kentucky. Then, at the beginning of 1854, just as state legislators were preparing to vote on his reappointment as keeper, a set of amorous letters from Craig to Webster began to circulate around Frankfort. They seemed to show that the keeper had engaged in an extramarital affair with the abolitionist.[9]

Craig and his friends quickly began a campaign to defend his honor. They argued that the letters had been misconstrued, or that they had been leaked by a rival for Craig's position—perhaps even a dark horse candidate named Zebulon Ward. Craig's problems were compounded, however, by evidence that Webster had resumed her abolitionist activities on the farm he helped her buy. Even to white Kentuckians who could look past adultery, letting an abolitionist loose in the state was an unforgivable sin—especially given the gathering signs that Webster and Fairbank were not acting alone.[10]

In 1845, for example, a Yale-educated Kentuckian named Cassius Clay had begun publishing an antislavery newspaper in Lexington. Only a few years later, a young man studying at Centre College in Danville told a group of seventy slaves that he could help them get across the river. Not long after that, Fairbank had also managed to secure his early release from jail. Two years later, the abolitionist minister was caught trying to help slaves escape again and was sentenced to fifteen more years in Frankfort; by December 1853, he was one of eleven inmates who had been convicted of assisting runaway slaves. And that same year, abolitionist John Fee established a free labor colony in Berea, Madison County, with the support of missionary groups in the North.[11]

These and other events had convinced many white Kentuckians that abolitionist conspirators were multiplying on both sides of the river. The present crisis needed a keeper who would punish agitators, not cozy up to them. On February 20, 1854, when legislators convened to consider Craig's reappointment, a first round of balloting showed that he lacked a clear majority. Zebulon Ward's name was put forward by a senator, and at last it rose above the fray. After eight rounds of voting, he emerged triumphant as the new penitentiary keeper.[12]

Ward would not assume his new duties until March 1, 1855. In the meantime, he remained at work as a deputy sheriff in Kenton County, where his activities could only have reassured white Kentuckians who wanted a tougher policy against the likes of Fairbank. One night in June 1854, Ward learned that nine enslaved people had escaped from Boone County to Ohio, first by crossing the river to Indiana in a skiff and then by walking to within five miles of Cincinnati. Wearied from carrying their bundles and at least three children, none older than seven, the leaders of the group stopped for rest in the stable of a farmer who promised them safety. The farmer betrayed them by crossing to Kentucky and informing locals there about the escape. By Wednesday, June 14, the group of slaves had been surrounded by a posse of white men that included Zeb Ward.[13]

Later that week, in Cincinnati, perfunctory hearings were held in which the runaways were never permitted to testify. Although their case was taken up by the ubiquitous Jolliffe, who argued that the slaves had become free the minute they touched free soil, the runaways' case proved hopeless under the Fugitive Slave Law. On Saturday, a federal commissioner announced his decision in the same courtroom where Boyd had been tried before Judge Flinn a few months before, and the commissioner remanded all nine people to Kentucky. They were driven across the river to the Covington jail. And exactly one week after that, by coincidence, the Fayette County Circuit Court finally ruled on the case of *Wood v. Ward*. The result was more good news for Kentucky's new keeper.[14]

Wood's day in court had been delayed for more than a year, but in the summer of 1854, she later told the *Ripley Bee*, "they had some kind of a trial." She was once again "taken to the Court house" and ordered not to speak. "I just sat there like a stick," she recalled, "and couldn't say nothing."[15]

What she could do was listen. "I tell you I recollect all that was said," Wood told the *Ripley Bee*, "every word that I could understand." She did not remember "all them law words," though she caught the gist of the arguments: "Old Zeb Ward, he claimed my mistress did not own me and had no right to emancipate me; but that I belonged to young master and mistress," that is, the Whites. Ward "said he had bought me in March 1853. He knew I was in Cincinnati, and he paid them $300 or was to, when he got me in Kentucky." Wood recalled that "Mr. Kinkead, he said a piece, then Ward's lawyer talked, and then Judge said I didn't make my case. I saw old Ward grin, and they took me back to jail." A clerk for the court recorded the suit as "dismissed."[16]

Kinkead objected to the ruling at once, successfully forcing the case to be sent to the state's Court of Appeals. The records of that court were the ones later lost in a fire leaving behind no clues about the arguments he made. Wood recalled that her freedom papers were never brought up in court. And the lower court had apparently accepted Ward's argument that Cirode had not been entitled to manumit her. Kinkead could have argued that Wood's extended residence in Cincinnati was enough to establish her freedom. After all, unlike the slaves who had just escaped from Boone County, Wood had clearly established domicile north of the river. Jane Cirode could have confirmed that when called to testify. But Cirode's testimony in the case was not preserved either, and her own feelings about the case are not known.[17]

Cirode's evidence might not have mattered anyway in the end. Even had Kinkead been able to prove that Wood had lived for a number of years on free soil, that fact might well have failed to win her sympathy. Nothing required a Kentucky court to honor Ohio's statutes concerning freedom, and Kentucky courts may have been less inclined to do so in 1854 than ever before. Wood's trial came, after all, at the end of a decade when the actions of abolitionists such as Fairbank, Webster, and Jolliffe had eroded interstate comity along the border.[18]

National politics deepened local distrust. The Fugitive Slave Law had only increased tension over slavery along the Ohio, and congressional conflicts over the westward expansion of slavery had also been rising since the Mexican War. Polarization in Washington reached a new peak with the 1854 passage of the Kansas-Nebraska Act, which would allow settlers in those territories to decide whether to allow slavery. The act became law just one month before *Wood v. Ward* was dismissed.[19]

After that dismissal, Wood remained imprisoned for another six months in Lexington, waiting for the Court of Appeals to hear her case. When it did, on January 20, 1855, it quickly upheld the decision. "The higher court said I was not free," she recalled.[20]

Thus, more than a year and a half after Ward paid $300 and set in motion the events that led to Wood's reenslavement, Kentucky's highest court decisively ruled that she belonged to him. He now possessed the power to sell her at once. Perhaps to her surprise, however, Ward decided not to take her to a trader. Instead, he "came and took me away to Frankfort, Kentucky," where, she told Hearn, he now "had charge of the Penitentiary." For the time being, she would be forced to labor for his family there.[21]

Ward's first day as keeper—March 1, 1855—was one his prisoners would not soon forget. The inmates, roughly numbering around two hundred, were all forced to gather inside the penitentiary chapel, where they saw that the governor of Kentucky had come to witness the proceedings. A hush fell over the room as Zeb Ward took the keys to the prison and turned to address the crowd.

"Men, I'm a man of few words, and prompt action," he bellowed. "Do your duties, or I'll make ye! Go to your work."[22]

Later, Calvin Fairbank, one year into his second stint in the penitentiary, remembered in his memoir that the speech passed over the captive audience like "hot shot." The direct hit came the next week, after the governor was gone. The convicts shuffled into the chapel again, a mass of striped uniforms and dark wool caps. As the men finally quieted and stilled, the keeper came to the front and removed the coat from his tall frame. "I came here to make money," Ward told them, "and I'm going to do it if I kill you all."[23]

The prisoners, Fairbank recalled, "all sat still and smiled," perhaps unsure if the new keeper's threat was serious. Soon enough they would learn he meant what he said.[24]

Outside the walls, Ward's term was being closely watched from the start, especially by former members of Newton Craig's staff who felt that the previous keeper had been unfairly deposed. Among them was a physician, W. C. Sneed, who later published a history of Kentucky's state prison from its founding up to the first year under Ward's successor. In that book, Sneed allowed that Ward had brought "great energy" to the post. He also observed that "Mr. Ward, though a thorough business man, had no previous experience in the management of such an institution" and wholly lacked Craig's concern for religious instruction. In a retrospective summary of Ward's treatment of convicts, Sneed concluded that "all the laws in relation to their moral condition were neglected, and only one great idea made prominent, and that was—work."[25]

Sneed was an apologist for Craig, of course; in Sneed's view, politicking had infected the appointment process, turning the prison from "a place for the reformation and restraint of criminals" into "a sink of corruption." A more careful critic could have seen that the convict lease arrangement was itself largely to blame. Kentucky's penitential system, which foretold the future of southern prisons during the late nineteenth century and well into the twentieth, was one that any "business man" could easily exploit. The keeper had too much unchecked power—and too many incentives to push his inmates hard.[26]

Rumors that Ward was abusing the prisoners began almost right away. In May 1855, a grand jury investigated the charges, having been impaneled by the same circuit judge who had dismissed the case of *Wood v. Ward* the year before. The grand jury reported that the cells in the prison were "miserably ventilated" and that many convicts had "to sleep on a cold, damp floor," though the jurors did not much blame Ward for conditions he had inherited. But the panel did express "disapprobation of the severity of punishment inflicted on the convicts, in more instances than one, amounting, if not to a violation of *law*," then at least "violating to the feelings of humanity."[27]

Fairbank, writing later, was much less restrained. He recounted a pattern of routine "barbarity" under Ward, particularly in the workshops where the prison's main product, hemp bagging, was made. Craig had required prisoners to weave 125 to 150 yards of hemp every day, Fairbank explained, "with two to two and a half threads or shots to the inch." Convicts had even earned twenty-five cents for every additional fifty yards that they weaved—a small gesture reflecting Craig's reformatory concerns. By contrast, Ward required the men in the hemp room to keep an impossible pace—"two hundred and eight yards a day, with five shots to the inch." Those who fell behind were mercilessly beaten.[28]

The result was what Fairbank described as a "rigorous, murderous rule." Though he had his problems with Craig as a keeper, too, Fairbank concluded that Ward "cared nothing for human life. Money was his religion." The abolitionist remembered being flogged "never less than twice" a day, usually with the kind of strap "commonly used by overseers of slaves." To avoid the punishing pace of work, more than one prisoner cut off his own hand, preferring to be sent to the infirmary as a partial amputee. Before Ward had even completed a year in the new post, thirteen convicts had died by the keeper's own report—a startling and unprecedented increase. In sum, Fairbank wrote, the lease by which Ward obtained control of the inmates "was virtually a sale, with very little difference between the condition of the prisoner and that of an actual slave."[29]

An "actual slave" might have questioned the comparison, but Ward might not have refused it. By July 1856, he was the owner of four slaves, seven by the following year—a rising number that signaled his increasing wealth. Zeb was growing accustomed to earning his bread from other men's sweat. The keeper and his employees also seemed to specially delight in persecuting antislavery convicts such as Fairbank or James Blackburn, a married "mulatto" man who had been convicted of assisting slaves to run away and who was identified in the register of inmates by the lash marks on his back. Thomas Brown, an alleged abolitionist who had moved from Cincinnati to Kentucky in 1850 and was sent to prison on May 8, 1855, later recalled being "stripped, and flogged" with a cat-o'-nine-tails, all while the guards joked that "'Old Brown had worn himself out stealing negroes, and would not work.'" Brown also recalled something Ward himself had said upon his arrival at the jail. "The head keeper was extremely glad to get another 'Abolitionist,' as he called him, in his power, expressing with an oath, a wish to be permitted to hang all such."[30]

Though Ward's treatment of his abolitionist inmates was not always as ferocious as that, his capriciousness was what kept them afraid.

Fairbank recalled the keeper pledging to allow the minister to correspond with his wife, only to withdraw the promise later. Ward was unpredictable in other ways, too. On Sundays, for example, he sometimes formed the inmates into lines and watched in amusement as they ran foot races in the yard. At other times the keeper himself played marbles with the men, using a plug of tobacco as the stakes. As a skilled gambler, Zebulon usually won the games, gave the tobacco back, and then won it all back again before lining the prisoners up and distributing it "to men whom he knew used the weed." At the same time, though, he might threaten them all with discipline for some minor infraction. The keeper could swerve, without warning, from "mirthfulness" to force, and to Fairbank, such vacillations only proved he was a "tyrant." Ward "played with his men as with his dogs," the minister concluded, "whipped them as a boy his top to make it spin." The keeper's main goals were "money, mixed with a little fun, provided it did not cost him too much."[31]

As for Thomas Brown, Ward did not hang him, whatever he may have said upon the inmate's arrival. In fact, Brown became a trusted prisoner who was one day sent on an errand to Ward's own house, wearing his "prison garb" all the way through town. There he spoke with the keeper's wife, Mary Worthen Ward, who said she was "sorry" to see a man of his age in jail, and Brown later recalled that the keeper's wife impressed him with her "womanly humanity" and concern. But hers was also the same house to which Henrietta Wood had been brought after losing her freedom suit. And her own recollections would paint a very different picture of Mrs. Ward.[32]

Wood was brought to Ward's house in Frankfort after his term as keeper began. She later told the *Ripley Bee* only that she worked for his family for seven months, but she gave Lafcadio Hearn a more extended account. Zebulon and Mary had two children at the time—an infant daughter and a toddling boy—and Wood said she was ordered to work as their "nurse." In both interviews, Wood also recalled that she and the children's mother "didn't get along."[33]

The conflict was hardly a surprise. Even under normal circumstances, caring for the children of another woman would have been challenging work, physically and emotionally. In Wood's case, the forced labor also came with the galling reminder that these were the children of a man who had stolen her liberty away.

Needless to say, she did not take cheerfully to the work. She remembered that Mrs. Ward quarreled with her "because I could not keep her little boy from crying," even though "she couldn't keep him quiet herself." Later, after the Civil War, the experiences of black women in positions like Wood's would be twisted beyond recognition by the myth of loyal black "mammies" whose diligent care for white children endeared them to their owners. In reality, many white slaveholding mothers felt simultaneously dependent on black women for child care and guilty about delegating their maternal duties; they often lashed out with violence and verbal assaults.[34]

One day, for example, Wood recalled that Mary Ward threatened to whip her for failing to keep the Wards' son happy. It may not have been the first such threat that Wood had received, yet something about that threat, on that particular day, brought Henrietta to what seemed, looking back, like a fork in the road.[35]

By then she could not see a clear way back to Cincinnati. In one direction now lay the path of least resistance, stretching into the distance with no end in sight. In the other direction was a road of refusal, resistance, retort.

"Guess not," Wood remembered finally replying to Mary Ward's threat. "It takes men to whip me."

Recalling that moment later in her interview with Hearn, Wood explained that she weighed two hundred pounds at the time and was "strong as most men." The idea that Ward, a woman four years younger, could overpower Wood struck her as ridiculous, both then and many years after the fact. Yet she also knew that her defiance had crossed a line. Mary told her husband what had happened, Wood recalled, and soon enough, the keeper came and took her "out in the Penitentiary yard."

"I'll have to learn you not to talk to Mrs. Ward that way," Zebulon said, while preparing "to whip her." But then Henrietta stepped farther down the fight-back road.

"Why, you know she can't keep the child from crying," she retorted. "And how can I do it?"

Ward seemed to pause at this—"kind of thought over the matter," she said—almost as if he, too, were at a fork in the road. Perhaps he was toying with the idea of letting her impudence go. Perhaps he was weighing the potential costs and benefits of a beating. Perhaps he simply enjoyed watching the woman who sued him squirm. In any case, Henrietta was most likely surprised when the keeper lowered his lash. He "let me off," she recalled.[36]

Two weeks after the standoff in the prison yard, however, Ward struck Wood with a different kind of blow. He took her back to Lexington and left her in the trading yard run by William Pullum—the one in which she had been imprisoned before the trial for her freedom. Together with his partner, a trader named Pierce Griffin, Pullum did a booming business buying slaves in Kentucky and selling them in the Deep South river town of Natchez, Mississippi. And before long, Griffin and Pullum took Wood there, too. It was the second time in her life that a sale sent her down the river, and this time she would not avoid the hell of the cotton fields.[37]

CHAPTER ELEVEN

NATCHEZ

More than seven hundred miles southwest of Lexington, the town of Natchez stood on a bluff high above the Mississippi River. It was the site of more than a thousand years of settlement, conflict, and trade. Native peoples had lived in the region since the seventh century at least, growing corn and other crops in the alluvial soil. Europeans arrived by 1700, beginning a hundred years of struggle over the hinterlands. Until the American War of Independence, the French and British Empires had each relied on native allies to wage war with the other—and to keep faraway colonists in line. Then Natchez was claimed by the Spanish crown, which offered land to eager American settlers from the East. A new generation of white migrants streamed into the area, dreaming of riches from cotton and heedless of native sovereignty. By 1798, when Natchez was ceded to the United States, the town was well on its way to being the city on a hill for an empire of cotton.[1]

American cotton growers produced about one million pounds of cotton in 1800; in 1860, the total would exceed one billion. By 1820, the crop already represented a majority of all American exports. Cotton was becoming king in the American South, and especially in the Natchez District—an area that encompassed the Mississippi counties of Adams, Jefferson, and Claiborne, as well as Louisiana parishes just across the river such as Concordia and Tensas. In 1840, the state of Mississippi accounted for almost a quarter of all American cotton grown. Three of the state's most productive counties lay around Natchez.[2]

That boom owed much to the political rise of Andrew Jackson in the 1830s and the Jacksonians who supported his signature policies: dispossession of native peoples and democracy for white men. In 1830, during Jackson's first term as president, white Americans used the Treaty of Dancing Rabbit Creek to seize eleven million acres from Choctaws in Mississippi, opening the state to cheap public land sales and feverish settlement by cotton planters. Migrants from the East poured into the state, including one North Carolina man who wrote home to say that he had found the best place he had "yet seen for making money." In 1834, a visitor to Mississippi predicted that the whole state would soon be "one vast cotton field."[3]

Many small planters quickly went bust after the Panic of 1837. The wealthiest Mississippians—especially those whose families were already well established in the region—were left to reap most of the profits from the cotton boom. In the Natchez District, an aristocratic planter elite invested its wealth in highly capitalized, sprawling plantations that were worked by hundreds of slaves. The richest was Stephen Duncan, who enslaved more than a thousand people and boasted an estate worth $1.3 million by the eve of the Civil War.[4]

Slaveholdings that large were highly unusual in the antebellum South. Even in Mississippi, fewer than nine hundred people in 1860 owned seventy slaves or more. Large slaveholdings were more common near Natchez than almost anywhere else; more millionaires lived there, it was said, than in any other place of comparable size. And between 1840 and 1860, those millionaires grew increasingly single-minded in their pursuit of wealth: their only goal, as one Louisianan put it in 1854, was "to buy Negroes to plant cotton & raise cotton to buy Negroes."[5]

By the time Henrietta Wood arrived, Natchez had therefore also become one of the largest slave markets in the nation, second only to New Orleans. Professional "Negro traders" had established a permanent market at the town limits, one mile east of the river. As early as 1834, one visitor observed slaves being sold there in "a cluster of rough wooden buildings, in the angle of two roads," one heading north to Washington, a former territorial capital, and the other heading east, toward a town called Liberty. Some local traders called the emporium "Niggerville." But the market was also known, in Natchez and beyond, by a more common name—Forks of the Road.[6]

Thousands of slaves from the Upper South ultimately came through the Forks of the Road slave market. Many were chained into coffles and forcibly marched over land from Maryland or Virginia, arriving "ragged & dirty," as one trader described them, and sometimes clinging to life. Others arrived by steamboat at the Natchez docks, climbing the bluff and walking the mile to the slave pens outside town. There, the traders stripped them down and replaced their clothes, sometimes blackening their hair with dye. Medicine was applied, skin was greased, bodies were readied for display and inspection by the buyers. And among the regular customers there, by 1855, was one of the wealthiest men in Mississippi, the scion of a former governor of the state, and the next man who would own Henrietta Wood: the planter Gerard Brandon of Brandon Hall.[7]

Wood came to Natchez by steamboat, but her journey began by train. Zebulon Ward took her back to Pullum's jail sometime in the fall of 1855, and she later recalled that Pullum and Griffin "were making up a gang" of slaves to take to Mississippi, where they operated a regular stand. One "drove" of slaves was sent down by land shortly after her arrival back in Lexington. Wood was taken by rail to Louisville and then to Natchez on a boat. She believed, in retrospect, that she had been separated from the others so that she "could have no chance to talk to anyone."[8]

Pullum's firm had been sending slaves south by steamboat for many years. In 1853, when Pullum was called to testify in a Kentucky lawsuit involving another slave trader, he explained that even after paying for passage down the river, traders in the 1840s could expect average profits of "$100 to $150 each" on slaves carried to Natchez. In another suit, an agent of Griffin and Pullum also detailed a typical journey: "On our trip South the negroes were put on [the] deck of [a] steamboat sleeping in bunks. They were chained together two by two till we got to the mouth of Ohio river, when they were unchained."[9]

The chains returned as soon as the boat reached Natchez. In Mississippi, Wood recalled, she was taken off the boat and brought "to the great trading yards at Fork roads." The slave market had not changed much since the early 1830s, except for a marked increase both in the number of slaves annually sold and in the prices they fetched. It was the start of the busy season for traders, and hundreds of enslaved people may have been there when Wood arrived, crowded into low-slung buildings marked on a map from 1853 as "Negro marts." Tied up outside the buildings would have been the horses of customers who were inside shopping for human beings.[10]

The buyers were usually greeted at the door by solicitous "Negro traders" such as Pullum, Griffin, or their local broker, Robert H. Elam. Such traders were expert salesmen who understood they were selling more than laborers or investments: they were selling, too, the fulfillment of wishes, the satisfaction of fantasies. In slave markets, white men and women could buy a pleasing image of themselves as discerning masters and mistresses who knew how to sniff out a deal, and traders knew just how to play upon their clients' vanities.[11]

Griffin and Pullum, for example, had published ads in Natchez papers as early as 1852, touting their "large and well-selected stock of Negroes" and promising to "sell as low or lower than any other house here or in New Orleans.... Our terms are liberal. Give us a call." In 1858, the firm would still be advertising its "choice selection" and "reasonable rates" for "SLAVES! SLAVES!! SLAVES!!!" at Forks of the Road—along with their promise of a warranty to any buyer who wanted one.[12]

The marketing only intensified once buyers arrived at their stand. Inside, people for sale were pressed into a line to await the buyer's queries and inspection. Were they good with children? With mules? Some were asked to bare their teeth or take off their clothes. Wood was likely forced into such a line, too, forced to answer questions about her past. In both of her interviews, she later recalled that a man named Wilson was the first to show an interest in buying her, and, all things considered, she may have preferred him over the others who entered. Wilson lived in town and wanted Wood to wash and iron, jobs she already knew. Yet she also remembered that her captors refused to sell her to Wilson. After he left, the traders revealed "that Ward had told them to get me out on a plantation, and not to sell me to any one in town, because I'd raise another suit in the Courts."[13]

on their valuation and price: manual dexterity was a must for slaves who were tasked with picking cotton. Brandon's eyes—and likely his hands—would have roved over her body, judging her heft, the fullness of her breasts, even, perhaps, the scars on her hand that Zebulon Ward had found. He reduced Wood to her body parts, appraising each one. And in the end, Brandon saw whatever he wanted to see.[19]

"He bought me at sight," she told Hearn in 1876. Then he took her out by wagon to the house where he lived, about eleven miles along one of the two roads that joined at the Forks.[20]

The wagon could not have gone far into the country before Henrietta began to notice the scenery starting to change. The path was lined with tall oaks, as well as towering hedges of Cherokee rose, some of them standing nearly as tall as Frankfort's prison walls. Travelers compared the roads around Natchez to wooded tunnels or darkened lanes; the routes were secluded and enclosed by design so they could be patrolled. "No residence is visible from the road," one visitor said, and no road was visible from within. It was as if the blinds had been buttoned down on the world at large.[21]

When Brandon and Wood finally arrived at their destination, probably passing through a gap within one of the fence-like hedges, she could see cleared fields, clusters of small cabins, outbuildings of various kinds—and enslaved people laboring everywhere she looked. "Brandon was a very rich man," as Wood told Hearn. "He had eight hundred working blacks, and more slave children than I could count."[22]

In time, she learned that he also owned more than one plantation— "four on the Louisiana side of the river, and three on the other side"— each one staffed by paid overseers who managed his crops and slaves. Brandon was among the wealthy planters who extended their operations across the Mississippi to the Louisiana parishes of Tensas and Concordia, places where slaves outnumbered white residents by eight or nine to one. Wood, however, was brought to the plantation in Adams County where he actually lived, a place known as Brandon Hall.[23]

Gerard and his wife, Charlotte, had received the land from her father, and in 1853, they had begun to have a large mansion built. Designed in the Greek Revival style, with a grand entrance hall and portico in the front, the two-story house was completed in 1856, about the time when Henrietta arrived. Brandon Hall was meant to display to all that the former governor's son was his own man, too. With a house like that, he was fully the peer of the other country nabobs—men who lived, in the later words of his nephew, as "veritable lords of the manor, surrounded by all the luxury and refinement which wealth and slavery could produce."[24]

For one lavish party held at Brandon Hall in the spring of 1858, for example, Brandon spared no expense. According to a guest named Benjamin L. C. Wailes, the entertainment was "elegant & sumptious." The tables were "laden with every delicacy brought from New Orleans." The food was served by waiters hired from the *Princess*, a palatial Mississippi steamboat that often carried the region's elite back and forth from the city. Musicians, including a harpist, performed. The event began at nine in the evening and lasted through the night.[25]

Eventually, though, the party guests left to return to their homes. Those who had come on horses guided them back through the hedges. Those who had come in carriages were driven away by liveried slaves. Wailes arrived at his own house as dawn began to break. But at Brandon Hall, the working day had just begun for Wood. And her work there would continue until the sun went down again.

CHAPTER TWELVE

BRANDON HALL

In retrospect, the voyage that took Henrietta Wood to Natchez was like the last leg of a journey back in time, to the mainspring of so much that had already happened in her life. In the beginning, settlers from the United States had poured into the Mississippi River valley, chasing cotton dreams. The southwestern population boom had helped to make Louisville an important river port, fueling Forsyth's wealth and eclipsing Touseytown. Global demand for cotton made New Orleans what it was, enticing William Cirode and his family down the river. Prices for cotton also buoyed the prices of slaves everywhere, tempting kidnappers across the Upper South and keeping Kentucky slavers such as Robards in business. By 1860, the nearly four million people enslaved in the United States would be worth an estimated $3 billion to their owners, more than all the factories, railroads, and banking capital in the country *combined*. White fears over the threats to all that wealth would soon spark a civil war.[1]

Now, by coming to Natchez, Wood had arrived close to the center of it all. "They put me to work at once in the cotton field," she told Lafcadio Hearn. "I sowed the cotton, hoed the cotton, and picked the cotton," she remembered. "I worked under the meanest overseers, and got flogged and flogged, until I thought I should die."[2]

Those memories echoed stories told by many people who were sold to the Deep South. In Adams County alone, more than fourteen thousand enslaved people lived in thrall to a white minority, and most had either begun their life in the Upper South or had parents and grandparents who did. Each of them had been forced to adjust to the unfamiliar routines and work of the cotton fields, just as Wood was now having to do. After leaving Touseytown as a girl, she had always lived in cities, working mostly in houses, and her labor had been structured by day-to-day rhythms. The rhythms were more seasonal in the cotton fields, beginning in February and March, when slaves were tasked with plowing carefully spaced rows and planting cotton seed. The next season's work, known as "hoeing" or "scraping," was often the most grueling. Slaves spent April through June walking through the rows to cut back weeds, sometimes digging ditches to help in draining the rows.[3]

Finally, in the searing heat of the summer, the bolls opened and picking began, continuing into the fall. Slaves ginned the cotton—a mechanical process that removed seeds and plant debris, or "trash," from the fibers. Then slaves packed the cotton into bales with bagging and rope, much of it made from Kentucky hemp in places like Ward's penitentiary shops, and hauled the bales by wagon to the docks under Natchez. There, the bales, each one weighing four hundred to five hundred pounds, were loaded on steamboats and taken down the river to New Orleans. Meanwhile, back at Brandon Hall, enslaved people began a new round of chores. They grew corn and peas that supplied the plantation with food. They foddered and tended to animals who aided the plantation's work. In the winter, they cleared land and prepared to plant cotton all over again.[4]

Wood confronted these new routines while also being forced to adjust to a whole new community, one that was unlike those she knew before. Slaves outnumbered whites by a factor of three to one in the rural districts surrounding the town of Natchez. By contrast, in Cincinnati, the free black community comprised about 3 percent of the city's population. Adams County was the first place she had ever lived where an overwhelming majority of the people around her were of African descent.[5]

Theirs was a complex communal world in which new bonds were often forged by telling the stories of the past. Many had experienced traumatic separations from kin and journeys much like hers. She also would have found people engaged in a range of romantic relationships, from temporary unions known as "sweethearting" or "taking up," to monogamous, extralegal marriages that sometimes crossed plantation borders—and remained resilient even in the face of frequent separations by sale. Enslaved people in Adams County carried mental maps in their heads of the neighborhoods to which they belonged, directories of who was who, who had been where, and who was newly arrived.[6]

New connections with neighbors may have helped somewhat to soften the worst shocks of Wood's arrival. In the fields people often helped each other to meet or resist the exacting demands of their overseers. But as in any community, the people Brandon enslaved were not immune to conflict. The sharing of stories sometimes turned to gossip with a sharper edge, or even violent quarrels. In December 1854, one of the men whom Brandon enslaved was indicted by the State of Mississippi for murdering another slave. Several other slaves belonging to Brandon—known only as Frances, Jamie, and Mary—were required to testify about the case in May 1855, not long before Henrietta came.[7]

In short, Wood had entered a social world that was largely unknown to her, all while being forced to learn new work routines, and *fast*. "I had to hoe, burn brush, and clear ground," she remembered, even though the latter jobs were typically assigned to men. The division of slave labor on a cotton plantation was another new rhythm. Men were responsible for ginning, and they also worked as teamsters, blacksmiths, and choppers; some men were assigned to be "drivers," tasked with keeping the pace of work in the fields. In the cotton fields, however, the women frequently outnumbered the men. Planters often preferred that women hoe and pick, and Brandon was evidently no exception to the rule.[8]

The reasons women were often preferred as pickers may not have been apparent to Henrietta at first, but making money from cotton was a risk-filled operation even for a man as rich as Gerard. It involved multiple layers of management and labor. Small changes in the fields could mean the difference between boom or bust for a planter. Raising cotton had only become more capital-intensive over the course of Brandon's life, and by the 1850s even the most well-endowed Mississippi planters usually worked closely with a factor or commission merchant firm that extended plantation supplies on credit to their clients. Over time, the firms became the closest thing that most planters had to banks.[9]

To settle accounts, planters depended on the quality of their crops. During and after picking seasons, Brandon sent bales of cotton down to New Orleans, where they were graded according to standards. The best cotton had been picked as soon as possible after blooming, before wind and rain could damage the fibers, and it was packaged with a minimum of dirt or debris from the stalks. Other bales might be judged only "middling" or "ordinary." Agents monitored the market for each grade of cotton and made the final decisions about when to sell a bale.[10]

In February 1854, for example, Brandon received notice from his factors in New Orleans, the firm of Buckner, Manning, and Newman, that they had sold 118 bales of his cotton for $5,208.70. The firm credited the money to Brandon's account. Then they wrote to reassure him that "the sale was made at the prices current prior to the decline of last week and we hope will give you satisfaction." When the "prices current" for cotton were high, planters were in the money. A factor might either forward the profit or credit it to his client's standing account. Brandon could order more supplies or make a draft on the factor for cash.[11]

On the other hand, there was always the danger of a price drop or a bad yield. If too many batches of cotton sold low or did not arrive in sufficient quantities, Brandon might find himself in the red with his suppliers—putting him at risk for a vicious cycle. He would need to grow more cotton to cover his expenses, and to grow more cotton, he needed the credit that factors could extend. For the wealthiest planters, however, disaster seldom came. In years with bumper crops, large slaveholders could mobilize more labor to take full advantage of the surplus. And in tough times, Brandon owned valuable land on both sides of the river that provided financial security. The hundreds of people he enslaved also served as insurance—assets he could sell or even mortgage to secure more credit. Those were among the reasons why he kept on buying more.[12]

In 1858, for example, Brandon returned to the stand where he had purchased Wood and bought eight slaves valued at $10,060 from

Griffin and Pullum. According to a receipt Brandon kept, he sold them "girl Marthy" in exchange, reducing his tab for the transaction to $9,210. Another receipt shows that the next year he paid the firm $6,700 for "five negroes to wit John at fourteen hundred & fifty dollars And Milly & child at fifteen hundred and fifty dollars And Thomas at thirteen hundred dollars, and John at twelve hundred dollars, and Matt at twelve hundred dollars." Prices like those encouraged Gerard to see the hundreds of people he owned as a bulwark against hard times. Like many planters, he kept two-columned lists of enslaved people's names—with their prices.[13]

Nonetheless, even with the multiple ways that Brandon could hedge risk, the cotton he raised still mattered to his bottom line. A bad crop or a dip in the market could always prompt an unhappy correspondence between Brandon and one of his merchant partners. During one stormy picking season in 1854, Brandon's commission firm blamed some lackluster proceeds from the sale of his cotton on the poor "quality of the last shipments," which "indicated very apparently the damages sustained" from recent bad weather.[14]

Six years later, Brandon wrote another commission firm to demand explanation for a recent disappointing sale they had made. He inquired whether the cotton was defective in some way and was told it was not. During the week preceding the sale, Brandon's firm had noticed a downward trend in the New Orleans cotton market, which was just then in "an unsettled condition." Graders had also been unusually exacting, so "that what is usually called 'Good Middling' would class scarcely as Strict Middling," as the firm explained. Rather than risk a poorer rating or a further drop in prices, the firm had decided to sell quickly and get the best deal they could: "We regret that the price obtained compares unfavorably with sales made since."[15]

Such letters showed how much remained outside of a Natchez planter's control—the weather, the ratings, the prices current for cotton. In the face of so much uncertainty, even well-off planters such as Brandon obsessed over the parts of the cycle that they *could* control. Which variety of cotton was easiest to pick, without mixing "trash" into the fibers? ("Petit Gulf" was the answer most planters gave.) Which enslaved people had the smallest hands, making it comparatively easier for them to yank the blossoms cleanly from the bolls? (It was usually the women, more than the men.) Most of all, what was the optimal number of bales a planter should produce in a season? Could the people he enslaved be forced to set a quick pace while keeping quality high?[16]

These were the kinds of questions that consumed planters, and violence was a common answer. To manage the day-to-day operations on his numerous farms, Brandon relied on overseers—men such as a Kentuckian named John Lyle, who appeared with Gerard's household in the 1860 Census. (Henrietta Wood recalled his name, or Hearn recorded it, as "Tom Lyles.") The overseers were also bent on productivity, and Brandon gave them authority to wield violence freely, punishing any slaves who were not keeping pace.[17]

Wood was not at Brandon Hall for long before she learned that almost any perceived infraction—or even nothing at all—might bring on a brutal outburst from an overseer such as Lyle, or Bill Gates, or Moore, men who (she later said) were "all nearly as bad." "If you did not walk fast enough to please the overseer, or pick quite enough cotton, or even looked away from your work, you got whipped," she told Hearn.[18]

The whippings were also inflicted in humiliating ways. "They used to throw the women down," she said, "pull their clothes over their heads," and "tie their legs and arms to four stakes, stuck in the ground." She knew women who had received hundreds of blows from "a long, heavy strap, made of harness leather" and "stuck full of tacks." The straps, she remembered, were usually less lethal than "bull whips," but they were no less painful, as she knew firsthand: "Every stroke would leave a gash just like you had drawn a knife across my back, and sometimes when they thought it didn't hurt me enough, they would sprinkle salt on the raw flesh" as mind and body reeled.[19]

"One got whipped for nothing," Wood recalled of her life outside Natchez when she spoke to the *Ripley Bee*. And she also recalled having to train her body to do new things, such as properly hoeing a row of plants. "After the cotton had come up about six inches above ground they would shear it off," she explained, "and then we would have to hoe it out, going backwards all day long." That way they could make sure the edge of the tool struck the ground at the proper angle.[20]

The work rewired her body and mind to perform unfamiliar motions: "I got so used to going backwards I pretty near forgot how to go forwards," she said. Swinging a hoe with enough precision to kill a weed, while not inflicting any harm on the cotton plant itself, was painstaking. "The stands are about two feet apart," Wood remembered, "and if you happen to cut one of them up they would take you back to it and whip you, sure. Many, many times have I been whipped for it."[21]

The memory showed how Brandon's men used terror and torture to exploit field workers, during the scraping season as well as during the harvest. The same patterns were repeated on many cotton plantations, and planters valued overseers who could push hands to the farthest extent without fatally hurting their investments. Wood remembered one, Bill Sandford, who "flogged so many to death that the boss had at last to get rid of him," though he may simply have been moved to another of Brandon's farms. A Sandford remained in his employ as late as 1863.[22]

Either way, the kinds of overseers preferred by the people in the fields usually could not keep their jobs at Brandon Hall. Wood recalled one overseer as "rather kind" because he rarely whipped women and never very hard. One day, though, Brandon's wife sent "a girl to him to be whipped," accompanied by another woman to see that it was done. The messenger reported back "that the new overseer wouldn't strip the girl below the waist." Wood remembered that "the mistress sent for him" and demanded an explanation, saying, "When I send a nigger to you to get whipped, I want it done right."[23]

"My mother wasn't a damned dog," the hired man retorted, "and I don't propose to treat any woman like a dog."

According to Wood, he "was at once paid off and sent away."[24]

Wood did not say whether she had witnessed the overseer's dismissal by Brandon's wife, or only heard about the story secondhand. At some point after her arrival in the cotton field, however, Brandon or his overseers determined that no amount of whipping would turn the newcomer from Kentucky into an effective hand. "I could not pick cotton to suit," Wood later explained to Hearn, "because my fingers were too big." After being whipped "almost to death," she was taken out of the fields and sent to work in the big house. There, in the kitchen and the laundry, she worked under the closer surveillance of Brandon and his wife and returned to tasks more like the ones she already knew how to do from years of experience: hauling water, tending fires, scrubbing clothes, preparing food. "I got along a little better," she recalled.[25]

The removal from the fields was not a reprieve from violence, however. As Charlotte Brandon's confrontation with the "rather kind" overseer showed, white women were as willing as men to deploy violence against black women. In the house, Wood also may have experienced new conflicts with the enslaved people with whom she worked. On a large plantation like Brandon's, slaves who worked in the house often came from families who had belonged to the master's family across generations, and who therefore identified themselves as different from common "field hands." The arrival of a virtual stranger could have upset norms within the enslaved community of which Henrietta was still only partially aware.[26]

She nonetheless preferred the work in the house, where her skills may have been recognized and more highly valued. For better and for worse, she also now had limited access to direct conversations with "the boss," something that the vast majority of the people he enslaved never had. In fact, Wood later said in her interview with the *Ripley Bee* that Charlotte, Brandon's wife, was the one who told her that Gerard had paid $1,050 for her purchase. Rather than conveying intimacy and trust, the revelation was more likely intended as a threat—a reminder that she was property and could easily end up back at the Forks of the Road, or under the lash.[27]

One day after Henrietta had been moved from the field to the house, she saw the overseer Bill Sandford come and grab an enslaved woman who had been accused of stealing a yard or so of fabric. The woman had wanted, Wood thought, to make a "dress or something" for herself. Sandford knew well what his employers expected in such a case, and the overseer had her taken out to the yard, stripped to her skin, and tied to the ground "face down." Sandford "whipped her with the strap till he got tired," Wood recalled. Then he forced two black men to continue the beating, turn by turn, until he was ready to retake the whip.[28]

The beating began at two o'clock in the afternoon, and Wood remembered the sound of the woman's yells from the yard. Two hours into the whipping, "she could not even scream, and would only shake and tremble when they struck her." At last one of the black men protested to Sandford that the woman appeared to be nearing death. Sandford said, "Go on, give her a little more. I'll tell you when to stop."

At that, "the colored fellow threw down the strap," Wood recalled, "and said he'd die rather than hit her again."

The woman was finally untied at about five o'clock. She was physically unable to stand, so a man from the field came to carry her back to the quarters.

"She died in a few minutes after," Wood said.

It may not have been the first death she saw in those days, and certainly it would not be the last. Apparently Wood even told Hearn much more about what she witnessed at the farm outside of Natchez, though he deemed the rest of "her pictures of the plantation life" to be "too horrible for publication." Wood, however, remembered those pictures all too well. And she never forgot whose fault it was that she came to Brandon Hall.[29]

CHAPTER THIRTEEN

VERSAILLES

Back in Frankfort, Kentucky, Zebulon Ward's term as keeper ended in the spring of 1859 after making him a newly wealthy and well-connected man. In 1856, one year into his term, Ward's contract had even been revised in his favor. Instead of splitting profits from the convicts' labor with the state, he began paying an annual rent of $6,000 to take total control of the prison and its proceeds. "No monarch ever had more unlimited control of his subjects" than Ward had over his convicts, observed William Sneed in 1860, "and no one ever exercised his own will more completely."[1]

The result had been more misery for the penitentiary's inmates. Convicts complained of lungs choked with hemp dust from the shops. Fairbank called 1856 "the most terrible of my whole life." Annual deaths at the prison grew, peaking at twenty-three in 1858, almost a tenth of the whole population. And at least some of the nineteen deaths in 1859, including the suspected suicide of a free woman of color who worked inside the walls as a cook, might also be traced to conditions left by Ward as outgoing keeper.[2]

Critics of Ward's regime concluded that he was a murderous tyrant. The keeper denied the charge. Prison doctors paid by him praised his "generous humanity" in their annual reports to the state, and Ward's own reports usually focused on improvements he had made. Still, it was clear to almost anyone else that his primary wish was to make the penitentiary pay. He often complained that the prison did not contain enough machinery or space to "furnish profitable employment to the number of inmates," as one of his reports put it, forcing him to concentrate more than he liked on making hemp products.[3]

Under the revised terms of Ward's lease, however, it was difficult for outsiders to know how much he was really raking in, and there was at least one sign that Zeb was making more than he let on. In February 1858, when the General Assembly had to vote on whether to renew his contract as keeper, Ward made clear that he wanted to stay. He even offered to pay the state twice as much in rent.[4]

That offer revealed just how highly Ward valued his profits. In fact, with his bid to pay the state $12,000 per year, he may have made the mistake of showing his hand. One Louisville newspaper sarcastically endorsed Ward with a modest proposal of its own: give Ward a rent of $8,000 per year, and then charge him $1,000 "for every prisoner who dies during his lease." Perhaps the deal would force the keeper to take "good care of his prisoners," who, "being civilly dead, have no right to object to this arrangement." But more likely, predicted the editor slyly, Ward would "think it more profitable" to keep working his prisoners until they were actually dead, netting the state another $25,000.[5]

In the end, state legislators decided in 1858 that the state should raise the rent to $12,000—while also replacing Ward. And when his successor took over as keeper in 1859, a new corps of physicians un-covered deplorable conditions. Reviewing the records they found at the prison's crowded infirmary, they noted the "fearful mortality" under Ward's tenure, a rate they called "unprecedented in the annals of prison discipline" in the United States.[6]

No matter to Ward. He had already gotten the riches he wanted. According to Sneed, he had made "a fortune variously estimated from fifty to seventy-five thousand dollars," practically spinning gold from straw. And after he was dismissed from his monarch-like post in Frankfort, Ward took the profits he had made at the penitentiary and retired to a sprawling estate in nearby Woodford County, just outside the tiny vil-lage of Versailles.[7]

Versailles sat on the western edge of the Bluegrass region of central Kentucky, an area known as the best in the country for breeding Thoroughbred horses. George Wilkes (the New York editor of *Wilkes' Spirit of the Times*, the most widely read sporting paper in the nation) referred to Woodford and the adjoining areas as ideal "race-horse counties," and in the spring of 1862, Wilkes himself would pay a visit to Zeb Ward's farm, describing to his readers what he saw on the turnpike from Frankfort: "On all sides, I beheld a beautiful rolling country, dotted with browsing stock, and already covered with a verdure not due to our more northern pastures for a month to come. This was the blue grass."[8]

The Bluegrass was also the region with the largest concentration of slaves in the state: in 1860, Woodford was the only Kentucky county in which they outnumbered free people. Compared to neighbors, a higher percentage of Woodford County's free residents lived in slaveholding households, too, on farms such as Airy Mount, Spring Hill, and Edgewood. Zebulon's estate, near the meeting of the Big Sink Road and the Frankfort pike, was known as "Ward Villa."[9]

Like Brandon Hall, Ward Villa embodied its owner's ambitions: to become a country squire with a force of valuable slaves. Ward also hoped to acquire a large stable of stallions, fillies, and mares—blooded stock that would make him the envy of other men. The horses would do much more for Ward than indulge his penchant for gambling. They would prove that he was now a member of the South's elite—no longer just a steamboat clerk who had to buy slaves at a discount, or a man who wielded his power only over the criminal set, but a master who controlled substantial wealth and commanded respect from his peers, including on the track as a "man of the turf."

Wealthy white southerners had raced horses for sport since colonial times, using the track to display the power of the planter class. By the time Ward moved to Woodford County, slaveholders remained, by and large, the only southerners with the means to invest in Thoroughbreds. In the first half of the nineteenth century, however, the center of gravity in American racing had moved west from the Atlantic seaboard to Kentucky and the Mississippi River. Sugar and cotton planters in the Deep South flaunted their wealth at elaborate racetracks such as the Metairie Course in Louisiana, and Bluegrass farmers paid to have their horses shipped by steamboat down the river to try their luck. In the spring of 1854, for example, while Wood was awaiting the outcome of

Wood v. Ward, a group of proud Kentucky turfmen had sent a horse called Lexington to race against two southern steeds, Arrow and Lecomte.[10]

Lexington bested his challengers, breaking world records for speed and appearing to vindicate the superiority of Bluegrass stables. Meanwhile, racing rivalries deepened the cultural ties between slaveholders in the Upper and Lower South, despite their regional differences. The planters who cheered Arrow and Lecomte came from states where slavery fueled monoculture on a massive scale. For the Upper South slaveholders who cheered Lexington, slave labor was part of a more diversified economy. Their slaves might work in a field, but they also might be hired out to work in a Lexington factory, in a house in Frankfort, or on a steamboat in Louisville, and some slaveholders even used enslaved men as jockeys at the track. But whether they hailed from Kentucky or Mississippi, when wealthy white slaveholders came to the races, they signaled their mutual membership in a master class.[11]

Zeb Ward now belonged to that class, too. He had acquired fifteen slaves by May 1859—nearly four times more than he had owned in 1856. He had also purchased nearly 450 acres of land, and both numbers grew by the 1860 Census, which valued his real estate at $60,000 and his personal estate at $30,000, including twenty-seven slaves. They worked on Ward's farm producing hemp and other crops, which he usually sold from a profitable store he ran in town, and by February 1862, his holdings included 581 acres.[12]

Ward had also thrown himself headlong into raising horses, though he remained several lengths behind the better-known turfmen around him. R. A. Alexander of Woodburn, an estate just up the road from Ward Villa, was heir to a British industrialist's fortune and had once paid the staggering sum of $15,000 to buy the champion Lexington, whose career was ended prematurely by blindness. Alexander had put the horse out to stud at Woodburn and soon became the most respected breeder in the state. Though Lexington died in 1875, the inaugural year of the Kentucky Derby, all but nine of the derby's first sixty-one winners would be directly descended from the "blind hero of Woodburn."[13]

Though Zebulon never owned a horse comparable to Lexington, he proved a quick study in the Thoroughbred business. He frequented Alexander's farm with his neighbor Willis F. Jones, and by the spring of 1859 he owned at least thirty-one horses. On October 6, 1859, Ward even exhibited some harness horses and two Thoroughbred mares at an agricultural fair in Mercer County, winning a prize. At the state fair that same year, he bought a prize-winning horse for $700, reselling it not long after for $1,000 to "a gentleman in the South," according to a newspaper report.[14]

The master of Ward Villa clearly remained a gambler at heart, but he hoped to prove that he was now a gentleman, too. All signs seemed to suggest that he would succeed. Zeb's future likely unfurled before him in a series of pleasing scenes: a generous pour of whiskey on the porch as twilight fell, the nickering of his pedigreed horses from the barn, the sound of his slaves breaking hemp and working in the kitchen. But the idyll, for Ward, would be disturbed almost as soon as it began—first by rumors of rebellion and war, and then by the realities.[15]

The rumors arrived in Woodford County in the fall of 1859. On October 16, in Harpers Ferry, Virginia, the abolitionist John Brown led an armed band of nineteen men, including five who were black, in a midnight raid on a federal armory, apparently intending to arm slaves for an insurrection. In the next few days, Kentuckians read reports of how Brown was surrounded and captured; how evidence of his plans was found among his possessions; how he appeared to have allies in numerous other states. On November 19, news arrived in Kentucky of a letter sent to Brown by a man named "Day," which seemed to contain plans for another operation. "The negroes, at the instigation of some white scoundrels, designed an attack" on the towns of Frankfort and Versailles—or so the *Louisville Daily Courier* reported. Then the rebels would proceed to "devastate the country."[16]

The idea did not seem far-fetched in those early days after the Harpers Ferry raid, which sparked hysteria across the South. The threat on Versailles appeared more credible than most; Virginia officials had intercepted the letter to Brown from Day and then sent it directly to their counterparts in Kentucky. Some concluded that the author must have been Norris Day, a friend of the notorious Delia Webster, whose alleged affair with Newton Craig had scandalized the capital, and many were prepared to suspect the worst about abolitionist infiltration in the state. John Fee, a Kentucky native, still ran a free labor colony in the Bluegrass. The black abolitionist John Parker of Ripley, Ohio, had crossed the river multiple times to assist fugitive slaves. And William Bailey, an editor in Newport, printed a radical paper that he called the *Free South*. At almost the same time as Brown's raid, he had even published an item urging the "champions of freedom" to make war on slavery "where it exists."[17]

Far more circumstantial evidence had led to panic in the Bluegrass before. In 1856, while Ward was still keeper, a fire broke out in Frankfort and a newspaper reported that "a negro was discovered, under suspicious circumstances," raising fears of a larger plan by black "incendiaries." Later that year, as Christmas approached, several counties along the Tennessee border were seized by reports that a group of slaves was planning to make for the North, slaughtering all the whites in their way. No armed rebellion had occurred, but many white Kentuckians thought they knew the cause of such alarms: as one paper remarked, there were too many people "with abolition proclivities" in the state, and they needed to be stopped.[18]

In 1859, therefore, vigilantes acted quickly to meet the threat, egged on by Kentucky governor Beriah Magoffin's warning that "our lives, and the lives of our wives and children, are threatened." Within two weeks of Brown's arrest, a mob led by two officers of the law attacked Bailey's press. Then, after reports that Fee had told an audience in New York that "we need more John Browns," sixty men on horses ran most of Berea's free labor colonists out of the state. Meanwhile, in Franklin and Woodford Counties, local authorities appointed a special police force and called up a militia in Versailles. Both stood ready to fight "at the first sound of the tocsin of war."[19]

Ward barely had time to celebrate his prizes from the Mercer County Fair before he was also swept up in the rush of events. Having wrangled with abolitionists before as a deputy sheriff along the Ohio River, and then as a jailor for "negro stealers" in Frankfort, Ward may well have taken part in the defensive preparations around Versailles. After all, he was now the owner of many valuable slaves himself, and he also knew that beneath the seemingly placid surface of the "race-horse counties," an undertow of resistance always lurked. One of his own enslaved men had escaped from Ward Villa earlier that fall, making it to neighboring Anderson County.[20]

White Kentuckians tried hard to keep their fears in check. One local newspaper editor in Frankfort warned other editors not to engage in loose talk about the recent reports, lest white Kentuckians begin to seem unsteadied. "Any Harper's Ferry scoundrel that turns up here," promised the *Yeoman*, "will be hung in front of the arsenal, over the banks of the Kentucky river."[21]

Zeb Ward, too, put on a brave face in the wake of John Brown's raid, but if a battle did occur with abolitionists in the South, the master of Ward Villa knew which side he would choose. In fact, a week after the warnings of insurrection in Versailles, Zebulon calmly sat down and addressed a letter, to be sent by express mail to "His Excellency" Governor Henry Wise of Virginia, where John Brown and other raiders had, by then, been sentenced to hang.

"Dear Sir," he began,

> I send you by Adams Express this morning a rope made expressly for the use of John Brown & Co. Kentucky will stand pledged for its being an honest rope. I had it made in her behalf & send it to show that we are willing & ready to aid our mother State in disposing of those who may attempt to destroy & overthrow her government. I hope you will use it.

The hemp rope, Ward explained, had been made at Frankfort for "the express purpose" of hanging the Harpers Ferry raiders. He hoped Wise would "pass it over to the proper authorities to be used," signing the letter, "Yours With Respect, Zeb Ward, Late Keeper, Kentucky Penitentiary, Versailles, Ky." It was dated November 23, 1859.[22]

Wise received the letter and the length of rope four days later, on a Sunday. On Wednesday, he entrusted the rope to a military officer headed to Charlestown, Virginia, where Brown was to be hanged on Friday, December 2. One reporter present said that several other ropes, including one made of South Carolina cotton, had been on display that week as Brown's date with the gallows approached. Each of the samples was tested in advance to check its strength. But only one proved to be strong enough for a hanging noose. In the end, the hangman chose the rope sent from Kentucky.[23]

The new year began with John Brown's body moldering in its grave, and Ward trying to revive his horse racing dreams. In February 1860, he spent time at Woodburn. In May, he purchased another 144 acres and entered a filly in a sweepstake race in Louisville. And in June, he raced his horses against Alexander's in a series of mile and two-mile heats. An announcement before the event promised "great sport ahead."[24]

On the political horizon, though, there were signs of trouble. Brown's execution had made him a martyr to many in the North. In the South, a vocal political movement, led by men called "fire-eaters," had seized on the Harpers Ferry raid to call for their states to secede. According to Virginian John Tyler Jr., the son of a former president, Brown had "invited the slaves throughout the South to rebellion and a feast of blood and rapine." When, Tyler wondered in April 1860, would the "People of the South" decide that they were "justified in the establishment of a new and independent confederation"?[25]

The answer was *not yet*, but some southern leaders had been pondering secession for years, tallying up what they perceived as the North's many sins: resistance to the enforcement of the Fugitive Slave Law; violence against proslavery settlers in the West; and most of all, the rise of the Republican Party. Founded in 1854, the Republicans drew together a wide range of exclusively northern supporters, from radical abolitionists to moderates who opposed the expansion of slavery, and the party's ranks had swelled after 1857 and the Supreme Court's decision in *Dred Scott v. Sanford*. That ruling said people of African descent had no rights that white Americans had to respect—and seemed to say that slaveholders had a right to take their slaves anywhere in the nation. Party leaders declared that an "irrepressible conflict" was coming with the slave states, and by 1858, Republicans had taken control of the House of Representatives. "Fire-eaters" denounced them as "Black Republicans" who preached racial equality and bore the blame for men such as Brown.

Many leading Republicans denied both of those charges, especially as the presidential campaign of 1860 began. The Republican candidate, Abraham Lincoln of Illinois, was on record distancing the party from Harpers Ferry and declaring that he did not support full racial equality. Secessionists in the South were not reassured. Republicans, including Lincoln, said that slavery was morally wrong, that there was no nationally protected right to property in slaves, and that slavery existed only as a creature of state law. The party wanted the federal government to withdraw support from slavery in every place that it legally could. And although Republicans said that Congress could not unilaterally abolish slavery in a state that wanted to keep it, their long-range strategy was clear to fire-eaters: the slave states would be surrounded and left to their own defenses, while Republican rhetoric incited a thousand more John Browns.[26]

The mere chance of such a result led secessionists to disband the Democratic Party's convention in Charleston that April, exploding a national party that still controlled the White House and the Senate. Three different presidential candidates would vie for Democrats' votes in the polls that November. In the end, Lincoln won the election, but without a single electoral vote from any slave state. Before he could even be inaugurated, seven southern states had seceded and declared themselves the Confederate States of America. A full-fledged rebellion in defense of slavery had begun.

The first rebels hoped that they could quickly persuade the other slave states to join them. Two days after Christmas in 1860, a commissioner sent to Frankfort by the governor of Alabama presented a long letter to Governor Magoffin, urging Kentucky's citizens to secede. "If the policy of the Republicans is carried out according to the programme indicated by the leaders of the party," warned the rebel commissioner, who was himself born in Kentucky, the result would be slavery's ruin and "an eternal war of races." Republicans would inevitably destroy the most valuable property of the South, while "consigning her citizens to assassinations and her wives and daughters to pollution and violation to gratify the lust of half-civilized Africans." Two weeks later, similar arguments persuaded Alabama to secede.[27]

Governor Magoffin leaned toward secession, too, though most white Kentuckians remained unconvinced. They shared Magoffin's fears about the Republicans, but not his faith in secession as the answer. For one thing, Kentucky was closer to the free states, more vulnerable to attack and to abolitionists than Alabama. To throw off the protection of the Union, as one Kentuckian put it, would be like "bringing the Canada line to the Ohio River," giving enslavers no hope of recovering runaway slaves from the North. In February, another Unionist, in Lexington, made the prescient point that "slavery could not long exist in a State bordering upon a hostile nation at war with her about the subject of slavery."[28]

Kentucky conservatives like these were proslavery *and* pro-Union. Believing that the Confederacy would fail, they hoped the country would soon return to the long tradition of compromise that had typified relations between Kentuckians and their neighbors to the north, people with whom they shared many ties of kinship. Lincoln himself, a man who had married into a Bluegrass family, leaned heavily on those connections as he made his way from Illinois to Washington after his election. Stopping on his birthday at Lawrenceburg, Indiana, just across the river from where Touseytown had once been, Lincoln told his listeners that he was sure "you are all Union men here." Then, gesturing to the Kentucky side of the Ohio, the president-elect said he was equally sure that "you are in favor of doing full justice to all...on that side of the river." Later that day, in Cincinnati, the president-elect assured Kentuckians that Republicans would "abide by all and every compromise of the constitution."[29]

Those pledges worked, for the moment. Even after Confederates fired upon Fort Sumter in April and Lincoln issued a call for seventy-five thousand volunteers, Unionists continued to predominate in Kentucky. By the middle of May, Arkansas and Virginia had joined the Confederacy, which had already mobilized sixty thousand soldiers for civil war. Kentucky's legislature instead endorsed a policy of neutrality, warning that soldiers, whether from the North or the South, would not be allowed in the state.[30]

Neutrality struck many Republicans as tantamount to treason, but the policy temporarily enabled the illusion that normal life could go on. In fact, on May 18, while politicians in Frankfort debated the state's next steps, Zebulon Ward was celebrating at the Woodlawn Race Course in Louisville. In a race for the Challenge Vase, a $1,000 trophy commissioned by R. A. Alexander and designed by Tiffany and Company in New York, Ward won his first big success on the turf. His horse Sailor, by Yorkshire, finished in third place, beating an offspring of Lexington in the fastest four-mile heat that had ever been run in Kentucky.[31]

Three days later, North Carolina seceded, bringing the number of Confederate states to ten. Tennessee soon became the last to leave the Union. Then, in late July, near a Virginia railroad junction called Manassas, US soldiers fought with Confederate troops around a stream named Bull Run. Spectators had come from Washington to watch, as though heading out to a day at the track. Some believed the rebellion would be crushed then and there. By the end of the battle, however, federal troops were falling back in disarray. The Union had suffered a shocking defeat.[32]

In the late summer of 1861, the embarrassment of US forces at Bull Run fueled a burst of outraged patriotism across the loyal states. Lincoln issued calls for a million recruits to enlist. In Kentucky, meanwhile, Bull Run served as a backdrop to state elections that were slated to be held on August 5. Even before the battle, Ward had decided to take a step that revealed his own political views: he ran for election as a state representative for Woodford County, running as a proslavery supporter of the Union.[33]

Ward opposed secession, though it must have been a difficult decision to make. Some of his neighbors, including fellow turfman Willis Jones, still hoped that Kentucky would secede. Zeb's many years on the

Mississippi River as a younger man also gave him reasons to sympathize with rebels in the states where he had often done business. Certainly, his 1859 pledge to help Virginia "in disposing of those who may attempt to destroy & overthrow her government" was one of many signs that he hated abolitionists. Now, however, it was the Confederates, not the abolitionists, who were trying to "destroy & overthrow" the government, and Lincoln continued to pledge that slavery in the loyal states would not be disturbed. With four slave states still in the Union, to be a Unionist did not require Ward to be antislavery.[34]

Kentucky voters also decisively rejected secession at the polls on August 5. Conservative Unionists swept into office, and Ward was among the winners. As he prepared to go to Frankfort for the start of the legislative session a month later, Ward nevertheless confronted new signs that proslavery Unionism would not be an easy position to maintain. The day after his election, Congress (now controlled in both houses by the Republican Party) passed the First Confiscation Act, providing that slaves used to support the rebellion would be subject to forfeiture. Instructions issued by the War Department two days later interpreted the law to mean that any enslaved people who came into federal lines should be sheltered there.[35]

Those steps outraged border Unionists who wanted the government to avoid disturbing slavery at all costs. Many were particularly worried about the effect of such steps on the people they enslaved. As one slaveholder in Bowling Green told a northern visitor that summer, "There has been so much talk about the matter all through the State that the niggers know as much about it as we do…and too much for our safety and peace of mind." In Woodford County, on August 17, a large anti-war barbecue was held in a pasture owned by Ward's neighbor Jones. Ward was probably there to witness the fear and anger in his new constituents' eyes.[36]

Two weeks later, as he arrived in Frankfort to sit in the General Assembly, talk of new crises swirled in the streets of the state capital. On August 30, the Republican general John C. Frémont issued a proclamation emancipating all the slaves of disloyal owners in neighboring

Missouri. And white Kentuckians barely had time to register that development before more troubling news arrived. On September 3, Confederate troops entered the state from the South. Three days later, federal soldiers also crossed into the state, under the command of a then little-known officer named Ulysses S. Grant.[37]

Those movements brought Kentucky's brief flirtation with neutrality to an end. On September 17, the General Assembly voted overwhelmingly to side with the Union, and Ward stood with the majority. For a few weeks at the beginning of September, however, anxious officials in Washington had waited in suspense to see how Kentuckians would react to a Confederate invasion. Having been warned by friends in Kentucky about the outrage there over Frémont's emancipation edict, Lincoln acted swiftly to overrule his general. When he explained his decision later to a friend who supported Frémont, Lincoln pointed to the precarious situation in the Bluegrass: "I think to lose Kentucky is nearly the same as to lose the whole game."[38]

Events that fall showed that Lincoln had less cause for worry about Kentucky than he initially feared. The General Assembly spent the remainder of its session supporting federal military activities in the state. Simultaneously, though, loyal Kentuckians resisted the steady creep of policies aimed at dissolving slavery. One state resolution, passed in December, opposed any emancipation of slaves in Kentucky; another praised Lincoln for his rebuff of Frémont's order. Zebulon Ward cast his vote in favor of both.[39]

Ward's proslavery Unionism would be further tested as the war effort hardened over the next winter. In March 1862, only a few days before the end of the General Assembly's session, Lincoln signed a law forbidding members of the military from enforcing the Fugitive Slave Law. At about the same time, the president gathered congressmen from the border slave states and encouraged them to consider a gradual emancipation plan in which slaveholders would be compensated.[40]

That plan got nowhere, but northern Republicans increasingly believed that the abolition of slavery was the only way to be sure that a loyal border state would remain that way. Still, for the time being, slaveholding Unionists in Kentucky had good reason to stand firm.

Confederate troops were driven out of Kentucky early in 1862, and during the campaign, many Union commanders in the state had actively returned runaway slaves to their owners or simply avoided the issue by refusing to allow escaping slaves into their camps. As the first year of the Civil War came to a close, slavery remained functional in Kentucky. That January, Ward even hired out four of his slaves to his rebel-sympathizing neighbor to help break hemp.[41]

The next month, a series of encouraging federal victories in the West also raised hopes that the war would be over soon. The Union might then be restored as it was, with the property rights of loyal slaveholders undisturbed. As his first session as a state legislator concluded, Ward looked forward to returning home to his stables. And he even had time, on March 17, to welcome the editor George Wilkes of New York to his house outside of Versailles.[42]

Wilkes had come to Kentucky on his way to Tennessee, hoping to cover news of the war for *Spirit of the Times*. Though antislavery in his politics, Wilkes remained a turfman first, and while in the South he hoped to persuade his fellow sportsmen there to attend upcoming meets in Boston, Philadelphia, and New York. His columns since 1859 had already alienated many of his southern subscribers, and the collapse of the Union had further roiled the racing community, so Wilkes hoped to shore up friendships in the Bluegrass state.[43]

The editor began his Kentucky tour in Frankfort, where he observed the final days of the General Assembly's session. He then rented a buggy and drove it to Ward Villa, relishing his first views of the "blue grass region" despite a "driving wind and rain." When he arrived, Ward refused to let the journalist lodge at an inn. Instead, Zebulon put him up as a guest in "his fine mansion," sending him off to bed after "an abundant supper" and a few glasses of "genial old Bourbon."[44]

Wilkes marveled at Ward's hospitality to his Yankee readers back home; as an aspiring horseman, Ward was probably grateful for the publicity. The next morning, Zeb took George on a tour of his racing farm. He ordered his best buggy to protect the men from the rain, "placing a little nigger boy behind in order that he might open gates," according to Wilkes, and as they rode, Ward whistled at horses to call them in from their pastures. The editor and politician chatted easily about the palmy days of racing before the war began, and they visited several area stables, including Alexander's Woodburn, where they laid eyes on "the old hero LEXINGTON, the true American 'King of the Wind.'" Wilkes then parted ways with his host, though not before securing a list of the "fine lot of horses" that Ward promised to bring to races in the North.[45]

Those promises suggest Ward's hope that the war and its threats to slavery would soon end. But three weeks after he hosted George Wilkes at Ward Villa, a gruesome battle near a small church in southwestern Tennessee would leave twenty thousand men wounded or dead—the bloodiest day of fighting, to that point, in all of American history. After the Battle of Shiloh, as it soon became known, the war would continue for three more years. And it would not end before it had brought revolution to the gates of Versailles and beyond.[46]

CHAPTER FOURTEEN

REVOLUTION

News of a civil war reached Henrietta Wood more slowly than it had
Zebulon Ward, and neither of her interviews said exactly when or how
she first learned of the fighting. Newspapers in Natchez covered the
march to secession, but the laws of Mississippi made it a crime to teach
enslaved people to read. In addition, most of the people with whom
Wood lived and worked remained relatively isolated in a rural world.
Though Natchez was fewer than a dozen miles away from Brandon
Hall, she remembered that slaves "in the country never got to town
more than once a year."[1]

That did not mean they were unaware of political events. Some enslaved people learned how to read in spite of the ban, and some also
did jobs that required moving about. Carriage drivers, wagoners, and
messengers all went frequently to town or to other farms, circulating
news, and by 1860, informal lines of communication crackled with
rumors of distant events. One day, a black woman named Dora Franks,
who lived even deeper in the countryside than Wood, heard her owner
tell his wife that "a bloody war" was coming. Franks and the other
enslaved women on the place "started praying for freedom" right away,
as she later recalled.[2]

Wood may have learned of the war in a similar way, eavesdropping
while at work in the laundry or the kitchen. In January 1861, delegates
to a secession convention in Mississippi voted to become the second
state to withdraw from the Union, declaring that "our position is thoroughly identified with the institution of slavery." Many large planters
in the Natchez District were initially opposed to the war, fearing that it
would jeopardize their wealth. Not the Brandons, though. Gerard

Brandon's uncle became a Confederate officer; two of his brothers enlisted. So the white folk at Brandon Hall had much to discuss in the war's first year—discussions that people who worked in the house were well positioned to hear.[3]

Enslaved people had to handle whatever they knew with care. Many planters around Natchez already feared that the black majorities in their counties knew too much. Only a few weeks after Fort Sumter fell, a group of enslaved men in Jefferson County were accused of forming a conspiracy "to march up the river to meet '*Mr. Linkin*' bearing off as booty such things as they could carry," as one accuser put it. Several suspects were put to death. At about the same time, across the river, a planter in Tensas Parish overheard a conversation among his slaves that revealed, according to him, that "the negros all knew of the war and what it was for." In nearby Claiborne County, an enslaved preacher named Anthony Lewis was taken into the woods and threatened because he had publicly expressed support for the Union to other slaves. Lewis recanted to save his life, but a fellow slave remembered the gist of what he had said: "if the Yankees whipped the Confederates we all would be free." An enslaved man in Adams County, under questioning in 1861, put more bluntly what he had heard from friends: "the Northerners make the South shit behind their asses."[4]

The white residents of the Natchez District reacted to such talk with heightened vigilance during the war's first year. In the village of Washington, for example, not far from Brandon Hall, a troop was created to defend against "such persons white or black as may be detected in causing or engaged in insurrection," and their menacing activities could not have escaped the notice of enslaved people. Benjamin Wailes even worried that excitable boys, witnessing the formation of the Washington Troop, would talk about it "indiscreetly with our servants."[5]

In 1861, however, enslaved people still had more to fear from panicked white residents than the other way around. After the war, many of the black men and women who lived through those harrowing days did recall talking about what would happen if faraway troops came. Most stopped short of acting before any arrived. Spooked planters saw little difference, though, between planning an insurrection and talking about politics. Five months after the war began, a group of planters near Second Creek in southern Adams County uncovered evidence that a network of enslaved drivers, including a teamster owned by Brandon, knew a great deal about the war and had been discussing what to do now that "freedom was at our door." A group of inquisitorial planters concluded that a massive plot was in the works. Over the next few months, dozens of enslaved men—by some accounts, hundreds—were executed, many of them strung up at a racetrack near Natchez.[6]

Littleton Barber, an enslaved man living in Adams County at the time, later testified that he "took good care that no white persons heard me say anything" about his "Union sentiments," especially after witnessing the rate of executions. Barber continued "to talk to a few of my own color about our chances for freedom." But his main advice, he remembered, was to "watch & pray" for "when the Union troops Came."[7]

Henrietta probably did the same: watched, listened, and prayed. She knew from her life in Ohio, and even her suit in Kentucky, that rumors of allies farther north had a degree of truth—but also that antislavery allies were not all-powerful. More than likely she kindled "Union sentiments" herself, sharing with others everything she already knew about liberty—both its flavor and its fragility. Perhaps she even dared to hope that she would taste it again, if the Union troops did come.

In any case, black Southerners saw from the start how the fighting might benefit them, and the hushed conversations among slaves in the Natchez District were echoed in most slave states during the Civil War. In September 1861, for example, as vigilantes hanged dozens—or hundreds—at the Natchez racetrack, enslaved people near Frankfort, Kentucky, gathered to greet the arrival of an Ohio infantry regiment. It was a pattern that would be repeated throughout the war: wherever federal armies went, they attracted freedom-seekers. By the middle of 1862, as one chaplain in the Army of the Tennessee reported, enslaved people were flocking to US military camps in such numbers that it was "like the oncoming of cities."[8]

That fact terrified large planters like Brandon in Mississippi, where the mass flight of slaves would mean the loss of millions of dollars—

not to mention the loss of the labor needed to bring in their cotton. For the first year of the war, Brandon and his overseers tried to continue business as usual, putting in crops on his various plantations. But a dry summer stunted the yields across the region, depressing an already sluggish market. "We are sorry to hear last accounts of your crop," a New Orleans cotton dealer wrote to Brandon in October 1861, "but it is the same everywhere." The dealer could only hope "the Almighty will overrule everything for good."[9]

The New Year brought Gerard few signs of the Almighty's favor. One of his ten-year-old daughters, a twin, died on January 19, 1862, plunging his household into grief. Then bad news began to arrive about the war. In February, Union forces captured Nashville, Tennessee, and Columbus, Kentucky. The Battle of Shiloh in April brought a huge army to within striking distance of Mississippi. Even worse for planters on the Mississippi River, federals took New Orleans on April 25. Within a month, their boats began to pass below Natchez.[10]

The recapture of New Orleans brought about the rapid dissolution of the plantation order in southern Louisiana, forcing many planters to flee up the river. Brandon must have watched with equal alarm as the federals inched down the river from above. Confederate forces abandoned Memphis and Fort Pillow that June, leaving the federal government in control of all but about two hundred miles of the Mississippi. Natchez, for the moment, remained in the segment of Confederate control that ran from Port Hudson to Vicksburg, but it was unclear how long that would last. That September, a gunboat fired on the town for several hours, starting a few fires.[11]

Still, Brandon had at least two reasons for hope in those (to him) dark days. Instead of mounting an assault on Vicksburg that summer, which would have meant the certain occupation of Natchez, the western armies of the United States moved toward middle Tennessee. Moreover, Confederate defeat seemed imminent to many at the time. It may have consoled Brandon to think that defeat would at least come while his closest relatives in uniform survived—and before a general emancipation could totally destroy his wealth.

* * *

Back in Kentucky, Zebulon Ward had the same hopes in 1862: quick end to the war, slavery still intact. Over the previous winter, his wife, Mary, had been pregnant with twins who died that spring in childbirth, bringing tragedy to Ward Villa not long after death also struck Brandon Hall. But in the case of Ward, a Union man, the personal loss was followed by cheering news from the front. By the end of June, after months of delay, US forces had advanced to within six miles of Richmond, the Confederate capital. "We shall be disappointed," said the *New York Tribune* on June 5, "if the National flag is not flying over every considerable city of the South by the 4th of July."[12]

Buoyed by the national mood, Zebulon decided in June to leave his convalescent wife at home and take some horses to a series of races in the North. A group of Northern turfmen had organized the races in the hopes of building new ties between Kentucky horse farms and sportsmen in the Northeast. The first was held in Philadelphia, where newspaper reports said that Ward's "fine horses" performed well—winning one "highly exciting" heat. He continued on from there to New York, where twenty-five hundred people turned out for the Fourth of July holiday to watch some of his horses race at the Union Course on Long Island.[13]

The success must have gratified Ward, who was introduced to readers by a *New York Times* journalist as "well-known in Kentucky and the adjacent country." The trip only boosted his reputation as a man of the turf, and even more gratifying may have been the signs that many white Northerners still welcomed loyal border-state slaveholders such as he.[14]

But the races in New York ended with news of shocking setbacks in the war. That week had begun with predictions that national troops would occupy Richmond within days. Instead, by July 6, the *New York Times* looked back on the previous seven days as "the heaviest week we have had since the war began." After a series of bloody battles, federal armies had been turned back from the Confederate capital, and as the races at the Union track came to a close, "a feeling of despondency" descended over New York.[15]

Ward's mood must have darkened, too, though he traveled on to Boston for another round of races. There he also received distressing news from home. Throughout the summer of 1862, as Union armies slowly made their way across Tennessee, roving Confederate cavalry regiments had been wreaking havoc on their supply lines—burning railroads, damaging bridges, picking off men and stock in guerrilla-style raids. One of the most infamous raiders was the Kentuckian John Hunt Morgan, and in mid-July, Morgan's men made it all the way to Lexington and Versailles, where he hoped to recruit more soldiers.[16]

While Morgan was welcomed by local secessionists, including Ward's neighbor Jones, he targeted Unionists in the area for punishment. Morgan set up his headquarters in the pastures at Ward Villa—arresting the stable manager, emptying the smokehouse, and "mutilating" the gardens. As a final insult, when leaving town, Morgan's cavalry stole six of Zeb Ward's horses.[17]

By the time Ward returned to Kentucky for a called session of the state legislature, which began August 14, it was clear that the war would not be over soon after all. Moreover, setbacks on the battlefield had only hardened the resolve of Republicans in Washington to attack slavery more directly. On July 17, Congress passed the Second Confiscation Act, declaring all persons held as slaves by traitors to the Union to be "forever free of their servitude," as well as a new militia act that allowed black men to serve in the military. Then, in September, President Lincoln announced his plans to issue an even broader Emancipation Proclamation on January 1, which would free all slaves in areas still in rebellion.

Unionist slaveholders howled with displeasure over the mounting signs that Lincoln wanted slavery abolished, though none of his steps should have been a complete surprise. In May, Lincoln had warned the border slave states that the "signs of the times" pointed to emancipation. On July 12, two days before Morgan's raiders arrived at Ward Villa, Lincoln had met with border state congressmen again, urging them to reconsider his offer to support gradual, compensated emancipation. Soon enough, he counseled, the "abrasions" of war would lead to the end of slavery by other means.[18]

Those abrasions came to Kentucky in full force that fall. Emboldened by the successful raids of cavalry officers such as Morgan, Confederate generals in the West launched a two-pronged attack on Kentucky. The rebels briefly occupied Frankfort in September, before fresh US troops swept across the state, repelling the rebels at the Battle of Perryville on October 8. As Northern regiments—many of them composed of abolitionist soldiers—moved across the Bluegrass, enslaved people reacted as they did elsewhere when the opportunity arose: they fled in large numbers to US Army lines.[19]

Kentucky slaveholders tried in vain to hold on to their human property. Even though Lincoln's forthcoming Emancipation Proclamation exempted loyal states, the application of military policy on the ground undermined slavery in Kentucky anyway. Soldiers in the Twenty-second Wisconsin, for example, sheltered fugitive slaves in their ranks as they marched across Kentucky that winter. In one case on the road between Lexington and Frankfort, a white Kentuckian appeared alongside a group of Northern troops on the march and found a man he claimed as his slave. Holding a gun to the black man's head, the enslaver demanded that he come along. A colonel appeared and sent the white man packing.[20]

Startled by such stories, conservative Unionists like Ward struggled to accept how dramatically things had shifted since 1861. A week before Christmas, even Wood's former lawyer George Kinkead lamented recent events in a letter to his brother-in-law. "The political skies look to me gloomy as midnight," he wrote. Noting rumors from the Deep South that "the negroes have broke loose and are with savage ferocity claiming their freedom," Kinkead bemoaned that each Union defeat emboldened abolitionists in Washington. "We are still annoyed here by the soldiers enticing our slaves" away.[21]

In Frankfort, Kinkead's dismay was echoed by the man he had once tried to defeat in *Wood v. Ward*. After Lincoln had issued his promised Emancipation Proclamation, Ward used a debate in the General Assembly over a military funding bill to launch into a tirade about "the unconstitutional and iniquitous course of the Radicals" in Washington. Then Ward registered his disgust by proposing an amendment making clear that Kentucky would not ask its soldiers to enforce emancipation. He still hoped slavery in Kentucky could survive the maelstrom of war.[22]

For Brandon, news of the Emancipation Proclamation could not have come at a worse time. The death of his other twin daughter on December 13, 1862, had cast a pall over Brandon Hall again. Embargoes and droughts had also weakened cotton production, and in 1862 the bottom had fallen out of the market, leaving bales in the field across the cotton kingdom. Brandon's hundreds of slaves provided a tenuous economic safety net as the new year began, but now Lincoln's proclamation threatened that capital, too.[23]

Most concerning were the signs that US military commanders were refocusing their attention on the Mississippi River. In November and December, federal forces from New Orleans pushed farther into the Louisiana interior, liberating slaves wherever they went. As 1863 began, Ulysses S. Grant developed new plans for besieging the Confederate stronghold of Vicksburg, Mississippi, the last significant obstacle to total Union control of the Mississippi River. Meanwhile, US commanders in Louisiana began to make extensive use of black regiments, for both military labor and combat operations.

The worst nightmares of white Confederates seemed to be coming to pass. From a Louisiana plantation just below Vicksburg, one diarist noted with concern the federal recruiters moving through the plantation districts and persuading slaves to join them, "the Negroes generally going most willingly, being promised their freedom by the vandals."[24]

Many slaveholders now determined that their only option was to run away themselves, forcing as many enslaved people as possible to come with them. That May, Brandon received a letter from T. C. Holmes, a planter who had lived in Natchez before moving to New Orleans. It informed him that Holmes had taken his slaves to a plantation Brandon owned on the Louisiana side of the river, near Waterproof. Holmes had tried to push on toward the Red River, but he backtracked when he discovered troops in the area and local residents "more panic stricken there than here." Hemmed in but hopeful that the Union forces would not come farther down the Mississippi, he asked Brandon permission to remain on his place. Holmes would start planting corn "if the yankees leave me alone."[25]

Before long the Yankees came. The town of Vicksburg surrendered to Grant on the Fourth of July. US troops in Pennsylvania won the pivotal Battle of Gettysburg on the same day. The last serious rebel garrison on the Mississippi fell a few days after, and the whole of the river now finally lay under federal control. Little more than a week after the capture of Vicksburg, Union soldiers arrived in Natchez and took it without a shot.

Afterward, enslaved people in the Natchez District fled their plantations by the thousands and streamed into town. Quickly overwhelmed by the refugees, US Army officers struggled to provide for the freedom-seekers in crowded, disease-ridden camps that were hastily organized under the bluffs. Fleeing from the countryside to Union lines remained dangerous even then. In one case, a group of twenty enslaved people were killed near Natchez while trying to get to town. According to Northern abolitionist Laura Haviland, who had arrived to help in the camps, slave owners also shot at an escaping black mother and hit a baby she was carrying. The mother continued to Union lines, Haviland reported, "with her dead child in her arms, to be buried, as she said, '*free.*'"[26]

The arrival of Northern troops and the flight of slaves brought revolution to Adams County at last. "Victory over the rebels in their own States," wrote one correspondent from Natchez to a Chicago newspaper, "is necessarily followed by the freedom of their slaves." Almost immediately, US officers in Natchez also began to enlist black men. A white officer in one of the new black regiments in Natchez described its operations for a Wisconsin paper in January 1864, reporting that "our first quarters were in a long range of barracks used for a number of years as slave pens." He referred to the buildings outside town that had once been Forks of the Road.[27]

"Very many of the men composing the regiment had been sold" in these pens, explained the correspondent to the *Milwaukee Sentinel*, "brought from Kentucky, Tennessee, Virginia and other slave States, in large gangs ironed." Because the ramshackle buildings at the Forks were exposed to attack, the regiment soon received orders to tear them down and use the lumber to construct new quarters in town. The order came "just at evening and was hailed with the wildest enthusiasm by these men," who worked throughout the night. "The morning sun saw the slave pens of Natchez leveled to the ground," a striking proof of the revolution emancipation had brought.[28]

Henrietta Wood, however, did not get to see the change, for by the time an army of liberation arrived in Natchez, she was already long gone. "When the news came to master that the Yankees were coming toward us," she recalled in her interview with the *Ripley Bee*, "his wife made him take us to Texas." For Wood, and a few hundred other people who lived at Brandon Hall, freedom was still years away.[29]

CHAPTER FIFTEEN

THE MARCH

Gerard Brandon was already on the run when he learned that Confederate forces had lost control of the Mississippi. He had made the decision to flee on July 1, 1863, leaving his wife and children behind and setting out for the West. He had forced a large group of slaves to go with him to the river—probably close to three hundred souls, maybe two hundred more. Overseers had also come with wagons and supplies. Then Brandon had paid to ferry them all across the water, mere days before Vicksburg fell to Grant.[1]

After the crossing, the caravan turned its back to the river and marched. Gerard marked their progress in a small leather book. In the first days they were slowed by more ferries at Cocodrie Bayou, Cross Bayou, and Little River, each one putting more distance between his slaves and the Yankees. Finally they got all the way to Alexandria, a Confederate military headquarters in the heart of Louisiana. And then he received the news of the defeat at Vicksburg.[2]

Going back now, he knew, meant surrender to the Republicans and losing his slaves. It meant going bust, which was why he had gone away. So Brandon ordered the people he enslaved back onto the road. His thought was to reach the Sabine River and cross it into Texas—the last refuge, it seemed, for a slaveholding refugee.

"Old Brandon picked out five hundred of his best slaves and went to Texas for safety," Lafcadio Hearn would write in 1876, and Henrietta Wood recollected it all, because she was one of the marchers. "When we had got about 100 miles from Natchez," she remembered, "Brandon got a dispatch that Vicksburg had fallen into the hands of the Yanks. When he read it he said, 'Oh hell! we are done for. We might as well go back.'" But instead, Wood continued, "we went on some 400 miles into Texas."[3]

By July 1863, Brandon was not the only Confederate planter in flight. As federal armies tightened their grasp on the Mississippi River, attracting fleeing slaves to their lines wherever they went, many slave-holders had decided to flee. Texas beckoned as one of the places where US troops had not reached, and where cotton continued to be grown and sold across the border to Mexico.[4]

One Confederate cavalryman reported from Arkansas in November 1862 that "every day we meet refugees with hundreds of Negroes, on their way to Texas." A few months later, a Massachusetts chaplain sta-tioned in southern Louisiana found it common to come across house-holds led by white women, each of whose husbands had "gathered together his best hands (the young, strong-limbed men), his finest horses, and all his mules, and started for the prairie near Alexandria, whose soil the foot of the Yankee, he thought, would never desecrate."[5]

Running was risky, however, and always a last resort. The crowded roads were often in total disrepair. Food, supplies, and medicine were scarce, making prices high, and avoiding Yankee troops was never guaranteed. Only a few months before Brandon and his caravan ar-rived in Alexandria, federal forces had briefly occupied the town, free-ing thousands of people in the parishes around.[6]

Even if a planter such as Brandon could get to northeastern Texas, refugees there also faced a different kind of threat. By the end of 1863, Confederate officials in Texas were pressuring planters to provide slaves for forced military labor, such as building fortifications to keep the Yankees out. Many believed that refugees should bear the brunt of the levies. In September 1863, a few months after Brandon began his own flight, planters around Alexandria were hearing troubling rumors from "persons returning from Texas" that as many as half of a refugee's slaves might be impressed by the state.[7]

Many planters left to take their chances in Texas anyway. One for-merly enslaved man in Mississippi later recalled his owner ordering his slaves to "git everything bundled up and in the wagons for a long trip." When one man refused to go along for the ride, the white man viciously flogged him. Other planters relied on different kinds of duress, such as separating spouses and families on the march, moving people too sick and too weak to resist, or telling lies about what Lincoln's men would do when they came. "We met several planters on the road," noted an eastbound traveler in Louisiana at the time, and one road seemed to be almost "alive with negroes, who are being 'run' into Texas.... We must have met hundreds of them." Tens of thousands of slaves eventually made the trek.[8]

As for Brandon, on July 8, 1863, he was still in Alexandria, ruing the news from home and the desperate road ahead. It was a Wednesday when he appeared at the military headquarters in town to get a "Pass" permitting travel through Confederate lines to Texas. A strange thing for a master: to be told where he could go. But Brandon counted himself lucky to have gotten off with his slaves. He even wondered now whether he should have brought more, though with Vicksburg lost, there was nothing to be gained by looking back.[9]

At last, on July 14, he reached the Sabine River. Two weeks after leaving Brandon Hall, Brandon had made it to Texas. But his slaves had barely managed to survive the grueling trip.

Henrietta Wood had never walked so many miles in her life, camping out on the road even in the worst of weather. Years later, she tried to convey the misery of the march. Brandon had brought some wagons on the journey, she said, together with what Wood recalled as "a whole drove of mules." Some people "rode one of them," she explained. Yet Henrietta refused to straddle a donkey "like a hair pin," and she only spent one day riding on the march. She also feared that a wagon would tip over, and not without reason. Brandon could have chosen to travel through Natchitoches, joining a very old road that snaked to Milam, Texas. But he may have decided instead to stay off the road altogether, moving due west from Alexandria to a crossing at Sabinetown. If so, the last week of the journey was across a gullied landscape not easy to navigate on wheels.[10]

The roads in Texas were not much better, especially under the increased wartime load. By the end of the war, somewhere between

50,000 and 150,000 slaves were "refugeed" to Texas by fleeing planters. No one was sure exactly how many came, but it was more than enough to make most of the state's roadways impassable. One newspaper editor in the town of Marshall, Texas, even proposed that all the incoming slaves be put to work on public roads, especially since "there are more negroes in the State now than were ever here before."[11]

Planters were more interested in renting land and putting their slaves to work producing cotton again. Brandon's first stop was near the town of Butler in Freestone County, the northern edge of rich cotton country known as the Bottomlands. Fed by the water of the Brazos River, the east-central counties of Texas had produced a profusion of cotton in the decade before the war, and Brandon encountered many refugees already in the region. He traveled around for several weeks looking for land to rent, before finding a farm owned by Joseph S. Able in Robertson County—right along the banks of the river Brandon misspelled as the "Brassos." A county tax collector found him settled there in 1864 along with 270 slaves.[12]

Wood was among them. She later told Hearn that "her health and strength were gone," but at least she had survived. Others had reached Texas just in time to die, such as Jack Mose, Dudly, and a baby belonging to Lucy. Brandon recorded their deaths and others in his small leather pocketbook, wedged between pages that listed his traveling expenses:[13]

> Thornton drowned on 24 July, found body next day
> William (7 years) died August 5th
> Winston (Mandy's) died August 10th '63

Winston's death "worries me," Brandon confessed. "It was a fine child, seemed but little sick at first."[14]

> Frances (Dicey's) (4 years) died August 15 '63
> Lucinda (Jane) (10 months) died August 15 '63
> Gerard (Dicey's) (2 years) died August 18 '63
> George (Palina) 6 years died September 13 ...

The list of deaths reached eighteen names as the days passed, often with no meat. Mules sickened, too, and by September Brandon seemed to give up on cataloging it all: "how many cases I have doctored of sick negroes swelled feet & legs—swelled stomachs—Diphtheria—fever." Wood herself was among the sick and the lame, later telling the *Ripley Bee* "I was sick a whole year from exposure."[15]

Yet in one significant way, at least, Henrietta had been spared. All around her now were women whose babies had died on the road, or on Able's land in the northwestern corner of Robertson County. There were also mothers whom Brandon had forced to abandon their children in Mississippi, and who wondered if they would ever be reunited. But Henrietta did not have that sorrow to add to her sufferings, for when Brandon fled, she later said, "I coaxed him to let me take my child with me."[16]

It was the first time in her story to the *Ripley Bee* that Wood had mentioned her son.

PART III

THE RETURN OF HENRIETTA WOOD

CHAPTER SIXTEEN

ARTHUR

Lafcadio Hearn knew that Henrietta Wood had a son, but he did not meet the man and he did not publish his name. What the Cincinnati reporter said in 1876 may have been all that he knew: her "only child, a boy," was "in Chicago, doing well."[1]

In 1948, however, more than seventy years later, a reporter named Dennis Murray *would* interview Wood's son, by then an elderly man named Arthur H. Simms. Wood had been dead for three dozen years, but Simms remained in Chicago. According to an article by Murray in the Sunday *Chicago Tribune*, he was just about to turn ninety-three years old and had worked for decades as a lawyer in the city.[2]

By that time, nearly a century had passed since Simms's mother was sold in Natchez, Mississippi. The world looked very different. People now listened to radios and traveled by cars and planes. Televisions were spreading into the homes of American families. Simms had been married, fathered two kids, and buried his wife and children. Atomic bombs had been dropped on Hiroshima and Nagasaki.

A photograph with Murray's article in the *Tribune* showed a dapper man with a serious face dressed in a three-piece suit—a "venerable barrister," Murray wrote, "who pulled himself up from slavery" and was *still* practicing law. The accompanying text focused mainly on his legal career and his advanced age; it said little about the woman who was his mother, whom Murray called "a laundress" and did not name, but census returns and other records showed that she was in fact Wood. The *Tribune* piece reported only that "Simms was born a slave in January, 1856, on a farm 11 miles from Natchez, Miss. His mother had been sold to the plantation owner only a month before his birth."[3]

If so, then Henrietta had become pregnant with Arthur even before she reached Forks of the Road. When he died in 1951, however, his own death certificate would provide few details about his birth. Place: Mississippi. Date: January 8, 1856. Mother's name: "Hattie Woods." Father's name: "unknown."[4]

Wood herself was the person who could have filled in the most blanks about Arthur's birth. Who the father was and why she had chosen his name. Whether she had been forced to work until her labor began, and who had attended the delivery. Whether she had been permitted to feed him herself or forced to give him to another woman to suckle, so that she could return more quickly to the cotton.[5]

Yet whatever she knew about the identity of Arthur Simms's father did not survive in the records that she or her son left behind. Although the surnames slave children bore sometimes told their paternity, that was not true in every case, and Wood herself might have preferred to keep the knowledge concealed. After all, if Simms remembered his birthday correctly, then she had been impregnated while imprisoned in a Lexington slave jail, or while laboring for a prison keeper who had abducted her. Remembering it, for her, was almost surely a torment.[6]

Wood might never have told her son exactly how it happened. It is difficult to imagine that she consented to his conception, given her captivity at the time. Becoming a mother would also have been shadowed by the recent terror and grief of reenslavement—as well as the knowledge that her child would now be born enslaved. Wood once told Mary Ward that only a man could whip her; perhaps the defensive boast was the scab for a deeper wound.[7]

Specific dates would help to clear up parts of the mystery. One possibility is that Arthur was actually born before 1856, maybe even before his mother's sale at Forks of the Road. After all, she told Hearn that she was forced to "nurse" for the Wards, an ambiguous term that could have meant she was forced to breastfeed their children, and if so, then she must have given birth before then.[8]

Another possibility is that Wood became pregnant after Ward had returned her to Lexington and the "negro traders," a class of men notorious for raping women they sold. Or Arthur could have been conceived on the way to Mississippi. A steamboat like the one that carried Wood down to Natchez would have had many corners where men could assault women. One formerly enslaved man who was forced to work for a slave trader remembered being ordered to put a particular woman, Cynthia, "in a stateroom...apart from the other slaves" on a riverboat. Then he listened as the trader made a series of "vile proposals" and forced himself upon her. Perhaps Pullum or Griffin or one of their firm's agents had a similar motive for taking Wood alone by rail and boat to Natchez, while the rest of the "gang" was marched overland from Kentucky.[9]

Henrietta's son might have been conceived in any of these ways, or another not already named. A rape at Brandon Hall may have been among the "pictures of plantation life" that were later deemed, by Hearn, "too horrible" to tell. Then again, Wood herself may never have told Hearn or anyone else about what had occurred. The mystery surrounding Arthur's birth could suggest a trauma that pained her too much to recount.[10]

Whatever the case, Simms was certainly not alone in having an "unknown" father. According to Henry Bibb, a former slave who wrote an autobiography and was born in Kentucky just a few years earlier than Wood, it was "almost impossible for slaves to give a correct account of their male parentage." After Bibb escaped from slavery in 1842, he wrote what he knew about his paternity: "my mother informed me that my father's name was James Bibb," a white slaveholder. Beyond that, Bibb knew little for sure.[11]

Even when it came to her own parentage, Wood knew only what her own mother had told her, though she passed that information down to her son. After her death in 1912, Arthur became the informant for his mother's death certificate, which listed her parents as "William Williams" and "Daphne Williams." "William" may have been Simms's own recollection of the name that Henrietta and her brother had remembered as "Bill." That name also appeared, with "Daphney," in the 1834 list of Moses Tousey's slaves. Her father's eponymous last name—"Williams"—may have stood in place of a surname that Simms never knew, or her parents never had. After all, Josh had said they were called by the last name Tousey.

Adding to the mysteries surrounding Wood's own paternity are the various words that were sometimes used to describe her appearance. After her kidnapping, for example, some court records and newspaper reports described her as a "mulatto" or "yellow girl," terms meant to convey that a person came from mixed-race parents. They could mean only that her skin did not seem very dark—racial ascription always depended on the eye of the beholder—but the terms might be a sign that white men were among her immediate forebears. Like her son, Wood had no official birth record, no way to check what her mother had told her about her father.[12]

Slaveholders, of course, wanted it this way. Their wealth depended on denying that it mattered who a slave's father was. Whenever a birth occurred in a slave state in the antebellum period, the laws were very clear. If the mother was enslaved, so was the child; if not, then neither was he—theoretically, at least. Either way, the status and race of the father were immaterial, as was the question of how a slave woman's child was conceived. Legally, her "increase" belonged to her owner, and owners used these rules to their financial advantage. One white Kentuckian, for example, once wrote of his desire "to obtain a negro woman about twenty four or five years of age of good qualities that would breed." Another advised his son, in 1825, that "there is no species of property...that improves an estate as fast as a healthy breeding negro woman whose children do well."[13]

Some enslavers grew their estates by encouraging the people they owned to procreate, exploiting their human longings for love, family, and marriage. But the law did not recognize slave marriage as an inviolate bond, or as the start of a family that could pass on an inheritance. Bibb, for example, recalled falling in love with an enslaved woman, Malinda, whose "master was very much in favor of the match, but entirely upon selfish principles." He knew that their progeny would bring him profit. Another enslaved man, also born in Kentucky, remembered his owner forcing him to "marry" a certain woman, hoping that their union would "enrich his plantation." Moreover, as Bibb's memoirs also pointed out, enslaved men and women had no legal power to prevent "licentious white men" from committing acts of rape that further increased their wealth when "mulatto" children were born. Even Malinda's master only consented to her union on a condition that Bibb deemed "too vulgar" to repeat.[14]

The white man likely made clear that Malinda's body remained his: he could use it however he pleased. Or perhaps he made a slur about what pleased her. Centuries of racist propaganda, dating to before the start of the transatlantic slave trade, maintained that women of color were naturally promiscuous. In an influential 1858 book, the Georgia attorney Thomas Cobb even questioned the need for laws against the rape of a female slave, since what he called "the known lasciviousness of the negro" made it unlikely that a black woman would not consent to sex. Only a few years after Wood was sold in Natchez, the Mississippi State Supreme Court had agreed, in a case called *George v. State*, that rape was not a crime that could occur between slaves.[15]

Such rulings strengthened a stigma around sex and black women, one that each resisted in her own way. In an 1861 narrative about her life, one formerly enslaved woman, Harriet Jacobs, openly described the sexual economy of the antebellum slave plantation, naming the dangers that black women faced, describing assaults that she suffered, and narrating her search for love even within bondage. "Slavery is terrible for men, but it is far more terrible for women," she said.[16]

Not all formerly enslaved women spoke as openly as Jacobs, however. Even after the Civil War and after emancipation, some black women held their intimate lives close, lest they be twisted by racists into "proof" of promiscuity. Reticent when it came to discussions of sex, these women used privacy as a shield to protect both their bodies and their interior lives.[17]

Wood may have wanted privacy, too, at least when it came to matters such as the name of Arthur's father. Some of the curtains around her story she may have drawn herself. And there were other parts of her past she may have chosen to keep concealed, including the origins of her own last name. She was already known as "Wood" by the time of her abduction. Some later records would call her a "widow," too. Her surname may have belonged to a partner whom she loved, maybe someone back in Louisville or even Cincinnati, maybe someone she was forced to leave behind by the Cirodes. But neither of her interviews ever said a word about a husband or a lover. And the surname "Wood" might instead be another clue about paternity, a sign that her biological father was someone other than the man she remembered.[18]

One thing at least is clear: Arthur was Henrietta's son. And his birth added the experiences of motherhood to all the other adjustments that her sale to Natchez brought. The future lawyer grew up around Brandon Hall.[19]

Simms himself, however, said little about that time. In 1948, he remembered being "just a 'skippin' baby'" when the Civil War began. "His only recollection of the crisis," according to Dennis Murray, "was of Confederate soldiers encamped near the plantation provided with provisions by the farm," a memory, perhaps, of militias that had formed in Adams County after the state seceded. The *Chicago Tribune* article said nothing about a forced march to Texas—or even, for that matter, about the suit that Simms's mother would later file against Zebulon Ward.[20]

Wood, though, remembered the days when Brandon's wife had told him to run off to Texas, taking slaves with him to keep them enslaved. She also made sure her interviewers knew that she had "coaxed" Brandon to let her take her child along on the journey, and that somehow she succeeded. Sometime after her sale to Natchez but before her march to Texas, Wood's story had become the story of a mother, too. From that point on, her struggle was for more than her life alone.

CHAPTER SEVENTEEN

ROBERTSON COUNTY

After marching hundreds of miles from Brandon Hall, Henrietta Wood arrived in Robertson County, Texas, in the summer of 1863, barely able to put one foot in front of the other. In 1876, Lafcadio Hearn reported that she had to walk on crutches for a year.[1]

That would have made it difficult for Wood to do the kinds of labor that Brandon most valued upon his arrival in Texas, where he hoped to be, as his journal put it, "at Home for the war." The refugee planter wanted his slaves to raise cotton there, though he also rented the labor of some of his slaves to locals desperate for help. On August 29, Brandon wrote in his small journal that he had been "besieged for two days by persons wanting to hire negroes, men & women," especially for domestic service. When healthy, Wood might well have been among the women he would have hired out.[2]

Injury did not exempt Henrietta Wood from hard work; it merely determined the kind of hard work she could do. Her recollections about the move to Texas—the coaxing of Brandon to bring her child, for example, and the mothers who had been forced to leave their children behind—suggest that she may have been expected initially to perform child care. In fact, it was likely Wood who confronted Brandon himself one day about the worsening health of the children he had marched from Mississippi.

The date was August 20, 1863, a Thursday, and Brandon had just returned from a short trip away from a campsite where he had left his slaves. He was still looking for a place to settle at the time, and while on the road, he had lodged in the houses of several hosts, recording the stops in his diary. In Belton, he had cornbread; in Salado, buttermilk. A man named Jones served watermelons and gave him a place to nap, rousing him from his sleep with a drink of strong whiskey and mint. With Jones he ate "good soup & a peach cobbler," and not much later, he would meet Joseph Able and arrange to rent his land.[3]

It was then that Brandon returned to his camp and learned that "Dicey's girl," a four-year-old, had perished after a twenty-four-hour illness. "Jane's baby," Lucinda, had also died. And as Brandon began to plan the move out to Able's place, another woman gave him news of yet another death. "Henrietta," he wrote, "has just come to say Dicey's little boy is dead."[4]

It was probably Henrietta Wood who delivered that somber message, given the evidence of her proximity to Brandon as a laundress and a cook. Enslaved women often took on the work of caring for children and the sick, even when they were sick themselves, and in her later comments about Robertson County, Wood focused on matters of health—not only on the breakdown of her own body, but also on what she later learned about the enslaved children left behind at Brandon Hall. (She told the *Ripley Bee* that many of those children "died of neglect before our return.") Evidently she was concerned, in Robertson County, that even children who had come to Texas with their mothers were dying, too.[5]

All the deaths did make Brandon nervous as well, though he counted the numbers as a capitalist, not as a caregiver. In his journal, Brandon acknowledged that his slaves were "dissatisfied" in Texas and living on "short rations." Yet he was still more concerned that he could not find enough work to keep his slaves busy, and he feared most of all "to feed them in idleness," for then they would "eat imprudently & in evry way keep themselves sick." Even if they were starving, he doubted their self-control—a perverse logic that was often embraced by large cotton planters. Better the slaves should be hungry—or so Brandon believed—than to overfeed and watch them "eat their heads off."[6]

The dilemma highlighted larger problems, as Brandon saw them. He had brought his slaves to Texas to preserve his wealth, both for his own use and the later use of his children. If the people he enslaved now died in great numbers, the loss to him would be the same as if he had stayed at Brandon Hall and watched them flee to the Yankees. Keeping them well in Texas was no easy task, however, given the expense of provisions in the state. The Confederate currency Brandon brought with him proved to be worthless, and that September he lamented that "I find my negroes out of doors, & stock poor, corn high & some difficulty to get it, & separated from my family."[7]

Brandon also discovered that many white Texans he met were openly hostile to refugees. Able, of course, was generous; so were several others. But one of the very first Texans he met told of "great opposition to new comers" in the state, especially those who were bringing in "large numbers of negroes." The man "had incurred the displeasure of the people around him by furnishing supplies to a *Mississippian*."[8]

That displeasure was common in many Texas counties with planter refugees. Amid wartime shortages of medicine and food, locals proved reluctant to give what they had for subsistence to strangers. Some of the people Brandon met were "hard on all who were not in the army," too. They suspected that the planters who had come from Mississippi were "too rich and cowardly to fight." As refugees arrived with hundreds of slaves, and Texas soldiers left their homes for war, the contrast seemed to prove, as Brandon heard it said, that this was "the 'rich man's war & the poor man's fight.'"[9]

While some Texans seemed to resent Brandon's riches, others simply feared the presence of so many slaves, viewing them as carriers of disease—or worse, the contagion of revolution and war. One day, four men called to tell him about a meeting happening soon, "for the purpose of passing resolutions" on matters of local concern. With "some 1000 or 1500 negroes moved into the region," they expected "that subject would be considered, and that no more would be allowed to come in." The men told Brandon that his slaves "looked 'clean & orderly,'" hinting at the rumors then swirling about the newcomers, but Brandon's informants "supposed all that were properly managed & controled would be let alone." They promised to put in a good word for his.[10]

Privately, though, Brandon knew that he and his overseer, a man named Poole, had only limited control over the people he had brought to Robertson County. Earlier in the month, one of his slaves had run away. One morning, Brandon had learned that another young slave from Mississippi had stolen eggs from a neighbor. The boy had also taken a chicken to one of the women Brandon enslaved, and "the supposition is she had sent him after the prize." Brandon subsequently learned that some of his slaves had gone begging for food, complaining that he did not feed them enough. One had "robbed a stack of Rye, to make coffee," and Brandon found that some of his men were engaged in the "hog business," by which he meant that they had "stolen meat."[11]

In retrospect, all these events hinted at the hunger of Brandon's slaves—as well as their determination to survive. Brandon only saw in them his own afflictions. Such actions would surely not quiet local white concerns about slave control, and upon learning about the men who had begged a neighbor for food, he confessed in his journal to being "vexed" to the point of "using profane words." He hoped to be forgiven by God for his tongue, though not for anything he had done to the hungry men; after everything he had gone through "to supply them & make them comfortable, I won't say satisfied, I feel I have done my duty." Brandon still explained his slaves' mischief by the absence of work. Idleness, he felt, enabled them to roam freely after the sun went down. And all of it confirmed, for him, what Brandon had already expressed a few weeks before, in a journal entry bemoaning life with his slaves—even those whom he felt, or hoped, that he could trust.[12]

"Henrietta conducts herself well," Brandon had written then, adding that "Harry & Will are fine boys." Even so, Brandon was "sick" of camping among his slaves and "being with them." He considered it "a perfect dog's life," and enough to "disgust anyone with the whole race." "My children must thank me for the attempt to save this property for them," Brandon then concluded, "for I have seen sights of trouble more than I can ever describe or make them sensible of." And that was even before Brandon learned of the stolen hen—before he learned his slaves had gone begging others for food—and even before the night at the very start of September, when Brandon was suddenly awakened by "the cry of dogs & the yelling of men."[13]

The commotion began at about midnight on September 1, 1863. Brandon shook off his sleep and went outside to find a large "crowd of dogs & men," headed by "Mr. Able." Poole had also been awakened, along with a slave named Sandy. But others in the camp might have heard barking, too, likely alarmed by the sound of angry white men in the dark.[14]

Brandon quickly learned the cause of the ruckus: a man owned by Able had recently stolen some of Able's money and run away. That man, Bill, had just been caught, but he did not have the cash. Bill claimed he had given it to two of Brandon's slaves, Anthony and Ben, who had sold Bill a suit of clothes before he ran. Both men were summoned; both denied the charge. Poole went with Able to look for the clothes, while Brandon remained behind, convinced that Ben had lied. Ben, despite being whipped, would not confess.

At last Anthony admitted that he was involved and produced the money, a total of $26. When Poole returned from the search for the clothes, however, Brandon learned that Bill's story had changed. Now the recent runaway said that Anthony, Ben, and two more of Brandon's slaves had been plotting that night to run away—back to Mississippi.

The news had further angered the crowd at Able's. Some, wrote Brandon in his journal later, "declared that the negroes must be sold out of this section, or hung." At the very least Brandon should leave, as his slaves were apparently the underlying cause of all the dissatisfaction. After two hours, the panic subsided for the night, and Brandon returned to his cabin to brood. "Now I was in trouble," he later remembered thinking.[15]

That night and into the morning, talk of what had happened also probably spread among the enslaved. Perhaps Ben showed his wounds from the whipping he had received. Maybe Anthony told the others what Bill had said. Rumors of imminent lynching would have made for a sleepless night.

The next morning, Able showed up at Brandon's door again, this time backed by a smaller group. He forced Bill to retell the whole story to Brandon, detailing the plot to flee to Mississippi. The slaves implicated were questioned one by one, but now Brandon's men had a different story to tell. They claimed Bill had told them he was planning to run to Mexico.

The dueling stories open a window onto relationships and conflicts already developing between the people Brandon enslaved and those they met in Texas. Slaves in Robertson County had likely learned that many of Brandon's slaves longed to return to Mississippi, where they had left family members, and where things had been dramatically changed by the war. That was how Bill knew his story would be plausible.

Conversely, Ben and Anthony had learned what many slaves in Texas knew: that slavery was illegal south of the border with Mexico. Even before the war, that knowledge had made Mexico a magnet for runaway slaves, and escape attempts continued during the war. In 1863, the same year when Able's Bill was accused of making a break for the Rio Grande, another enslaved man in Robertson County also fled for the border, making it as far west as Menard County before being caught. Now Ben and Anthony said that Bill had invited Brandon's men to join him in a similar runaway attempt, claiming (they said) "that when we got to the middle of a certain river, we were as free as any man."[16]

In the end, the white men's suspicions turned back on Bill, and Brandon breathed a momentary sigh of relief. In his journal Brandon nonetheless used the incident to show "some of the many annoyances I suffer." While he had once thought he should have brought more slaves to Texas, he now was glad he had not. In addition to lacking enough work for them all, the cost of feeding them for one or two years made them pricey to maintain. Brandon noted, parenthetically, that he doubted whether the war would even continue that long. "I sometimes wish it was over now," he admitted, giving full vent to his homesickness and dread.[17]

"Story of a Slave," *Cincinnati Commercial*, April 2, 1876.

LAFCADIO HEARN
About 1873

Lafcadio Hearn about 1873. From Elizabeth Bisland, *Life and Letters of Lafcadio Hearn* (1906).

Zebulon Ward. Courtesy of Arkansas State Archives, G4543.55.

Moses Tousey
Inventory

A True and just inventory and appraisement of the personal property and slaves of Mons Tousey Decd which were produced to us by
Ann Tousey and Thomas Porter his administrators

Property appraised   Value

			Value
1.	Negro man Bill		150 00
for hire 1.	Negro woman Daphney		100 00
1.	Negro woman Eliza and Child		325 00
1.	" " Dicey		300 00
1.	" Agness		250 00
1.	" Ellen		180 00
1.	Negro Boy Mason		225 00
1.	" Joshua		150 00
1.	Negro Girl Jane		110 00
50.	head of Hogs & Pigs		80 00
1.	Red Cow with white Back		10 00
1.	Brindle Cow with do do		11 00
1.	Red Cow		10 00
1.	Spotted Cow		10 00
1.	Large Red Bull		10 00
2.	Yearling heifers & Bull		17 00
4.	Calves		8 50
1.	yoke of Oxen		45 00
1.	Sorrel Horse with Blaze face		35 00
1.	Blind bay Horse		18 00
1.	Bay filly		30 00
1.	Black Mare		20 00
9.	Sheep		9 00
1.	Cart		8 00
1.	Large Harrow		3 00
1.	Pair Stretchers Clevis, 2 Singletrees &c		2 00
1.	Log Chains, and draught chain		5 00
4.	Old ploughs		4 00
6.	Hoes		2 00
2.	Sets of Gear		5 00
1.	Broad Axe and Shovel		3 00
1.	Lot of Old Tools		5 00
1.	Large Auger and Crank		1 00
2.	Mowing Scythes and hangings		75
1.	Lot of Old Irons		2 00
1.	Grind Stone		1 00
1.	Lot of Tubs & Bbl		4 00
1.	Washing tub 4. Buckets & churn		4 00
1.	Cooking Stove		25 00
1.	Lot of Castings & Brass Kettle		7 00
1.	Lot of Tin ware		4 00
1.	Lot of Stone ware		2 00
1.	Tin Baker		1 25
3.	Smoothing irons 4 candlesticks, Shovel tongs &c		3 00
4.	Augers, 4 chisels, 2 Handsaws, Axe, Churn irons &c		3 00
3.	Half bushel, 1 Peck, & Gal Measure &4 Baskets		2 00
1.	Large Spinning wheel		2 25

Moses Tousey Estate Inventory. Courtesy of the Boone County Public
Library, Kentucky.

Probable site of William Cirode's house in New Orleans. Photograph by author.

Photograph of house formerly used by Lewis Robards as part of his slave jail. Courtesy of John Winston Coleman Jr. Collection on Slavery in Kentucky, University of Kentucky Archives.

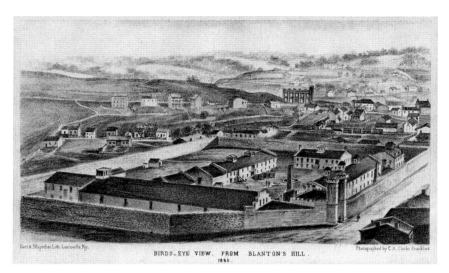

The Kentucky State Penitentiary in Frankfort, 1860. Courtesy of Kentucky Historical Society, 2004.41.85.

View of the entrance to the Kentucky Penitentiary. Courtesy of Kentucky Historical Society, 2004.41.54.

Kentucky Penitentiary inmates outside workshops, 1860. Courtesy of
Kentucky Historical Society, 2004.41.84.

Drawing of a Kentucky convict laborer published in 1860, one year after Zeb
Ward's term as keeper ended. Courtesy of Kentucky Historical Society,
2004.41.7.

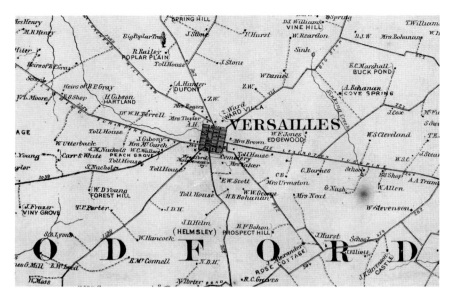

Map of Versailles showing Ward Villa. From E. A. Hewitt and George Washington Hewitt, *Topographical Map of the Counties of Bourbon, Fayette, Clark, Jessamine, and Woodford, Kentucky from Actual Surveys* (New York: Smith, Gallup, 1861). Courtesy of Library of Congress, Geography and Map Division.

Artist's depiction of Natchez, circa 1856. Courtesy of Miriam and Ira D. Wallach Division of Art, Prints, and Photographs: Print Collection, New York Public Library.

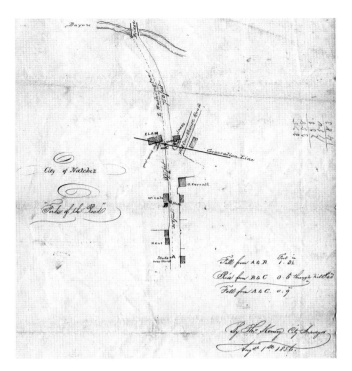

Survey of the Forks of the Road slave market from 1856, with the stand of Robert H. Elam, the local broker for Griffin and Pullum, shown. Courtesy of the Mississippi Department of Archives and History.

Daguerreotype of man identified by descendants as Gerard Brandon. Courtesy of Gerard B. Rickey.

Brandon Hall in 1936. Library of Congress, Prints and Photographs Division, Historic American Buildings Survey, HABS MISS,1-WASH.V,1—1. Courtesy of Library of Congress, Prints and Photographs Division.

Late nineteenth-century photograph of women picking cotton. Courtesy of Miriam and Ira D. Wallach Division of Art, Prints, and Photographs: Photography Collection, New York Public Library.

Arthur H. Simms. Courtesy of David
M. Blackman.

Caroline Person Simms. Courtesy of
David M. Blackman.

Union College Law Class of 1889, with Arthur H. Simms pictured third from the right, second row from the top. Courtesy of Northwestern University Archives.

Arthur H. Simms in 1883 or 1884. Courtesy of Winona Adkins.

Arthur Simms Jr. and Neata Simms, children of Arthur and Caroline Simms. Courtesy of Winona Adkins.

Neata Simms Adkins, granddaughter of Henrietta Wood. Courtesy of Winona Adkins.

Arthur H. Simms Sr. with Lawrence Adkins, circa 1948. Courtesy of Winona Adkins.

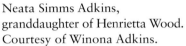

Lucinda Tousey's letter to Henrietta Wood. Courtesy of David M. Blackman.

Case file for *Wood v. Ward* at the Chicago branch of the National Archives and Records Administration. Photograph by author.

Affidavit in case file for *Wood v. Ward*, signed by Henrietta Wood with her mark. Photograph by author.

Jury's verdict in *Wood v. Ward* in 1878. Photograph by author.

Partly to salve those feelings, Gerard left for a trip back to Brandon Hall in February 1864, a journey of just over four hundred miles. Henrietta and her son, Arthur, were left behind in Texas, still struggling to survive. And they would remain there, in Robertson County, for almost two more years, far from the famous battlefields of the Civil War, and far from the military camps where hundreds of thousands of freed people were now seeking protection—and claiming new rights.

CHAPTER EIGHTEEN

DAWN AND DOOM

By the beginning of June 1865, the last major Confederate armies in the field had surrendered, but in many ways the Civil War went on. Civilian authority was not yet restored and violence continued across the seceded states. John Wilkes Booth had assassinated Abraham Lincoln in April. Hundreds of thousands of soldiers had been killed or would die soon from injuries and disease. And millions of men and women were also still enslaved—including Henrietta Wood. Gerard Brandon had returned to Texas after his brief visit home in 1864, and as Wood later recalled in 1879, he kept his slaves working on his rented plantation for three more years after the Emancipation Proclamation—in other words, until the year 1866.[1]

Her experience underscored what refugee planters such as Brandon had known from the start. Lincoln's proclamation had technically freed all the slaves in disloyal states, beginning on January 1, 1863. *Actual* emancipation depended, however, on federal troops who could enforce that order. By the time of the Confederate surrender at Appomattox, the US Army and Navy had only reached and liberated, at most, one million people. That left as many as three million still enslaved when surrender came. As new state constitutions were drafted by former Confederate states in 1865, slavery's last legal props began to disappear, and the Thirteenth Amendment to the US Constitution, passed by Congress at the start of 1865, would abolish slavery throughout the country, including loyal border states. But it would not be ratified until the end of the year. Even as the laws allowing slavery were overturned, many white Southerners held people in bondage for as long as they could.[2]

Texas in particular remained a last resort for diehard enslavers. Although Union forces had briefly occupied Galveston in 1862, most of the cotton counties in Texas never saw a federal until after Confederate surrender. For a brief period in the spring of 1865, it even appeared that the remnants of the Confederate military might attempt to regroup in the Lone Star State and fight on.[3]

Meanwhile, planters in Texas went on growing cotton. Working in partnership with another refugee from Mississippi, Brandon had produced at least 215 bales of cotton by the end of the 1865 season, using the forced labor of his slaves on the land he had rented. He moved the cotton by rail from Millican, in Brazos County, to a firm based in Houston: Ranger and Company. During the war, Texans had managed to export cotton around the US Navy's blockade of the Confederacy by transporting much of their crop across the border to Mexico, and after the war, Galveston resumed an important role as a cotton port.[4]

Still, even Texas could not remain forever unaffected by the Confederate surrender. Federal troops arrived in Galveston in June 1865 under the command of Major General Gordon Granger, who issued a famous order on June 19 reminding Texans that slaves had been declared free. The next few months saw a rapid buildup of troops inside the state, eventually peaking at about fifty thousand men, and as the army began to venture out from command posts in places such as Houston and Hempstead, soldiers informed any slaves who had not heard about the Confederate defeat. They were then followed, in the fall of 1865, by agents of the Bureau of Refugees, Freedmen, and Abandoned Lands, or the "Freedmen's Bureau," which was created by Congress the previous March and charged with overseeing relations between white planters and newly freed people.[5]

These developments heralded the dawn of the same revolutionary shifts that had already begun uprooting slavery in other parts of the South. Many years later, Hattie Cole, born enslaved in Robertson County, remembered that her owner never did tell his slaves of their freedom. But she also recalled what happened when "Bluecoats" finally arrived: a soldier read a paper to all of the enslaved people on the place where she lived, near Hearne. The paper said she was free and could go wherever she liked.[6]

The reading of a paper did not, however, make its promises real—not for Cole and not for Wood. "Life changed some" in Robertson County after surrender, Cole said, but how much would depend on the use of state power to back up abolition, especially in the state's interior. Henrietta Wood recalled of those days in Texas that "at last the white folks there run one overseer clean off, and told the other one if he didn't tell us we was free, they would have him arrested." After that, as she later told the *Ripley Bee*, "he called us all up in line and read it to us."[7]

Wood no doubt referred to a paper like the one that Cole remembered. But Henrietta had also experienced a taste of liberty before, had once even had a paper that declared she was free. Time would tell if this one was more powerful than the last.

In the fall of 1865, as Wood began to measure the meaning of a new freedom, Gerard Brandon struggled to accept that slavery was dying. In one letter from Texas to his daughter back home, Brandon mockingly referred to the ex-slaves working his rented plantation as "my free gents & ladies." Like other planters, Brandon assumed that he would never produce as much cotton as before, and like other refugees, he was uncertain whether to continue in Texas. "I do not hope to make more than a living from free negro labor any where," he lamented in October, as the season for picking cotton was ending.[8]

Brandon also lamented the wealth he lost by the legal end of slavery, which white Mississippians grudgingly acknowledged in a state constitutional convention held in August 1865. "The institution of slavery having been destroyed in the State of Mississippi," said the state's new constitution, it would not "hereafter exist in this State." Brandon had stored an immense amount of capital in his slaves, and now all that property, legally speaking, was gone.[9]

The loss was especially on Gerard's mind in September 1865, because his oldest daughter, Ella, was engaged to be married soon. In a letter, he wrote that "I cannot feel well for any measure that robs my family of so many valuable negroes as I had collected for them, particularly when such a measure brings them from affluence to a very limited means." Now, he would only be able to send Ella a "trifle" for a wedding gift. Brandon grieved about losing the wealth he had inherited from his own father, and he regretted having invested so heavily in slaves—all those trips he had made to the pens at Forks of the Road. He regretted, too, the delusion that refugeeing slaves would somehow save his wealth, when he could have sold them instead during the war, even at a steep discount, "but then I had confidence in the powers & people who have lost us our cause." Now he feared the whole family would have to accept that they were poor.[10]

While Brandon and other planters plotted their next moves, newly freed people faced decisions of their own. Some who had been forcibly brought to Texas decided to hit the road after the "Bluecoats" came, hoping to reunite with family members left behind or at least to find work far away from their former owners. On one road that crossed the Louisiana border, some observers saw hundreds of former slaves leaving Texas every day by the end of 1865. Other black men and women stayed put, working cotton fields in exchange for pledges from white planters that they would receive wages or a share of the crop at year's end. Some were even convinced by rumors that the federal government planned to seize the white planters' lands and distribute plots to freedpeople at about Christmastime.[11]

Many of those who stayed had no other choice, and those who tried to leave risked violent reprisals. The roads leading out of the state were plagued by desperadoes and gangs of white gunmen, many of them veterans returning home from the war. The lawlessness was prevalent enough to worry even white Texans, but black men and women were most vulnerable by far. Some white planters were abducting freedpeople and attempting to take them to Cuba or Brazil, where slavery was still legal. Others were using violence to make freedpeople stay. As one Freedmen's Bureau agent reported from Houston in November 1865, "Committees have been established in some counties to prevent the freedmen from going to their homes in other states," by any means necessary. One formerly enslaved woman in northeastern Texas later remembered the sight of black people's bodies hanging from trees in the Sabine bottoms "right after freedom." White vigilantes left the corpses there as warnings to ex-slaves who might try to leave.[12]

Planters also resisted emancipation in interior counties such as Robertson. One anonymous correspondent to a Galveston newspaper wrote from "Middle Texas" on August 2, 1865, to report that many freedpeople were still "under the bondage of their former not unfrequently cruel masters," while others had been punished for seeking "a more humane employer." In the days immediately after "the 19th of June," many angry planters had told their former slaves to leave. Soon enough, however, the same planters organized and agreed to stop such movements. They resolved that "every negro, if he or she attempts to leave the premises, shall be brought back and chastised in the most severe manner." The most recalcitrant offenders would "be *put out of the way*." Already, reported the "Middle Texas" writer, "more than twenty dead negroes have drifted down the Brazos."[13]

Fearing death if they left and bondage if they stayed, many black people in Texas remained where they were in 1865. "We didn't know what to do with ourselves," Wood recalled of those days, after she had heard a freedom paper read, but Brandon interpreted that indecision in ways that aligned with his interests. "Most are anxious to make a crop here next year," he wrote in a letter home in October 1865, referring to his former slaves. "My mind is relieved on that subject for the present, until they change theirs again."[14]

Brandon was "relieved" because his own mind was made up. In September, he had informed his daughter that he planned to work a cotton crop in Texas for a year, vowing to try something else if the 1866 crop failed. Although the 1865 season disappointed many Texas planters, he was optimistic about the coming season, even despite the US Army's growing footprint in the state.[15]

In truth, the army had proven friendlier than most white Texans had expected. Even before Granger's arrival in Galveston in June, Lieutenant General Ulysses S. Grant had urged his subordinates to "encourage the Shipment of Cotton from Louisiana and Texas," hoping that a successful crop would stabilize the state. Fearing a mass exodus of laborers from the fields at the very moment when cotton needed to be picked, the military urged freedpeople to enter into contracts with planters through the end of the year.[16]

Even in his June 19 proclamation affirming an end to slavery, for example, Granger declared that the "freed are advised to remain at their present homes, and work for wages." The general also warned that "they will not be allowed to collect at military posts, and that they will not be supported in idleness." In Washington County, one army official delivered a speech explaining that although former slaves might desire to rest from labor, perhaps even to "celebrate their emancipation by a day or two of recreation," such an "indulgence" could not be allowed: "The holidays must be put off until the crops are gathered."[17]

Freedpeople in Texas had to wait until September to meet a more sympathetic authority. Edgar M. Gregory, a firm abolitionist, arrived in Galveston in September to serve as the state's assistant commissioner of the Freedmen's Bureau and promptly took a tour of eastern Texas plantations. What he saw convinced him that many planters still acted as though the war had never ended, and that impression was strengthened by a more extensive tour in November. Gregory moved quickly to dispatch bureau field agents—subassistant commissioners—to the interior of the state. By January, he reported to his superior that hundreds of crimes against the freedpeople had been reported to the bureau, "ranging from downright murder, savage beatings, merciless whippings, hunting men with trained bloodhounds, through all the lesser degrees of cruelty and crime."[18]

Gregory was determined to ensure that no such crime would be allowed to go unpunished. But he emphasized that although white planters should be restrained from violence, the "freemen should be enjoined to work." True to those orders, the army and the bureau worked together throughout the fall to make "vagrant" workers return to their plantations, to continue cotton production, and—above all—to dispel the persistent rumors that a vast redistribution of land to freedpeople would occur.[19]

William E. Strong, another bureau agent who toured the state in late 1865, reported that he and Gregory frequently addressed groups of freedpeople on these points in the small towns between Galveston and Millican, often at nighttime assemblies after the working day. The hopeful crowds were probably disappointed, however, to hear part of the message brought by Gregory and Strong: that there would be no division of property on New Year's Day; that the government owned no lands in Texas to distribute to former slaves; and that in return for being freed by the government's actions, "they must show by their industry and perseverance that they were worthy of freedom."[20]

The recently enslaved people who heard such lectures were then left to absorb what the government's kind of freedom meant. While undoubtedly glad to learn of slavery's legal end, they could not have helped noticing that even their professed friends only spoke of the former slaves' present circumstances and future. They did not say what the freed might be owed for the past.

During his tours of the countryside in the fall of 1865, Assistant Commissioner Gregory never made it as far as northern Robertson County. For that entire year, Wood remained in an area remote from the bureau's operations. Just before the New Year, a bureau agent finally did appear in Robertson in the form of William H. Farner. Farner only won the job, however, by lying to Gregory about his past and representing himself as an Iowa Republican. In fact, Farner had served during the war as a Confederate surgeon, and in 1863 he had even moved twenty slaves from Louisiana to Brazos County, Texas.[21]

Farner was hardly the man most likely to hold other refugee planters to account. Before long, his superiors were hearing reports of Farner's neglect of orders, abuse of whiskey, and brutal application of the bureau's instructions to make the freedmen work. He reportedly punished freedpeople who violated the terms of their contracts by suspending them from their thumbs for long periods of time.[22]

By May 1866, Farner had been replaced as subassistant commissioner, but his successor, Champe Carter Jr., was not much better. Carter was a Robertson County local who disobeyed instructions from headquarters and protested that "physical punishment—or the fear of it"— was the only way to control the "fickle nature" of "stupid, ignorant" black men and women. He claimed, implausibly, that most of the cases of violence he heard were instances of freedpeople attacking each other.[23]

By August, Carter, too, had been relieved of duty, though his letters to superiors throughout the summer complained that "demoralization"— a euphemism for black laborers who refused to work—was "deep & wide-spread." Carter wanted a guard of soldiers sent to help him force freedpeople to honor their contracts, though he added another reason that unintentionally revealed the thinking of former slaves. "Some freedmen," he wrote, found it "hard to believe that the orders I read are true & that I am the proper agent of the Government." According to Carter, a few had warned that "if another agent comes around without *Yankee Soldiers*," it would not go well for the white man.[24]

If true, Carter's report suggests that Robertson County's freedpeople, perhaps including Wood, still looked to the federal government as their primary ally in an ongoing struggle with local whites. As during the war, the arrival of Bluecoats seemed their best hope. But the US military answered, ultimately, to the White House. And as time went on, its occupant, President Andrew Johnson, proved to be no better friend of the freedpeople than Farner or Carter had been.[25]

Elected as vice president in 1864, Johnson had been elevated to the presidency after Lincoln's assassination, and at first he had seemed prepared to take a hard line against former Confederates. In 1865, he used his war powers to appoint provisional governors in some states, including Texas. There, his appointee, Andrew Jackson Hamilton, was a loyal Unionist determined to stamp out slavery. In October, Hamilton wrote Johnson warning that many owners of former slaves "still claim and control them as property, and in two or three instances have recently bought and sold them as in former years."[26]

By the end of 1865, however, and despite cautions from men such as Hamilton, Johnson revealed his desire for a quick "Reconstruction" of the seceded states. In parts of the Confederacy where former slaves had been resettled by the military on abandoned lands, Johnson quickly ended those programs of land redistribution. The president granted amnesty to thousands of former Confederates. And he also encouraged southern states to elect new state governments, signaling that Washington would look favorably on the readmission to the Union of any state that ratified the Thirteenth Amendment. In April 1866, he declared that peace had returned to all of the states of the Confederacy except Texas. In August, he proclaimed peace in Texas, too.[27]

In Congress, Johnson's steps alarmed members of his own party. Congressional Republicans feared that presidential Reconstruction would allow former secessionists and slaveholders to quickly regain control of their states. In early 1866, outraged by reports of the violent abuse and continued enslavement of black Southerners, Republicans passed a bill to reauthorize the Freedmen's Bureau, along with a Civil Rights Act that enabled people of African descent to file federal lawsuits, testify in court, make contracts, and hold property. Johnson vetoed both, widening a rift within the Republican ranks.[28]

Republicans in Congress managed to overturn Johnson's vetoes in 1866. In June, Republicans passed the Fourteenth Amendment, which would enshrine birthright citizenship regardless of race in the Constitution. The party also won sweeping victories in midterm elections that November. Yet white reactionaries across the country were mobilizing to fight back, and the consequences could be seen in all of the places where Wood had once lived. In Cincinnati and Louisville, white crowds cheered President Johnson when he arrived in their cities on a western tour, shortly after his vetoes of the Freedmen's Bureau and Civil Rights Acts. In Frankfort that May, a black man was lynched, one in a grim litany of murders across the Reconstruction South. That same month, in New Orleans, a white mob disrupted a constitutional convention and massacred radical Republicans, many of them people of color, who had hoped to extend the protections of citizenship to ex-slaves.[29]

Reactionary forces were also gaining strength in central Texas, where Wood and others had only just been told they were free. In February 1866, conservative white Texans gathered to draft a new constitution, and although they acknowledged emancipation, they stopped short of ratifying the Thirteenth Amendment. The new state constitution also paved the way for elections in the fall that handed the governorship to

James Throckmorton, a former Confederate who opposed the continued presence of the army and the Freedmen's Bureau. Publicly, Governor Throckmorton accepted the end of slavery. In a private communication, though, he reasoned that white Texans, once in control of their state, would "be enabled to adopt a coercive system of labor" that would look much like slavery. By the end of 1866, the state legislature had followed many other newly elected governments in the South by passing draconian "Black Codes," so called because they were designed to subjugate former slaves.[30]

Through all this, Brandon continued to keep some of his former slaves at work in Robertson County, where most probably remained unaware of the political events swirling in Austin or Washington. What they saw was likely enough for them to know that real freedom, wherever it was, was definitely not in Texas. On June 17, 1866, almost exactly one year after the arrival of federal troops in the state, Brandon wrote to his new son-in-law that "most of my Freedmen are determined to leave Texas at the end of this season."[31]

The reasons for that determination should have been obvious, though Brandon did not see them. "They are a queer people," he wrote of "my" men and women, alleging that they "seem to consider every thing on the place as free for them, take many liberties." In reality, though, the people whom Brandon still called "my Freedmen" had little opportunity in Robertson County to exercise their new, theoretical rights.[32]

Even the Yankee soldiers who eventually arrived in the county, as requested by Carter, did not bring greater freedom to all. In a July letter to Ella, Gerard related the story of a freedman who had recently received "an old fashioned whipping" from a white neighbor for leaving the plantation. When the man complained to federal officers in the area, a cavalryman "tied the fellow up for two hours telling him to do his duty, conduct himself right, then if Dr. Jones or any one whipped him they should suffer but that he was not there to protect niggers in idleness, meanness or impudence." On another occasion that summer, the local bureau agent—presumably Carter—"hung Ben up for several hours" and then proceeded to give Ben and Brandon's other laborers "a long talk explaining the law." "How learned they are becoming," Brandon sneered.[33]

The formerly enslaved were indeed learning a great deal about "the law," especially its limited power to protect them after slavery. Brandon, on the other hand, was relatively pleased by the positions of the bureau. Gregory was replaced early in the year by Major General Joseph Kiddoo, and Brandon approved of the change. Kiddoo "conducts matters on the white man principal," Brandon explained to his daughter in July, and was not afraid to scare black laborers into contracts. Sometimes, Brandon added, federal troops beat freedpeople with their military swords "in place of our old strap."[34]

Even so, by mid-1866, Brandon had begun to tire of Texas and began making plans to leave. A litany of complaints made him restless to go home, including a generally disappointing 1866 season. The low yields were caused by sluggish prices and excessive rains that filled the fields with weeds. Planters, however, blamed the harvest on lazy workers. "They do try my patience greatly," Gerard told Ella's new husband. "I am disgusted & think often this is my last attempt at managing Freedmen." Yet he also admitted that he could not do without their continued labor. Perhaps that was why, as Wood recalled, Brandon eventually approached the former slaves still on Able's place and floated a proposal: anyone who would work for him for three years could come back with him to Natchez.[35]

He may have intended the offer more as a command. In letters to each other, refugee planters predicted that even though slavery was destroyed, they would be able to control "free labor" using state legislation. If they could get back home with black laborers in tow, they were optimistic, as one put it, that they could create "a good substitution for the late institution." Many of the refugee planters who came to Texas also used promises of transportation to coerce former slaves into unfavorable contracts; in one case, a planter returning to Louisiana with slaves he had refugeed threatened to leave them all on the road, in the middle of nowhere, if they did not agree to his terms.[36]

The three-year deal Wood remembered being offered would commit her to work for Brandon much longer than the bureau-approved, one-year contracts most freedpeople signed. On the other hand, Wood and the others may have preferred Brandon's proposal over the uncertain alternatives in Texas. Some other refugee planters in Robertson County had simply left the state at the end of 1865 without paying anything to the freedpeople who had worked on their crop. At least Brandon offered to help them get back to Natchez. Maybe conditions back in Mississippi would be different, and maybe those who had been forced to leave family and friends behind would finally have a chance to reunite.[37]

In the end, whether they had much of a choice in the matter or not, many of the people Brandon had brought to Texas did return to Mississippi in 1866—including Henrietta Wood. "We all took up the line of march," she remembered, "and came back to Natchez with him." And there she would remain until 1869, the year before she would cross paths again with an older enemy.[38]

CHAPTER NINETEEN

NASHVILLE

One week in November 1864, after Henrietta Wood had been in Texas more than a year, a rumor spread in racing circles that Zebulon Ward was dead—shot down by a posse at his house near Versailles. On November 19, his friend George Wilkes was relieved to report in *Spirit of the Times* that Ward himself had written to a local paper to say that he was "a living witness to the incorrectness of the rumor." The turf-man was already turning the mixup into a punch line.[1]

Ward was not dead, but by then his hopes for slavery's survival were dying. Throughout 1863, the year of the Emancipation Proclamation, Ward and other proslavery Unionists in Kentucky had continued to hope that slavery in their state might live on after the war, and state leaders had rebuffed several proposals by Lincoln for a gradual, compensated abolition. They had also managed to forestall the enlistment of black Kentuckians in the US Army. In February 1864, however, provost marshals in the state began to accept black soldiers. In June, a military order offered the chance of enlistment—and, by extension, liberation and citizenship—to "any slave who may present himself" at certain army posts. One such post was Camp Nelson, not far from Versailles.[2]

As news of the order spread, hundreds of enslaved men streamed from hemp fields and horse farms into the army's lines, eagerly volunteering to fight. By the time of Confederate surrender less than a year later, nearly twenty-four thousand black Kentuckians had joined up— more than half of the eligible black men in the state. Camp Nelson alone received about a tenth of the total number of Kentucky's black recruits before the summer ended in 1864. Their actions dealt a shattering blow to slavery in the Bluegrass State.[3]

Some of Ward's own slaves were part of the rush to enlist. In June, William Simmons enlisted at Camp Nelson as a private in a regiment of US Colored Troops; on his muster sheet, Zeb Ward was listed as his "reputed owner." By September, six other men whom Ward still technically owned had all escaped from Ward Villa and gone to Camp Nelson, too, joining a wave of enslaved men from Woodford County. D. C. Humphreys of Waverly, just north of Midway, bemoaned the situation in a letter to a neighbor: "We are in danger of losing every hand on our farms, by harvest," thanks to the recruitment of federal troops. "There is a perfect stampede of 'darkies' in Franklin & Woodford."[4]

These changes represented a revolution that was hard for slaveholders to stomach; to Humphreys, it was a "sickening business," and white Kentuckians continued to resist black enlistment and abolition. The state would not ratify the Thirteenth Amendment until 1976—a symbolic protest that did not stop its implementation, but signaled the danger ahead for the formerly enslaved in Kentucky. In one incident typical of wartime Woodford County, a black soldier was shot by a white vigilante while traveling through the state with official army documents. In Versailles, in the summer of 1866, another black man attempted to buy a meal in town, probing what was possible in the postwar world. He "coolly sat at the table and ordered supper," but for his nerve he was beaten and thrown into jail.[5]

Such incidents were the first shots in a war after the war, one that raged in Kentucky no less than in Texas. It was a white supremacist rebellion against a new world where black men were issued army rifles and where people of color demanded seats at white men's tables. Proslavery Unionists had resisted calls for secession; now nostalgia for slavery made them pine for "Southern Rights." In memory, some Kentuckians even rewrote the Civil War years, claiming that the state had been closer to seceding than it ever was in fact.[6]

As for Ward, while many of his neighbors reimagined themselves as dyed-in-the-wool rebels, for the second time in his life he decided to leave Kentucky, and he relocated to a state that actually had seceded. In 1866, Ward announced that he had "determined to quit farming," closing up his business in Versailles by May. That summer, he put his entire Woodford County estate up for sale—all 580 acres of it, including a "good two-story brick house," outbuildings, orchards, and "eight or ten negro houses," now presumably empty—along with another tract of five hundred acres and nearly fifty horses. By December, he had sold his house and at least a hundred acres of the farm to a buyer from New Orleans for $250 an acre. Then he moved south to Nashville, Tennessee.[7]

Ward moved because he chose to, not because he had to, though he had experienced financial losses during the war, even beyond the loss of the slaves he had owned. Morgan's raiders stole more Thoroughbreds from Ward when they returned to Kentucky in 1864, and Ward later claimed to have given some of his best horses to Union cavalrymen while serving as an aide-de-camp during the last months of the fighting. Still, Ward remained able to pay all his debts, and his land alone still represented substantial wealth.[8]

There were other forces, though, impelling Zebulon to leave. The destructive impact of the war on the South had boosted the Thoroughbred business in New York, which quickly became a new mecca for turfmen. Except for the largest stables, such as Woodburn, horse farms in Kentucky would find it hard, for a time, to compete.[9]

Ward's Unionism also may have branded him as out of step with the times, particularly as postwar white Kentuckians embraced a "Southern" cultural identity. In 1866, Ward found himself named as a defendant in several lawsuits for false imprisonment during the war, filed by residents of Woodford County. According to Ward's supporters, what had happened was this: in 1862 he had been ordered by a general to escort disloyal persons from his county to Louisville under arrest. Ward at first refused, but eventually he complied. Then, at his own expense, he put his prisoners up in the Galt House hotel for a night before they were sent to military prison. For this reputed "kindness" he was repaid by postwar lawsuits demanding $140,000.[10]

Ward successfully fought off those suits, but they showed how much the war had alienated neighbors. More than that, emancipation had soured Zeb himself on the federal government's conduct of the war. The postwar world of free labor and black citizenship that Republicans now envisioned was not the antebellum Union that he had hoped to preserve. Yet Ward also knew from experience that there was more than one way to exploit black labor, and that was one reason why he now moved to Nashville, Tennessee. Zeb had lived in the city before, during his steamboat days on the Cumberland River. This time, though, he went to resume his more recent career as a keeper.

Located on the outskirts of Nashville, the Tennessee penitentiary had been organized on the Auburn Plan in 1831. Like the convicts whom Ward had once managed in Kentucky, prisoners in Tennessee generated revenue for the state by working, primarily inside the walls and occasionally outside them. Unlike in Kentucky, the state legislature had resisted leasing convict labor to private contractors until the 1850s. After the war, though, Tennessee decided to lease out the entire penitentiary. Two businessmen, C. M. Briggs and J. L. Hyatt, won the lease in June 1866—at about the time when Ward began planning his move to Nashville.[11]

Several factors motivated the state's decision to lease. Postwar Tennessee faced a debilitating debt crisis, and the prison itself was at least $50,000 in arrears after four years of fighting. The grounds had been used by the US military to hold prisoners of war, and the state had no funds to repair the war-torn prison.[12]

Tennessee officials also had bigger problems. A state government headed by Governor William Brownlow, a Unionist, had been established in 1865. Tennessee, the last state to join the Confederacy, became the first to rejoin the Union. Many white Tennesseans, however, hated Brownlow's government, which disfranchised all ex-Confederates and rebel sympathizers. In 1865 and 1866, large numbers of Confederate veterans were returning to the battle-scarred state, along with prominent rebel generals such as Nathan Bedford Forrest, Gideon J. Pillow, and John C. Brown. Emboldened by the conciliatory proposals for Reconstruction being proposed by President Andrew Johnson, himself a Tennessean, these former Confederates chafed at what they considered Brownlow's illegitimate rule.[13]

All of this occurred while rampant crime and violence in the countryside stretched the resources of Freedmen's Bureau agents, often overwhelming black communities' means of self-defense. Formerly en-slaved people left plantations and crowded into cities such as Nashville and Memphis, but they found little refuge there. Over several days in the spring of 1866, white mobs in Memphis killed almost four dozen black residents, destroying their neighborhoods, raping black women, and sparking outrage in the North. Threatened by a total breakdown of order, Brownlow's government needed a functioning prison fast. In a May circular calling for bids on the lease, the prison directors assured interested applicants that the number of convicts—then standing at 220—"will probably be very largely increased at an early date."[14]

Ward may have decided to move to Nashville after seeing that circu-lar in Kentucky. Or he may have been recruited by Briggs and Hyatt after their bid for the lease was accepted. Both men hailed from Kentucky and had no prison experience of their own, though one local editor noted that the new plan for leasing the prison had "been found to work very well in Kentucky." They may well have turned to Zebulon for help.[15]

In any case, by mid-1867, Ward had become a full partner in the les-sees' firm, which advertised the sale of cedarware, cotton scrapers, and threshers made by convicts. The terms of the lease were not exactly as Ward might have wished: instead of paying a flat annual rent (as he had done in Kentucky), Hyatt, Briggs, and Ward paid the state forty-three cents per day for each of the convicts in the prison. The lessees were also denied the total control of the prison that Ward had eventually enjoyed in Frankfort. A warden hired by the state remained responsible for overseeing the general welfare of the convicts, who were not al-lowed to work for more than "ten hours per day." Nevertheless, Ward knew how much money a hard-driving man could make by pushing convicts. His interest in the job did not waver even after a disastrous fire at the prison in July 1867. Hyatt decided to leave the firm at that time, but Briggs and Ward expanded production from furniture and farm implements to hemp bagging and rope—the products that Ward had specialized in making at Frankfort. By September, Ward was adver-tising the sale of bagging "of the celebrated 'Z. Ward' Brand," made by convict labor.[16]

Meanwhile, the number of convicts was rapidly increasing—and most of the newcomers were black. The power to prosecute criminals was still in the hands of county officials and juries who mostly opposed Brownlow's government and emancipation, and they used their powers to indict freed people on minor or spurious charges and then sentence them to hard labor in Nashville. By the end of 1866, more than half of the inmates in the state penitentiary were black, and three years later, the prison population had grown from 311 to 551, of whom 62 percent were listed in prison rolls as "Negro." The black prison population had doubled while white convicts increased by no more than a third.[17]

These disparities confirmed the warnings of many—Freedmen's Bureau agents, northern Republicans, and freedpeople themselves—that white Southerners were attempting to re-create slavery under the guise of law and order. Most of Tennessee's black convicts were incarcerated for charges such as petty larceny, as the directors of the penitentiary noted in an annual report from 1868: "it is a matter of documentary proof that many criminals are sent here for offences ranging from eight cents, the value of a fence rail, to all intermediate sums not reaching $5." Most were "formerly slaves; and are sentenced, in most cases for 'taking,' as they express it, some article of provision or clothing from their employer, who refuses to pay them."[18]

As similar reports multiplied across the South, Republican resistance to presidential Reconstruction grew. After Johnson's critics gained seats in the fall elections of 1866, Congress passed a Reconstruction Act in early 1867, overturning a veto by the president. The act divided ten southern states into five military districts and required former Confederate states to ratify the Fourteenth Amendment before they would be allowed to rejoin Congress. Unreconstructed states were also required to draft new state constitutions at conventions elected by loyal male voters—without regard to race. These acts ushered in a new era of Congressional, or Radical, Reconstruction.[19]

The case of Tennessee would foreshadow the fate of the radical program as a whole. On the one hand, Brownlow's Republican government broke with Johnson and sided with Republicans in Congress. Tennessee quickly ratified the Fourteenth Amendment in July 1866, becoming the first former Confederate state to do so, and then removed racial bars to voting.[20]

On the other hand, although Congressional Reconstruction began in Tennessee, so did the backlash against it, led by the Ku Klux Klan. Originally founded in 1866 as a secretive club in Pulaski, Tennessee, by the end of 1868 the Klan encompassed a large, loosely organized network of white terrorist groups determined to fight Reconstruction. The Klan used brutal violence, nighttime raids, and public spectacles such as parades to intimidate the enemies of conservatives in the state, targeting the Republican political mobilization that had led to a large turnout of new black voters in state elections held in 1867. The Klan's emergence prefigured a coming reaction across the South: the more a state inched toward a true, biracial democracy, the fiercer the forces of white counterrevolution became.[21]

By early 1868, prominent ex-Confederate generals such as Forrest, a former slave trader from Memphis, were also connected to the Klan, though their precise roles were kept obscure. White elites such as Forrest (later remembered as the first grand wizard of the Klan) alternated between disavowing any control over the group, describing it as a needed check on alleged black criminality, and using the specter of the Ku Klux to pressure Brownlow into restoring the vote to former Confederates.[22]

What could not be denied was the rising tide of violence by nightriders. In July 1868, a twenty-year-old black man was seized from his home by a posse of fifty or sixty white men, strangled to death, and dumped into a river with a stone tied to his corpse. The month before, in Pulaski, a hundred masked men took a black man from the local jail, cut him to pieces with gunshots, and left his body in the street until the next day as a warning. Similar lynchings terrified black families across the region.[23]

White allies of the Brownlow regime were also attacked. In April, forty or fifty Ku Klux men, "dressed in masks," entered the house of sixty-year-old state senator William Wyatt in Lincoln County. "Afterwards," Wyatt later said, "I heard of their raid through the country, whipping some negroes very seriously." Later, another "band of disguised Ku

Klux" returned to Wyatt's house, pulled him from his bed, and pistol-whipped the old man, citing his support of "negro equality."[24]

By the summer of 1868, attacks like these had convinced the head of the Freedmen's Bureau in Tennessee that the Ku Klux could only be put down by "Powder and ball." But because it had already been readmitted to the Union, Tennessee had also been exempted from the federal military occupation of the old Confederacy that began in 1867. Governor Brownlow had no recourse but to call a special session of the legislature and ask it to give him the power to call out the state militia and suppress the violence.[25]

Brownlow had already used the militia before to protect the integrity of elections held the previous year. Now, the prospect of the militia's return further enraged white reactionaries, who threatened the resumption of civil war. In late August, Forrest gave an interview to the *Cincinnati Commercial* hinting that the Klan was forty thousand strong. He predicted pitched battles in the state if the militia bill was passed.[26]

In reality, though, most of Brownlow's critics were terrified by the possibility that the governor might use state troops—including black soldiers—to wreak vengeance on his enemies. Forrest's threats in the *Commercial* came only after a group of more than a dozen former Confederate generals, including Forrest himself and several others suspected of belonging to the Klan, had gone to Nashville on August 1, hoping to convince the General Assembly that there was no vast Ku Klux conspiracy afoot. Most outrages would cease, the generals said, if former Confederates could only vote. On the eve of the arrival of this "Peace Council," led by Forrest, an advance delegation of former Confederate officers came to Nashville to press the same case at a meeting with state legislators.[27]

Zebulon Ward was at that meeting, too—a telling sign of his own position on Reconstruction. Addressing the group of lawmakers and rebels, Ward told them he was a "businessman" who hoped for "a peaceful solution of the existing state of affairs." He deplored "such outrages as that recently committed on Senator Wyatt." But the best solution, Ward thought, was to believe the pledges of loyalty from the former rebel generals. Instead of calling out the militia, he favored asking President Johnson (who had recently been impeached by Congress) for federal troops.[28]

That was a solution favored by other reactionaries, too. They knew that the state militia would have more power to stamp out the Klan than troops controlled by Johnson. Despite all the evidence to the contrary, Ward claimed that "there are now but few left who would want to fire on the old flag," downplaying the rising violence in the state. And after the meeting ended, he invited the other men in attendance to have a drink at his home, where, according to newspaper accounts, they "renewed over the social glass the pledges of moderation and good faith which had been exchanged at the capitol," setting the stage for the arrival of Forrest the next day.[29]

Ward's involvement in the meeting between lawmakers and Forrest's men, which became known as the Peace Conference of 1868, typified the roles he would thereafter play in the politics of Reconstruction. In the words of his obituary, he became a "red-hot Democrat" after the war, but instead of returning to office, he usually stood on the sidelines, exerting his influence as a "businessman" and a master of the "social glass." The Conference nevertheless showed clearly enough where he stood. Once a Unionist legislator, he now took Confederates and terrorists at their word. Preaching moderation and order, he winked at the counterrevolutionary movements that were rising in the South.[30]

That counterrevolution eventually triumphed in Tennessee earlier than anywhere else, though not without another year of political struggle. That fall, national elections elevated Ulysses S. Grant to the White House and handed sweeping victories to Republicans. Their share of the vote declined in Tennessee, a harbinger of things to come.[31]

The fall of 1868 also brought to a boil long-simmering tensions between the lessees of the Tennessee penitentiary and the state legislature. Ward and Briggs had argued with the state for months over who was responsible for repairs after the fire in 1867. The lessees had also lobbied unsuccessfully for total control over the prison for a flat rent. Instead, as evidence grew that many of the convicts in the penitentiary were there on "frivolous charges," as one legislator put it, state Republicans took steps to pardon hundreds of prisoners, reducing the workforce available to the lessees.[32]

Tensions also arose between Ward and the state over Thomas McElwee, a former state senator who was appointed warden in the middle of 1867. McElwee soon discovered that the keepers were treating many of their inmates like slaves. Some convicts were sent to work with a ball and chain. Others were suspended by their thumbs for thirty minutes to two hours at a time, just for talking back to Ward or laughing at a guard. Many were hung up or dragged out of their cells at night and whipped with a leather strap for failing to complete tasks that McElwee believed impossible, such as weaving 150 yards of hemp bagging a day.[33]

What the warden found suggested that Ward was up to the same habits of driving inmates that Calvin Fairbank had experienced in Frankfort. In 1868, McElwee's reports found their way into the hands of the reform-minded New York Prison Association, drawing unwanted attention to the penitentiary at a time when northern outrage was already growing over events in Tennessee. As a report by the association noted, it was clear that under the regime of Briggs and Ward, "nothing but work, work, work, could shield the prisoner from the lash." Ward and Briggs responded with a smear campaign against McElwee, accusing him in the press of incompetence and even of allowing "lewd women" into the prison—charges reminiscent of the salacious rumors that had tanked Newton Craig's career in Kentucky and cleared the way for Ward's first penitentiary job.[34]

Eventually the state and the lessees agreed to end the contract early, on July 1, 1869. It proved to be one of the final acts of Brownlow's government, which was swept out by statewide conservative victories in August. The new state legislature temporarily banned the lease of convicts but later leased to another firm in 1871, at a flat rate just like the one that Zeb had always wanted.[35]

By that time Ward had returned to Kentucky, leaving the penitentiary business for the second time in his life and landing, softly, in the Bluegrass again. He began to manufacture his signature hemp bagging in Lexington, using steam machinery, and all the evidence shows that he prospered. In 1870, he appeared in the census as a "Hemp Manufacturer," with real estate valued at $50,000 and personal property worth $10,000. Then, two years later, Ward and Briggs won a colossal lawsuit against the state of Tennessee for outstanding debts, receiving $132,000 in settlement money for improvements they had made to the penitentiary.[36]

Ward used his wealth to refocus on gambling and the turf, first loves that he had never lost. While living in Tennessee, Ward had continued to attend horse races across the country. He also served as an officer in the Turf Congress, an organization of Southerners from various states. They aimed to demonstrate their section's independence from the North, even at the track, though secession was not really possible in the sport. In November 1867, while serving as secretary of the Turf Congress, Ward showed a Nashville editor "a magnificent gold mounted riding whip" that would serve as the prize for an upcoming race in Memphis, where speeches were given by Ward and by Nathan Bedford Forrest. The golden whip was made by a firm in New York.[37]

The Turf Congress did not survive in its sectional form, but Zebulon's attachment to the track did not dim. In May 1870, his horses won a few races in Nashville. He would return for more races in Tennessee that fall. And in between, Ward also traveled to Ohio to watch a race, most likely the spring meeting of the Buckeye Club at Carthage, just outside Cincinnati.[38]

It was probably while he was there, however, that a local sheriff found Ward and officially informed him of a lawsuit just filed against him in the Superior Court of Cincinnati. The date of the summons was June 3, 1870, a Friday, and when he was told the name of the plaintiff, a woman of color who claimed that she was Ward's former slave, even a betting man such as Zeb must have been visibly shocked. The Civil War had changed his world in many ways, but Ward had never wagered that he might see *her* again.[39]

CHAPTER TWENTY

A RATHER
INTERESTING CASE

On June 8, 1870, five days after Zebulon Ward received notice of being sued, the *Cincinnati Enquirer* published an item titled "A Case of Alleged Kidnapping." "A rather interesting case has been commenced in the Superior Court of this city," the *Enquirer* reported, noting that it arose "out of the custom of slavery, now supposed to be extinct." The plaintiff was "a mulatto woman, formerly a resident of this city, who brings suit against Zeb. Ward" on charges that she had been abducted, reenslaved, and then sold to a plantation owner in Mississippi before being taken to Texas, "remaining there in the bonds of slavery until her shackles were knocked off by the lamented Mr. Lincoln." Now the woman had returned to Cincinnati and sued Ward for $20,000 in damages, including the years of wages she had lost because of her reenslavement.[1]

The *Enquirer* story contained a number of errors about details—a flaw that would also plague subsequent accounts of the case. It named the plaintiff as "Henrietta Ward," and Brandon became "Gerard Bronson." Rebecca Boyd was wrongly identified as a defendant. Nonetheless, the *Enquirer* captured accurately enough the basic, startling truth: Henrietta Wood had filed a lawsuit against Ward in Cincinnati. "The case," concluded the paper, was bound "to attract some attention."[2]

The reasons why were not hard to see in 1870. Before abolition, freedom suits in the slave states had sometimes included claims for monetary damages, but the amounts paid or even requested in such suits had never been as high as five figures. And although some abolitionists and radical Republicans had advocated reparations of some form to the enslaved, previous efforts had fallen short.[3]

In 1853, for instance, not long after Wood's abduction, a man named Solomon Northup published a memoir of his own "twelve years a slave" after being kidnapped as a free man in New York and sold to a planter in Louisiana. Abolitionists signed petitions calling for reparations for Northup, to no avail. Some abolitionists also knew the case of John Lytle, a free American kidnapped and eventually enslaved in Cuba. He was later freed and paid $2,211.33 by the Cuban government, but such an outcome had never been matched in the United States. After the Civil War, some white Republicans joined freedpeople in calling for abandoned Confederate lands or homesteads on public lands to be allotted to former slaves. Those proposals, too, had withered on the vine, along with the promises of "forty acres and a mule" that had been made by government officials during and immediately after the war.[4]

Everyone who heard of it knew, therefore, that Wood's legal claim was extraordinary. Even apart from that fact, her story piqued curiosity. It stretched from Ohio and Kentucky to Mississippi and Texas. It included a colorful turfman and prison lessee. And last but not least, it featured a woman who had somehow managed to make it back from some of the darkest corners of the cotton kingdom to the city where she had been abducted seventeen years before.

Wood had returned to the Cincinnati area in the spring of 1869, three years after she had returned from Robertson County to Brandon Hall. At the end of his interview with her in 1876, Lafcadio Hearn explained to his readers how Brandon had extracted a promise of three years' labor from his former slaves, and how Wood had "kept the promise," though without being paid for her work. Then, in 1869, Henrietta had moved to Cincinnati with Arthur.[5]

In both of her later interviews, she was tight-lipped about what had happened in the three intervening years back in Mississippi, a time of radical transformation in that state. More revealing was a labor contract between Wood and Brandon from that time, a copy of which survived into the twenty-first century. The contract, written in Brandon's hand, said that after returning to Natchez from Texas, "Henrietta Wood, a free woman," had to "wash and iron" for his family and milk their cow twice a day. In return, Brandon pledged to give her a "comfortable house," food, two suits of clothing, and a pair of shoes, along with $10 per month, paid out four times a year. In addition, he agreed to clothe and board "Arthur son of Henrietta."[6]

The contract, dated January 1866 and signed by a witness in Adams County, offers a clue about when Henrietta and Arthur had made their return trip to Natchez, though it may have been backdated to the start of the year. It also revealed her importance to Brandon's household as a laundress. Unlike many labor contracts drawn up by former enslavers with large groups of freedpeople, this contract mentioned Henrietta Wood and her son alone. The agreement was Brandon's grudging concession to the outcome of the war and the policies of Republicans, for whom a written contract was the hallmark of free labor.[7]

Brandon made the concession partly because, unlike Tennessee, Mississippi *was* occupied by federal troops during Reconstruction. Under the terms of the Reconstruction Act of 1867, Mississippi was not readmitted into the Union until 1870, after the state had enfranchised black men with a new constitution. The result was an efflorescence of black institutions in Reconstruction Natchez during the years Wood was there. New schools for black children (some founded by missionary organizations and the Freedmen's Bureau, but many supported by freedpeople themselves) might even have given Arthur his first exposure to formal education. African Americans also formed numerous churches, Republican clubs, and mutual aid societies, all of which facilitated political mobilization. On July 4, 1867, close to eight thousand black men and women converged on a public square in Natchez—near the very place where Wood had once been sold—to celebrate the removal of racial barriers to voting in the state.[8]

These collective efforts quickly bore fruit. David Young, for example, had a story similar to Wood's. Born enslaved in Kentucky, he had escaped to Ohio in about 1850 before being kidnapped, reenslaved, and sold down the river to Forks of the Road. By 1868, he was a local Republican operative in Concordia Parish and soon became a state legislator in Louisiana. John Roy Lynch, a former slave, was elected justice of the peace in Natchez in 1869. The next year, Mississippi Republicans sent Hiram Revels, then a resident of Natchez, to the US Senate, where he became the first African-American congressman by taking the seat Jefferson Davis had abandoned in 1860 to lead the Confederate States. Lynch would later be elected to Congress, too.[9]

Yet Reconstruction in Mississippi did not immediately alter the circumstances of a woman such as Henrietta Wood. Her economic position remained precarious, even with a contract in hand. For one, she likely remained unable to read that contract, which she could only sign by putting an "X," her legal mark, at the bottom. And instead of having the contract approved by a Freedmen's Bureau official, Brandon had it witnessed by the local justice of the peace, W. N. Whitehurst, who was a fellow planter.[10]

Clearly Brandon also still had a large degree of power to interpret, enforce, and manipulate the terms of Wood's contract. In its first draft, the contract obliged Brandon to "pay expenses of" Arthur, but at some point, perhaps after Henrietta had signed, those three words were crossed out. That may mean Arthur's expenses were taken out of her wages. Brandon also expected eleven-year-old Arthur to work: the contract said he would serve as a "nurse," presumably caring for children on the plantation, and would have to make "himself generally useful (as a child may do)" to Brandon's family. Like many newly freed women, Henrietta Wood still found herself without full control over her son. Finally, Brandon's contract obligated her to perform her work "in a prompt and satisfactory manner, deporting herself with respect & politeness" toward all the Brandons. In the end, she told Hearn that Brandon "never paid her a cent."[11]

That was not because Brandon was unable to pay. White planters were already starting to regain their footing in the three years after the war's close. On Christmas morning in 1868, the extended Brandon family gathered at Brandon Hall for a "delightful" holiday, as one family letter put it, and Gerard's granddaughter Charlotte discovered that "old Kris" Kringle had stuffed her stocking. Given that Brandon did not pay her, Henrietta's ability to provide such delights to Arthur would have remained limited, and there was only so much she could do about the quality of her life. Although black men had acquired the vote in Mississippi, women remained disfranchised, whether white or black.[12]

Freedwomen in the South did take part in Reconstruction politics by other means, including as teachers and leaders in churches and voluntary associations. Black women also made claims on the Freedmen's Bureau, which was overwhelmed after the war by applications for marriage licenses. Formerly enslaved women in Natchez, Memphis, Little Rock, and elsewhere frequently petitioned the bureau and the military to protect them from sexual assault and other forms of violence, to address shortages of food and medical care, to help them find children, and to force employers to pay them. Black women appeared as plaintiffs, too, in hundreds of lawsuits against white defendants across the Reconstruction South, making them active participants in an ongoing grassroots struggle to secure civil rights. Meanwhile, outside the courtroom, many in Mississippi and elsewhere voted with their feet, engaging in various kinds of independent commercial activity.[13]

Still, the taste of liberty Wood got in postwar Mississippi must have been more bitter than the taste she had in Ohio. In Hearn's recounting, even after several years of raising pigs and poultry for sale around Natchez, she had only accumulated $25 in savings.[14]

As in Texas, Kentucky, and Tennessee, whites in Natchez also violently resisted the gains made by former slaves. Paramilitary groups such as the Klan roamed widely in Mississippi, especially during elections. By 1875, white Democratic conservatives would manage, by a combination of fraud and force, to topple Mississippi's Reconstruction government, defying the federal government, and John Roy Lynch would lament that the "war was fought in vain."[15]

By then, however, Henrietta had already decided to get out. On a spring day in 1869, sixteen years after she had stepped into a curtained carriage, she walked with her son to the bluffs of Natchez, bought tickets for a steamboat, and journeyed back up the river to the place she still considered her home.

Wood returned to a Cincinnati very different from the one she had last seen from an upper room in Covington. The small antebellum city where business was centered on the waterfront was already transforming into an industrialized and sprawling urban area, now more reliant on railroads than on steamboats. The last time she had crossed the Ohio River, it was on a steam ferry. Now that same quarter mile was spanned by a suspension bridge.[16]

On the northern side of that bridge was a Cincinnati whose black population had also grown significantly, the result of a broader migration to cities in the Ohio River valley. Louisville's black population had risen from 6,800 to nearly 15,000 during the war; Cincinnati's climbed from about 3,730 to 5,900. A similar increase occurred in Covington, which accounted for nearly 70 percent of the total black population in Kenton County. These growing populations were also now concentrated in particular neighborhoods. In the early 1850s, free black men and women had been dispersed throughout Cincinnati, but by 1870, black households were more likely to be clustered in enclaves such as the one known at the time as Bucktown.[17]

Not everything about the river cities had changed. Jobs for black residents, especially for women, were scarce. Even before the war, female wage earners in the city had usually been limited to low-paying work, and that pattern continued after the war. In 1860, about fifteen percent of the black women who worked in Cincinnati had jobs as domestic servants; by 1890, almost half did, and most of the remainder worked as launderers. The only jobs likely to be available to Wood were the same ones that she had done before, and often during, her long reenslavement.[18]

Cincinnati also remained a dangerous place for people of color. In July 1862, a fight broke out between Irish and black dockworkers on the city's public landing, where the two groups competed for a dwindling number of steamboat jobs. Over the following weekend, white rioters rampaged through Bucktown, beating black residents in the streets and destroying their property. By Tuesday, angry gangs of white men were gathering throughout the city, inciting each other with shouts that the "Niggers would be cleaned out."[19]

Even so, reaching the banks of the Ohio River, after years spent along the Mississippi and the Brazos, must have been a significant moment for Henrietta Wood. Just having survived, and with Arthur by her side, was a personal triumph, but she aimed to do more than survive. Many years later, Simms would claim that he and his mother left Mississippi in search of relatives, a common goal for many freedpeople on the move in those years.[20]

No record shows if they ever found the family members they sought, but evidence of the search survives in a brief letter dated March 7, 1870, and written in Lawrenceburg, Indiana. It was addressed to Henrietta by Lucinda Tousey, the widow of Omer Tousey, Moses's son. Lucinda wrote to inform her that she had "received your letter," a proof that Wood had somehow managed to have a letter sent. Evidently Wood had contacted Tousey hoping to learn more about her childhood in Touseytown, including the year she was born. But Lucinda's reply disappointed. She informed Henrietta that Omer had been dead for two years and was buried across the river. Meanwhile, the rest of his family had dispersed. "Your old mistress Ann Tousey is living in New York," Lucinda said, "and I have no way of telling your age." She said nothing of what she knew, if anything, about what had happened to the rest of Wood's family after Omer had sold Henrietta, back when she was about as old as Arthur was now.[21]

Meanwhile, Henrietta had a more immediate problem: the search for paying work to support herself and her son. But on that front, at least, she had more success, and on June 25, 1870, she was counted for the first time by name in the US Census, another sign of the changes that abolition had wrought. "Wood, Henrietta" appeared (along with "Simms, Arthur," age fourteen) as the "Domestic" employees of a white Kentuckian in Covington named Harvey Myers.[22]

Myers had been born in New York State but had moved to Covington by 1853. By 1870, the value of his personal property and real estate exceeded $40,000, enabling him to employ, in addition to Wood and her son, three Irish domestic workers and two other black employees. More important for Henrietta, though, was Harvey's occupation— Myers was a lawyer, and earlier in the same month when the census taker came, he was the one who had helped her to file her suit against Zebulon Ward.[23]

Myers brought to that task a reputation as a lawyer's lawyer. He had run a thriving practice with his partner, John W. Stevenson, who became Kentucky's governor in 1867, and proceeds from that work had enabled Myers to purchase his elegant house on the waterfront in Covington, near the corner where the Licking River and the Ohio meet. Yet Myers also had a reputation as a political outsider in a town where most of his peers were conservative Democrats, and where even those who had remained loyal to the Union were nostalgic about the Confederacy. The war split Myers's own law firm down the middle. His partner Stevenson was a native Virginian who blamed Republicans for bringing about the war; as governor, he urged amnesty for former Confederates and opposed the extension of civil rights to former slaves. Another lawyer in Covington, John G. Carlisle, ran for state office by promising to save Kentucky from the imposition of "martial law," warning that enfranchising black men—a step that Republicans in Washington eventually took when the Fifteenth Amendment was passed in 1869—would leave white men "enslaved" by the "domination of the freed negro."[24]

Harvey Myers was different. Not only had he been "an active Union man" during the war, according to the *Enquirer*, he also remained a loyal Republican after it. In fact, until the very end of his life, he held out hope that Republicans could win in the border South. That view required a considerable amount of optimism, given that most white Kentuckians at the time viewed any postwar election won by a Republican as stolen. In August 1865, Myers himself ran for office in the General Assembly and won, but the result was immediately challenged by Democrats "on the ground of military interference" by federal troops, who were rumored to have kept Democrats from the polls. Rather than taking a seat whose legitimacy was in question, Myers resigned and agreed to run in another election. This time he lost.[25]

Myers's decision won him some praise from local Democrats, who viewed it as a vindication of their claims of federal interference, but the defeated lawyer's principles did not waver. In 1871, for example, he joined a committee of Kenton County lawyers who called for Kentucky to allow witness testimony in court without regard to color. Of all the lawyers whom Wood might have found in Covington after her return from Mississippi, it would have been hard to imagine an attorney more likely to help. So when she met Myers, sometime between April 1869 and June 1870, she decided to do what she had done so many times before. She told him her story.[26]

Lack of evidence makes it hard to know if Wood began working for Myers before he began working for her. One of her interviews suggests that she may have sought him out for help. "I found Mr. Myers, of Covington," she told the *Ripley Bee* in 1879, "and he commenced the suit for me."[27]

Certainly she did not need a white lawyer to introduce her to the concept of restitution for slavery. Enslaved people—women in particular—had always understood slavery as a crime that demanded reparation. Near the close of the American Revolution, for example, a manumitted woman named Belinda had successfully petitioned the Massachusetts legislature for a small pension paid out of the estate of her former owner, on the grounds that his wealth had been partly "accumulated by her own industry," as the petition stated, and "augmented by her servitude."[28]

Now, seven decades later, many formerly enslaved people were arguing the same thing. In August 1865, one former slave in Dayton, Ohio, heard that his past owner wished him to return and work for him in Tennessee. In reply, Jourdon Anderson dictated a letter to "My Old Master." First published in the *Cincinnati Commercial* and then widely reprinted, the letter from Anderson explained that he and his wife deserved back wages for their decades of enslavement, an amount that he calculated at $11,680, plus interest.[29]

The idea of reparations grew out of enslaved people's experiences, and it was not original to Henrietta Wood's particular suit. However, she did possess specific and hard-won knowledge. She knew from experience that courts could not be depended on absolutely, yet she also knew them as places where her claims could be heard. Perhaps she retained a childhood memory of Sampson's success in suing for his own abduction to Touseytown, and she might have heard of more recent suits in the South as well. In one 1857 case in Louisiana, near the Natchez District, Joseph—a free black man—had sued two white men for kidnapping and wrongful enslavement, winning $500 in a verdict against them. Rumors of such successes could have made their way to Wood along the same information networks that had spread news to slaves about the Civil War.[30]

She did need a lawyer like Myers, though, to help commence her suit. Having lived in Kentucky since 1853, Myers very likely recognized the former penitentiary keeper's name and knew that he now lived in Lexington. In addition, Myers knew good lawyers in Cincinnati, and he linked her to the law firm that would officially take her case: Lincoln, Smith & Warnock—fellow Republicans all.

Then, on June 3, 1870, Wood appeared as a plaintiff at the Superior Court of Cincinnati "by Lincoln, Smith & Warnock her attorney and filed in the office of the Clerk of said court, her certain petition," to wit:

> The above named plaintiff a single woman says, that she was on or about the day of _____ in the year 1853, and for many years previous thereto a free mullato woman residing in the city of Cincinnati in the State of Ohio, and that the defendant Zeb Ward, together with one Rebecca Boyd and other persons, whose names are to the plaintiff unknown, contriving to deprive the plaintiff of her liberty, and to convey and sell her into slavery for life, for gain and profit to themselves, did cause the plaintiff to be kidnapped and abducted from her place of abode in Cincinnati, and to be delivered to the defendant Zeb Ward in the State of Kentucky, and the said defendant Ward, well knowing that the plaintiff was a free woman, and a resident of Cincinnati, kept her in slavery for the space of seven months, and then under a pretended sale, delivered her to one William Pulliam a slave trader, to be by the said Pulliam, taken to the State of Mississippi and there sold into slavery and thereafter the said

Pulliam did take her to the State of Mississippi and there sold her into slavery to one Gerard Brandon, for the price of $1050, under the pretence that she was a slave, and then and there delivered the plaintiff into the possession of the said Brandon, who imprisoned her and forced and compelled her, to labor on his plantations in Mississippi and Texas, as a common field hand for the space of fifteen years.

As a result of these crimes, the petition continued, Wood had been deprived of the value of her services, which were worth "at least the sum of five hundred dollars per year." Those lost wages, combined with all the damages she had suffered during this time, meant that she was owed "the sum of twenty thousand dollars."[31]

Below that petition, the names of "Lincoln, Smith & Warnock" and "Harvey Myers" were listed as the plaintiff's attorneys. And then came an affidavit stating that the plaintiff herself agreed with the facts in the petition. Henrietta Wood remained unable to sign her own name below the oath. But she did write the "X" that served as her legal mark—and signaled her determination to hold Zebulon Ward to account.[32]

Ward received the notice of Wood's suit as he was going to the horse races in Cincinnati, according to her interview with the *Ripley Bee*. As defendant, he was given until July 2, 1870, to answer her in court. Court records show that the deadline came and went. Finally, though, on December 7, 1870, the Cincinnati law firm of Hoadly, Jackson & Johnson appeared on Ward's behalf and declared that their client wished to transfer the suit to a federal court—the US Circuit Court for the Southern District of Ohio. It was the opening salvo in what would become a legal war of attrition. The primary strategy of Ward's team would be to confuse and delay.[33]

When demanding a removal of the case to federal court, Hoadly, Jackson & Johnson cited recent changes to judiciary laws that made it easier for defendants to move cases from local courts to federal ones—even though those changes were irrelevant in Ward's case. In 1867, Republicans in Congress had passed a law providing that defendants could remove cases to federal courts when they believed that they would not get a fair hearing in a state court due to "prejudice or local influence." Though the law was intended to protect Republican officials and black defendants in the Reconstruction South, Ward's petition to the Superior Court turned the rule around. He claimed that "prejudice or local influence" in Cincinnati would work against *him*.[34]

In truth, Henrietta had more reasons to fear local prejudice than Zeb, even in Ohio. The Superior Court judge who received her petition was Alphonso Taft, a staunch antislavery Republican, but men such as he were becoming less popular in postwar Cincinnati, and any jurors would be drawn from a city rife with antiblack sentiment. Indeed, by the end of 1870, even local white Republicans who had supported the expansion of black civil rights were having second thoughts about Reconstruction. Disillusioned by the presidency of Ulysses S. Grant, conservative Republicans spoke of joining with like-minded Democrats to form a third party. In May 1872, these independents would nominate newspaper editor Horace Greeley for president at a convention held in Cincinnati, and their platform preached reconciliation with the white South. "Gentlemen, the past is past," Greeley told his supporters in 1871, after a trip to Texas and Mississippi. He added that "I am weary of fighting over issues that ought to be dead."[35]

Those words were music to former Confederates, of course. That fall, Greeley would lose to Grant in a landslide, but Greeley's movement did well in Kentucky, Tennessee, and southern Ohio, where the Republican Party had been splintering for years. In fact, another prominent critic of Grant was the lawyer George Hoadly, who led the firm that represented Zebulon Ward.[36]

Hoadly had been an antislavery Democrat before the war and studied law with the abolitionist Salmon P. Chase. In September 1853, as a young attorney, Hoadly had even been a leading member, together with John Jolliffe, of the efforts to impeach Judge Jacob Flinn, the proslavery Democrat who later acquitted Wood's kidnappers. Though Hoadly became a Republican after 1854 and voted for Grant in 1868, by 1872 he had migrated back into the Democratic fold. He agreed with those who believed, as one anti-Grant resolution put it, in "the disappearance of political issues arising out of the institution of slavery and resulting from the war which slavery entailed."[37]

The number of white men in Cincinnati who shared Hoadly's views made it far from certain that "local influence" would hurt Ward. Either way, his motion to move to a federal court succeeded on December 21, 1870. Three weeks later, on January 12, 1871, Wood's petition was duly transcribed into the record of the US Court, Sixth Circuit, for the Southern District of Ohio, which met in Cincinnati, and the case was assigned a number: 1431.[38]

The move prompted a new round of articles about the unusual suit. A headline in Nashville, where Ward was still embroiled in litigation against the state over the end of his convict lease, reported "Zeb. Ward in Trouble." A Cincinnati paper called the case "The Dregs of American Slavery." By January 15, papers as far away as Washington, DC, New Orleans, and New York had begun to reprint the story. After that, however, the pace of the suit suddenly slowed to a crawl. It was not until November 4, 1871, that lawyers filed Wood's "Declaration," the formal statement by a plaintiff that initiated a suit. Then, on February 7, 1872, Ward's lawyers filed a motion to dismiss the case, citing a procedural error in Wood's declaration. Her lawyers had filed her complaint as "a plea of trespass on the case," a form of legal action rooted in common law traditions that dated back to the Middle Ages. Ward's lawyers said the charges should have been filed as a plea of "trespass," plain and simple.[39]

It took yet another year before the court heard arguments about this issue. Finally, on March 30, 1873, the court sustained the motion against Wood's declaration, and her lawyers were instructed to amend the petition. They did so, quickly, on April 9, and a week before it was filed, she appeared again before a notary public in Hamilton County and once again signed her "X." Almost three full years after her lawsuit had begun in the Superior Court of Cincinnati, and four years after she made it back from Mississippi, the real fight with Ward was only beginning.[40]

CHAPTER TWENTY-ONE

STORY OF A SLAVE

If Henrietta Wood asked her lawyers why she had to sign a new petition in 1873, essentially restarting the whole process of litigation, she could not have been pleased when she heard their response. Her first declaration had been set aside by the US Circuit Court because of only three words: "on the case."

For Harvey Myers, that development would have been frustrating, too, but also more familiar. At the time, most lawyers still learned their art not in a formal law school, but by "reading" in a law office, studying records of past cases, practical treatises, and tomes such as Blackstone's commentaries on English law. In the process, they learned to swim, or at least to paddle, in an ocean of jargon—trover, *vi et armis*, *assumpsit*, demurrer—and to fit their pleadings into templates dating back to medieval England. Successful lawyers acquired a high degree of technical skill, and cases were often decided or disrupted on minor points of procedure such as the one that now threatened Wood's case against Ward.[1]

Legal reformers in the nineteenth century sought to correct that trend by developing less technical codes of civil procedure. By midcentury their efforts to establish what was known as simple "code pleading" had begun to sweep the nation. A code of procedure adopted by the State of New York in 1848 was adopted rapidly by other states, with minor alterations. By 1853, state courts in both Kentucky and Ohio had also switched to code pleading in civil actions.[2]

Procedural reform proceeded more slowly in the federal courts. Many federal trial judges still expected lawyers to file common law pleas, which meant first deciding which of about ten forms of legal action best described a plaintiff's cause. In 1871, therefore, when Wood's attorneys filed her declaration before the Circuit Court, they had to do more than simply describe what Zebulon Ward had done. They had to classify what he had done according to abstruse common law categories such as detinue or replevin.[3]

One obvious choice her lawyers could have made would have been to file a plea of *trespass*, a relatively simple category covering cases in which a plaintiff had been harmed by the use of force. Assault, battery, and false imprisonment were all examples of trespass. Wood's story included examples of each. Instead, her lawyers chose to label her declaration as *trespass on the case*, a different kind of common law plea.[4]

"On the case" pleas typically covered situations where direct, physical force had not been involved. Over time, they had also evolved into a more flexible, open-ended category, one that plaintiffs used when they had been injured by the later consequences, intentional or not, of a defendant's original act. Plaintiffs also turned to *trespass on the case* when their complaint seemed to deal with a new kind of harm, one that did not fit precisely in any other category. The move was risky, however. If the opposing side could convince a judge that the cause of a plaintiff's action *was* already covered by a different plea, such as trespass, a "case" declaration might be thrown out.[5]

Wood's lawyers thus would not have made the choice lightly to file a plea of *trespass on the case*. More probably, it was a deliberate choice reflecting what they intended to show. Myers and his colleagues apparently believed that their client's story raised a new and unique civil claim—a claim to reparations that went beyond the damages caused by Ward's original trespass. Her case was not just about an abduction or one violent act, but about the long period in which she was "deprived of her time and the value of her labor" by someone *other* than Ward. The case, in other words, was about slavery itself.[6]

Ward's lawyers, on the other hand, objected to this theory. By arguing that Wood's declaration was a plea of trespass, they hoped to confine the court's attention to the original act of alleged kidnapping in 1853. Evidently, by requiring Wood to amend her petition in the spring of 1873, the Circuit Court agreed with the defense.

Only a few years before, her suit might well have foundered on this procedural disagreement. Instead, it was probably saved by an obscure act of Congress passed on June 1, 1872. The so-called Conformity Act required federal courts in most cases to adopt the procedural rules already in use by state courts. So in April 1873, when Wood's lawyers amended her petition, they simply dropped any reference to *trespass on the case* and used Ohio's state court procedures to write a new petition, giving a straightforward description of the harms Wood had suffered. Ward's lawyers tried to complain that the new petition, filed "according to the Civil Code of Ohio," was "not a declaration in Trespass." In obedience to the new Conformity Act, however, the court allowed the new petition to stand.[7]

That decision resolved the technical issue that nearly doomed her case. It did not resolve the deeper issues between the two parties. On April 14, 1873, Ward's lawyers filed an answer to Wood's petition, asserting that he had legally obtained possession of her by paying Robert White, and also that too much time had passed between the alleged kidnapping and Wood's suit, and further, that the issue between them had been settled by the Kentucky freedom suit that she had lost back in the 1850s.[8]

Wood's lawyers, for their part, rejected this narrowing of the issue. In their amended petition, they added a line estimating that Wood had lost $500 a year in wages for each year she had been enslaved after 1853. They intended to make Ward liable for that harm as well as her abduction.[9]

Those who knew Harvey Myers could have predicted that he would not concede an inch. "He was not of engaging address," according to one remembrance of the Republican lawyer, "but rather clumsy in carriage, unconventional in manner, and reserved and gruff in tone. Indeed in the Courtroom he was almost without courtesy, giving no quarter to his opponent and asking none, but mercilessly prosecuting every case as though it were war." Outside the courthouse, Myers also remained a foot soldier in the political fight to defend Radical Reconstruction. During the election season of 1872, as Horace Greeley gathered supporters across Kentucky, Myers had run for Congress as

STORY OF A SLAVE

a Ulysses S. Grant man. At one campaign event in Covington, he declared that the "Republican party was founded in justice and equality to all men" and would not rest until Kentucky was no longer "benighted" by Democratic rule. At another, Myers joined a procession of Grant supporters, black and white, through the streets of Covington. That parade almost sparked a riot when a white onlooker threw a stone at one of the black marchers, but Myers succeeded in addressing the group and received their strong endorsement. He was not one to retreat from threats.[10]

After Ward's answer was filed in April, however, the proceedings in Wood's case ground to a halt again. Things stalled for more than a year. And then, on March 28, 1874, the estranged husband of one of Myers's clients in an unrelated case—an ugly suit for divorce—pushed his way into the lawyer's office in Covington, pulled out a gun, and shot him in the stomach.[11]

Within half an hour, Harvey Myers was dead.

After the murder, Wood left Covington and moved across the river, settling near the neighborhood where she had lived and worked the last time she was in Cincinnati, before her abduction. Myers's death may have left both Henrietta and Arthur bereaved and unemployed, forcing them to look for new work. An 1875 city directory listed "Henrietta Woods" at 19 Harrison Street, and for a time, Arthur Simms lived at the same address, having found work in the city as a "coachman." The murder nevertheless robbed Wood of her legal champion. Technically, she was still represented by Thomas D. Lincoln, Fayette Smith, and their new legal partner, but 1874 passed by without her lawyers filing any pleadings on her behalf.[12]

That may have been because the defendant had left Kentucky once again. In 1873, Ward learned that Arkansas was leasing its state penitentiary for ten full years, giving total control of the convicts to a private contractor with the best bid. He closed his bagging firm in Kentucky and quickly moved to Little Rock, joining another lessee as a partner. Then, in 1875, he bought his partner's stake. Zeb Ward had taken control of his third state prison.[13]

By then the State of Arkansas was in the hands of Democrats like him and had passed a law sentencing petty thieves to years in jail—an arrangement that promised to add to Ward's considerable wealth. The number of convicts he controlled doubled in just two years, to about four hundred, and Ward began to build yet another fortune with their labor. By 1878, a credit reporting agency estimated that he was worth at least $150,000 and predicted that the keeper would soon be worth twice that amount.[14]

Wood's lawyers may have seen that wealth as harder to reach once Ward had relocated to Little Rock, or they may have begun to weigh the costs of assisting a poor black woman against the uncertain benefits of continuing her suit. Even so, there was finally movement in the case on January 30, 1875. That was the day when Wood's lawyers filed a reply to Ward in the Circuit Court.[15]

Almost two years before, Ward's lawyers had argued that his title to Wood was settled by the freedom suit she had lost in 1854, a loss confirmed on appeal in 1855. Ward denied the allegations that he had abducted Wood, insisting that he had purchased her legally from Robert White. Last, he claimed that the statute of limitations protected him from action. Wood had waited too long to sue.[16]

In reply, Wood's lawyers now pointed out that she had not been able to file suit any earlier because she was "in duress, having been kidnapped by the procurement of the defendant" and imprisoned as a slave. She denied that the Fayette County court had jurisdiction over the wrongs raised in her petition "or that the judgment therein alleged is a bar to the present action." Below these arguments, Wood once again made an "X" for her mark. Henrietta and her lawyers still intended to fight.[17]

Ward's team continued a strategy of delay. They filed a successful motion in March arguing that the plaintiff needed to amend her reply, making sure that each item in it was clearly numbered. The tactic forced her attorneys to file an amended pleading on April 6, 1875. On the same day, Ward's lawyers filed a new demurrer to stop the amended document, on the grounds that it contained "facts insufficient in law to constitute a reply." After that flurry of motions in April 1875, the case stalled again until the end of the year. Then, in December, the court sustained the motion made by Ward. The plaintiff was now required to amend her pleading *again*.[18]

Henrietta Wood must have despaired of ever getting a hearing, much less the justice she desired. As winter turned to spring, the suit had been dragging on for more than seventy-two months, with nothing yet gained, and no end in sight. On April 1, 1876, however, an unexpected opportunity came to revive attention to her case. That evening, a reporter for the *Cincinnati Commercial* appeared at her door on Harrison Street. It was Lafcadio Hearn.[19]

By then, Hearn was a fairly regular presence in Wood's neighborhood, one noted for its poverty and crime and largely avoided by more respectable journalists. Hearn was one of the few reporters who took an interest in profiling the people who frequented the city's dingiest streets, its brothels and asylums and shabby, dark hotels—the sort of places where Lafcadio himself felt less self-conscious, more at ease.[20]

He had lived in Cincinnati since 1869, the same year Wood returned there from Natchez, Mississippi. Arriving in the city penniless as a nineteen-year-old immigrant, Hearn had since worked as a reporter for the *Cincinnati Enquirer* and the *Cincinnati Commercial,* despite a disability that made it hard to read and write. Lafcadio's left eye had been severely injured in childhood and then became infected; it quickly clouded over and went completely blind. The resulting strain caused his right eye, already severely nearsighted, to bulge out from its socket for the rest of his life. In conversation, he usually tried to cast his eyes downward and away, convinced that his own appearance would strike others as monstrous.[21]

The habit gave the man who appeared on Wood's doorstep that night the air of a painfully shy person, though the persona seemed to help him find stories that other white reporters in the city seldom told. Sometimes sensationalistic and marred by stereotypes, sometimes written in the mold of Edgar Allan Poe, his stories could also be sensitive and even sociological. And by the time he found Wood, he had come multiple times to the block between Sixth and Seventh Streets, bisected by Harrison and bounded on either side by Broadway and Culvert.[22]

Hearn described that block in 1875 as one of the city's most polluted, crowded, and policed. "Ten, twelve, or even twenty inhabitants" might live in houses barely fit for habitation, with "two or three stories under ground." In an alley at Fifth and Culvert was a "long, stagnant pool of execrable stench" in which "the foulest" bugs liked to breed, and at the corner of Culvert and Harrison was "the lowest thieves' hole in Bucktown." At Culvert and Sixth he found a miasmatic trench "running into the sewer," the perfect place, he mused, to "dispose of a body in," and in "the lots opposite Harrison and Culvert" were the ruins of burned-out factories and an "immense well uncovered save by some charred beams."[23]

Here was a block, Hearn reported, where the ministrations of the city's Board of Health were especially needed—but seldom given. Yet Lafcadio was fascinated by the people he met in the neighborhood, including the formerly enslaved black woman, Alethea Foley, to whom he had been briefly married. He eventually found a number of other ex-slaves also willing to speak about their life "'Before Freedom,' as the colored folks say." And it was there, in one of the most impoverished parts of a highly stratified city, that he also met and interviewed Henrietta Wood.[24]

It was a Saturday when Hearn arrived and asked Wood to tell about her own life "before freedom." That night he found Henrietta alone without Arthur, who was then in Chicago. She may have regarded the reporter warily at first, given how often she had recounted her story to white men who promised to help but did not succeed.

Had she been able to read some of the other stories Hearn had published, she also might have been less willing to trust him with hers. Hearn had been known to exoticize the black women of Bucktown, describing the "immense stature and phenomenal muscularity" of the "negresses" and "the supple pantherish strength" of "neatly built mulatto girls." With such lines, Hearn played to the prejudices of his white reading audience—and betrayed racial prejudices of his own. In one article published in the *Commercial* on August 22, 1875, Hearn referred to the black residents of Bucktown as "Pariah People," low sorts who lived in a sink of turpitude and debauchery.[25]

Nonetheless, something about Hearn or her own situation made Henrietta decide to tell her story once again. It was what she had done before when she had been in desperate straits, and this time, Hearn wrote the interview up for publication. The next morning, on April 2, 1876, the nearly four-thousand-word story appeared on the second page of the *Cincinnati Commercial*, under a headline sure to attract the interest of Hearn's many readers:

STORY OF A SLAVE.
Kidnaped in Covington Twenty Years Ago,
AND ILLEGALLY SOLD IN THE COTTON STATES.
Horrible Experiences in Mississippi—Recent Suit Against the Kidnapers.

"I can't quite tell my age, she said, in commencing her story, but I guess I must be about fifty eight or fifty nine years old..."[26]

CHAPTER TWENTY-TWO

THE VERDICT

The story was unlike any that Lafcadio Hearn had known. He told his readers that "narratives innumerable of slave life" had been written; he had published several such narratives himself. But none was quite like that of Henrietta Wood, which was full of "shocking incidents" and had ended in a lawsuit for a huge sum. In "Story of a Slave," Hearn reported that the case had been taken up by the law firm of Lincoln and Smith, and that Harvey Myers was to have represented her but for his "tragical death."[1]

Hearn himself probably knew something about that murder. The enraged husband who shot Myers was a former correspondent for the *Cincinnati Commercial,* and his lengthy trial had been covered by the *Enquirer* while Hearn was still working on that rival paper's staff. Other facts in the story, though, were totally new to him, including the name of the man at the center of Wood's abduction. A more established resident of Cincinnati might well have recognized Ward—former sheriff in Covington, current man of the turf. Hearn, a relative newcomer, misidentified Zebulon throughout as "Jabez."[2]

Similar, small errors peppered Hearn's piece. He was on surer footing, though, when it came to the places that Wood mentioned in Cincinnati: Fifth and Broadway, Fourth Street near Main, or the ferry that took Henrietta over the river to Covington—"guess it was the old ferry," Hearn reported Wood saying, "that used to run from the foot of Vine street." He knew Cincinnati's streets well, and when she spoke of Boyd's place, the interview noted that it was "not far from where the St. James is now," possibly a reference to a ramshackle restaurant that he had written about only a few weeks before in a piece for the *Commercial*, "Levee Life."[3]

The other details were more than enough to attract notice on both sides of the Ohio River. Commenting on Hearn's story, the *Covington Journal* recognized the "Frank Russ" he mentioned as "undoubtedly...Frank Rust, who died three or four years since." Meanwhile, in Cincinnati, the mention of Wood's lawyers by name may have given them new motivation to resume her case. On April 10, one week after the publication of "Story of a Slave," Lincoln and Smith filed to amend her latest pleading, four months after the court had required the revision.[4]

For the first time, Zeb Ward's lawyers did not make any motions objecting to the new filing. This time there would be no demurrers, no amendments—no arguments that might have further delayed a trial. Instead, the defense team proceeded to gather evidence, and in December, depositions were taken from F. K. Hunt, a former mayor of Lexington, Kentucky, and also George B. Kinkead, Wood's now elderly former lawyer. Both men likely testified about their knowledge of the freedom suit in the 1850s—a case that would soon feature prominently in this one.[5]

Still, it was not until Monday, April 15, 1878—two years after Hearn had interviewed Wood, nine years after she had returned from Mississippi—that Case 1431 was brought before a jury of twelve white men for trial. A reporter present for the *Cincinnati Enquirer* noted that Henrietta herself—"a spectacled negro woman, apparently sixty years old"—took the witness stand on the very first day. "Her only son," Arthur, was present in the courtroom, too, evidently having returned from Chicago. Though a full quarter of a century had passed since the carriage ordered by Boyd had crossed the Ohio River and stopped on a road outside of Covington, Wood now finally had a chance to tell her full story in court.[6]

One day would not be enough for a jury to hear everything. So on April 15, the court adjourned. At 9:00 a.m. the next morning, the jurors returned to the courtroom. Then the trial went on.[7]

Reporters in Cincinnati were the first to notice that the trial had begun. On April 16, the *Commercial* even remembered that Wood had been interviewed two years before by Hearn, who had since left the city and moved to New Orleans. The paper briefly summarized "Story of a

Slave," and news of the case spread across state lines, too. It was a "curious suit," said the *Brooklyn Daily Eagle* on April 18. "Remarkable," the *New York Herald* agreed.[8]

The case was remarkable partly because it focused attention on slavery at a time when the drift of national politics was in the opposite direction. In 1871, Republicans had passed the Ku Klux Klan Act to protect newly enfranchised black citizens from violence. Congress followed that with an expanded Civil Rights Act in 1875. But by the time Wood testified in court in 1878, those laws looked like the high water marks of Reconstruction.[9]

Democrats and white southern conservatives had waged war on Reconstruction from the start, of course, but its doom in the 1870s was sealed by quarrels among Republicans themselves, who were divided between supporters and critics of President Ulysses S. Grant. Satisfied that the Thirteenth, Fourteenth, and Fifteenth Amendments had fully discharged whatever debt the nation owed to former slaves, Grant's critics wanted Republicans to stop antagonizing white Southerners with interventions on behalf of freed people, whom many denigrated as unprepared for citizenship, and instead to move on to what they saw as more pressing national issues—civil service reform, labor disputes, and economic depression after the Panic of 1873.[10]

The turn against Grant from within his own party had roots in Horace Greeley's failed campaign for the White House in 1872, but it also began even earlier. In 1867, Republicans associated with the *Nation*, an increasingly conservative journal, had concluded that the "removal of white prejudice against the negro depends almost entirely on the negro himself," and not on federal power. Even the American Anti-Slavery Society, founded in 1833 by radical abolitionists, disbanded in 1870, declaring its work finished. In 1871, Carl Schurz, a former radical during the war, argued that it was time for the "questions connected with the Civil War to be disposed of forever." The *Nation* agreed the following year in an editorial: "Reconstruction and slavery we have done with," it announced.[11]

As calls for conciliation toward former Confederates gained steam in the North, the result was disaster for the formerly enslaved. In 1873,

Alexander Stephens, the former vice president of the Confederacy, was elected to the House of Representatives; Andrew Johnson would briefly join him in Congress as a senator in 1875. In 1874, Congress failed to do anything to stop the failure of the Freedman's Bank, whose managers had accepted and then squandered more than $2 million in deposits from freedpeople since 1865. Tens of thousands of former slaves who had entrusted their savings to the bank lost almost everything they had put in. The next year, Democrats used armed violence to overthrow the legitimate Republican government in the State of Mississippi, defying federal authority, but President Grant, fearing backlash from his critics, refused to send federal troops. Mississippi's embattled Republican governor, Adelbert Ames, warned that "an era of second slavery" was descending across the South.[12]

Abolitionists returned to their barricades to denounce all these atrocities. Yet most Republicans were glad for the signs, as one put it, that the nation was beginning to move "out of the region of the Civil War." Most white Americans viewed an end to military intervention in the South as already overdue. In 1877, Grant was replaced in the White House by Ohio Republican Rutherford B. Hayes, who had previously assured white Southerners that Northerners intended to extend them only "good will" and to pursue a "let alone policy" with the states.[13]

With Hayes's inauguration, military Reconstruction effectively came to an end, and the "era of second slavery" that Ames predicted seemed to begin. The Civil Rights Act was treated with contempt across the country. Republican state governments in the South were overturned, one by one, by Democrats who claimed to be the "Redeemers" of white rule. New waves of violence against black men and women swept across the states of the former Confederacy. In April 1878, one Pennsylvania newspaper's report on Wood's lawsuit appeared immediately beside the story of "an unfortunate colored woman named Charlotta Harris" who had just been lynched in Virginia. Her name joined a lengthening roll of black casualties in what seemed like an ongoing war.[14]

It therefore seemed exceedingly unlikely in the spring of 1878 that Wood could bring a suit for damages related to slavery, much less that she could win—especially since federal courts had also played a role in the retreat from Reconstruction. In the *Slaughterhouse* cases of 1873, and again in the *Cruikshank* case of 1876, the Supreme Court had significantly narrowed the protections offered to individual citizens by the Fourteenth Amendment, to the detriment of black litigants. Far from becoming friendlier to plaintiffs such as Wood, federal courts often remained hostile to them during the 1870s, the very years in which she had been waiting for a trial.[15]

Now that the trial had begun, her lawyers would have to row against powerful currents in both politics and the law—all while trying to show that Ward was liable for wrongful acts that were twenty-five years old. Truly, the case of "A Slave's Claims" was "a singular one," as one newspaper put it, both "because of the length of time that has elapsed since the occurrence, and as being a relic of the slavery system now dead." The *Cincinnati Enquirer* predicted that it would "probably be a little bit slow in the motions through the Courts." After the jury was named, however, on April 15, 1878, Wood's case practically hurtled toward a conclusion. After eight years of watching the case creep along, she would receive a verdict in three short days.[16]

By the end of the day on April 16, 1878, the court had already heard all of the evidence in *Wood v. Ward*. The next morning, a Wednesday, the jurors filed back into the courtroom to hear closing statements from the attorneys. Then the Circuit Court judge, Phillip B. Swing, delivered final instructions to the jury.[17]

Henrietta Wood was in the courtroom again that day, and in many ways her fortunes hinged on what Swing decided to say. Theoretically, the role of the judge in a federal civil action was to instruct the jury about legal principles relevant to the case. Jurors had the responsibility of deciding questions of fact. In practice, though, the line between the two often blurred, especially in cases like this where questions of fact—*was she a free woman when she was abducted?*—were directly related to questions of law—*did the earlier adjudication of her freedom suit bar her from recovering damages now?* In the second half of the nineteenth century, fears about juror bias had also contributed to a legal culture in which judges assumed more power to instruct juries. Increasingly, judges even claimed the power to direct a verdict.[18]

Swing was one of three judges who could hear cases before the Sixth Circuit Court for the Southern District in Ohio, though his primary post was as the judge of the federal District Court. Appointed in 1871 by Ulysses S. Grant, a close friend, Swing had a reputation as a fairly conservative judge. On other matters, Swing was more forward-looking. In 1871, he appointed George W. Hays, a formerly enslaved man, to the position of court crier, making Hays the first African American to work in the District Court. Ward's lawyers may have had some reasons to worry that the Grant appointee would take Wood's case seriously.[19]

Swing did take the case seriously, but he delivered a long, convoluted set of instructions to the jury. On the one hand, Swing dispensed quickly with Ward's argument that Wood was barred by statutes of limitations. Swing replied that the statutes did not begin to run until after her enslavement ended and she returned to Ohio. She also had no opportunity to file her suit until Ward himself visited Ohio in 1870.[20]

On the other hand, Swing told the jurors to weigh carefully the question of whether she was free in 1853. Swing believed that the case "has, perhaps, more of the elements of false imprisonment than any other," focusing the jurors' attention on the initial trespass of abduction instead of on the many years of lost wages during her enslavement. "To entitle the plaintiff to recover," Swing explained, "the evidence must satisfy your minds that at the time of the alleged injury she was a free woman." Swing granted that, "Freedom being the natural right of man," and slavery being outlawed by the Constitution of the State of Ohio, the jury should presume that Wood was a free woman if she had resided in Ohio for several years. "That presumption would, however, be rebutted," the judge continued, "by showing that by the laws of Kentucky she was a slave and was in Ohio without the consent of her owner." This, of course, was precisely the rebuttal that Ward had always offered in his defense: that Henrietta had belonged to Robert White, had gone to Ohio without his consent, and then had been purchased by Ward. Swing left it to the jury to decide if that story was true.[21]

In doing so, he also seemed to affirm the antebellum principle—ratified by the Supreme Court—that states had been able to decide cases of freedom and slavery on the basis of their own laws. Citing the "full faith and credit" clause of the Constitution, Swing quoted from an antebellum decision by the Kentucky Court of Appeals in which a woman of color who had spent two weeks in Ohio was reenslaved upon her return to Kentucky: "If the laws and Courts of Ohio will determine the condition of the slave while in that State, they can not, by their own force, determine what shall be his condition when beyond their control." In other words, antebellum Kentucky courts did not have to abide by the Ohio principle that a slave who stepped on free soil was automatically free.[22]

As a southern Ohioan born in 1820, Swing was unsurprisingly familiar with the principles of compromise and interstate comity embodied in such decisions. Those principles had been essential to the survival of slavery in the borderlands between Ohio and Kentucky. More surprising, though, was that Swing went out of his way to affirm them now. By doing so, he may have planted a seed of doubt about Wood in the jurors' minds, suggesting that Ward had been acting within his rights at the time.

Next, Swing turned to consider one of Ward's most important defenses: that the decisions of the Kentucky courts in Wood's earlier freedom suit disqualified her from suing now. Could a plaintiff's suit against a defendant be stopped by the adjudication of a different suit between the same parties? "The question has been recently before the Supreme Court," Swing informed the jury, referring especially to its ruling in *Russell v. Place* (1876). The Court held there that a plaintiff could sue a defendant, even after losing an earlier case, as long as the earlier case was a suit for a different cause. And on this point, Swing was clear: Wood's suit against Ward now was "for personal wrongs and injuries," whereas the earlier case was a suit for freedom. The two causes of action were distinct.[23]

Not content to leave matters there, Swing next suggested that any questions of fact settled by the earlier case might be considered binding if they could be determined. The judge believed that the earlier court had likely decided how long Henrietta Wood had resided in Cincinnati and whether Ward had purchased her from White or Boyd, but the case file for her freedom suit had been lost near the end of the Civil War in that 1864 courthouse fire. And even if the earlier court's findings of fact could be determined, Swing suggested, they might not matter if the jurors accepted Wood's claim that her 1853 petition "was not filed by her, nor by her procurement; that she was kept in close restraint and in fear of personal injury, and had no control over, and took no part in, said proceedings." If so, Swing told the jurors, then she was not bound by anything the earlier court had said.[24]

At this point, the jurors in *Wood v. Ward* could have been forgiven for some confusion about Swing's many instructions. He had begun by telling them that they should decide whether Wood was in fact free in 1853. Then he implied that the question of her freedom was decided by the earlier Kentucky court, whose findings of fact were conclusive even if they did not bar Wood from seeking damages for injury. Yet Swing also said that if she did not begin the earlier suit herself, "then it is a nullity as far as she is concerned, and the recital of any fact in the record will not affect this record."[25]

Instead of closing with a helpful summary, Swing finished with a warning against jury bias in the assessment of any damages in the case. "Fortunately for this country the institution of slavery has passed away," Swing intoned, reflecting the consensus among white Americans at the time, "and we should not bring our particular ideas of the legality or morality of an institution of that character into Court or the jury-box in assessing penalties upon those who may have been connected with it." Swing went so far as to speculate that many former beneficiaries of slavery "regret its existence as much as any of us." Even if the plaintiff had proved her case, the jury should refrain from an excessive award.[26]

Whatever else the jurors took away from Swing's instructions, they evidently took this last caution to heart, for after a brief deliberation, the jury returned with its verdict written on a small slip of paper, signed in a shaky hand by the jury foreman. At the top of the paper was the title of the case and the case number, followed by a single sentence:

> We, the Jury in the above entitled cause, do find for the plaintiff and assess her damages in the premises at Two thousand five hundred dollars $2,500.

Henrietta Wood had won her case. But she was awarded only a small fraction of the $20,000 that her suit had asked—much less than the $500 per year that she estimated her labor to have been worth while she was held in slavery. And even that proved to be more than Ward wanted to pay.[27]

The verdict from the jury had scarcely been read before Ward's attorney gave notice that he would be filing a motion for a new trial. Two months later, on June 29, 1878, Hoadly, Johnson and Colston, attorneys for the defendant, filed a bill of exceptions that quivered with unpunctuated outrage over the verdict. "And now comes defendant & moves for a new trial," the pleading read, "because":

First The verdict is contrary to the law.
Second The verdict is contrary to the Evidence
Third Error of Court in admission of testimony
Fourth Error of Court in rejection of testimony
Fifth Error of Court in refusing to charge jury as requested by defendant
Sixth Error of Court in charging jury as requested by plaintiff
Seventh Error of Court in general charge to jury
Eighth The damages are excessive
Ninth Newly discovered evidence
Tenth Other grounds

Zeb Ward was not finished fighting yet.[28]

Meanwhile, news of Swing's instructions and the jury's decision was spreading rapidly in the press. Within a little more than a year, more than fifty newspapers in at least twenty-one states would mention the case. The stories united in calling the case extraordinary—"remarkable" and "curious" continued to be common words in reports—though editors often misreported details, either in their haste or their desire to punch up the story. One Chicago newspaper, deciding that the case was not dramatic enough, turned Jane Cirode into a violent prostitute, claiming that Wood had belonged "originally to a woman of ill-fame at Lexington, Ky., who, after having been charged with complicity in a murder, left Lexington and came to Cincinnati."[29]

Even those papers that got the facts mostly right did not agree entirely on how to regard the outcome. Some headlines spoke of "An Old Wrong Righted," "A Slave's Triumph," "Heavy Damages," and "Retribution at Last." A Cincinnati paper called it a "righteous verdict," and in San Francisco, the verdict was celebrated as a case of "Long-Delayed Justice."[30]

Other papers, however, contrasted the $2,500 with the amount that Henrietta Wood had asked—$20,000—and wondered how that fraction could possibly be fair. "It is said," reported a Massachusetts journalist, "that the jury computed the damages by taking the price for which she was sold as a basis, and computing simple interest upon it…but it seems a strange rule to apply to this case." A Republican newspaper in Chicago was more direct: the award "should have been $25,000," especially since "the kidnapper is said to have grown wealthy." The *Inter Ocean* considered the case "a pointed commentary on the kind of government we had under the rule of the old pro-slavery Democracy" and found it "humiliating" that "human liberty" could be regarded as "so cheap."[31]

Many reports identified Ward as the lessee of the Arkansas state penitentiary, noting the wealth that he had amassed since 1853. In comparison, $2,500 seemed meager, even minuscule. One paper edited by former abolitionists believed that "Zebulon may congratulate himself on having gotten off cheap." Others compared the award not to Zeb's riches but to all that Henrietta had been forced to endure. Yet that made the amount she won seem all the more "trifling." As the *Cincinnati Gazette* put it, "the damages awarded the twice emancipated colored woman seem trivial in comparison to the amount of suffering she underwent."[32]

Another paper, the *New York Herald*, agreed that the amount Wood won was insufficient, though it still considered the victory significant in the end. "This is not a liberal equivalent for the loss of liberty and for fifteen years' hard labor on a Gulf State plantation," conceded the *Herald*, "but it is far better in the circumstances than no equivalent at all, and it is large enough to cover the principle that the wrongdoer must pay." Indeed, given "the many histories that were formerly circulated of life in the border States," the *Herald* predicted that the principle would "be applicable to a great many cases yet untried. Here is a field in which the speculative attorney may run down many a nimble six-pence."[33]

Concern about that possibility may be one reason why many reports emphasized that Wood's suit was an "old case," described it as a "relic of slavery times," and called her an "old" woman. "Not so many complications of a legal nature arise out of the old relations of master and slave as might have been expected," noted the *New York Tribune*, before reporting on Wood's case as an exception to the rule. Some editors sought to distance the horrors in her story from the present; one observed that it was "pleasant to reflect that such days will come again no more to her or any of her race," and Swing had made much the same point in one of his final instructions to the jury. Slavery was regrettable, he had said. "But its history has been written, and it is never again to be reinstated upon this continent."[34]

Some commentators, on the contrary, saw Wood's victory as a rebuttal to the idea that slavery was a thing of the distant past. "We would willingly close this dark chapter in American history," said the *New York Times* in its commentary on the case, except that Henrietta Wood had "opened it again," raising some difficult questions about the nation's "unsettled account" with the formerly enslaved. As the *Times* noted, former Confederates and Democrats could still be heard arguing, on occasion, that they were owed compensation for the loss of their slaves or forgiveness of their debts from the war. To them, the *Times* asked, what about compensation to ex-slaves?[35]

Newspapers raised that question and many others in the months after the verdict, debating whether the amount Wood won was a trifle or a triumph. Yet what no journalist appears to have wondered or tried to discover—at least not in 1878—was how Henrietta herself felt about the jury's decision. In fact, only one local journalist claimed to have observed her reaction to the verdict, and though his report mangled some facts and relied more on racial stereotype than on deep insight, it provides the only glimpse of what she thought on the day when her trial concluded.

"Henrietta Woods, waiting for the jury, sat like a black marble statue," wrote the court reporter for the *Cincinnati Enquirer*, "till it was announced that the jury were ready. As they filed past her to the seats she surveyed them one by one and grew a little bit nervous. When the verdict was announced not a lineament of her dark face changed. She had lost her nervousness and relaxed into Henrietta Woods."[36]

Wood had good reason to be impassive when the jury's verdict was read. It was not the first time she had been promised money, only to discover later that the pledges meant nothing. And Ward's attorney had filed a motion for a new trial, preventing the immediate payment of the damages. She waited almost another year before the motion for a new trial was heard, this time by John Baxter, another Circuit Court judge.

Unlike Swing, Baxter was a Southerner by birth, having been born in North Carolina before moving to Knoxville, Tennessee, on the eve of the Civil War. After that, Baxter had moved all over the political map: a Unionist who opposed secession, he ran unsuccessfully for the Confederate Congress anyway, but then defended East Tennessee Unionists from persecution. A Whig before the war, Baxter migrated into the Republican Party, but he opposed the Emancipation Proclamation and supported Democrat George McClellan's campaign against Lincoln in 1864. Baxter returned to the Republican fold but became a fierce critic of Tennessee governor William G. Brownlow during the very same years when Zebulon Ward was running the Tennessee penitentiary. In 1872, he supported Greeley's campaign against Grant, siding with opponents of Reconstruction, and he was appointed to the Circuit Court by Rutherford B. Hayes in 1877. Probably most encouraging of all, from Ward's perspective, was the fact that Baxter had once owned slaves himself.[37]

On February 15, 1879, however, when Baxter took up the motion for a new trial, the judge quickly dispelled any suspicions that he might be partial to Ward. He described Wood's ordeal as "a case of peculiar and complicated oppression" and Wood herself as the victim of "a most grievous wrong." And he showed little patience with "Defendant's exceptions upon the trial," which were many and, in Baxter's view, frivolous.[38]

Baxter conceded that Judge Swing may have "indulged in instructions upon immaterial and abstract matters" in his charge to the jury. Still, Baxter said that most of the complaints raised by Ward were irrelevant, and the "damages are not excessive." The only real controversy, Baxter believed, concerned the question of whether plaintiff was "precluded from a re-examination" of her case by the previous decisions of Kentucky courts in the 1850s. That question was significant, he said, and rightly deserved "thorough consideration."[39]

Swing had made that issue a question of fact: did Wood initiate the freedom suit in Kentucky herself, or was it initiated on her behalf? But Baxter settled the question by turning to the law. The judge concluded that if Wood was a slave in 1853, "she was a chattel, a mere piece of property, without civil rights, and incompetent to prosecute or defend a suit." Baxter provided a lengthy survey of Southern antebellum laws to show that slaves could not "appear as suitors, either in Court of law or equity."[40]

Clearly, if Ward had hoped that Baxter's Southern background would help him, that hope had backfired. Baxter knew the laws of slavery well, and he knew the legal fictions that many Southern courts used to treat slaves as property for some purposes and as persons for others. It was true that a freedom suit had been prosecuted in Wood's name in Kentucky, Baxter said. "Similar suits were not infrequent in the Courts of the slave States." He added accurately, however, that "these suits were always entertained upon the allegation that the plaintiff was free." As soon as a plaintiff was proven to be a slave, "the litigation, whatever its scope, necessarily ceased for the want of a competent plaintiff."[41]

That was exactly what had happened in Wood's case in Kentucky, Baxter believed. "Plaintiff alleged her freedom. This, prima facie, gave jurisdiction. But as soon as the Court reached the conclusion that plaintiff was a slave, it found itself without jurisdiction for the want of a plaintiff competent to sue, and did the only thing which, under the circumstances, it could have done—struck the case from the docket."

Legally speaking, according to the laws of slavery, it was as though the suit had never been filed at all.[42]

For that reason, Baxter concluded, the earlier decree of the Kentucky Court of Appeals had no bearing on the present case. By logic at once tortuous and indisputable, the decision in 1855 that Wood was a slave gave her the ability to argue in 1878 that she was actually free in 1853. Ward had offered no opposing testimony in court to rebut that point, resting all his arguments on the earlier judgment. And given that Baxter considered that judgment immaterial, "the verdict of the jury must stand." There would be no new trial.[43]

Baxter's decision briefly brought the case of *Wood v. Ward* into the public eye again—not least because of its ingenious reasoning, which seemed to echo the controversial *Dred Scott* decision made by the Supreme Court in 1857. One legal reporter questioned "the rather novel theory, that the judgment of the Kentucky court did not bind the plaintiff, because a slave could not bring suit, thus assuming conclusively that she was a slave in order to permit her to show that she was not." That a former slaveholder and conservative Republican had ruled in favor of a formerly enslaved woman was not the only irony in the case.[44]

The irony was also noted by a pseudonymous correspondent for the *Ripley Bee*, "Cincinnati," who found Henrietta Wood in the aftermath of the latest decision and interviewed her in 1879. The interview, when published, stretched across several issues of the small-town paper, adding new details to her story that had never been reported before, even by Lafcadio Hearn. "Little was it thought," concluded "Cincinnati" in the article's final installment, "when Judge Taney, of the U.S. Supreme Court, decided that Dred Scott could not sue as a citizen in the U.S. Courts, that that decision and its reasoning would someday operate in favor of one who had been a victim" of slavery.[45]

As for Henrietta, she continued to reserve judgment on what had occurred until she was convinced that the money would appear. She told the *Bee* that she was still waiting for Ward to "pass over them checks," and perhaps that was why she had agreed—once again—to sit and tell her story, reviewing all her claims. How she had been enslaved and then freed and enslaved again. How she had been taken to Mississippi and Texas. How she had made it back to Cincinnati and "found Mr. Myers, of Covington, and he commenced the suit for me, but he was killed…before anything could be done, and you know the rest."[46]

Henrietta had told it all so many times, rehearsed her memories for so many men over the years, that she may well have wondered, even in her moment of triumph, whether she would ever be able to stop. If so, her answer came on July 10, 1879, when a final document was filed with the Circuit Court—a "receipt" acknowledging that Ward had paid a last installment of $2,000 to the plaintiff, completing his payment in full.[47]

When the clerk for the court received the receipt, he folded it carefully into fours. The clerk stamped his name on the outside of the folded sheet, along with the filing date. He wrote the number of the case and the title one more time, "Henrietta Wood vs. Zeb Ward." And then he carefully penned the proper legal name for the document.[48]

It was a "Satisfaction."

Cover sheet for the proof of Zebulon Ward's payment to Henrietta Wood. Photograph by author.

EPILOGUE

After finally winning her lawsuit against Zebulon Ward, Henrietta Wood moved to Chicago with her son. In June 1880, a US Census taker found them both living on Fourth Avenue, lodging in the home of a black cook and his family.[1]

Chicago was still emerging from the Great Fire of 1871 and the national railroad strikes of 1877. Already, though, it was attracting many African American migrants who were looking for better lives. Henrietta took in laundry while Arthur, then in his twenties, found various jobs working as a janitor and a waiter, including on Michigan Avenue at the Gardner House hotel. He later said he had served prominent Chicago men such as Joseph Medill, the newspaperman and former mayor, as well as George Pullman, who was just starting to manufacture and market his luxury sleeping cars for trains.[2]

Pullman staffed each of those cars with a black attendant, and Arthur Simms took one of those jobs, too, as did thousands of other African American men over the next few decades. The reporter who interviewed Simms for the *Chicago Tribune* in 1948 wrote that Pullman hired Simms to work on "de luxe" trains running from Chicago to Philadelphia and New York. The Census of 1880 also noted his occupation as "Porter on RR," though city directories in later years still sometimes had him listed as a janitor or waiter.[3]

Yet Simms aspired to something more secure than service jobs, especially once he had a family of his own to support. In 1883, he returned to Cincinnati and married his longtime sweetheart, Caroline Person. He then brought his bride back with him to Chicago, where his mother remained, and in 1884, Simms's wife gave birth to a son they named Arthur H. Simms Jr.[4]

By then, Arthur Sr. had surely noticed, with dismay, that employers often preferred former slaves for jobs like his. Pullman expected the porters he hired to perform the role of an obsequious "negro," indulging white riders' nostalgia for slavery, and Simms had a different idea of who he was and who he could be. A friend from his days at the Gardner House told him that he should consider studying the law. So in 1887, he enrolled as a student at Chicago's Union College of Law, beginning his pursuit of the two-year degree he needed to become an attorney.[5]

How he paid for that schooling is not specifically recorded, but a clue can be found in a purchase he made on July 24, 1885. On that day, two years before he entered Union College, Simms managed to buy a house at 5759 South State Street. The house was south of downtown Chicago and just west of Washington Park, and available records show that he paid $1,150 outright for the deed.[6]

It is possible that Simms had saved that much money from his previous ten years of railroad and restaurant work—possible, but implausible. Very few wage-earning families in Chicago at the time could afford to purchase homes without a loan from a friend or family member. The number of black homeowners was especially small—amounting to about 1 or 2 percent of the people in a community that made up only 1 or 2 percent of the city's whole population. Arthur Simms must have turned to someone with enough capital to help him buy the real estate and begin his education—someone such as his mother, Henrietta.[7]

Wood had come to Chicago with the damages won from her suit against Ward, though not with the whole amount. Late in 1879, one of her lawyers sued to recover some legal fees, winning $400. Even so, she still had a substantial amount left from the $2,500 award. Her long determination to get back to Ohio with her son by her side makes it hard to believe she would not have given Arthur what he needed to change his work, and to buy a home that she and his family could share.[8]

It seems more than possible that his mother's story also played a greater role in his interest in the law than his interview with the *Chicago*

Tribune let on. "He mightily believes in the power and insight of judges," Dennis Murray would report of Simms in 1948—a belief possibly seeded, though the *Tribune* did not say it, by the rulings of Phillip Swing and John Baxter in his mother's suit for restitution in the 1870s. Her case had taught him what the law could do—and may have made it possible for him to do law.[9]

Indeed, the home Simms purchased in 1885 proved to be a fruitful asset, particularly as a means of acquiring cash. Using his equity in the house, he borrowed $800 in 1888, midway through his legal studies. It was the first of several mortgages Simms would take out and pay off before the century turned, taking advantage of rising property values. Simms eventually sold his property on State Street in 1909 for $6,500. By then, his investments had paid off with further real estate purchases, some of which he made in advance of the World's Columbian Exposition of 1893, which brought huge crowds to Chicago and boosted real estate prices.[10]

He had also begun a long and successful legal career. In 1889, Simms became one of the first African American graduates of Union College of Law, which was soon thereafter absorbed by Northwestern University. He took a temporary job as a clerk at the Harrison Street Police Court, an unfavorable post but necessary to complete his legal training. By 1909, the year he moved to 4917 South Dearborn Street, he had established a thriving legal practice. Simms buttered his bread with the cases of a working people's lawyer. Divorces were a staple, but his own marriage to Caroline lasted until her untimely death in 1929. She was survived by two of the four children she had borne—Arthur Jr. and a girl named Neata. Arthur Sr. never married again.[11]

In short, by moving to Chicago and then buying a house, Simms had been able to achieve a great deal. As a lawyer, he also threw himself into race-conscious causes. He joined mercantile associations (serving as secretary in one and president of another) that preached the benefits of black-run businesses and of tapping the growing purchasing power of some black consumers. In 1905, he spoke about the topic at one of the literary societies that frequently met at black churches in the city, titling his lecture with one word: "Progress." That same year, Simms also took part in a debate at another literary society, on the question "Which had the hardest struggle, man or woman?" Simms and a debating partner took the "woman" side and won.[12]

As for his mother, her struggle had ended differently than she probably could have imagined in the laundry at Brandon Hall, or on the land that lay on the Brazos River in Robertson County, or even in the home of William and Jane Cirode in New Orleans. Henrietta had survived slavery and seen her grandchildren born in freedom. She was still alive in 1912 when her granddaughter, Neata, got married in the home where the Simms family lived on Dearborn Street. When Wood died later that year, at the same address, her son paid for a notice to be printed in the *Chicago Defender*, the voice of the city's growing African-American community. Arthur buried his ninety-two or ninety-four-year-old mother—she could never be sure which—in a grave in Lincoln Cemetery on the South Side.[13]

Arthur Simms would live in Chicago for four decades more, practicing law and presiding over a large clan that included grandchildren and great-grandchildren, one of whom remembered him as a "taciturn" man who "radiated gravitas." His descendants included a grandson trained as a Tuskegee airman during World War II, a jazz musician well known in postwar Chicago, and a host of African-American professionals, including a librarian, a doctor, and a great-granddaughter who grew up attending Bud Billiken parades, practically "lived in the library" where her mother worked, graduated from the University of Chicago, and died in 2018, after a long career in computers.[14]

That great-granddaughter was also born in time to know Simms, who died at age ninety-five and was memorialized in *Jet* magazine as the "nation's oldest practicing Negro lawyer." His life ended in 1951, almost a century after his mother had been reenslaved. By then, however, her suit had been long forgotten by almost everyone except, perhaps, Arthur Simms himself. The case file remained folded up in a box of court records. Those records were moved to Chicago in 1953. And there the file likely stayed untouched, collecting layers of dust in the archive where it was stored, for more than sixty years, until a visit to that archive by the twenty-first-century historian who has been telling this story to you.[15]

* * *

It was a warm September day in 2015 when I arrived in Chicago to look for the original case file for *Wood v. Ward*, which I believed would be housed in the regional branch of the National Archives and Records Administration there. In the reading room, I soon found court order books that mentioned the major dates and turning points in the case. Unfortunately, the case file itself seemed to be lost. I filled in a slip with the case number, 1431, and the box where I thought it resided. But several archivists returned from the stacks empty-handed.

"It's not looking good," one said.

The day before, I had driven from Cincinnati just to find the file. I fairly begged the archivists to look one more time. There was nothing to do except to wait as they searched.

At the time I did not yet know that Wood had ever lived in Chicago or that she was buried there, only a few miles from where I sat. Nor did I know anything substantial about her son. I was still in the early days of my research on Wood, which had started in the fall of 2014 when I learned about her interview with the *Ripley Bee* and then found a transcript of Judge Baxter's decision online. I had not yet heard of Lafcadio Hearn or his interview with Wood. I had not yet visited Natchez or seen Brandon Hall, which is now a bed and breakfast and boutique wedding venue. I was still some years away from the sorts of empathy and closeness that biographers sometimes come to feel about the people they study. Back then, Henrietta Wood was never Henrietta in my mind, and I was still wrestling with the sorts of questions that come at the beginning of a research project. What about her case was so compelling? Were there enough sources to do her story justice?[16]

The first question was easier to answer than the second. At the time, Americans had just finished observing the sesquicentennial of the Civil War, and the anniversary coincided with ongoing debates over how to interpret the end of the war and emancipation. One side sees triumph, describing the nationalization of freedom that came with the Thirteenth Amendment as a revolutionary victory won by the Republican Party, the abolitionists, and the African Americans who struggled to win freedom and citizenship for themselves. Others stress how much the war and emancipation left undone, highlighting the continuities between slavery and what came after. Thousands of enslaved people were not even immediately freed by the war, and not all were given the full rights of citizens—least of all black women. Those who were freed had to survive violence, displacement, and disease.[17]

After freedom, moreover, white supremacy took new forms that seemed like slavery in all but name. Even the Thirteenth Amendment that abolished slavery made an exception for involuntary servitude imposed as punishment for crime. Southern states took full advantage of that loophole by crowding their prisons with black prisoners. Many then leased the convicts to private contractors such as Zebulon Ward, often to do the same sorts of work they had done as slaves. African Americans continued to struggle in the generations after against white terrorism, lynchings, poverty, disfranchisement, Jim Crow segregation, and the "new Jim Crow" of mass incarceration.[18]

In view of all this, by 2015 many were beginning to ask whether "freedom" should still be seen as the landmark achievement of the Civil War and an organizing theme of African-American history, or whether the war was part of a larger struggle for something more than freedom—for national belonging; or bodily integrity; or citizenship; or justice; or, to use a word that encompasses more than one of these things, reparations. I had been drawn to Wood's story in the first place because it seemed to bring many of these questions into better focus through the lens of one woman's life.[19]

By 2015, talk of reparations for slavery in the United States had also gained increasing public attention. Since 2000, there had been unsuccessful class action lawsuits filed against corporations with ties to slavery, renewed debates about a national apology for slavery, renewed struggles over the display of Confederate symbols in public spaces, and new investigations into the historic investments of universities and other institutions in slavery. One of the latest entries in debates over reparations had appeared only a year before I arrived in Chicago, when the writer Ta-Nehisi Coates published an award-winning magazine article, "The Case for Reparations." After surveying what he called the "plunder" of black men and women under slavery and Jim Crow, Coates highlighted the continued "quiet plunder" of their descendants through twentieth-century housing discrimination. And he pointed particularly to Chicago, where federally approved "redlining" in the mid-twentieth century had weakened the ability of black homeowners to build heritable wealth.[20]

For me, it was impossible to learn about Henrietta Wood without thinking of the recent debates about reparations, even if what I knew of her case so far suggested a range of possible conclusions. On the one hand, her experience could be read as a cautionary tale about the limited ability of a lawsuit to redress the harms of slavery and white supremacy in American history. Absent an honest acknowledgment of slavery's evils and a full reckoning with its consequences, individual payments such as the one that she received seemed unlikely to result in the things that many advocates for reparations most desire: apology, respect, recognition, truth-telling, and truth-hearing. I already knew that while Zebulon Ward admitted, in 1887, to having written a check to Wood, he also laughed her off with his friends as the "the last negro to be paid for," belittling her suit as a transactional exchange, a cheap payoff to make her finally go away. He never admitted fault. He never said her name.[21]

Concerns about a similar outcome may be why many twenty-first-century advocates of reparations question the wisdom of pursuing redress for slavery through the courts. On the other hand, what I knew of Wood's story did address a popular argument often made by opponents of reparations in any form: that because slavery was in the distant past, it would be too difficult to determine who should pay restitution, how much it should be, and who should receive it. The time for reparations, according to this argument, was *back then*, when the wounds of slavery were fresh and perpetrators were living, not *now*, more than a century and a half later.[22]

Whatever the merits of this argument on legal or practical grounds, it encourages a historical assumption that I already knew to be flawed: that it would have been easier to win or enact reparations in an earlier era. Wood sued Ward for restitution decades before 1916, the date of the failed "cotton tax" lawsuit that is often cited as the first case of reparations litigation. She sued before Callie House rallied a movement of ex-slaves that lobbied for pensions in the 1890s. She sued before the 1886 speech of Ohio state legislator Benjamin William Arnett, who called for an "indemnity" to be paid to former slaves as "a settlement for the years of unpaid labor in the South." She began her suit as early as she possibly could have, during the small window of opportunity created by Reconstruction. And even then she had encountered a host of legal, practical, and political obstacles—any one of which could easily have derailed her whole case. In the end, she received only a fraction of the damages she claimed.[23]

It was difficult to imagine *when* most former slaves could have advanced cases for restitution, given all that it seemed to have cost Henrietta Wood to make Ward pay anything at all. Even so, I was drawn to her story partly because it was so rare and so early. It seemed to offer a case study of the differences that even a small amount of money might have made to the material prospects of a formerly enslaved woman and her family. On that September day at the archives, however, I was not yet even sure whether Wood had ever received the money she won. That was one reason why I was so anxious to find the file that appeared to be lost.

As I waited for the archivists to return from their search for the missing file, I knew quite a bit more about Zebulon Ward. I knew that he had taken over the Arkansas penitentiary in 1873, and I knew that he had died a very wealthy man, partly because of that prison lease. The white Southerners who took over the state after Reconstruction had passed harsh new sentencing laws for petty crimes and used them as dragnets for freedpeople. By 1880, the prisoners under Ward's control numbered six hundred, most of them black men, and hundreds were put to work growing cotton for him under the watch of armed guards.[24]

Ward relied on violence to make those prisoners work, as he did in both of the prisons he had run before. In 1885, not long after the end of Ward's lease, George Washington Cable published an exposé on prisons in the South arguing that black people there were "freed—not free," and he named Arkansas as an example of the convict lease system "at its worst." Mortality rates for convicts were staggering, he said, and amounted to "brutal slavery." Five years later, Albion Tourgée, a Northern reformer, examined recent public penitentiary reports from Arkansas and found evidence of black prisoners who had been shot, hung, and whipped to death while leased to a coal mine. Tourgée noted pointedly that Zeb Ward had resisted even making such public reports when he served as a lessee. In 1882, in response to a request for information from Cable, Ward replied in a letter that the "business of the prison is my private business."[25]

The brutality of Ward's regime was already notorious in 1875, when the state launched an investigation into allegations of mismanagement. It found extensive evidence of "unusual and unwarranted whipping" since Ward had taken over, along with other abuses. Ward also faced criticism in Arkansas from white laborers who resented the fact that convict labor forced their own wages down. Nonetheless, he held the lease until 1883. Seeking to cut costs, the state gave Ward control of the prison and responsibility for the prisoners without his having to pay anything in return. Then, when the state approved an expansion of the penitentiary's buildings to deal with its exploding population, Ward won the construction contract on the strength of his inherent advantage: the ability to use forced labor for the work. Political enemies suspected him of securing such favorable deals by entertaining legislators at boozy parties in his Little Rock mansion, using his well-known charm as a raconteur to line his own pockets.[26]

No class of people had a more clear-eyed view of the man than black Arkansans. In 1880, when Ulysses S. Grant visited Little Rock, Ward—whom many thought resembled the former president—offered to stand in a receiving line to greet a long line of Grant's black admirers, supposedly to give the general a rest from shaking hands. It was not long, though, before a black man "drew back" when he recognized Ward—or so the story went. The possibly apocryphal incident lived on in numerous retellings by white humorists who often rendered the words of the man who discovered Ward's ruse in racist dialect. "Uch oh!" the man was supposed to have said, in one popular version. "Git back you fool niggers. Dis ain' no Gen'l Grant. Dis is ole Zeb Ward an' he gwine

march you all right straight inter de pennytenchy." While contemporary white readers had a laugh at the expense of the caricatured "negro,"
few stopped to consider a more serious moral of the story: that white
Southerners like Ward *were* increasingly taking the place of men like
Grant after Reconstruction.[27]

Instead, in his later years Zeb Ward was reborn in the national press
as a harmless, walking stereotype: that of the genial Kentucky colonel
who liked to sip mint juleps and talk about horses. He was "a splendid
specimen of a vanishing type, the country-bred American horseman,"
as one paper put it, just a few weeks before he told his distorted version
of Wood's story at the St. James Hotel in Manhattan. Two years later,
the *Cincinnati Enquirer* reported, of a recent horse race in the city, that
the "typical Southerner, middle-aged, with low-crowned, wide-brimmed,
soft white hat, who has attracted so much attention at the quarter-stretch,
is Zeb Ward, a wealthy Arkansas planter and enthusiastic admirer of
thorough-breds." His connection to the lawsuit that Wood had won ten
years before was not mentioned at all.[28]

Meanwhile, back in Little Rock, Ward had become a celebrated representative of the New South. "No state in the Union has a better citizen than Zeb Ward," effused the *Arkansas Gazette*, and the *Memphis
Ledger* agreed: a model of "energy, good spirits and go-aheadativeness,
he is a splendid type of the American citizen and example for young
men." Using his skills as a promoter and a businessman, Ward had facilitated the construction of new railroads using convict labor. He
helped pay for paving stones for the capital. His greatest civic achievement would be his construction, in 1887, of huge, cement-lined water
reservoirs outside of Little Rock, providing the city with its first modern
waterworks.[29]

Even in his new business ventures, Ward continued to rely on prison
and "negro" labor. As the penitentiary lessee, he could promise railroad
companies the use of cheap convicts, and he took out subleases to use
inmate labor even after his prison lease ended. In 1886, a Little Rock
newspaper reported on a small strike for better wages by "some colored
laborers employed by Col. Zeb Ward on a ditch" for his waterworks.

Ward ended it quickly by dismissing the strikers and replacing them with convicts, whom he also leased to work the large cotton plantations he owned near Morrilton.[30]

In earlier years, Ward had even conspired with white labor recruiters hired by railroad companies to go to black laborers in one part of the South and falsely promise them better wages in another part, where the railroad could transport them. One notorious recruiter, named Peg Leg Williams, brought "250 negro laborers" to Ward's plantation in Morrilton in 1884. When a South Carolina newspaper took notice of an exodus of black laborers in its county, it discovered that Ward, "the largest planter in Arkansas, and by report the wealthiest man in that State, is the chief engineer of this negro emigration."[31]

Ward was still producing cotton when he died in 1894, leaving his heirs an estate worth some $600,000. In today's terms he was a multimillionaire, and his legacy would live on in the prison labor systems he had helped to pioneer. Though convict leasing eventually grew unpopular enough with white Southerners to spell its end, Ward's spirit haunted prisons and prison farms such as Parchman in Mississippi, Angola Prison in Louisiana, and the Imperial Prison Farm in Sugar Land, Texas. In all the states where Henrietta Wood had lived as a slave, state governments and former Confederates used Jim Crow laws and incarceration to maintain white supremacy.[32]

Hoping to escape those conditions, thousands of black Southerners eventually did what Henrietta and Arthur had done: they moved to Chicago. The so-called Great Migration brought waves of black migrants to northern cities at the dawn of the twentieth century. They came fleeing lynching, disfranchisement, debt peonage—pursuing a taste of liberty, wherever it might be found. But Chicago turned out to be a troubled land of promise. In 1919, a bloody race riot enveloped the city, stretching into the Washington Park neighborhood where Simms lived. When the dust settled, twenty-three black Chicagoans had been killed by white rioters, while more than three hundred had been injured. Though most of the violence was provoked by white mobs and fueled by the police, media reports cast the riot as alleged proof of rampant black criminality.[33]

The riot came close to Arthur Simms's own door, and the lawyer played a small role in the aftermath. He helped to successfully defend four African Americans, including a woman named Emma Jackson, who were charged in the death of a white man named Harold Brignadello. Simms and two cocounsels argued that the defendants had fired in self-defense at a mob surrounding their house, and the jury took little more than an hour to acquit them of the charges. After the riots, though, black Chicagoans continued to be stigmatized as criminals and singled out for policing; Simms increasingly found himself taking up the task of defending young black men and women caught up, as the *Chicago Defender* put it, "In the Grip of the Law."[34]

The riot also accelerated the transition of the once multiethnic neighborhoods where he and his family members lived into a predominantly black, poorer area of the city. Simms moved into a house on Wabash Avenue with his son-in-law, who had purchased the place in 1921 for approximately $1,850. Many black newcomers to Chicago, however, were increasingly pushed into ghettos on the South Side and would find homeownership to be an impossible dream. After the Great Depression, the Home Owners Loan Corporation—a product of Franklin Roosevelt's New Deal—drew up maps for use in determining where federally approved mortgages would be granted. "Hazardous" areas for lenders were colored in red and were usually those with the densest concentrations of black residents. The neighborhood where Simms and his son-in-law had owned property was one of those marked as red on the maps and described by surveyors as "a blighted area, 100 percent negro." "Washington Park is already doomed," warned the white appraisers who made the redlined maps. The park, they said, had been "almost completely monopolized by the colored race."[35]

Such descriptions facilitated the rise of predatory lending practices that prevented black citizens from acquiring real estate and widened the racial wealth gap in the twentieth century, even in the northern cities where the descendants of former slaves had fled. The Natchez-born writer Richard Wright, grandson of a soldier in the US Colored Troops, would use the Washington Park streets that Simms knew well as the setting for his 1940 novel *Native Son*, a searing indictment of the strategies of containment that white Americans still used to keep black people in place. And in 1966, Martin Luther King Jr. would come to Chicago as part of his campaign against housing discrimination, only to be pelted by stones. Invoking the "fierce urgency of now," King told his audiences Americans would never "make real the promises of democracy" until meaningful civil rights were coupled with equal economic opportunity for all. He also urged black Americans not to wait for whites to act, pointing for inspiration to "our great heritage" of struggle. History showed that "freedom is never voluntarily granted by the oppressor," King famously thundered. "It must be demanded by the oppressed."[36]

Few stories better illustrated King's point than the one I had come to Chicago to find in 2015, only to be stopped, it seemed, by a missing file. The archivists at the reading room made several more attempts to locate Case 1431. Eventually, though, they turned to the director of the branch, Douglas Bicknese, who told me he would try again, one last time. He did not sound optimistic.[37]

Finally, Bicknese returned from the stacks with his hands coated in dust and a cautious smile on his face. At some point long ago, perhaps even in the nineteenth century, Wood's case had been misfiled in the records of the federal *District* Court in Ohio. Bicknese had looked in those long undisturbed boxes and caught a glimpse of the names Wood and Ward. He ran a vacuum cleaner over the soiled files, clearing away decades of dust and flakes of brittle paper. The name "Henrietta" materialized before our eyes.

The case file that Bicknese found was still incomplete. A small note inside said that depositions were stored separately in the "South Closet, East Side, 2nd row," and those have never been found. Yet the file bulged with new clues about Wood's story. Inside, for instance, was her first petition to the Superior Court. At the bottom of several pleadings, a small "X" marked the spots where she had attested her claims. The file also divulged a crucial fact that her interview with the *Bee* did not: Ward had eventually passed over those checks.[38]

Excited by these discoveries, I told the director a little about Wood's long struggle. I told him what I already knew and what I still hoped to learn. I spoke about what her case might show about slavery, freedom, reparations—and the differences they made or did not make for her and for others. When I finished, his question for me was brief, and proved harder than it seemed.

"Did she win?"

ACKNOWLEDGMENTS

The writing of this book was supported by a Public Scholar grant from the National Endowment for the Humanities. I thank the staff of the NEH and the anonymous reviewers of my proposal for helpful feedback early on. I am also grateful for the support I received from the Humanities Research Center; Dean Nicholas Shumway and Dean Kathleen Canning in the School of Humanities at Rice University; my department chairs Alida Metcalf and Carl Caldwell; and Provost Marie Lynn Miranda, who supported a faculty writing retreat, led by Louma Ghandour, Tracy Volz, and Jennifer Wilson, where the proposal for the book took shape. Over the years I have been at Rice, generous funding from the Mosle family made possible the many research trips and purchases of materials that were essential to my search for the story of Henrietta Wood.

That search never would have begun were it not for Richard Blackett, who first shared with me Wood's interview in the *Ripley Bee* and then watched in mild bemusement as I went down a rabbit hole looking for more. His encouragement and sustained support for the project over the years have been just as crucial as that first tip. Likewise, the support I received from Ta-Nehisi Coates meant more than I can adequately convey.

I have been joined on the search by talented undergraduate and graduate students at Rice who served as research assistants or pointed me to sources. I especially thank Lucy Codron, Blake Earle, Ashley Evelyn, Clair Hopper, William D. Jones, Mikayla Knutson, Maria Montalvo, Christina Regelski, Ryan Shaver, Wes Skidmore, and Edward Valentin.

Archivists in nine states helped me track down documents and cheerfully answered follow-up questions. In particular, I thank Douglas

Bicknese, Stephanie Hillyard, Jeremy Farmer, and Lorraine Bates at the Chicago branch of the National Archives; Walter Bowman, Trace Kirkwood, and Jennifer Patterson at the Kentucky Department of Libraries and Archives; Christina Bryant of the New Orleans Public Library; Hillary Delaney of the Boone County Public Library in Kentucky; Jack Dempsey of the Hamilton County Genealogical Society; Chelsea Farron of the Historical Collections Department at Baker Library, Harvard Business School; Helen Hanowsky at the Newberry Library; Jim Holmberg of the Filson Historical Society; M'Lissa Kesterman of the Cincinnati History Library and Archives; Kevin Leonard of the Northwestern University Archives; Janet McGill of the Dearborn County Historical Society in Indiana; Mimi Miller of the Historic Natchez Foundation; Jennifer Navarre of the Historic New Orleans Collection; Sally Reeves of the New Orleans Notarial Archives; Cathy Schenck of the Keeneland Library in Versailles, Kentucky; Michael Vetman of the Indiana State Archives; Elizabeth Freeman of the Arkansas State Archives; De'Niecechsi Layton of the Mississippi Department of Archives and History; and the staffs of the Kentucky Historical Society, the Cook County Recorder's Office in Chicago, the University of Kentucky Archives, the Ohio History Connection, and the Rice University Interlibrary Loan Office. Thanks also to Mike Calcote and Ron Garber for the tour of Brandon Hall.

I first presented my preliminary research in 2015 at a conference in Seattle honoring my late and greatly missed colleague Stephanie Camp. I often wished I could have talked with her about this book as I was writing it; I hope that she would be pleased with the result. I am grateful to the organizers, Ed Baptist and Barbara Krauthammer, for inviting me to participate and for commenting on my paper, and to my fellow conference presenters and attendees from whom I learned so much at the very start of this project, especially Luther Adams, Celso Castilho, Sharla Fett, Aisha Finch, Kali Gross, Vanessa Holden, Jessica Marie Johnson, Robin D. G. Kelley, Rafael Marquese, Jennifer Morgan, Sowande' Mustakeem, Deirdre Cooper Owens, Elizabeth Stordeur Pryor, Chandan Reddy, and Stephanie Smallwood. Luther Adams and Liz Pryor got me thinking in new ways about the larger implications of the question I often heard from people when I started telling them about Wood's case: "Did she win?"

Numerous people helped me by answering queries, offering encouragement, or sharing research of their own. I am particularly grateful to Pat Dale, Gerard Rickey, and Susan vonKersburg for their help and their interest in my work. Thanks also to Justin Behrend, Daina Ramey Berry, Tony Curtis, Erica Armstrong Dunbar, Kellen Funk, Robert Gudmestad, Stan Harrold, Tera Hunter, Martha Jones, the late Tony Kaye, Debian Marty, Katherine Mooney, Lou Moore, Sue Peabody, Giuliana Perrone, Christopher Phillips, Stacey Robertson, Adam Rothman, Beryl Satter, and Kim Welch. I owe a great debt, as well, to the colleagues and friends who read drafts of the manuscript, either in whole or in part, and offered valuable feedback: Aaron Astor, Richard Blackett, Carl Caldwell, Nathan Citino, John Crum, Daniel Dominguez, Greg Downs, Caitlin Fitz, Elaine Frantz, Craig Friend, Randal Hall, Scott Heerman, Kim Jones, Jennifer Lackey, Ken Liddle, Maria Montalvo, James Myers, Caitlin Rosenthal, Jim Sidbury, Kidada Williams, Diane Wolfthal, and Fay Yarbrough. Thanks also to Emily Conroy-Krutz and Jessica Lepler for organizing the inaugural Second Book Workshop at SHEAR, and to Bronwen Everill, Sean Harvey, Matt Mason, and Gautham Rao for commenting on an early piece of the manuscript presented there. Of course, any errors of fact or interpretation remain my responsibility alone.

I consider it a great honor to have had the Strothman Agency in my corner from the beginning. In addition to helping me develop the proposal for the book, Wendy Strothman suggested the book's title and, with her colleague Lauren MacLeod, guided me through the publication process. At Oxford University Press, my editor, Tim Bent, believed in the promise of the proposal and improved the book immeasurably with his suggestions for revision. My thanks to him, Joellyn Ausanka, and Mariah White for shepherding the manuscript along, and also to Jean Aroom and Naomi Hausman at Rice University for producing the maps.

From start to finish, this book was made while I was living at Duncan College, and I enjoyed talking about my findings and trying out my ideas in conversations with "Duncaroos." Questions, comments, and encouragement from these outstanding Rice University students had a greater impact on the book than they may realize. I am especially thankful to the group of students who read a partial draft of the manuscript and shared their thoughts with me: Lizzie Bjork, Megan Gordon, Aanu-Oluwa Jibodu, Victoria Johnson, Mikayla Knutson, Ridge Liu, Areli Navarro, Jaewoo Park, Brianna Satow, Erika Schumacher, and Erik Wu. My fellow "A-Team" members at Duncan also provided camaraderie and support throughout; thanks to Vicki Woods, Jenifer Bratter and Noe Perez, Bojan Szumanski and Maggie Pamula, Rich and Lauren Spain, and Courtney Stefancyk and Myron Clemence.

As always, friends and family members provided support throughout the research and writing. Special thanks to Jacob Benjamin and Shannon Johnson for their hospitality and interest in the book when I visited Oakland, as well as to Margala and Kelly Woods during my trip to Sacramento. Robert Icsezen, David Pybus, and Brent Spivey answered questions about law, and I enjoyed sharing my latest finds with James Denham, Steve Sargent, and Michael Tucker over coffee at Fioza. Cactus Music (thanks, Michael Bell) and Brazos Bookstore provided respite, community, and incentives to keep on writing. My parents, in-laws, siblings, and Southwest Central family cheered me on. Above all, I am grateful to Ellery and Carter for the ways they have graced my life with joy, and to Brandy, the love of my life.

The greatest privilege of writing this book was the chance to meet David Blackman and Winona Adkins, descendants of Henrietta Wood. Although I was introduced to David in the book's late stages, he graciously read the manuscript and provided me with two extraordinary documents that I had not yet seen—Wood's 1866 contract with Gerard Brandon, and Lucinda Tousey's 1870 letter to Wood—as well as several beautiful photographs of his ancestors. I am deeply thankful, too, for my conversations and correspondence with the late Winona Adkins and her husband, Bill Spight. My great regret is that the manuscript was not completed in time for Winona to see the whole thing, but her sense of humor, her hospitality, and her memories of her family and her great-grandfather Arthur Simms will remain with me forever. This book is gratefully dedicated to her.

APPENDIX: AN ESSAY ON SOURCES

Picture again a carriage, with all of its curtains drawn, as it rattles through Cincinnati with Henrietta Wood inside. You will form a fitting image of the challenges involved in reconstructing an enslaved woman's life. Slavery concealed many of the things that historians most want to know about enslaved people: their experiences, their feelings, their family histories, in many cases even the names they preferred. Nineteenth-century records about black women in particular faced an uphill battle for survival in the archives. Glimpsing their stories now requires peering through and around a multitude of blinds.[1]

Slaveholders themselves are largely responsible for those blinds. Recent scholars have emphasized that the archive of slavery we have is itself an artifact of slaveholders' power and violence in the past. That is, the seeming silence or invisibility of enslaved people in archival records tells us a great deal about how slavery worked. Denying a past to enslaved people was not incidental to slavery, but essential to the whole system of dispossession and domination. It was and remains a pillar of white supremacy, too.[2]

Former slaves understood this reality from the beginning. Wood's own interviews with Lafcadio Hearn and the *Ripley Bee* frequently called attention to the precariousness of documents about her life and connected it to her own vulnerability. She knew instinctively how the burning of the Hamilton County courthouse endangered her and evidently talked with others about what might have happened to the "big book" containing records of freedom. And she knew that records about enslaved people were subject not only to the dangers faced by all written records—decay, misplacement, and natural disaster—but also to the deliberate efforts of slaveholders to silence black women.

In her interviews, Wood bore witness to many of those efforts to silence her: the theft of her freedom papers, the orders not to speak, the disappearance of family members by sale. Reflection on these experiences contributed to her trenchant observations about slavery and about the kind of freedom that could only be tasted, depending as it did on papers that could be stolen from a trunk. Recall that in one description of a courtroom experience, Wood remembered that "I just sat there like a stick and couldn't say nothing," a statement that went to the heart of slaveholders' power over the archive. Meanwhile, her efforts to preserve her own memories and the few documents she did possess also testify to a different kind of fragmentary archive built by the enslaved themselves, one in which even bodily scars might serve as records of the past. Think of the disfiguration on her brother Joshua's chin.[3]

In the end, connecting the dots among the many archives of slavery—some kept by enslavers, others kept by the enslaved—is not always possible. During the course of my research for this book, I sometimes came across potentially relevant sources that I decided not to include in the main text because I could not identify the people in them with confidence. Three examples illustrate the kinds of dilemmas that historians often confront.

Example one: While Zebulon Ward was serving as keeper of the Kentucky penitentiary, Franklin County briefly maintained a state-required register that combined the births of free and enslaved children in the same book. I studied the register with interest, hoping I might learn whether it contained any evidence that Henrietta gave birth to her son, Arthur, or another child while still in Kentucky. (Recall that Arthur Simms placed the date of his birth in 1856 in Mississippi; that date is the most likely one, but chapter 16 discusses some of the reasons Wood might have chosen to tell him that his birth occurred at a different time than it actually did.)

Along the top of the register's pages, available in digitized form on Ancestry.com, are the preprinted column headings one would expect in such a volume: "Name," "Sex," "Date of Birth," "Maiden Name of

Mother." But the column for paternity was headed with an ambiguous yet revealing label: "Name of Father or Owner of Child." In one birth recorded in 1856, a boy named George appeared with "Zeb Ward" in that column. Only the word "Slave" appeared in the column for his mother, just to the left of the column that recorded "Color of Child"— white, mulatto, or black.[4]

In George's case, a "W" for "white" was at some point crossed out and replaced with "B." Other corrections on the same page suggest that the original marking of the child as "white" was a clerical error. Yet the document illustrates what the marking of a child as "black" entailed: no mother's name was recorded, and the precise relationship of the father/owner to the child was left unclear. Clarity did not matter in the eyes of the law—as long as the mother of the child was one of Ward's slaves, Ward would be the owner even if he were the father, too. The register is an example of how the laws of slavery governing the reproduction of slaves shaped the documentary record about enslaved women and their children.[5]

A second example can be found in a document that may be the closest thing to a birth certificate Wood ever had: a minute book kept by the Bullittsburg Baptist Church, which was founded in Boone County, Kentucky, in 1794. The church stood only a few miles up the road from Touseytown, the place where Wood remembered growing up, and although there is no evidence of Touseys in the church, many white slaveholders in the area were listed as members—along with some of the people they enslaved. Like many other proslavery churches at the time, the Bullittsburg Baptists believed it their duty to evangelize and baptize the people they owned. Member John Terrill, for example, joined the church in 1809 after moving to Boone County from Virginia, and within a few years, several of his slaves had been "receiv'd for Baptism," including "Daphny," "Will," and "Bill."[6]

Daphny, Will, and Bill were only three of the more than a hundred enslaved people who were listed as members of the Bullittsburg church by May 1813, though it is difficult to know how many of those who were baptized did so only under duress. Some doubtless took some solace from a genuine Christian faith, and church minutes sometimes spoke of black members as "brothers" and "sisters." But there were still clear gradations within this spiritual family. The baptisms of slaves were recorded, for example, but minute books also still identified enslaved members as the possessions of their white owners: "John Graves's Lucy," "Fanny belonging to John Cave." In 1817, black members asked for the privilege of assembling by themselves "for the purpose of worship in the night," but they were refused by the white leadership of the church.[7]

Inclusion in the church did offer some potential benefits to black members, however. The minutes of the Bullittsburg church contain examples of enslaved black members bringing complaints of "unseemly conduct," "fornication," and adultery against themselves or members of the opposite sex, though men most often brought the charges. Such complaints show the efforts of enslaved people to win some public recognition for marital rights and relationships that were denied them under the law, which also denied them the right to sue for injuries done to each other. In one entry in the church's minutes, for example, "Bill and Will belonging to brother John Terrill" came before the congregation to confess "very unpleasant feelings toward each other" and to seek a resolution—though the source of their conflict was not recorded.[8]

Ultimately, however, the church's judicial procedures served primarily as a theater in which slaveholders could enforce their own understandings of morality—and their own preferences about who should "marry" whom. In 1826, Bill ran away to Indiana with an enslaved woman other than the one recognized by white church members as his wife. They were captured, disciplined by the church, and returned to Terrill. Twelve years before, in 1814, "John Terrill's Daphny" had been expelled from the church after being found guilty of "fornication," perhaps with "John Terrill's Sam," who was convicted of "the sin of adultery" at the same time. In 1817, "Daphny was restored to fellowship by repentance." But then, in June 1819, Terrill returned to the church with a "complaint against Dafney a black member of this church for having an eligitimate [sic] child."[9]

No name was recorded for the child born in 1819 to Dafney, sometimes spelled "Daphney" or "Daphny" in church records. The father was not named, though another complaint brought to the church the following month could have been related: a man named "Billy" (also belonging to Terrill and perhaps one of the two men mentioned elsewhere as "Bill" or "Will") accused another enslaved man named Jesse of "abuesing [sic] his wife and him self." Maybe Terrill's "Billy" considered Dafney "his wife." Maybe Dafney considered Jesse her husband or her lover. Maybe the abuse of which Billy accused Jesse was a sexual assault, or maybe Jesse attacked Dafney's character after the birth of her child.[10]

Maybe the "eligitimate" child whom Dafney was accused of having in 1819 grew up to become Henrietta, who remembered being told she was born in about 1818 or 1820.

All of those maybes must remain speculations. The woman known to us only as Terrill's Dafney was expelled from the church after the birth of her unnamed child and no longer appeared in the Bullittsburg minutes. She could have been sold by Terrill to nearby Touseytown, there to become known as Daphne Tousey, the woman whose record in the 1850 census said she was born in Virginia, Terrill's home state. The father at Touseytown whom Wood recalled as William or Bill could even have been the "Billy" mentioned in the Bullittsburg Baptist Church's minutes. He, too, could have been sold to the Touseys by John Terrill, who moved away from Boone County sometime in the late 1820s. The records that white Kentuckians chose to keep about enslaved people omitted surnames that could have helped to solve such mysteries, to identify a "Dafney" with a "Daphne," or to distinguish between "Billy" or "Bill" and "William" or "Will." While the minute book at first seemed to offer me some clues about Wood's birth, in the end it is another example of records that were ambiguous by design.[11]

A final example of such records is the diary that Gerard Brandon kept of his journey to Texas during the Civil War. As described in chapters 15 and 17 of this book, that diary contains information about enslaved people who died on the forced march west, as well as about some of the people who survived, including "Henrietta," who was mentioned by name in the journal three times. In the case of this source, unlike the case of the Bullittsburg minutes, I decided to cite two of those instances as references to Wood. Given the other evidence of Wood's proximity to the Brandon family as a laundress and cook, it seems more likely than not that Wood was the Henrietta mentioned.[12]

Still, the identification cannot be made certain, nor can the references in Brandon's text be tied definitively to the third mention of a "Henrietta" in the journal. In a list of babies born to Brandon's slaves during their sojourn in Texas, Brandon said "Henrietta's" came in October 1863.[13]

By then, given her age, Wood would have been an unlikely new mother, but a pregnancy was not impossible. And perhaps, if Wood was with child on the journey, that contributed to her wariness about riding rough wagons and mules across Louisiana. Perhaps a pregnancy even played a role when she "coaxed" Brandon to grant her what some other mothers on the trip were denied.

On the other hand, neither of Wood's interviews mentioned her giving birth to more than one child. Only one later source, the 1900 Census, said that she had borne four children, only one of whom (Arthur Simms) survived. That one record may have been made in error, but if it was not, then Wood may have wanted the enumerator to record that she had three other children, about whom nothing is known. If so, maybe each of her other children's lives had been short and their deaths traumatic for Wood, who never mentioned them to Hearn or the *Ripley Bee*. Another enslaved woman who was brought by a different enslaver to Cherokee County, Texas, during the Civil War, all the way from Mississippi, later remembered her own child with pain. "I lost my baby," she said, while on the road to Texas; the child was "buried somewhere" along the "Red River," though no record or tombstone marked the spot.[14]

These three examples are only a few of many that show the challenges involved in genealogical research about enslaved women and their children. The archives built by slaveholders were not designed to enable their stories to be told. Usually, as Saidiya Hartman writes, "the stories that exist are not about them, but rather about the violence . . . that seized hold of their lives, transformed them into commodities and corpses, and identified them with names tossed-off as insults and crass jokes," much like Ward's attempt to reduce Wood to "the last slave to be paid for in this country." Even when the curtains can be pulled back for a moment, revealing an insight into an enslaved woman's experience, the archival traces do not tell anything like the whole story. As historian Marisa Fuentes puts it, "These fleeting glimpses from a historical aperture that closes too fast make it nearly impossible to string together events into a neat narrative."[15]

Not all the curtains on the past are totally drawn, however. In the research for this book, for example, databases of digitized sources such as the ones provided by FamilySearch.org, Ancestry.com, and Newspapers.com brought countless clues about Wood's life to the surface through keyword searches for names that were fortuitously unusual, such as "Zebulon," "Cirode," and "Daphne Tousey." More digitization and improved search technology cannot overcome all obstacles to discovery, of course, since the sources they uncover were still not created to reveal much about enslaved people in the first place. (Worth noting, too, is that some of the digitization on which these sites rely was done by unpaid or underpaid inmates in twenty-first-century prisons.) But digital tools can help, especially when paired with traditional archival research and guided by sources that *do* purport to tell the story of an enslaved woman from her own perspective.[16]

In Wood's case, such sources thankfully exist in the form of the two lengthy interviews she gave in 1876 and 1879 to Lafcadio Hearn and the *Ripley Bee*. Neither one makes it possible to recover her thoughts or experiences in their entirety. But internal and external evidences offer good reasons to rely on these sources, as I have done throughout this book.

First, comparing the two interviews makes clear that they were conducted independently by the two reporters. The second interview, for example, contained incidents that were not present in the earlier one. Each was sometimes wrong about details, but they were wrong in different ways—as in their misspellings of Tousey as "Tauser" (Hearn) and "Touci" (*Bee*). As another example, in 1876, Wood identified the two men who drove her as Scott and "Frank Russ," adding that they were joined in Florence by a man named "Bolton." Her interview three years later identified Bolton and Scott as the men who drove her to Florence. That pattern suggests that instead of copying from another source, the interviewers were trying to transcribe what they heard Wood say, as when Hearn referred to Zeb Ward as "Jabez" and to Lewis Robards as "Nick Roberts."

Rather than decreasing confidence in the interviews, small discrepancies such as these indicate authenticity. In my judgment, the general accuracy of her recollections, many of which are corroborated by other sources, overshadows her interviewers' mistakes and the things she may have misremembered. Indeed, the source independence of the two interviews makes all the more amazing the close similarities between them, including some almost identical passages. Consider the ways her interviews recorded the words of the innkeeper, Williams, as Wood left Florence for Lexington on the morning after her abduction:

Hearn: "Don't you be afraid, if I can do you any good I will, and if I can't I won't do you any harm."

Ripley Bee: "I'll see you in Lexington, and if I can't do you any good, have no fears. I'll do you no harm."

While the exact words Williams spoke may well have been different from either of those versions, the passages could not have been totally untethered from Henrietta's memory. At the very least, their similarity was the product of the many times she must have recalled that conversation over the years—first, perhaps, to her lawyer George B. Kinkead, then to her mother in Pullum's jail, then to Harvey Myers, then to Hearn and the *Ripley Bee*, and doubtless to many others she met along the way.

The interviews are not unproblematic sources. First, they were conducted by other writers, one of them a white man and the other a pseudonymous writer who was probably white as well. The same was true of many sources recording the stories of former slaves—ranging from some of the autobiographical narratives published with the help of white abolitionists before the Civil War, to the interviews of former slaves conducted by employees of the Works Progress Administration

(WPA) during the Great Depression. In each case, working with such sources requires attention to how the writers' own ideas may have shaped the interview and its publication.[17]

Such editorial interventions undoubtedly shaped Wood's interviews, in ways both large and small. When Wood remembered one of her captors cursing at her the morning after her abduction, the *Ripley Bee* printed the curse as "G–d d–n you." But the *Bee* did not similarly abbreviate the many times she remembered being insulted with a racist epithet, the n-word. The small difference tells a great deal about what the writer or editor for the *Bee* found more offensive.[18]

The beliefs and sensibilities of Wood's interviewers left other imprints, too, though they are easier to discern in the case of Lafcadio Hearn. As a prolific Cincinnati reporter, he was especially known for writing macabre and gruesome stories about the seamier sides of life in the city. A typical article was the one he published at the end of 1874: a ghoulish, true crime story of a man who was murdered by being burned alive at a city tanyard. He later returned to investigate reports that the tannery was haunted, one of several articles showing a long-standing interest in ghosts. Among the other topics he explored were ones that few other reporters considered: for example, the nauseating steps by which animals were butchered, or the dizzying work of men who cleaned the steeples of Cincinnati, or the sanitation problems in the poorest parts of the city.

In one muckraking piece called "Haceldama," or "Field of Blood," Hearn described how cows were cruelly bludgeoned to death at a slaughterhouse whose floor was slick and reeking from animal entrails. Then he contrasted the scene to that in a Jewish slaughterhouse, where a kosher butcher described to Hearn the benefits of drinking blood from his more humanely slaughtered bulls. The reporter took a glass, gulped it down, and described the drink to his readers as like "the richest cream, warm, with a tart sweetness." The next month, he wrote of a factory where dead animals were boiled to make tallow, fertilizer, and soap, re-creating the scene, as usual, in stomach-turning detail.[19]

As noted in chapter 21, Hearn's coverage of "Bucktown" sometimes betrayed his signature gruesome style—as well as the prejudices that he and many white contemporaries shared about the poorest black residents of Cincinnati. He began one piece with the story of "a certain low brothel" where "a negro levee hand blew a brother roustabout's brains all over the bar," leaving the waitress to wipe them up "like so much spilt beer." He closed the piece describing an assault on a drunken white woman by "some roughs" in the neighborhood, concluding, "It is comforting to think that in ten years hence Bucktown will have ceased to exist."[20]

That coverage must be kept in mind when reading Hearn's interview with Wood, whom he described as a woman with "features rather regular for one with so large a preponderance of colored blood in her veins." Hearn's documented interest in Cincinnati's Jewish community may also explain an otherwise curious detail in "Story of a Slave." According to Hearn, when Wood spoke of Touseytown she said that the "farm was owned by Moses Tauser, who, I believe was a Jew." Having found no evidence to support this, I suspect that Wood was responding to a question from Hearn, prompted perhaps by Tousey's first name and Hearn's journalistic interests. While questioning Wood, Hearn might also have focused more than she would have on the most lurid parts of her memories, such as the description of a woman flogged by the overseer at Brandon Hall until her "skin slipped and cracked apart and fell off as though she had been scalded."[21]

On the other hand, Wood shared similar memories about Mississippi when she later spoke to the reporter from the *Ripley Bee*. Scenes like the flogging at Brandon Hall were also attested by many other autobiographical narratives of slavery. On the whole, in fact, Hearn's style in the interview with Wood was remarkably restrained and matter-of-fact, compared to most of the other pieces he wrote about Bucktown. A man who was willing to drink warm cow's blood for his readers did not believe there was much that was "too horrible for publication," yet Wood told of some horrors that Hearn chose to withhold.[22]

Compared to other reporters at the time, Hearn also frequently challenged white prejudices about the African Americans he met. In the article describing Bucktown as a vice district, for instance, Hearn also took his readers inside a restaurant known as "Butler's," an establishment that most whites would assume to be "a den of infamy unutterable" from the outside looking in. "But this is far from being the truth," Hearn reported, inviting his readers to "take a peep" inside. In such places, his reporting argued, there were people with rich inner lives, complex communities, and fascinating stories to tell.[23]

In another "peep" inside a well-known Bucktown saloon, patronized almost exclusively by black river workers, Hearn interviewed the proprietor, "Ole Man Pickett," and then related, in detail, his former life as an enslaved Virginian who had purchased his own freedom before the Civil War and then established himself in Ohio. Another *Enquirer* profile featured a black barber and ex-slave named William Handy. In that piece, headlined "Mr. Handy's Life," Hearn dispensed entirely with his sensationalistic style and put down Handy's story of slavery "in his own words." Hearn called the story of "how an energetic colored man has got on in the world" a "remarkable" one and "thoroughly creditable" to him.[24]

Though Hearn arrived in the United States after the abolition of slavery, he may have been familiar with the antebellum abolitionist literary tradition, too. The subtitle for his article on "Ole Man Pickett," which appeared in 1875, was "Life Among the Lowly," and that was also the subtitle for Harriet Beecher Stowe's *Uncle Tom's Cabin*. The same phrase appeared in 1873 as the title for a series of articles in an Ohio newspaper written by former slaves at Thomas Jefferson's Monticello, including Madison Hemings, Jefferson's son by Sally Hemings—a woman he enslaved. Whether Hearn knew of that specific series, he must have had a passing familiarity with the literary genre of slave narratives, which appeared with some regularity in newspapers during Reconstruction.[25]

As reported earlier in this book, in 1871 Hearn also began a long-term romantic relationship with a woman of color named Alethea Foley, whom he met while lodging at a boardinghouse where she worked in the kitchen. In 1874, not long after he was brought on staff by the *Enquirer*, Hearn asked Foley to become his wife. Ohio laws banned such interracial marriages, but the couple persevered. Through Foley's friends, they found a black minister who performed the marriage rites, solemnizing a relationship that was several years old. The union did not last, but in 1875, after the marriage had already effectively ended, enemies of Hearn's iconoclastic reporting discovered and publicized the relationship.[26]

Soon after his secret life with Foley was exposed, Hearn was fired by the *Enquirer* and hired by the *Commercial*. There he would work for another two years, further honing his trademark, grotesque style. One of his first pieces for his new employer was "Pariah People," whose occasionally vicious portrayal of Bucktown may have been intended partly to distance himself from the recent scandal of his marriage.

Yet Hearn never lost his genuine interest in ex-slaves' stories. In "Levee Life," published in March 1876, he transcribed some of the "old Kentucky slave songs" that black river workers often sang along the waterfront, praising the "strange, sad sweetness" of the music. One of the "plaintive airs" Hearn most admired evoked experiences that might have been about the life of a roustabout, or about the memory of the domestic slave trade, or about both:

> I'm going away to New Orleans!
> Good-bye, my lover, good-bye!
> I'm going away to New Orleans!
> Good-bye, my lover, good-bye!
> Oh, let her go by!

Despite Hearn's own, undeniable racism, such ethnographic pieces gave his readers and later historians some of the few depictions of poor black people's urban life in the North during Reconstruction. While at the *Commercial*, Hearn also published the long narrative of a boardinghouse cook who told of whippings she had seen and ghost stories she had heard as a slave in Kentucky. The woman, though never identified, was probably Foley, and when Hearn shared her memories, he used the same format he would later use when he published "Story of a Slave"—a brief introduction followed by Foley's story, as told by her.[27]

In conclusion, Lafcadio Hearn's interview with Henrietta Wood was more like his descriptions of "Ole Man Pickett" or Foley's experiences than his caricatures of life along the Ohio levee—more like "Mr. Handy's Life" than "Pariah People." Read alongside his other work from that period, it is clear that Hearn saw something unique in Wood's tale and decided to relate her struggle with comparative respect.

Or so it seems to me, after reviewing all the evidence. In this book, I have sometimes quoted dialogue and statements in Wood's interviews as though they came directly from her memory, knowing full well that to see her through such sources is still to glimpse her through a veil. There is no way to interview her today, nor would such an exercise necessarily give a more direct access to her beliefs and experiences than we have through her interviews with Hearn and the *Ripley Bee*.

Ultimately, even with all that *can* be corroborated about Wood's story, not every scrap of dialogue or detail in her interviews can be verified somewhere else in the archive, but most archives were not built for the purpose of recording her point of view. To refuse the attempt to "imagine what cannot be verified," as Hartman writes, is to leave Wood's story where her captors wanted it: curtained and curtailed. I have tried to write of her experiences and her feelings about them in a way "that is accountable to the enslaved," in the words of historian Stephanie Smallwood. But I conclude knowing that others might find different paths through the archive and might come to different judgments about the sources I have used.[28]

That is one reason why, throughout the research for this book, I decided to make the majority of my sources and archival notes available online. Interested readers can visit http://wiki.wcaleb.rice.edu to explore the research that supported *Sweet Taste of Liberty*, and to consider alternative ways that Henrietta Wood's story might have been, or might still be, told.[29]

NOTES

PROLOGUE

1. *Indianapolis News*, December 31, 1887, 4; "The Last Slave Buyer," *Wilmington (OH) Journal*, February 1, 1888.
2. "Last Slave Buyer." For physical description, "Col. Zeb Ward," *Louisville Courier-Journal*, December 30, 1894; Helen Ward Lafferty Nisbet, *Ward* (n.p.: [Helen Ward Lafferty Nisbet], 1961), 67, Kentucky Historical Society. On resemblance to Grant, *Ottawa (IL) Free Trader*, February 9, 1889, 6; "Great Men's Doubles: Stories About Resemblances That Cause Confusion," *Bismarck (ND) Tribune*, February 15, 1889, 4; "Their Doubles: Public Men Who Are Mistaken for Other Fellows," *Cleveland Plain Dealer*, September 2, 1888, 10; "A Story of Col. Zeb Ward," *Little Rock Daily Arkansas Gazette*, October 3, 1888.
3. "Philadelphia Races," *New York Herald*, June 11, 1863; "Turf News," *Louisville Courier-Journal*, January 17, 1888, 4.
4. "Stealing Asteroid," New York Sun, February 12, 1888 ("reminiscent mood"); "Col. Zeb Ward [by] an Observant Citizen in New York World," *Louisville Courier-Journal*, December 14, 1887 ("old-school eloquence"). On Wall, see E. Berry Wall, *Neither Pest nor Puritan: The Memoirs of E. Berry Wall* (New York: Dial Press, 1940), 63–65, 77, 111; "Berry Wall Returns to His Friends: Greeted at the St. James Hotel by Some of His Club Members," *New York Tribune*, December 24, 1887, 5. On Ward's arrival at St. James, "Last Slave Buyer"; "Written on Hotel Books," *New York Evening World,* December 9, 1887, 2. On the hotel, Andrew Wiese, "St. James Hotel," in *The Encyclopedia of New York City*, 2nd edition, ed. Kenneth T. Jackson (New Haven, CT: Yale University Press, 2010), 1139; Moses King, ed., *King's Handbook of New York City* (Boston: Moses King, 1893), 148, 226, 857. On Ward as raconteur: "Col. Ward in Louisville," *Arkansas Gazette*, May 9, 1890; "Bad Day for Packing Ham: Col. Zeb Ward Perpetrates a Pun on Col. B. D. Williams," *Arkansas Gazette*, January 8, 1890; "A Stiff Game of Poker," *Rochester (NY) Democrat and Chronicle*, June 28, 1889; "Joined at Last," *Daily Arkansas Gazette*, February 26, 1881, 4.

5. *Rochester (NY) Democrat and Chronicle*, December 20, 1887, 4. I have changed "sewed" in the original to "sued" for clarity.

6. See "Last Slave Buyer"; *New Orleans Daily Picayune*, December 27, 1887, 4; *San Francisco Bulletin*, January 9, 1888; *Biloxi (MS) Herald*, January 14, 1888; *Chicago Tribune*, December 23, 1887, 4; *Cleveland Leader*, December 19, 1887, 4; *Worcester (MA) Daily Spy*, December 28, 1887, 2; *Indianapolis News*, December 31, 1887, 4; *New York Sportsman*, January 21, 1888, 63; *Wilmington (DE) Morning News*, January 27, 1888, 3; *Indiana (PA) Weekly Messenger*, February 1, 1888; "Paid for the Last Negro," *Waco (TX) Morning News*, October 25, 1888.

7. "Kidnapped and Sold into Slavery," *Ripley (OH) Bee,* February 27, 1879.

8. The lawsuit is documented in Case File 1431, US Circuit Court, Southern District of Ohio, Cincinnati, RG 21, Civil Records, Civil Case Files (New Series), National Archives at Chicago, hereafter cited as "Chicago Case File."

9. The first interview, conducted by the famous journalist Lafcadio Hearn, appeared as "Story of a Slave," *Cincinnati Commercial*, April 2, 1876, 2, hereafter cited as "LH-1876." Though "Story of a Slave" was unsigned, like most of Hearn's newspaper work, it is attributed to him by Hearn scholars based on its time of publication, comparison to his other articles, and context. The second interview, hereafter cited as "RB-1879," appears in the February 27, March 6, and March 20, 1879, issues of the *Ripley (OH) Bee*, always under the headline "Kidnapped and Sold into Slavery." The first installment of the article likely appeared in the February 20 issue, but no copy of it has been found. I thank Richard Blackett for first informing me of the *Ripley Bee* articles by email on September 24, 2014. On Ripley's Underground Railroad history, Keith P. Griffler, *Front Line of Freedom: African Americans and the Forging of the Underground Railroad in the Ohio Valley* (Lexington: University Press of Kentucky, 2004), 61–64.

10. Simon J. Bronner, ed., *Lafcadio Hearn's America: Ethnographic Sketches and Editorials* (Lexington: University Press of Kentucky, 2002), 13. See also Jonathan Cott, *Wandering Ghost: The Odyssey of Lafcadio Hearn* (New York: Alfred A. Knopf, 1991). Many of Hearn's themes continued to occupy him as a journalist in New Orleans, where he moved in 1877. See Adam Rothman, "Lafcadio Hearn in New Orleans and the Caribbean," *Atlantic Studies* 5, no. 2 (August 2008): 265–83.

11. LH-1876; "Claim Made by a Negress That She Is the Lawful Wife of Lafcadio P. Hearn," *Cincinnati Enquirer*, July 14, 1906.

12. LH-1876.

13. LH-1876; RB-1879.

14. LH-1876. For 1820 birth record, see US Census, 1910, Chicago, Ward 7, Cook County, Illinois, Sheet 12A, Family 266, NARA microfilm T624, roll 247, accessed on FamilySearch. Her son estimated her birthdate as 1818 on the full certificate of her 1912 death: "Henrietta Wood," Registered No. 30774,

downloaded from Cook County, Illinois, genealogy site, hereafter cited as "Wood Death Certificate."

15. On testimonies of slavery and racial violence in the period, see Kidada E. Williams, *They Left Great Marks on Me: African American Testimonies of Racial Violence from Emancipation to World War I* (New York: New York University Press, 2012). On the strengths and weaknesses of postbellum newspaper interviews in particular, see John W. Blassingame, ed., *Slave Testimony: Two Centuries of Letters, Speeches, Interviews, and Autobiographies* (Baton Rouge: Louisiana State University Press, 1977), lvii–lix.

16. Hearn collectors: Lafcadio Hearn, *Barbarous Barbers and Other Stories*, ed. Ichiro Nishizaki (Tokyo: Hokuseido Press, 1939), 172–85; Jon Christopher Hughes, ed., *Period of the Gruesome: Selected Cincinnati Journalism of Lafcadio Hearn* (Lanham, MD: University Press of America, 1990), 224–30, 314; Robert L. Gale, *A Lafcadio Hearn Companion* (Westport, CT: Greenwood Press, 2002), 211–14. The case received one sentence in Charles Theodore Greve, *Centennial History of Cincinnati and Representative Citizens*, vol. 1 (Chicago: Biographical Publishing Company, 1904), 884. For a few recent notices of Wood's story, see R. J. M. Blackett, *The Captive's Quest for Freedom: Fugitive Slaves, the 1850 Fugitive Slave Law, and the Politics of Slavery* (New York: Cambridge University Press, 2018), 241–42, 244; "Wood vs. Ward," *Antebellum Cincinnati: Social Intersections in the Queen City*, http://curiosity.cs.xu.edu/blogs/antebellumcincinnati/topics/wood-vs-ward/, accessed January 28, 2015; Reinette F. Jones, "Wood, Henrietta," *Notable Kentucky African Americans Database*, August 19, 2016, http://nkaa.uky.edu/nkaa/items/show/3155, accessed September 8, 2016.

17. "An Unsettled Account," *New York Times*, April 21, 1878.

18. Saidiya V. Hartman, *Scenes of Subjection: Terror, Slavery, and Self-Making in Nineteenth-Century America* (New York: Oxford University Press, 1997), 125–37; Mary Frances Berry, *My Face Is Black Is True: Callie House and the Struggle for Ex-Slave Reparations* (New York: Vintage, 2005).

19. RB-1879. The conversion of $2,500 in 1879 to more than $60,000 in real wage or real wealth value in 2017 is based on Samuel H. Williamson, "Seven Ways to Compute the Relative Value of a U.S. Dollar Amount, 1774 to present," *MeasuringWorth*, https://www.measuringworth.com/calculators/uscompare/relativevalue.php, accessed December 12, 2018.

CHAPTER ONE

1. LH-1876.
2. Ibid.
3. Boyd's husband is identified as a dentist in LH-1876. On boardinghouse work, see Wendy Gamber, *The Boardinghouse in Nineteenth-Century America* (Baltimore: Johns Hopkins University Press, 2007), 60–76. Boyd's address is

listed under "Mrs. Rebekah Boyd" in the 1853 Cincinnati City Directory, Cincinnati History Library and Archives. The events described here took place on April 10, 1853, according to Chicago Case File; in LH-1876, Wood accurately remembered that date being a Sunday.

4. In LH-1876, Wood recalled that Boyd "asked me if I wouldn't like a nice carriage ride." For recollection of Sarah Spears, the other employee: "The Kidnapping Case," *Cincinnati Enquirer*, June 8, 1853.

5. John H. White Jr., "Let Us Cross over the River: Cincinnati's Ferryboats," *Timeline: A Publication of the Ohio Historical Society* 23, no. 1 (January–March 2006): 48–51. The following Tuesday there was a blinding dust storm in the city caused by several days without rain: "River and News Items," *Cincinnati Enquirer*, April 13, 1853, 3.

6. Gilbert, the driver, is described as a "colored man" in "Kidnapping," *Cincinnati Gazette*, June 3, 1853. He is not mentioned in Wood's interviews.

7. LH-1876. Spears said she heard Boyd say there were two men in Kentucky, but Wood remembered three. Hearn mistakenly recorded Ward's name as "Jabez Ward." Willoughby Scott was a farmer and slaveholder who had lived in Harrison County. See "Willoughby Scott," US Census, 1840, Harrison County, Kentucky, NARA microfilm M704, reel 113, FamilySearch.

8. LH-1876.

9. RB-1879. LH-1876 places the room on the "fourth story of a high building."

10. LH-1876.

11. Ibid.

12. Ibid.

13. RB-1879.

14. Ibid. Wood rightly remembered the river being high: "River and News Items," *Cincinnati Enquirer*, April 12, 1853.

15. RB-1879. The *Bee* printed the curse as "G–d d–n you," which I have spelled out for clarity.

16. RB-1879; Paul Tanner, "Florence, Kentucky: The First Century, 1830–1930" (Frankfort, KY: n.p., 1993), 6, 8. In LH-1879, Wood identified the two men who drove her as Scott and "Frank Russ," adding that they were joined in Florence by a man named "Bolton." But in RB-1879, she identified Bolton and Scott as the men who drove her to Florence. For more on discrepancies such as these, see the appendix.

17. LH-1876; RB-1879.

18. RB-1879.

19. Sven Beckert, *Empire of Cotton: A Global History* (New York: Alfred A. Knopf, 2014).

20. Ira Berlin, *Generations of Captivity: A History of African-American Slaves* (Cambridge, MA: Harvard University Press, 2003), 161–230; Michael Tadman, *Speculators and Slaves: Masters, Traders, and Slaves in the Old South* (Madison: University of Wisconsin Press, 1996).

21. On formation of new communities, see Damian Alan Pargas, *Slavery and Forced Migration in the Antebellum South* (New York: Cambridge University Press, 2015), 232–41. On suicides, see Terri L. Snyder, *The Power to Die: Slavery and Suicide in British North America* (Chicago: University of Chicago Press, 2015); Thomas C. Buchanan, *Black Life on the Mississippi: Slaves, Free Blacks, and the Western Steamboat World* (Chapel Hill: University of North Carolina Press, 2004), 86–87.

22. RB-1879.

23. Wood reported the conversation in both LH-1876 (which identified him as the landlord's son) and RB-1879 (which called him the landlady's son and identified him as Williams). A Jonathan Williams appears in the 1850 and 1860 censuses, which give his birthplace as Pennsylvania, and he is listed in an 1859 business directory as the proprietor of an inn in Florence. He also appears in Boone County's 1853 tax list with a town lot, a slave, and a tavern license. Williams managed the inn that later became the Southern Hotel. See Tanner, "Florence, Kentucky," 13; 1853 Boone County Tax Rolls, Boone County Public Library (BCPL); "Jonathan Williams," US Census, 1850, Town of Florence, Boone County, Kentucky, Family 433, NARA microfilm M432, roll 192, FamilySearch; US Census, 1860, Town of Florence, Boone County, Kentucky, Family 21, NARA microfilm M653, roll 355, FamilySearch.

24. RB-1879.

25. On slavery as kidnapping, see Adam Rothman, *Beyond Freedom's Reach: A Kidnapping in the Twilight of Slavery* (Cambridge, MA.: Harvard University Press, 2015), 8–9; Edward E. Baptist, "'Stol' and Fetched Here': Enslaved Migration, Ex-Slave Narratives, and Vernacular History," *New Studies in the History of American Slavery*, ed. Baptist and Stephanie M. H. Camp (Athens: University of Georgia Press, 2006), 243–74. On slavery as the robbing of black women's wombs, see Daina Ramey Berry, *The Price for Their Pound of Flesh: The Value of the Enslaved from Womb to Grave in the Building of a Nation* (Boston: Beacon Press, 2017), 10–32.

26. RB-1879.

27. LH-1876.

CHAPTER TWO

1. LH-1876; Bridget B. Striker, ed., *Lost River Towns of Boone County* (Charleston, SC: History Press, 2010), 49–57; Theodore Cuyler Rose, *The Tousey Family in America* (Elmira, NY: Osborne Press, 1916), 108.

2. Craig Thompson Friend, "'Work & Be Rich': Economy and Culture on the Bluegrass Farm," in Craig Thompson Friend, ed., *The Buzzel About Kentuck: Settling the Promised Land* (Lexington: University Press of Kentucky, 1999), 126–51. On population growth, see Honor Sachs, *Home Rule: Households,*

Manhood, and National Expansion on the Eighteenth-Century Kentucky Frontier (New Haven, CT: Yale University Press, 2015), 71.

3. "Fire," *Indiana Palladium*, November 25, 1825, 3 (quotes). On land and settlement, see Craig Thompson Friend, *Along the Maysville Road: The Early American Republic in the Trans-Appalachian West* (Knoxville: University of Tennessee Press, 2005); Stephen Aron, *How the West Was Lost: The Transformation of Kentucky from Daniel Boone to Henry Clay* (Baltimore: Johns Hopkins University Press, 1996).

4. On slavery in early Kentucky, see Ellen Eslinger, "The Shape of Slavery on the Kentucky Frontier, 1775–1800," *The Register of the Kentucky Historical Society* 92, no. 1 (Winter 1994): 1–23; Matthew Salafia, *Slavery's Borderland: Freedom and Bondage Along the Ohio River* (Philadelphia: University of Pennsylvania Press, 2013), 72–78.

5. LH-1876. Population figures from Lowell H. Harrison and James C. Klotter, *A New History of Kentucky* (Lexington: University Press of Kentucky, 1997), 71–72, 167. For the Touseys' slaveholdings, see US Census, 1820, Boone County, Kentucky, NARA microfilm M33, roll 18, FamilySearch; US Census, 1830, Boone County, NARA microfilm M19, roll 33, accessed on Ancestry.

6. RB-1879. For William and Daphne, see Wood's death certificate.

7. Berry, *The Price for Their Pound of Flesh*, 33–41.

8. On dual sense of "belonging," to owners and to family members, see Rothman, *Beyond Freedom's Reach*, 6–7. I thank Kidada Williams for making this point to me.

9. Eslinger, "The Shape of Slavery on the Kentucky Frontier, 1775–1800"; Thomas D. Morris, *Southern Slavery and the Law, 1619–1860* (Chapel Hill: University of North Carolina Press, 1996), 43–49; William Littell, *The statute law of Kentucky: with notes, prælections, and observations on the public acts . . .*, 5 vols. (Frankfort, KY: William Hunter, 1809–1819), 2: 113–23.

10. For the Touseys' likely route to Kentucky, see Melinda Sartwell, "Pioneers from the East: The Percival Family in Boone County" (n.p, n.d.), 9-10, BCPL. On gradual emancipation, Ira Berlin, *The Long Emancipation: The Demise of Slavery in the United States* (Cambridge, MA: Harvard University Press, 2015), 67–71.

11. Patrick Rael, *Eighty-Eight Years: The Long Death of Slavery in the United States, 1777–1865* (Athens: University of Georgia Press, 2015), 126–59; Stephen Middleton, *The Black Laws in the Old Northwest: A Documentary History* (Westport, CT: Greenwood, 1993). State-by-state gradual emancipation created a patchwork of policies that often left the freedom of particular people at the mercy of owners who could move from one state to another. One of the slaves whom Zerah Tousey owned in Kentucky, a man named Thomas, was born in New York and would have been freed there on his twenty-eighth birthday had he remained. In recognition of that fact, Tousey's son Erastus did set Thomas free in 1833, though he acknowledged that in Kentucky, where no

such emancipation law existed, other heirs might still be able to claim some title to the man. See Boone County, Kentucky, Will Book B, 585–87; Boone County, Kentucky, Deed Book H, 599, available at BCPL.

12. Aron, *How the West Was Lost*, 89–95; Luke E. Harlow, *Religion, Race, and the Making of Confederate Kentucky, 1830–1880* (New York: Cambridge University Press, 2014); Craig Thompson Friend, *Kentucke's Frontiers* (Bloomington: Indiana University Press, 2010), 177–84, 193–95, 208–10, 214–19.

13. "Running Away to Get Married," *Indiana Palladium*, June 3, 1826; Stanley Harrold, *Border War: Fighting over Slavery Before the Civil War* (Chapel Hill: University of North Carolina Press, 2010), 33. See also Salafia, *Slavery's Borderland*, 15–107, 129–53.

14. Dearborn County Circuit Record (Complete), Book #3, 479–84, Dearborn County (Indiana) Courthouse. On kidnappings, see Carol Wilson, *Freedom at Risk: The Kidnapping of Free Blacks in America, 1780–1865* (Lexington: University Press of Kentucky, 1994).

15. See Sampson's name on a list of taxpayers in *Indiana Palladium*, November 14, 1829; Dearborn County Circuit Record.

16. On *Sampson v. Tousey*, see *Lawrenceburg Western Statesman*, December 10, 1830, 3; case file for "Sampson, a man of color, vs. Zerah Tousey," Indiana Supreme Court Records, Indiana State Archives, 1831 Term, Original Box Number 34; Indiana Supreme Court Order Book 3, 503, Indiana State Archives. Tousey's lawyer moved to quash the proceedings in September 1831, and Sampson's lawyer withdrew the case, after reporting Tousey's death to the court, in November. Some accounts claim that Sampson, who later called himself Thomas Record, went (or tried to go) to Liberia after the case. See Chris McHenry, "African-Americans' Contributions to the County," *Lawrenceburg Journal-Press*, February 3, 2009, 8. On Indiana jurisprudence on slavery at the time, see Randall T. Shepard, "Slave Cases and the Indiana Supreme Court," *Traces of Indiana and Midwestern History* 15, no. 3 (Summer 2003): 36–39.

17. No surviving record shows whether Sampson was actually paid.

18. "Notice," *Indiana Palladium*, November 12, 1831. See Rachael L. Pasierowska, "Up from Childhood: When African-American Enslaved Children Learned of Their Servile Status," *Slavery and Abolition* 37, no. 1 (2016): 94–116.

19. On lessons imparted by enslaved parents to children about their "soul value," see Berry, *The Price for Their Pound of Flesh*, 58–69. Other historians have noted that for many enslaved mothers, the impulse to teach their children what to expect competed with an opposing impulse to protect them from that knowledge for as long as possible. See Deborah Gray White, *Ar'n't I a Woman? Female Slaves in the Plantation South*, rev. ed. (New York: W. W. Norton, 1999), 95–97; Marie Jenkins Schwartz, *Born in Bondage: Growing up Enslaved in the Antebellum South* (Cambridge, MA.: Harvard University Press, 2000), 173.

20. "Caution," *Indiana Palladium*, January 7, 1832; "Fire," *Indiana Palladium*, August 31, 1833; obituary in *Indiana Palladium*, September 20, 1834. On Tousey children's departures, see Rose, *Tousey Family*, 95, 102; ads placed by Omer, George, and Erastus Tousey in *Indiana Palladium* between 1825 and 1834.

21. LH-1876. Moses Tousey's grandson Albert Gallatin Porter became governor of Indiana in 1881. See Charles W. Taylor, *Biographical Sketches and Review of the Bench and Bar of Indiana* (Indianapolis: Bench and Bar, 1895), 241; *History of Dearborn and Ohio Counties, Indiana, from Their Earliest Settlement* (Chicago: F. E. Weakley, 1885), 874–75.

22. List by Thomas Porter and Anne Tousey of the Estate of Moses Tousey, Boone County, Ky., Register of Appraisal, October 19, 1834, Series II, Box 1, Folder 7, Albert Gallatin Porter Papers, Indiana Historical Society; "Sale of Property," *Indiana Palladium*, October 25, 1834.

23. LH-1876.

CHAPTER THREE

1. LH-1876. On the complex decision to share traumatic stories, see Williams, *They Left Great Marks on Me*, 1–15.

2. Harriet A. Jacobs, *Incidents in the Life of a Slave Girl, Written by Herself*, ed. Lydia Maria Child (Boston: For the Author, 1861), 44, online at https://docsouth. unc.edu/fpn/jacobs/jacobs.html. See also Berry, *The Price for Their Pound of Flesh*, 78–83; Wilma King, "Within the Professional Household: Slave Children in the Antebellum South," *Historian* 59, no. 3 (March 1997): 523–40.

3. Caleb Atwater, *Remarks Made on a Tour to Prairie du Chien; Thence to Washington City, in 1829* (Columbus: Isaac N. Whiting, 1831), 15–22 (quotes); John E. Kleber, ed., *The Encyclopedia of Louisville* (Lexington: University Press of Kentucky, 2001), xvi–xviii. On adjustments from the country to the city, see Pargas, *Slavery and Forced Migration in the Antebellum South*, 72ff, 159, 166.

4. *The Louisville Directory, for the Year 1832: To Which is Annexed, Lists of the Municipal, County and State Officers* . . . (Louisville: Richard W. Otis, 1832), 34; Jefferson County Tax Assessment Rolls, Microfilm Reels 008053 and 008054, Kentucky Department for Libraries and Archives (hereafter KDLA). See also Forsyth's many advertisements for goods and steamboat bookings in the *Louisville Daily Journal* and *Louisville Public Advertiser* between 1830 and 1837.

5. Jefferson County Tax Assessment Rolls; John E. Kleber, ed., *The Encyclopedia of Louisville* (Lexington: University Press of Kentucky, 2001), 457; Lawrence M. Crutcher, *George Keats of Kentucky: A Life* (Lexington: University Press of Kentucky, 2012), 220; "An Act to Incorporate the Galt House Company," *Acts Passed at the* . . . *Forty-Second General Assembly for the Commonwealth of Kentucky* (Frankfort, KY: Albert G. Hodges, 1834), 502–5.

6. Kleber, *The Encyclopedia of Louisville*, xvi–xviii; Allen J. Share, *Cities in the Commonwealth: Two Centuries of Urban Life in Kentucky* (Lexington: University Press of Kentucky, 1982), 31; Keith C. Barton, "'Good Cooks and Washers': Slave Hiring, Domestic Labor, and the Market in Bourbon County, Kentucky," *Journal of American History* 84, no. 2 (September 1997): 436–60.

7. Forsyth disappears from the Jefferson County Tax Assessment Rolls after 1838. See suits listed in Chancery Defendants Index for 1835–1860, Jefferson County, KDLA. For his shifting addresses, see Louisville city directories for 1838, 1841, and 1843 (the last of which lists him as a "clerk at David L. Adams"). He had rebounded to his business as a grocer on Third between Main and Water by 1848 (see city directory and "Steamboat Journal" listings for *Daily Courier* in the mid-1840s). For dissolution of his firm and his attempt to sell off real estate after the Panic of 1837, see *Louisville Daily Journal*, January 1, 1839; January 18, 1839; and November 25, 1839.

8. LH-1876.

9. Eric Saugera, *Reborn in America: French Exiles and Refugees in the United States and the Vine and Olive Adventure, 1815–1865*, trans. Madeleine Velguth (Tuscaloosa: University of Alabama Press, 2011), 119–20; François Furstenberg, "The Significance of the Trans-Appalachian Frontier in Atlantic History," *American Historical Review* 113, no. 3 (June 2008): 647–77; Furstenberg, *When the United States Spoke French: Five Refugees Who Shaped a Nation* (New York: Penguin, 2014).

10. Rafe Blaufarb, *Bonapartists in the Borderlands: French Exiles and Refugees on the Gulf Coast, 1815–35* (Tuscaloosa: University of Alabama Press, 2005); *Letter from the Secretary of the Treasury, transmitting information of the progress that has been made, under the act of Congress of the 3d March, 1817, entitled "An act to set apart and dispose of certain public lands for the encouragement of the cultivation of the vine and olive"* . . . (Washington, DC: E. De Krafft, 1818), 15.

11. J. Winston Coleman Jr., comp., *Lexington's Second City Directory* (Lexington, KY: Winburn Press, 1953), 6; Kentucky Historical Society, *Kentucky Marriages, 1797–1865* (n.p.: Genealogical Publishing Company, 1966), 19; *Frankfort Commentator*, December 13, 1823; "Leather, Shoes, Boots, &c.," *Frankfort Argus*, May 31, 1826. See also *Frankfort Commentator*, September 11, 1824.

12. Cirode reported the events in a paid advertisement that he signed on August 30, 1824, and published for several months. See, for example, *Kentucky Gazette*, October 14, 1824, 4.

13. *Kentucky Gazette*, October 14, 1824, 4. On tanning, see Peter C. Welsh, "A Craft That Resisted Change: American Tanning Practices to 1850," *Technology and Culture* 4, no. 3 (Summer 1963): 299–317. On class conflict, see Stephen Aron, "'The Poor Men to Starve'": The Lives and Times of Workingmen in Early Lexington," in Friend, *The Buzzel About Kentuck*, 179–93.

14. *Kentucky Gazette*, October 14, 1824, 4.

15. "William Cirode," US Census, 1830, Louisville, Jefferson County, Kentucky, NARA microfilm M19, roll 38, accessed on Ancestry; *Louisville Directory, for the Year 1832*, 22; *Louisville Daily Journal*, January 2, 1837.

16. Harry Smith quoted in Salafia, *Slavery's Borderland*, 171. See also Pargas, *Slavery and Forced Migration in the Antebellum South*, 57–67; Steven Deyle, *Carry Me Back: The Domestic Slave Trade in American Life* (New York: Oxford University Press, 2005).

17. "100 Dollars Reward," *Louisville Daily Journal*, July 1, 1836.

18. LH-1876. On the *William French*, see "A New Steamer," *New Orleans Daily Picayune*, May 13, 1838; William M. Lytle, comp., *Merchant Steam Vessels of the United States, 1807–1868* (Mystic, CT: Steamship Historical Society of America, 1952), 203.

19. Rothman, *Beyond Freedom's Reach*, 35–36; Deyle, *Carry Me Back*, 153–54; Walter Johnson, *Soul by Soul: Life Inside the Antebellum Slave Market* (Cambridge, MA: Harvard University Press, 1999), 51–52.

20. Judith Kelleher Schafer, "New Orleans Slavery in 1850 as Seen in Advertisements," *Journal of Southern History* 47, no. 1 (February 1981): 33–56.

21. "For Sale," *Lexington Reporter*, December 10, 1828; Notarial Records of J. B. Marks, vol. 14, act 104 (August 1, 1839), New Orleans Notarial Archives (hereafter NONA). This act notarizes sale of Caroline to William Erskine Camp. Includes receipt for sale of Caroline, age thirteen or fourteen, to Cirode from Tilman Magruder & Co. for $550, dated Louisville, March 9, 1837.

22. LH-1876. For descriptions of housework done by black women, see Jacqueline Jones, *Labor of Love, Labor of Sorrow: Black Women, Work, and the Family, from Slavery to the Present* (New York: Basic Books, 2010), 24–25; Tera W. Hunter, *To 'Joy My Freedom: Southern Black Women's Lives and Labors After the Civil War* (Cambridge, MA: Harvard University Press, 1997), 51–57.

23. Cirode's firm advertised in the *New Orleans Commercial Bulletin*: see, for example, January 1, 1839, 1. See *Daily Picayune* reports on sluggish "Western produce" during those years. On the retail economy and the panic, see Scott P. Marler, *The Merchants' Capital: New Orleans and the Political Economy of the Nineteenth-Century South* (New York: Cambridge University Press, 2013), 27–28; Jessica M. Lepler, *The Many Panics of 1837: People, Politics, and the Creation of a Transatlantic Financial Crisis* (New York: Cambridge University Press, 2013).

24. See Notarial Records of J. B. Marks, vol. 12, act 3 (December 4, 1838), NONA; ads in *New Orleans Commercial Bulletin* from January through June 1838, as well as January through November 1839; quote from testimony of Joseph F. Kelly, *Parish v. Cirode*, Image 00535, Historical Archives of the Supreme Court of Louisiana, LASC Case Files, University of New Orleans, http://dspace. uno.edu:8080/xmlui/handle/123456789/20469. "Parish" is sometimes spelled "Parrish" in the records. On living arrangements, see advertisement placed in

Commercial Bulletin, August 30, 1843; Richard Campanella, *Geographies of New Orleans: Urban Fabrics Before the Storm* (Lafayette: Center for Louisiana Studies, 2006), 297. The address provided for Cirode in *Parish v. Cirode* records (No. 243 Dauphin Street) places him on or near the site of three two-story brick buildings built in 1833 by Pierre Forestier. (See Stanley Clisby Arthur, *Old New Orleans: A History of the Vieux Carré, Its Ancient and Historical Buildings* (New Orleans: Harmanson, 1936), 233.) Each had a detached three-story kitchen.

25. See ad in the *Louisville Daily Journal* beginning on January 20, 1837, and running through the end of the month, advertising his store for rent; "G. B. & R. J. Didlake" had apparently become the renters by March, according to an ad that ran on March 6, 1837. See also *Louisville Daily Journal,* October 23, 1839, 2. Josephine's marriage: "Kentucky Marriages, 1785–1979," database, FamilySearch (https://familysearch.org/ark:/61903/1:1:F43L-B8Li), Robert White and Josephine Cirode, 01 Sep 1840; Cirode's naturalization: "United States Passport Applications, 1795–1925," database with images, FamilySearch, (https://familysearch.org/ark:/61903/1:1:Q295-NYQ4), William Cirode, 12 Mar 1844; citing Passport Applications, 1795–1905, 14, NARA microfilm publications M1490 and M1372 (Washington, DC: National Archives and Records Administration, n.d.). The application indicates that he received a naturalization certificate in Louisville on September 17, 1840.

26. See *Mobile Directory, 1842,* arr. Mrs. John H. Mallon (Mobile: Mrs. Lester E. Taylor, n.d.), 7; "U.S. Customs Service, Slave Manifests—Mobile, Alabama Inward (By Owner Name)," National Archives at Atlanta, RG 36; *Samuel Bell v. William Cirode,* Commercial Court of Orleans Parish, Case 6207, Louisiana Division, City Archives, New Orleans Public Library; *Parish v. Cirode.*

27. Sheriff's summons, *Parish v. Cirode,* Images 00530 and 00531.

28. *Parish v. Cirode;* "Pennsylvania, Philadelphia Passenger Lists, 1800–1882," database with images, FamilySearch, https://familysearch.org/ark:/61903/1:1:K8CQ-DM8, William Cirode, 1844; citing NARA microfilm publication M425 (Washington, DC: National Archives and Records Administration, n.d.). See also "Cleared" and "Arrived" in *Philadelphia Public Ledger,* September 7, 1844, which reports the boat left Santiago on August 17. According to the July 18, 1844, edition of the *Public Ledger,* the boat had left Philadelphia for Cuba on July 18.

29. LH-1876.

30. Jane Cirode's younger children, William and Louisa, are listed in "Jane Cerode [*sic*]," US Census, 1850, Cincinnati, Ward 4, Hamilton County, Ohio, NARA microfilm M432, roll 688, FamilySearch.

31. Ad placed by James Barbee, address on Seventh between Walnut and Chestnut, *Louisville Morning Courier,* June 14, 1844, 3; ad placed by James H. Bagby, general agent, *Louisville Morning Courier,* February 20, 1845, 3. On hiring out labor, see Stephanie Cole, "Servants and Slaves in Louisville: Race, Ethnicity,

and Household Labor in an Antebellum Border City," *Ohio Valley History* 11, no. 1 (Spring 2011): 3–25; Jonathan D. Martin, *Divided Mastery: Slave Hiring in the American South* (Cambridge, MA: Harvard University Press, 2004), 34–36; Bridget Ford, *Bonds of Union: Religion, Race, and Politics in a Civil War Borderland* (Chapel Hill: University of North Carolina Press, 2016), 95.

32. Cole, "Servants and Slaves in Louisville," 10–13, newspaper quoted on 11. Lyons is mentioned in LH-1876; Thruston in RB-1879.

33. LH-1876.

34. RB-1879.

35. All quotations above concerning the meeting with Joshua are in RB-1879. On "ambiguous loss" following the separation of slave families, see Heather Andrea Williams, *Help Me to Find My People: The African American Search for Family Lost in Slavery* (Chapel Hill: University of North Carolina Press, 2012).

36. RB-1879.

CHAPTER FOUR

1. "Col. Zeb Ward," *Louisville Courier-Journal*, December 30, 1894, 3.

2. For Ward's family history, see David G. McDonald, *Zebulon Headington* (n.p.: David G. McDonald, 1983), 1–8, 15–16; Nisbet, *Ward*; Maude Ward Lafferty, *Life and Times of Andrew Harrison Ward* (n.p.: Maude Ward Lafferty, 1945). Also see the marriage record for Andrew and Elizabeth Ward, dated September 27, 1803, in "Kentucky, County Marriages, 1797–1954," database with images, FamilySearch.

3. Old War Invalid File 25,915, Military Pension Records, National Archives and Records Administration. On family stories of Ward's penchant for drink, see Nisbet, *Ward*, 53. On ideas about manhood and dependence in Kentucky, see Sachs, *Home Rule*.

4. McDonald, *Zebulon Headington*, 15–16, appendix to McDonald's work.

5. Zebulon Headington, Harrison County Will Book D, 465–68, KDLA; Lafferty, *Life and Times of Andrew Harrison Ward*, 75–76; McDonald, *Zebulon Headington*, 17.

6. Robert H. Gudmestad, *Steamboats and the Rise of the Cotton Kingdom* (Baton Rouge: Louisiana State University Press, 2011), 31–38.

7. Lafferty, *Life and Times of Andrew Harrison Ward*, 76; Gudmestad, *Steamboats and the Rise of the Cotton Kingdom*, 44–46, quote on 46.

8. Interview with Calvin Fairbank in Norman B. Wood, *The White Side of a Black Subject: Enlarged and Brought Down to Date; A Vindication of the Afro-American race, from the Landing of Slaves at St. Augustine, Florida, in 1565, to the Present Time* (Chicago: American Publishing House, 1897), 216. See also Gudmestad, *Steamboats and the Rise of the Cotton Kingdom*, 47–52; Buchanan, *Black Life on the Mississippi*.

9. Gudmestad, *Steamboats and the Rise of the Cotton Kingdom*, 140–58; Walter Johnson, *River of Dark Dreams: Slavery and Empire in the Cotton Kingdom* (Cambridge, MA: Harvard University Press, 2013), 73–125.

10. Letter from Thomas Falconer to John David Falconer, December [January] 5, 1841, Southwestern University Special Collections, http://texashistory.unt.edu/ark:/67531/metapth586980/. On snags and explosions, see Gudmestad, *Steamboats and the Rise of the Cotton Kingdom*, 97–116; Johnson, *River of Dark Dreams*, 103–19.

11. "River News," *New Orleans Times*, November 6, 1874. See also Lafferty, *Life and Times of Andrew Harrison Ward*, 76; Nisbet, *Ward*, 67.

12. Nisbet, *Ward*, 67; "Busy Life Ended," *Arkansas Gazette*, December 29, 1894. Ward later appeared at some meetings of Mexican War veterans, but no official record of his service has been found. See "Meeting of Mexican War Veterans," *Arkansas Gazette*, January 20, 1878.

13. "Busy Life Ended"; *New Orleans Daily Picayune*, May 11, 1850, 1; Malcolm J. Rohrbough, *Days of Gold: The California Gold Rush and the American Nation* (Berkeley: University of California Press, 1997), 58–60; John Haskell Kemble, *The Panama Route, 1848–1869* (Berkeley: University of California Publications in History, 1970). Between 1846 and 1851, published hotel arrivals and letters received show Ward in Louisville, New Orleans, and Sacramento at various times: see *Sacramento Transcript*, March 4, 1851; *New Orleans Daily Picayune*, April 19, 1850; *Louisville Daily Courier*, December 31, 1846, and July 3, 1848. The dates make it possible that Ward could have returned to Kentucky in about 1846 and then left for the US–Mexican War and the gold rush that followed.

14. *San Francisco Alta California*, October 31, 1850, 5; "Kentucky, County Marriages, 1797–1954," database with images, FamilySearch (https://familysearch.org/ark:/61903/1:1:V5ZD-YW4); "Kentucky Births and Christenings, 1839–1960," database, FamilySearch (https://familysearch.org/ark:/61903/1:1:FWVL-5F7); Kenton County Tax Assessment Rolls, 1853, Microfilm 008091, KDLA. Ward's arrival in California coincided with a violent confrontation between gold field squatters and the Sacramento government, which may have influenced his decision to leave. See Mark A. Eifler, *Gold Rush Capitalists: Greed and Growth in Sacramento* (Albuquerque: University of New Mexico Press, 2002).

15. Kenton County Court Order Books, 1853–1854, Reel 551,071, KDLA.

CHAPTER FIVE

1. LH-1876; *Haldeman's Picture of Louisville, Directory and Business Advertiser, for 1844–1845* ... (Louisville: W. N. Haldeman, 1844), 118. Also see Louisville Hotel Company Records, Book 2, 19, at the Filson Historical Society, Louisville, Kentucky. Bishop was given a five-year lease on the hotel in 1845, but was also listed as proprietor in 1844.

2. LH-1876.

3. Julie Roy Jeffrey, *Abolitionists Remember: Antislavery Autobiographies and the Unfinished Work of Emancipation* (Chapel Hill: University of North Carolina Press, 2008), 61–154.

4. Nikki M. Taylor, *Frontiers of Freedom: Cincinnati's Black Community, 1802–1868* (Athens: Ohio University Press, 2005), 2, 10–27; Matthew D. Smith, "The Specter of Cholera in Nineteenth-Century Cincinnati," *Ohio Valley History* 16, no. 2 (Summer 2016): 21–40, quote on 26.

5. Salafia, *Slavery's Borderland*.

6. See Taylor, *Frontiers of Freedom*, 2, 64–80; Salafia, *Slavery's Borderland*, 9, 129–30; Harrold, *Border War*, 20–21, 55, 65–66, 72–93.

7. Taylor, *Frontiers of Freedom*, 118–23; Harrold, *Border War*, 67, 113; Middleton, *The Black Laws in the Old Northwest*, 6, 144.

8. LH-1876. See Cincinnati City Directory, 1849–1850 and 1851–1852, Cincinnati History Library and Archives. Cirode may have had another boardinghouse as well, on Pearl, between Race and Elm. See Cincinnati City Directory, 1850–1851 and 1853.

9. LH-1876.

10. Notarial records of J. B. Marks, vol. 32, act 103 (May 6, 1843), NONA. See also Conveyance Records Books, Orleans Parish, vol. 34, 138, NONA, which describes Margaret as a "negress" and Eliza as "her daughter a griffonne." The price is listed as $450 cash. For her seizure and sale by the sheriff, see *Samuel Bell v. William Cirode*, Commercial Court of Orleans Parish, Case 6207, Louisiana Division, City Archives, New Orleans Public Library; Conveyance Records Book, Orleans Parish, vol. 36, 495, NONA.

11. The Weathered document is in *James C. Johnston v. William Cirode*, Jefferson County Chancery Court, Case #4648 (March 1848), KDLA.

12. *Johnston v. Cirode*. See also William C. Williams vs. William Cirode, Case #3766 (September 1842) and Case #4368 (June 1844), Jefferson County Chancery Court, KDLA.

13. *Johnston v. Cirode*.

14. *Pierre Roy v. William Cirode*, Case #6511 (July 1849), in Chancery Court for Jefferson County, KDLA.

15. On enslavers' savvy use of movement across jurisdictional lines, see Anne Twitty, *Before Dred Scott: Slavery and Legal Culture in the American Confluence, 1787–1857* (New York: Cambridge University Press, 2016), 54–55, 180–82.

16. For descriptions of boardinghouses, see Gamber, *The Boardinghouse in Nineteenth-Century America*; Joseph J. Mersman, *The Whiskey Merchant's Diary: An Urban Life in the Emerging Midwest*, ed. Linda A. Fisher (Athens: Ohio University Press, 2007).

17. LH-1876.

18. Ibid.; Steven McQuillin, "Hamilton County Courthouses," https://www.probatect.org/about/history-of-records; date from "Kidnapping Case," *Pittsburgh Legal Journal*, June 18, 1853.

19. Taylor, *Frontiers of Freedom*, 2–9.
20. Ibid., 102–3.
21. LH-1876.
22. Ibid. On these conflicts, see Hunter, *To 'Joy My Freedom*; Thavolia Glymph, *Out of the House of Bondage: The Transformation of the Plantation Household* (New York: Cambridge University Press, 2008).
23. LH-1876.
24. Ibid.
25. A. G. W. Carter, *The Old Court House: Reminiscences and Anecdotes of the Courts and Bar of Cincinnati* (Cincinnati: Peter G. Thomson, 1880), 12–14.
26. John Niven, ed., *The Salmon P. Chase Papers*, vol. 1: *Journals, 1829–1872* (Kent, OH: Kent State University Press, 1993), 216–17.
27. LH-1876. Few record books like the one Wood remembered have survived the Hamilton County courthouse fires of 1849 and 1884, and available indexes do not contain references to Wood. Email from Jim Dempsey, Hamilton County Genealogical Society, to author, April 12, 2016.

CHAPTER SIX

1. "Grocers," *Covington Journal*, January 8, 1853, 1. The same ad was a fixture in that space from February 8, 1851, to April 23, 1853. Before that long run, a much smaller business card also appeared beginning as early as January 1849. White remained in Mobile until at least 1844, when his name appeared in the city directory. The 1850 Census found a household headed by Robert White, a grocer born in England, and his wife, Josephine, born in Kentucky, living in Covington; see "Robert White," US Census, 1850, Covington, Kenton County, Kentucky, NARA microfilm M432, roll 208, FamilySearch.
2. *Covington Journal*, April 16, 1853; July 23, 1853. The ostensible reason given for White's closure in April was the owner's poor health; illness may have played some role in his latest moment of crisis. But White opened a smaller store in May before it was closed out, too. The final July notice called on his debtors and creditors to settle with him at his store. On reports that he had "assigned" and "stored away his ppy [property]," see Kentucky, Kenton County, 1855–1861, vol. 19, 218, R. G. Dun & Co. Credit Report Volumes, Baker Library, Harvard Business School. The Dun reports listed White on a page headed "Traders out of bus[iness] Kenton Co. Ky," and said he had been in business in Covington from July 1849 to July 1853.
3. LH-1876.
4. "Horrible Murder," *Cincinnati Enquirer*, May 20, 1848; "*Sarah W. Bolton, Executrix, etc., v. Thomas Dickens et al.*," *Central Law Journal* 2 (July 23, 1875), 477. On Bolton, Dickens, and Company, see also Frederic Bancroft, *Slave-Trading in the Old South* (Baltimore: J. H. Furst Company, 1931), 250–68; Deyle, *Carry Me Back*, 94–95. On slave traders in Kentucky, see J. Winston Coleman Jr., "Lexington's Slave Dealers and Their Southern Trade," *Filson*

Club History Quarterly 12, no. 1 (January 1938): 1–23; T. D. Clark, "The Slave Trade Between Kentucky and the Cotton Kingdom," *Mississippi Valley Historical Review* 21, no. 3 (December 1934): 331–42. For price swing, see Salafia, *Slavery's Borderland*, 175. The boom had followed a lifting, in 1849, of a ban on the nonimportation of slaves into the state for purposes of sale.

5. This reconstruction of what happened is based on Zebulon Ward's claims in Chicago Case File.

6. Chicago Case File. Wood also remembered Ward saying "he had bought me in March 1853" in RB-1879. On law officers along the border, see Harrold, *Border War*, 46–47.

7. On the range of methods used to recover runaway slaves, see John Hope Franklin and Loren Schweninger, *Runaway Slaves: Rebels on the Plantation* (New York: Oxford University Press, 1999), 149–81.

8. For traders' use of steamboats, see Gudmestad, *Steamboats and the Rise of the Cotton Kingdom*, 56–57; Calvin Schermerhorn, *The Business of Slavery and the Rise of American Capitalism, 1815–1860* (New Haven, CT: Yale University Press, 2015), 204–39.

9. Blackett, *The Captive's Quest for Freedom*, 233; William Wells Brown, *Narrative of William W. Brown, an American Slave, Written By Himself* (London: Charles Gilpin, 1849), 32, https://docsouth.unc.edu/fpn/brownw/brown.html.

10. Coleman Jr., "Lexington's Slave Dealers and Their Southern Trade," 13–15, quote on 15, n. 45; Robert H. Gudmestad, *A Troublesome Commerce: The Transformation of the Interstate Slave Trade* (Baton Rouge: Louisiana State University Press, 2003), 97–100; Clark, "The Slave Trade Between Kentucky and the Cotton Kingdom," 339.

11. Coleman Jr., "Lexington's Slave Dealers and Their Southern Trade," 15.

12. Ibid., 15, 19. For other examples of kidnappings in the region, many orchestrated by gangs and some resembling the ploy to abduct Wood, see Blackett, *The Captive's Quest for Freedom*, 241–43. For receipts of transactions in 1852 and 1853 between Robards, Scott, and Rust, see Lewis Robards Receipt Book, Box 2, Black History Collection, 1700–2008, Library of Congress. My thanks to Adam Rothman for finding this book and sending me images of the records described here. On black kidnappers, see Richard Bell, "Counterfeit Kin: Kidnappers of Color, the Reverse Underground Railroad, and the Origins of Practical Abolition," *Journal of the Early Republic* 38, no. 2 (Summer 2018): 199–230.

13. Harrold, *Border War*, 54. See also Blackett, *The Captive's Quest for Freedom*, 154–55.

14. Richard S. Newman, *The Transformation of American Abolitionism: Fighting Slavery in the Early Republic* (Chapel Hill: University of North Carolina Press, 2002).

15. Manisha Sinha, *The Slave's Cause: A History of Abolition* (New Haven, CT: Yale University Press, 2016); Stacey Robertson, *Hearts Beating for Liberty: Women*

Abolitionists in the Old Northwest (Chapel Hill: University of North Carolina Press, 2010).

16. Harrold, *Border War*, 58.

17. Ibid., 72–93; Salafia, *Slavery's Borderland.*

18. Griffler, *Front Line of Freedom*, 109; *Williams' Cincinnati Directory and Business Advertiser, for 1849–1850* (Cincinnati: C. S. Williams, 1849), 129; Benjamin Drew, *A North-Side View of Slavery. The Refugee: or the Narratives of Fugitive Slaves in Canada* (Boston: John P. Jewett, 1856), 363–64; "John Hatfield," US Census, 1850, Hamilton County, Cincinnati, Ward 2, NARA microfilm M432, roll 687, FamilySearch; Blackett, *The Captive's Quest for Freedom*, 223–24. See also "Proceedings of the Convention, of the Colored Freemen of Ohio, Held in Cincinnati, January 14, 15, 16, 17 and 19, 1852," *ColoredConventions.org*, http://coloredconventions.org/items/show/250, accessed August 14, 2018.

19. Harrold, *Border War*, 10, 54, 58–59, 85.

20. On Chase, see Taylor, *Frontiers of Freedom*, 114–15; Middleton, *The Black Laws in the Old Northwest*, 144. The 1837 case was *Matilda v. Lawrence.*

21. Blackett, *The Captive's Quest for Freedom*, 204–5, 226–29.

22. "Kenton County Association," *Licking Valley Register*, November 27, 1841; Harrold, *Border War*, 47–48. For Rust's association with the group, see *Boone County Recorder*, July 11, 1906, 5. Debian Marty confirms in an email to author, dated May 23, 2017, that Rust was one of the slave-catchers involved in the so-called Kentucky Raid. Rust was also a material witness in a later lawsuit filed by Thornton Timberlake against the Michigan abolitionists who had intervened. For a summary of the raid, see Debian Marty, "The Kentucky Raid," in *The Kentucky African American Encyclopedia*, ed. Gerald L. Smith, Karen Cotton McDaniel, and John A. Hardin (Lexington: University Press of Kentucky, 2015), 307–8.

23. Quotes in this and the next few paragraphs are from "A Negro Kidnapped," *Cincinnati Gazette*, May 11, 1850.

24. Ibid.

25. *Covington Journal*, April 23, 1853.

26. Harrold, *Border War*, 138–58; Blackett, *The Captive's Quest for Freedom*, 3–87.

27. Griffler, *Front Line of Freedom*, 105–30; Wilson, *Freedom at Risk*, 54–55; Blackett, *The Captive's Quest for Freedom*, 50, 182–85.

28. Griffler, *Front Line of Freedom*, 108–109; Blackett, *The Captive's Quest for Freedom*, 46–49.

29. For an example of how the Fugitive Slave Law aided kidnappers, see Lucy Maddox, *The Parker Sisters: A Border Kidnapping* (Philadelphia: Temple University Press, 2016).

30. For overviews of resistance to the law, see Blackett, *The Captive's Quest for Freedom*; Don E. Fehrenbacher, *The Slaveholding Republic: An Account of the*

United States Government's Relations to Slavery (New York: Oxford University Press, 2001), 231–51.

31. "Horrible Murder"; "Bloody Tragedy," *Lancaster (OH) Gazette*, June 2, 1848.

32. "Horrible Murder"; "Murder and Attempted Suicide," *Anti-Slavery Bugle*, June 2, 1848; "Most Sad and Bloody Tragedy," *Sandusky (OH) Clarion*, June 5, 1848. Eight years later, abolitionists would rehearse the same points to explain the more famous case of Margaret Garner, a woman who had escaped slavery in Boone County, near the place where Wood was born. After she and her family were surrounded in Ohio by white men who came to recapture her, Garner cut her own daughter's throat. She was later returned to the South because of the Fugitive Slave Law. On Garner, see Nikki M. Taylor, *Driven Toward Madness* (Athens: Ohio University Press, 2016); Steven Weisenburger, *Modern Medea: A Family Story of Slavery and Child-Murder from the Old South* (New York: Hill & Wang, 1998). On abolitionist interpretations of slave suicide, see Snyder, *The Power to Die*, chap. 6.

33. On the continued financial value of slaves after death, see Berry, *The Price for Their Pound of Flesh*, 148–93.

34. RB-1879.

CHAPTER SEVEN

1. RB-1879.

2. Ibid.; LH-1876.

3. LH-1876. On Tuttle: *Williams' Cincinnati Almanac, Business Guide and Annual Advertiser* (Cincinnati: C. S. Williams, 1850), 71; "Sarah A. Tuttle," US Census, 1850, Cincinnati, Ward 1, Hamilton County, Ohio, NARA microfilm M432, roll 687, FamilySearch. There was also a Dennis Tuttle who kept an inn called the City Hotel near the boardinghouse of Rebecca Boyd; see "Dennis P. Tuttle," US Census, 1850, Cincinnati, Ward 2, Hamilton County, Ohio, NARA microfilm M432, roll 687, FamilySearch. On Swormstedt: *Williams' Cincinnati Directory . . . for 1849–1850*, 279.

4. See Susan V. Spellman, *Cornering the Market: Independent Grocers and Innovation in American Small Business* (New York: Oxford University Press, 2016), 19–20; *Williams' Cincinnati Directory . . . for 1849–1850*, 305.

5. Taylor, *Frontiers of Freedom*, 117–37.

6. LH-1876. I have not been able to discover the identity of the Leonard Armstrong whom Wood and Williams knew, or even if they were both referring to the same person.

7. RB-1879. In LH-1876, the pledge is rendered only slightly differently: "I must go away right now, for the men will be here soon, but I'll tell you what you do. Go with the men to Lexington without a word, and as soon as they are gone I'll go over to Cincinnati, and see what I can do for you, and if I find you are a free woman, I'll have you stopped at Lexington."

8. RB-1879. The parting word is rendered slightly differently in LH-1876: "Don't you be afraid, if I can do you any good I will, and if I can't I won't do you any harm." In LH-1876, Wood recalled the men returning at ten o'clock.

9. LH-1876; RB-1879. On stagecoaches, see J. Winston Coleman Jr., *Stage-Coach Days in the Bluegrass: Being an Account of Stage-Coach Travel and Tavern Days in Lexington and Central Kentucky, 1800–1900* (1935; Lexington: University Press of Kentucky, 1995).

10. RB-1879.

11. Coleman Jr., "Lexington's Slave Dealers and Their Southern Trade," 10–12; Clark, "The Slave Trade Between Kentucky and the Cotton Kingdom," 334; "New Jail," *Kentucky Statesman*, May 28, 1851. Robards purchased the old Lexington Theater for use as a jail in 1849, later selling it to the firm, Bolton, Dickens & Company.

12. "Notes, 1784–1940, Trials and Suits, 1822–1858," Folder 12, J. Winston Coleman Collection, University of Kentucky Special Collections.

13. No other records I have found identify "Beck" Robards, whom Wood said was known as his wife, but Robards did buy an insurance policy on an enslaved woman named "Rebecca" at about this time. See "Slavery Era Insurance Registry," California Department of Insurance, http://www.insurance.ca.gov/01-consumers/150-other-prog/10-seir/. Other slave traders also owned women who were sometimes known in the community as their sexual partners or common-law wives, with power over other enslaved people, though in many cases they were themselves enslaved. See also Alexandra Finley, "'Cash to Corinna': Domestic Labor and Sexual Economy in the 'Fancy Trade,'" *Journal of American History* 104, no. 2 (September 2017): 410–30; Richard Bell, "'Thence to Patty Cannon's': Gender, Family, and the Reverse Underground Railroad," *Slavery and Abolition* 37, no. 4 (2016): 661–79.

14. RB-1879; Coleman Jr., "Lexington's Slave Dealers and Their Southern Trade," 12. See also Finley, "'Cash to Corinna'"; Edward E. Baptist, "'Cuffy,' 'Fancy Maids,' and 'One-Eyed Men': Rape, Commodification, and the Domestic Slave Trade in the United States," *American Historical Review* 106, no. 5 (December 2001): 1619–50; Pargas, *Slavery and Forced Migration in the Antebellum South*, 101–103.

15. RB-1879.

16. On enslaved women's labor in the marketing of slaves, see Finley, "'Cash to Corinna.'"

17. LH-1876; RB-1879.

18. Ibid. On Rodes Woods, see Coleman Jr., "Lexington's Slave Dealers and Their Southern Trade," 15.

19. RB-1879. Other enslaved people also recalled reflecting on the differences between their condition and that of animals such as birds: see Johnson, *River of Dark Dreams*, 209–10.

20. RB-1879.

CHAPTER EIGHT

1. LH-1876.
2. Ibid. The curse was printed as "G–d d–n," which I have spelled out for clarity.
3. LH-1876.
4. Ibid.
5. "Kidnapping," *Cincinnati Daily Gazette*, June 3, 1853, 2; "Deception," *Cincinnati Daily Enquirer*, June 3, 1853, 3; "Kidnappers Arrested," *Frederick Douglass' Paper*, June 24, 1853.
6. Jolliffe is identified with the case in RB-1879; "The Kidnapping Case," *Cincinnati Enquirer*, June 8, 1853, 3. For his fiction, John Jolliffe, *Belle Scott, or Liberty Overthrown!: A Tale for the Crisis* (Columbus, OH: D. Anderson, 1856), 19, 82. Also see William Jolliffe, *Historical, Genealogical, and Biographical Account of the Jolliffe Family of Virginia, 1652 to 1893* (Philadelphia: J. B. Lippincott, 1893), 223–31; Weisenburger, *Modern Medea*, 86–108; Taylor, *Frontiers of Freedom*, 115; John Wertheimer, Daphne Fruchtman, et al., "*Willis v. Jolliffe:* Love and Slavery on the South Carolina–Ohio Borderlands," in *Freedom's Conditions in the U.S.–Canadian Borderlands in the Age of Emancipation*, ed. Tony Freyer and Lyndsay Campbell (Durham, NC: Carolina Academic Press, 2011), 257–84.
7. "The Kidnapping Case." See "Ellen Hamilton," US Census, 1850, Cincinnati, Ward 9, Hamilton County, Ohio, NARA microfilm M432, reel 690, FamilySearch. A partial repeal of the Black Laws by Ohio's state legislature in 1849 enabled women of color to testify in court.
8. The thirty-five-year-old "Sarah Speers" appears in Ward 9 with a forty-year-old "mulatto" Virginian, likely her husband, and their one-year-old daughter, in a section of the city surrounded by black or mulatto households. Ellen Hamilton is listed as living only a few households away. "Sarah Speers," US Census, 1850, Cincinnati, Ward 9, Hamilton County, Ohio, NARA microfilm M432, reel 690, FamilySearch.
9. "The Kidnapping Case"; "Held to Answer," *Cincinnati Daily Gazette*, June 7, 1853, 2.
10. LH-1876. Wood told Hearn that "I think the Sheriff's name was Rhodes." Contemporary records confirm that it was Waller Rodes. See Fayette County Clerk Order Books 13 and 14, KDLA.
11. Fayette County Circuit Court Order Book, vol. 37 (March 4, 1853–March 3, 1855), 75, KDLA. Unfortunately, other than the notations about the Kentucky case of *Wood v. Ward* found in the Fayette County Circuit Court order book from that period, no case file survives. The file was already missing by the time historian J. Winston Coleman Jr. tried to find it in the 1930s while conducting research for his book on slavery in Kentucky; he knew of the case and its number (1271) from the order books, but marked it down as "Not Found" and "Contents Known" on a list documenting his search for cases involving Lewis Robards. The case had probably gone missing long before, since the court in

ne 1 – July 31; all ages welcome
untaindale.org/summeradventure
are your adventure!
PLDadventure

78–81

also mentioned that it was not
file was passed up to the Appeals
ls Court fire of 1864. See J. Winston
versity of Kentucky, 46M53, Folder
1822–1868." On the fire, see email
author, September 18, 2015.
r Wrongful Enslavement and the
British Journal of American Legal
in other states, see Twitty, *Before
n Songs: Suing for Freedom Before
Press, 2014); Kelly M. Kennington,
reedom Suits and the Legal Culture
ens: University of Georgia Press,
ants in the Antebellum American
Carolina Press, 2018).
5).
r, 1 B. Monroe 130 (Ky., 1840);
y., 1809).
ery, Federalism, and Comity* (Chapel
981), 190–96, 200; Salafia, *Slavery's
The Dred Scott Case: Its Significance
k: Oxford University Press, 1978),
ct of Laws," *Columbia Law Review*

al Enslavement and the Doctrine of
rew Fede, *Roadblocks to Freedom:
tates South* (New Orleans: Quid Pro
nd the Law*, 21–29.
rmer Slaves," *Boston University Law
Robert Westley, "The Accursed Share:
m of Value in Black Reparations
2005): 81–116; Westley, "Restitution
the Doctrine of the Master's Good

ham: Kentucky's Contribution to
red Scott Decision," *Kentucky Law
Fehrenbacher, *The Dred Scott Case*,
t Union.
lescribed in Finkelman, *An Imperfect

nmonwealth of Kentucky: December
ges, 1840), 172–73.
Lexington, Kentucky, 1850–1860"
1931), 37–42.

22. Ibid., 62–69; LH-1876.
23. LH-1876.
24. Ibid.
25. Ibid. A twenty-four-year-old "stage driver" named William White appears in the Kenton County Census from 1850; a "retired merchant" named William White appears in the 1860 Census. Both were found on FamilySearch. For the White who became Bolton's partner, see *Sarah W. Bolton, Executrix, etc., v. Thomas Dickens, et al.*, 574.

CHAPTER NINE

1. Fayette County Circuit Court Order Book, vol. 37, 75, KDLA.
2. Because the case file from 1853 is no longer extant, I have been forced to extrapolate Ward's defense from Wood's interviews and his later arguments in Chicago Case File.
3. RB-1879.
4. LH-1876. See Kinkead's profile in *The Biographical Encyclopedia of Kentucky of the Dead and Living Men of the Nineteenth Century* (Cincinnati: J. M. Armstrong, 1878), 163; "Transylvania Law School," *Daily National Intelligencer*, September 23, 1854. On the case in which Kinkead represented Abraham Lincoln, see William H. Townsend, *Abraham Lincoln, Defendant: Lincoln's Most Interesting Lawsuit* (Boston: Houghton Mifflin, 1923); Letter from Abraham Lincoln to George B. Kinkead, May 27, 1853, in Roy P. Basler, ed., *The Collected Works of Abraham Lincoln*, vol. 2, 194–95, online at http://quod.lib.umich.edu/l/lincoln/.
5. Fayette County Circuit Court Order Book, vol. 37, 44, KDLA. The family's correspondence is preserved in the Bodley Family Papers, Filson Historical Society.
6. George Blackburn Kinkead, *Address Delivered before the Kentucky Colonization Society: in the Representatives' Hall, January 10, 1850* (Frankfort, KY: A. G. Hodges, 1850), 4–5, 18. See also James Ann Pearce to her sister Molly, January 11, 1850, Bodley Family Papers, Mss. A/B668e, Folder 47, Filson Historical Society. Kinkead's brothers-in-law Pindell and Bodley were also colonizationists. See William S. Bodley, *Address of the Hon. W. S. Bodley, before the Kentucky Colonization Society, in the City of Frankfort, February 23, 1852* (Frankfort, KY: A. G. Hodges, 1852).
7. Kinkead, *Address*, 14; "Geo. B. Kinkead," US Census (Slave Schedule), 1850, Fayette County, Kentucky, NARA microfilm M432, FamilySearch. On the context in which views such as Kinkead's developed, see Harlow, *Religion, Race, and the Making of Confederate Kentucky, 1830–1880*, 16–106.
8. Nicholas Guyatt, "'The Outskirts of Our Happiness': Race and the Lure of Colonization in the Early Republic," *Journal of American History* 95, no. 4 (March 2009): 986–1011; Eric Foner, *The Fiery Trial: Abraham Lincoln and*

American Slavery (New York: W. W. Norton, 2010), 17–22; Lacy K. Ford, *Deliver Us from Evil: The Slavery Question in the Old South* (New York: Oxford University Press, 2009), 299–389.

9. Blackett, *The Captive's Quest for Freedom*, 88–134.

10. Kinkead, *Address*, 5, 7.

11. Ibid., 7. For more on the motives of Upper South lawyers who took on freedom suits despite conservative views, Twitty, *Before Dred Scott*, 96–125; Kennington, *In the Shadow of Dred Scott*, 69–78. On the 1847 case, Foner, *The Fiery Trial*, 47–50.

12. "Thruston, Hon. Charles Mynn," *Biographical Encyclopedia of Kentucky* (Cincinnati: J. M. Armstrong, 1878), 458–59; "Charles Mynn Thruston," in M. Joblin, *Louisville Past and Present: Its Industrial History* (Louisville: John F. Morton, 1875), 183–89. RB-1879 misspelled his name as "Thurston," but Kinkead's letter confirms it was Thruston.

13. Letter by G. B. Kinkead to W. S. Bodley, Esq., September 14, 1853, Bodley Family Papers, Mss. A/B668e, Folder 55, Filson Club Historical Society. I have changed the abbreviation "recd" to "received" for clarity. No earlier letter about the case exists in the collection, so it is not clear when Kinkead or Bodley deposed Thruston.

14. LH-1876.

15. RB-1879; Fayette County Circuit Court Order Book, vol. 37, 181, KDLA. In both of her interviews, Wood did not specify exactly the amount of time that passed between many of the events she recalled from the summer of 1853. For example, her memory of the court order moving her to Pullum's pen was shared immediately after her recollection of being brought back from Harrodsburg, though the court's order book shows the motion about custody occurring much later. My account represents a best effort to harmonize Wood's memories with the evidence from the court, and requires only the assumption that varying spans of time likely passed between the events that Wood briefly recounted in her interviews with Hearn and the *Bee*. But the possibility remains that she was moved more than once, first to Pullum's jail immediately after returning to Lexington, and again somewhere else (or even into the sheriff's custody) after the September court order. Erring on the side of parsimony, I conclude that she was moved to the Pullum jail once leased temporarily by Robards: Coleman Jr., "Lexington's Slave Dealers and Their Southern Trade," 11.

16. LH-1876. For description of the cells, see Coleman Jr., "Lexington's Slave Dealers and Their Southern Trade," 11.

17. LH-1876; Fayette County Circuit Court Order Book, vol. 37, 75, KDLA.

18. LH-1876.

19. Ibid.

20. RB-1879.

21. "Daphne Tousey," US Census, 1850, District 2, Scott County, Kentucky, Household 255, NARA microfilm, roll 218, FamilySearch.

22. The white woman was sixty-three-year-old Eleanor Fugate.
23. RB-1879. On enslaved people's search for lost loved ones, see Williams, *Help Me to Find My People*.
24. RB-1879.
25. Ibid.

CHAPTER TEN

1. See reports about the case under regular "Court Matters" column in the following 1853 issues of the *Cincinnati Gazette*: June 23, 1853; July 19, 1853; September 17, 1853; November 17, 1853; and December 15, 1853.
2. Weisenburger, *Modern Medea*, 95–98.
3. "Court Matters: Criminal Court—Before Judge Flinn," *Cincinnati Gazette*, December 16, 1853, 2; "Criminal Court—Before Judge Flinn," *Cincinnati Enquirer*, December 14, 1853, 3. The decision Flinn cited was *Prigg v. Pennsylvania*. See Fehrenbacher, *The Slaveholding Republic*, 219–25.
4. Letter by G. B. Kinkead to W. S. Bodley, February 4, 1854, Bodley Family Papers, Mss. A/B668e, Folder 57, Filson Club Historical Society. For Thruston's deathdate, see Charles Mynn Thruston tombstone in Cave Hill Cemetery, Jefferson County, Kentucky, Find a Grave Memorial no. 100562482, https://www.findagrave.com/memorial/100562482.
5. Fayette County Circuit Court Order Book, vol. 37, 193, KDLA. The lack of a recorded deed is inferred from Bodley's lack of a reply to Kinkead about it. I also conducted my own search in Jefferson County records at KDLA but found no deed.
6. "Keeper of the Penitentiary," *Covington Journal*, February 25, 1854. For cited amounts, see E. C. Wines and Theodore W. Dwight, *Report on the Prisons and Reformatories of the United States and Canada, made to the Legislature of New York, January, 1867* (Albany: Van Benthuysen & Sons, 1867), 260. On the spread of the Auburn Plan in this period, see Rebecca M. McLennan, *The Crisis of Imprisonment: Protest, Politics, and the Making of the American Penal State, 1776–1941* (New York: Cambridge University Press, 2008), 53–86. For the towers, see lithograph by C. A. Clarke included in some editions of William C. Sneed, *A Report on the History and Mode of Management of the Kentucky Penitentiary from its Origin, in 1798, to March 1, 1860* (Frankfort, KY: State of Kentucky, 1860).
7. On Craig, see Randolph Runyon, *Delia Webster and the Underground Railroad* (Lexington: University Press of Kentucky, 1996), 56–58.
8. Runyon, *Delia Webster and the Underground Railroad*, 1–57; Harrold, *Border War*, 122–23.
9. Runyon, *Delia Webster and the Underground Railroad*, 59–67, 174–83; Sneed, *Report*, 524–25.
10. On suspicions of Ward's involvement in the letters' release, see Runyon, *Delia Webster and the Underground Railroad*, 175.

11. Sneed, *Report*, 504; J. Blaine Hudson, *Fugitive Slaves and the Underground Railroad in the Kentucky Borderland* (Jefferson, NC: McFarland, 2002), 136–38; Harrold, *Border War*, 116–17, 122–31. Citing figures on the Kentucky penitentiary compiled by James Pritchard, Richard Blackett notes that "between 1844 and 1870, forty-four men and women were incarcerated for 'assisting slaves to run away,' sixteen of them in the 1850s. Of the forty-four, twenty-four were white." See Blackett, *The Captive's Quest for Freedom*, 231–32.

12. Sneed, *Report*, 516.

13. "Stampede of Slaves—Arrest of the Fugitives," *Covington Journal*, June 17, 1854. See also "Nine Fugitive Slaves," *St. Albans (VT) Messenger*, June 22, 1854 (which mentions involvement of "Sheriff Ward, of Covington Ky."); "The Fugitive Slave Case," *Cincinnati Enquirer*, June 16 and 17, 1854. A clipping about the case that mentions Ward's presence can also be found in Thomas Foraker Scrapbook, 1844–1854, Cincinnati History Library and Archives.

14. "The Slave Case—The Fugitives Remanded," *Cincinnati Enquirer*, June 18, 1854. A similar case involving a group of runaways from Kentucky who were betrayed by Ohio locals occurred in 1851. As Richard Blackett notes, under the terms of the Fugitive Slave Law "locals [in Ohio]...were perfectly within their rights to capture, hold, and return fugitives without recourse to a hearing." See Blackett, *The Captive's Quest for Freedom*, 70.

15. RB-1879. Wood recalled the trial beginning in July 1854. According to court records from the time, the trial actually started on June 24.

16. RB-1879; Fayette County Circuit Court Order Book, vol. 37, 372, KDLA.

17. LH-1876.

18. Finkelman, *An Imperfect Union*; Kennington, *In the Shadow of Dred Scott*, 104–6; Alfred L. Brophy, *University, Court, and Slave: Pro-Slavery Thought in Southern Colleges and Courts and the Coming of the Civil War* (New York: Oxford University Press, 2016), 267–74.

19. On the role of national crises in local tensions, see Harrold, *Border War*.

20. RB-1879; Fayette County Circuit Court Order Book, vol. 37, 372, 541 (which reports the Appeals Court decision), KDLA. Don Fehrenbacher claimed, "Except in Missouri, as a result of the Dred Scott case, there appears to have been no decision of a southern appellate court that denied a suit for freedom in a clear-cut case of permanent residence on free soil." According to Paul Finkelman, "Unlike most other slave states, neither the courts nor the legislature in Kentucky succumbed to the pressures of the era to the point of denying freedom to slaves who had lived in free states." Wood's defeat challenges both generalizations, which are based on reported cases and do not take into full account lower-court dismissals. See Fehrenbacher, *The Dred Scott Case*, 60; Finkelman, *An Imperfect Union*, 205.

21. LH-1876.

22. Calvin Fairbank, *Rev. Calvin Fairbank during Slavery Times: How He "Fought the Good Fight" to Prepare "The Way": Edited from his Manuscript*

(Chicago: Patriotic Publishing, 1890), 116–17. Fairbank misremembered the starting date of Ward's term.

23. Fairbank, *Rev. Calvin Fairbank*, 117.

24. Ibid.

25. Sneed, *Report*, 526, 554.

26. Ibid., 522–23. On the spread of the lease system, see Matthew J. Mancini, *One Dies, Get Another: Convict Leasing in the American South, 1866–1928* (Columbia: University of South Carolina Press, 1996).

27. Sneed, *Report*, 526–27.

28. Fairbank, *Rev. Calvin Fairbank*, 118–19; Norman B. Wood, *The white side of a black subject: enlarged and brought down to date: a vindication of the Afro-American race, from the landing of slaves at St. Augustine, Florida, in 1565, to the present time* (Chicago: American Publishing House, 1897), 216.

29. "Twelve and a Half Years in Prison," *St. Johnsbury (VT) Caledonian*, March 3, 1865, 1, reprinted from the *New York Independent*; Fairbank, *Rev. Calvin Fairbank*, 118–22; Sneed, *Report*, 546, 567, 569. With the exception of one outbreak of cholera during Craig's term, the three preceding keepers had usually reported one to four deaths a year and never more than six.

30. Franklin County Tax Assessment Rolls, Microfilm 007980, KDLA; "Register of Prisoners Confined in the Kentucky Penitentiary, on and after the First Day of September 1848," KDLA, Reel 7,009,891; [Thomas Brown,] *Brown's Three Years in the Kentucky Prisons: from May 30, 1854, to May 18, 1857* (Indianapolis: Indianapolis Journal Company, 1858), 16–17. Brown is not explicitly identified as the author of the pamphlet, which often refers to him in the third person, though the narrative of his time in prison clearly relies on his testimonies.

31. Fairbank, *Rev. Calvin Fairbank*, 123–28.

32. Brown, *Brown's Three Years*, 17–18.

33. RB-1879.

34. LH-1876. See Stephanie Jones-Rogers, "'[S]he Could…Spare One Ample Breast for the Profit of Her Owner': White Mothers and Enslaved Wet Nurses' Invisible Labor in American Slave Markets," *Slavery and Abolition* 38, no. 2 (2017): 337–55; Micki McElya, *Clinging to Mammy: The Faithful Slave in Twentieth-Century America* (Cambridge, MA: Harvard University Press, 2007); Kimberly Wallace-Sanders, *Mammy: A Century of Race, Gender, and Southern Memory* (Ann Arbor: University of Michigan Press, 2008).

35. Quoted dialogue in the following paragraphs is from LH-1876.

36. LH-1876.

37. Ibid.

CHAPTER ELEVEN

1. Brandon Layton, "Indian Country to Slave County: The Transformation of Natchez During the American Revolution," *Journal of Southern History* 82,

no. 1 (February 2016): 27–58; D. Clayton James, *Antebellum Natchez* (Baton Rouge: Louisiana State University Press, 1993), 1–53; Beckert, *Empire of Cotton*, 101–4; Adam Rothman, *Slave Country: American Expansion and the Origins of the Deep South* (Cambridge, MA: Harvard University Press, 2005); John Craig Hammond, *Slavery, Freedom, and Expansion in the Early American West* (Charlottesville: University of Virginia Press, 2007), 13–29.

2. Edward E. Baptist, *The Half Has Never Been Told: Slavery and the Making of American Capitalism* (New York: Basic Books, 2014), 113–14; Joshua D. Rothman, *Flush Times and Fever Dreams: A Story of Capitalism and Slavery in the Age of Jackson* (Athens: University of Georgia Press, 2012), 3–5; Anthony E. Kaye, *Joining Places: Slave Neighborhoods in the Old South* (Chapel Hill: University of North Carolina Press, 2007), 3–4.

3. Rothman, *Flush Times and Fever Dreams*, 2–5, quotes on p. 5. On the Treaty of Dancing Rabbit Creek, Johnson, *River of Dark Dreams*, 30, 36–47; Baptist, *The Half Has Never Been Told*, 249.

4. Baptist, *The Half Has Never Been Told*, 261–307; Beckert, *Empire of Cotton*, 113; Michael Wayne, *The Reshaping of Plantation Society: The Natchez District, 1860–1880* (Baton Rouge: Louisiana State University Press, 1983), 9–12; Joshua D. Rothman, "The Contours of Cotton Capitalism: Speculation, Slavery, and Economic Panic in Mississippi, 1832–1841," in *Slavery's Capitalism: A New History of American Economic Development*, ed. Sven Beckert and Seth Rockman (Philadelphia: University of Pennsylvania Press, 2016), 122–45.

5. Johnson, *River of Dark Dreams*, 12. See the similar formula by an earlier visitor to Natchez, quoted in Rothman, *Flush Times and Fever Dreams*, 10: "to sell cotton in order to buy negroes—to make more cotton to buy more negroes, 'ad infinitum,' is the aim and direct tendency of all the operations of the thorough-going cotton planter; his whole soul is wrapped up in the pursuit."

6. Jonathan H. Ingraham, *The South-West, by a Yankee* (2 vols.; New York: Harper & Brothers, 1835), 2: 192–93. For descriptions of the market, see Jim Barnett and H. Clark Burkett, "The Forks of the Road Slave Market at Natchez," *Journal of Mississippi History* 63, no. 3 (Fall 2001): 169–87; Bancroft, *Slave-Trading in the Old South*, 300–311; Gudmestad, *A Troublesome Commerce*, 17, 24–25, 93–95; Calvin Schermerhorn, *Money over Mastery, Family over Freedom: Slavery in the Antebellum Upper South* (Baltimore: Johns Hopkins University Press, 2011), 124–68.

7. "Ragged & dirty" from a letter by Isaac Franklin, quoted in Schermerhorn, *The Business of Slavery and the Rise of American Capitalism, 1815–1860*, 141. On preparations for slave sales, see Johnson, *Soul by Soul*, 118–21. See also Deyle, *Carry Me Back*, 145–49.

8. RB-1879; LH-1876. On Pullum's stand at Natchez, see Coleman Jr., "Lexington's Slave Dealers and Their Southern Trade," 17; Clark, "The Slave Trade Between Kentucky and the Cotton Kingdom," 333.

9. Deposition of William Pullum in *Hughes' Administrator v. Salem Downing* (1853), and deposition of S. Wood in *Griffin and Pulliam [Pullum] v. C. C. Morgan* (1855), Fayette County Circuit Court, Box 145, Drawer 1279–81, both in KDLA. For use of steamboats by traders, see Gudmestad, *Steamboats and the Rise of the Cotton Kingdom*, 56–57.

10. LH-1876. For map, see Barnett and Burkett, "The Forks of the Road Slave Market at Natchez," 168. Busy season: Gudmestad, *A Troublesome Commerce*, 1–2.

11. Johnson, *Soul by Soul*, 78–116.

12. "Slaves! Slaves!," *Natchez Free Trader*, June 14, 1853 (the ad was placed in October 16, 1852); "Slaves!! Slaves!! Slaves!!!," *Natchez Daily Courier*, November 27, 1858. On traders' marketing practices, Johnson, *Soul by Soul*, 117–34.

13. LH-1876; RB-1879. Wilson could have been Andrew L. Wilson, a prominent citizen of Natchez who acquired the Rosalie mansion in 1857. For a description of an inspection at the Griffin and Pullum stand that involved the stripping of a slave, see *Coffey v. Griffin and Pullum* (1858), Group 1850, Box 25, File 49, Adams County Court Records, Historic Natchez Foundation (hereafter HNF).

14. LH-1876. Examples of Griffin and Pullum suits: *State of Mississippi v. Pierce Griffin and William Pullum* (1854), Box 26, File 101; *John Tucker v. Griffin and Pullum* (1855), Box 26, File 84; *Benjamin Gilbert v. Griffin and Pullum* (1854), Box 26, File 93; *Cicero Stampley v. Griffin, Pullum & Co.* (1857), Box 27, File 62, all in Group 1850, Adams County Court Records, HNF. See also Welch, *Black Litigants in the Antebellum American South*.

15. LH-1876. Gerard C. Brandon was elected to two terms as governor, each two years long, beginning in 1828. He had also been lieutenant governor for his two predecessors and served as acting governor during large parts of both men's terms. See Gerard Brandon, *The Brandon Family*, ed. Daisy Patterson Brandon Dale (1932; Natchez, MS: Daisy Patterson Brandon Dale, 2007).

16. Claude E. Fike, "The Gubernatorial Administrations of Gerard Chittocque Brandon, 1825–1832," *Journal of Mississippi History* 35, no. 3 (August 1973): 247–66.

17. Brandon quoted in Charles S. Sydnor, *Slavery in Mississippi* (New York: D. Appleton-Century, 1933), 161–62. For similar alarms from some of Governor Brandon's contemporaries, see Gudmestad, *A Troublesome Commerce*, 102–17; Lacy Ford, "Reconsidering the Internal Slave Trade: Paternalism, Markets, and the Character of the Old South," in Walter Johnson, ed., *The Chattel Principle: Internal Slave Trades in the Americas* (New Haven, CT: Yale University Press, 2004), 157–59.

18. William Kauffman Scarborough, *Masters of the Big House: Elite Slaveholders of the Mid-Nineteenth-Century South* (Baton Rouge: Louisiana State University Press, 2003), 432; *Biographical and Historical Memoirs of Mississippi*, vol. 2 (Chicago: Goodspeed, 1891), 817.

19. See Johnson, *Soul by Soul*, 135–61; Johnson, *River of Dark Dreams*, 152–63, quote on 160.

20. LH-1876.
21. Frederick Law Olmsted, *The Cotton Kingdom: A Traveller's Observations on Cotton and Slavery in the American Slave States*, ed. Arthur M. Schlesinger (1861; New York: Alfred A. Knopf, 1953), 422. On the roads around Natchez, see Charles S. Sydnor, *A Gentleman of the Old Natchez Region: Benjamin L. C. Wailes* (Durham, NC: Duke University Press, 1938), 79–80; Winthrop D. Jordan, *Tumult and Silence at Second Creek: An Inquiry into a Civil War Slave Conspiracy*, rev. ed. (Baton Rouge: Louisiana State University Press, 1995), 10. On the use of landscaping to turn plantations into a "carceral" space and southern roads into routes that were easy to patrol, see Johnson, *River of Dark Dreams*, 221–28. Even today, the approach to Brandon Hall along the Natchez Trace Parkway retains the occluded look that nineteenth-century visitors noticed.
22. LH-1876.
23. Ibid.; Herbert Weaver, *Mississippi Farmers, 1850–1860* (Nashville: Vanderbilt University Press, 1945), 108–10; Joseph Karl Menn, *The Large Slaveholders of Louisiana, 1860* (New Orleans: Pelican, 1964), 196, 202, 393, 399; Ralph A. Wooster, "Wealthy Southerners on the Eve of the Civil War," in *Essays on Southern History Written in Honor of Barnes F. Lathrop*, ed. Gary W. Gallagher (Austin: University of Texas at Austin General Libraries, 1980), 144, 147.
24. Gerard Brandon, Esq., "Historic Adams County," *Publications of the Mississippi Historical Society* 2 (1899): 216. See also Steven Brooke, *The Majesty of Natchez* (Gretna, LA: Pelican, 2007), 92; "Brandon Hall," in Reid Smith and John Owens, *The Majesty of Natchez* (Montgomery, AL: Paddle Wheel, 1969).
25. Sydnor, *A Gentleman of the Old Natchez Region*, 288.

CHAPTER TWELVE

1. On combined value of slaves, see James L. Huston, *Calculating the Value of the Union: Slavery, Property Rights, and the Economic Origins of the Civil War* (Chapel Hill: University of North Carolina Press, 2003), 27–29.
2. LH-1876.
3. On the labor routines of Adams County cotton plantations in this period, see Kaye, *Joining Places*, 83–118. See Pargas, *Slavery and Forced Migration in the Antebellum South*, 135–48, on the adjustment of Upper South slaves to cotton cultivation. Kaye notes that "most slaves [in the Natchez District] were only a generation or two removed from the Upper South" (Kaye, *Joining Places*, 3).
4. Weight of bales from Johnson, *River of Dark Dreams*, 251. On hemp, Andrew Patrick, "Clothing King Cotton: Kentucky Hemp in the Atlantic World," paper presented at Atlantic Environments and the American South conference, Rice University, February 5–6, 2016.
5. Kaye, *Joining Places*, 3; Taylor, *Frontiers of Freedom*, 2.
6. Baptist, *The Half Has Never Been Told*, 187–92; Kaye, *Joining Places*, chap. 2; Tera W. Hunter, *Bound in Wedlock: Slave and Free Black Marriage in the*

Nineteenth Century (Cambridge, MA: Harvard University Press, 2017), chap. 1.

7. *State of Mississippi v. Little Jordan, a Slave* (1854), Group 1850, Box 26, File 68, Adams County Court Records, HNF. On conflicts, see Pargas, *Slavery and Forced Migration in the Antebellum South*, 220; Baptist, *The Half Has Never Been Told*, 148–53; Jeff Forret, *Slave Against Slave: Plantation Violence in the Old South* (Baton Rouge: Louisiana State University Press, 2015).

8. RB-1879; LH-1876. On gendered division of labor: Kaye, *Joining Places*, 95–96; Johnson, *River of Dark Dreams*, 161.

9. Johnson, *River of Dark Dreams*, 151–208. On factor-planter and credit relationships, see Weaver, *Mississippi Farmers, 1850–1860*, 107; Beckert, *Empire of Cotton*, 204; Richard Holcombe Kilbourne Jr., *Debt, Investment, Slaves: Credit Relations in East Feliciana Parish, Louisiana 1825–1885* (Tuscaloosa: University of Alabama Press, 1995). On management, see Caitlin Rosenthal, *Accounting for Slavery: Masters and Management* (Cambridge, MA: Harvard University Press, 2018).

10. On grades, see Johnson, *River of Dark Dreams*, 251; Beckert, *Empire of Cotton*, 207–12.

11. Buckner, Manning, and Newman to Gerard Brandon Esq., February 4, 1854, Forrest Flinn Collection, HNF. The same collection contains other correspondence between Brandon and that firm, as well as two others: Mandeville & McIlhenny and George Connelly & Co. The collection includes examples of detailed cotton bills of sale made out by Mandeville & McIlhenny.

12. On mortgages and slaves as collateral, see Bonnie Martin, "Neighbor-to-Neighbor Capitalism: Local Credit Networks and the Mortgaging of Slaves," in *Slavery's Capitalism*, ed. Beckert and Rockman, 107–21; Jonathan Levy, *Freaks of Fortune: The Emerging World of Capitalism and Risk in America* (Cambridge, MA: Harvard University Press, 2012), 89–97. On advantages of large slaveholders, see Gavin Wright, *Slavery and American Economic Development* (Baton Rouge: Louisiana State University Press, 2006), 93.

13. Receipts from Griffin and Pullum by Gerard Brandon, dated April 26, 1858, and January 19, 1859, Forrest Flinn Collection, HNF. See also other transactions made in 1859 for $5,850 and $13,750, also in Forrest Flinn Collection, HNF. The collection also contains a list of slaves and prices or values, apparently made in 1859. On planters' frequent valuations of enslaved people, see Berry, *The Price for Their Pound of Flesh*, 83–86, 94–97.

14. R. M. McIlhenny to Gerard Brandon, October 28, 1854, Forrest Flinn Collection, HNF.

15. Letter from New Orleans by Herndon to Gerard Brandon, October 23, 1860, Forrest Flinn Collection, HNF.

16. On these calculations, see Johnson, *River of Dark Dreams*, 151–75; Caitlin Rosenthal, "Slavery's Scientific Management: Masters and Managers," in Beckert and Rockman, *Slavery's Capitalism*, 62–86.

17. LH-1876. "John Lyle, Overseer," under "Gerard Brandon," US Census, 1860, Adams County, Mississippi, NARA microfilm M653, roll 577, FamilySearch.
18. LH-1876.
19. Ibid.; RB-1879.
20. RB-1879.
21. Ibid. Wood's memories reflect a theme in other slave narratives of what historian Walter Johnson calls "forced neuro-muscular transformation." See Johnson, *River of Dark Dreams*, 151–75; Baptist, *The Half Has Never Been Told*, 136–39.
22. LH-1876. See receipt for payment to B. J. Sandford, dated February 6, 1862, in Forrest Flinn Collection, HNF; entry for September 15, 1863, Gerard Brandon Diary, HNF. See also Baptist, *The Half Has Never Been Told*, 111–44.
23. LH-1876.
24. Ibid.
25. Ibid. On size of hands, see Johnson, *River of Dark Dreams*, 152–53. In RB-1879, Wood recalled of Brandon that "I worked in the field for him till they thought I was going to die, and then they changed my work to the house. The work in the field was too hard for me."
26. See Kaye, *Joining Places*, 85–89. On violence of slaveholding women, see Glymph, *Out of the House of Bondage*.
27. LH-1876; RB-1879.
28. LH-1876.
29. Ibid.

CHAPTER THIRTEEN

1. Sneed, *Report*, 537.
2. Fairbank, *Rev. Calvin Fairbank*, 122. See mortality figures compiled in Sneed, *Report*, 564–69. Twenty-three deaths took place over a little more than a year, between December 1, 1857, and March 1, 1859. Nineteen more deaths were reported from March 1, 1859, to December 1, 1859; thirteen of those were casualties of lung disease in the first four months after Ward's departure. The average number of prisoners in 1856 and 1857 was 240; in 1858, 284.
3. Sneed, *Report*, 535, 546, 543–44. See also 529–30.
4. Ibid., 558.
5. "We Go for Zeb Ward!," *Louisville Daily Courier*, January 25, 1858.
6. Sneed, *Report*, 537, 564–69.
7. Ibid., 554. Fairbank estimated Ward's fortune at $100,000, though that was likely an exaggeration. See Fairbank, *Rev. Calvin Fairbank*, 119.
8. "Letters from the Editor," *Wilkes' Spirit of the Times*, March 29, 1862.
9. On Woodford slaveholdings, see Aaron Astor, *Rebels on the Border: Civil War, Emancipation, and the Reconstruction of Kentucky and Missouri* (Baton Rouge: Louisiana State University Press, 2012), 22. Names and locations of

farms come from E. A. and G. W. Hewitt, *Topographical map of the counties of Bourbon, Fayette, Clark, Jessamine, and Woodford, Kentucky from actual surveys* (New York: Smith, Gallup, 1861), online at http://hdl.loc.gov/loc.gmd/g3953b.la000225.

10. See Katherine C. Mooney, *Race Horse Men: How Slavery and Freedom Were Made at the Racetrack* (Cambridge, MA: Harvard University Press, 2014), 1–116; Maryjean Wall, *How Kentucky Became Southern: A Tale of Outlaws, Horse Thieves, Gamblers, and Breeders* (Lexington: University Press of Kentucky, 2010), 28–29. On colonial racing, see Rhys Isaac, *The Transformation of Virginia, 1740–1790* (1982; New York: W. W. Norton, 1988), 98–101, 118–19.

11. Mooney, *Race Horse Men*, 38–54.

12. Franklin County Tax Assessment Rolls, Microfilm 007980, KDLA; Woodford County Court Order Book vol. L, 258, 318, KDLA; "Zeb Ward," US Census, 1860, Woodford County, Kentucky, NARA microfilm M653, reel 400, FamilySearch; "Zeb Ward," US Census (Slave Schedules), 1860, Woodford County, Kentucky, 72, Ancestry.com; deed of property by H. H. Culbertson to Zeb Ward, Woodford County Deed Book W, 488, KDLA; Kentucky, Franklin County, 1848–1880, vol. 13, 111, and Kentucky, Woodford County, 1852–1878, vol. 41, 263, R. G. Dun & Co. Credit Report Volumes, Baker Library, Harvard Business School.

13. Mooney, *Race Horse Men*, 89–95; Wall, *How Kentucky Became Southern*, 28–29, 42–48; Peter Chew, *The Kentucky Derby: The First 100 Years* (Boston: Houghton Mifflin, 1974), 7, 14.

14. Woodford County Court Order Book L, 258; Mary E. Wharton and Ellen F. Williams, eds., *Peach Leather and Rebel Gray: Bluegrass Life and the War, 1860–1865* (Lexington, KY: Helicon, 1986), 19; "Mercer County Fair," *Louisville Daily Courier*, October 8, 1859; "Second Annual Exhibition of the Salvisa Stock Association," *Louisville Daily Courier*, October 10, 1859; "Splendid Geldings," *Cleveland Ohio Farmer*, November 19, 1859.

15. On the sensorium of planters at home, see Johnson, *River of Dark Dreams*, 199.

16. "Another Insurrection Case," *Louisville Daily Courier*, November 22, 1859. On Brown's raid, see Tony Horwitz, *Midnight Rising: John Brown and the Raid That Sparked the Civil War* (New York: Henry Holt, 2011); Robert E. McGlone, *John Brown's War Against Slavery* (New York: Cambridge University Press, 2009), 246–306. For Kentucky coverage, see *Louisville Daily Courier* for October 18, 19, and 20, 1859.

17. See Harrold, *Border War*, 179, 187–93, Bailey quoted on 191; Griffler, *Front Line of Freedom*, 58–61, 120–23. For Norris Day, see "Another Insurrection Case"; Runyon, *Delia Webster and the Underground Railroad*, 166–72. See also David S. Reynolds, *John Brown, Abolitionist: The Man Who Killed Slavery, Sparked the Civil War, and Seeded Civil Rights* (New York: Alfred A. Knopf, 2005), 334–37.

18. "Another Fire in Frankfort—Arrest of the Incendiary—Negro Excitement," *Louisville Daily Courier*, September 17, 1856; Harrold, *Border War*, 185–86; Charles B. Dew, "Black Ironworkers and the Slave Insurrection Panic of 1856," *Journal of Southern History* 41 (August 1975): 321–38. *Western Recorder* quoted in Harlow, *Religion, Race, and the Making of Confederate Kentucky, 1830–1880*, 101.

19. Harrold, *Border War*, 192–93; "Frankfort and Versailles Insurrection," *Louisville Daily Courier*, November 26, 1859.

20. "A Judicial Decision in Anderson," *Louisville Daily Courier*, November 17, 1859.

21. *Frankfort Yeoman* quoted in "Frankfort and Versailles Insurrection."

22. Zeb Ward to Henry A. Wise, November 23, 1859, Executive Papers of Governor Henry A. Wise, Library of Virginia, Series II, Subseries B, Microfilm Reel Misc 4219, Frames 270–71.

23. Though Ward is not named, the rope "sent by Express" from Kentucky is accurately described, along with a report of its being handed by Wise to Major John Newton Brown, in "Execution of John Brown," *Raleigh (NC) Standard*, December 7, 1859, 3. For the various samples of rope and the tests, see "John Brown's Invasion," *New York Tribune*, December 6, 1859, 6, which describes the rope chosen as "of hemp, made in Kentucky, and sent in a box to Sheriff Campbell by a planter for this express purpose"—possibly a distortion of the story about Ward's rope. It was reported that after the hanging, the rope was cut up and distributed to observers. See *Portsmouth (OH) Daily Times*, December 10, 1859, 2. Several reports describe the rope used as unusually short. See also Reynolds, *John Brown, Abolitionist*, 396.

24. Wharton and Williams, *Peach Leather and Rebel Gray*, 19; deed of property from H. H. Bohannon to Zeb Ward, Woodford County Deed Book X, 197, KDLA; "The Woodlawn Race Course," *Louisville Daily Courier*, April 18, 1860; "Races at Woodburn—Great Sport Ahead," *Louisville Daily Courier*, June 18, 1860.

25. John Tyler Jr., "The Secession of the South," in John Stauffer and Zoe Trodd, eds., *The Tribunal: Responses to John Brown and the Harpers Ferry Raid* (Cambridge, MA: Harvard University Press, 2012), 329–32. See also William Freehling, *Road to Disunion*, vol. 2: *Secessionists Triumphant, 1854–1861* (New York: Oxford University Press, 2007), 205–21.

26. On the Republican antislavery plan, see James Oakes, *Freedom National: The Destruction of Slavery in the United States, 1861–1865* (New York: W. W. Norton, 2013), 1–83; James Oakes, *The Scorpion's Sting: Antislavery and the Coming of the Civil War* (New York: W. W. Norton, 2014).

27. Charles B. Dew, *Apostles of Disunion: Southern Secession Commissioners and the Causes of the Civil War*, Fifteenth Anniversary Ed. (Charlottesville: University of Virginia Press, 2016), 51–56, 112–25.

28. Quotes from Astor, *Rebels on the Border*, 45.

29. Christopher Phillips, *The Rivers Ran Backward: The Civil War and the Remaking of the American Middle Border* (New York: Oxford University Press, 2016), 145; "Speech at Cincinnati, Ohio," in Basler, ed., *Collected Works of Abraham Lincoln*, vol. 4, 197–99. On the complexities of Unionism in Kentucky, see Astor, *Rebels on the Border*; Patrick A. Lewis, *For Slavery and Union: Benjamin Buckner and Kentucky Loyalties in the Civil War* (Lexington: University Press of Kentucky, 2015); Stephen I. Rockenbach, *War Upon Our Border: Two Ohio Valley Communities Navigate the Civil War* (Charlottesville: University of Virginia Press, 2016); and Ford, *Bonds of Union*, 203–94.

30. On "armed neutrality" as a policy, see Phillips, *The Rivers Ran Backward*, 120–37.

31. "Woodlawn Races, First Day," *Louisville Daily Courier*, May 20, 1861; Tim Talbott, "Woodlawn Race Course," *ExploreKYHistory*, http://explorekyhistory. ky.gov/items/show/329, accessed October 20, 2017.

32. James M. McPherson, *Battle Cry of Freedom: The Civil War Era* (New York: Oxford University Press, 1988), 339–47.

33. "Covington," *Cincinnati Daily Commercial*, July 16, 1861, 2. On aftermath of battle, McPherson, *Battle Cry of Freedom*, 348–50.

34. Ward to Wise. On Jones, see Wharton and Williams, *Peach Leather and Rebel Gray*.

35. See Oakes, *Freedom National*, 106–44; McPherson, *Battle Cry of Freedom*, 295–96.

36. Victor B. Howard, *Black Liberation in Kentucky: Emancipation and Freedom, 1862–1884* (Lexington: University Press of Kentucky, 1983), 4; Wharton and Williams, *Peach Leather and Rebel Gray*, 65.

37. Oakes, *Freedom National*, 145–66; Phillips, *The Rivers Ran Backward*, 142–44.

38. Oakes, *Freedom National*, 160–63.

39. *Journal of the House of Representatives of the Commonwealth of Kentucky, Begun and Held in the Town of Frankfort, on Monday, the Second Day of September…1861* (Frankfort, KY: John B. Major, 1861), 503, 537–38.

40. Phillips, *The Rivers Ran Backward*, 144–62, 214–16; Oakes, *Freedom National*, 188–89.

41. Wharton and Williams, *Peach Leather and Rebel Gray*, 79–80. On Union commanders and fugitive slaves, see Phillips, *The Rivers Ran Backward*, 218; Oakes, *Freedom National*, 171–86.

42. Phillips, *The Rivers Ran Backward*, 169, 199; James M. McPherson, *Crossroads of Freedom: Antietam* (New York: Oxford University Press, 2002), 19.

43. On Wilkes, see Mooney, *Race Horse Men*, 104–8; Alexander Saxton, *The Rise and Fall of the White Republic: Class Politics and Mass Culture in Nineteenth-Century America* (1990; London: Verso, 2003), 205–25.

44. "Letters from the Editor."

45. Ibid.
46. McPherson, *Battle Cry of Freedom*, 405–14.

CHAPTER FOURTEEN

1. RB-1879. See Justin Behrend, *Reconstructing Democracy: Grassroots Black Politics in the Deep South After the Civil War* (Athens: University of Georgia Press, 2015), 14; Kaye, *Joining Places*, 21–50.
2. Armstead L. Robinson, "In the Shadow of Old John Brown: Insurrection Anxiety and Confederate Mobilization, 1861–1863," *Journal of Negro History* 65, no. 4 (Autumn 1980): 41–45, Dora Franks quoted on 42. On literacy laws, see Charles S. Sydnor, *Slavery in Mississippi* (New York: D. Appleton-Century, 1933), 53–55. On wartime networks of information among enslaved people in the Natchez District, see especially Kaye, *Joining Places*, 177–83; Behrend, *Reconstructing Democracy*, 15–20; Jordan, *Tumult and Silence at Second Creek*. On those networks in the South more generally, Steven Hahn, *A Nation Under Our Feet: Black Political Struggles in the Rural South from Slavery to the Great Migration* (Cambridge, MA: Harvard University Press, 2003), chap. 1; Stephanie McCurry, *Confederate Reckoning: Power and Politics in the Civil War South* (Cambridge, MA: Harvard University Press, 2010), 226–33; Thavolia Glymph, "Rose's War and the Gendered Politics of a Slave Insurgency in the Civil War," *Journal of the Civil War Era* 3, no. 4 (December 2013): 501–32.
3. Mississippi Declaration of Secession, Avalon Project, http://avalon.law.yale.edu/19th_century/csa_missec.asp. On the Brandons' politics, see Scarborough, *Masters of the Big House*, 329–38.
4. Kaye, *Joining Places*, 179–80; Jordan, *Tumult and Silence at Second Creek*, 11–15, 292. See also Behrend, *Reconstructing Democracy*, 20–21.
5. Jordan, *Tumult and Silence at Second Creek*, 75–80, 311.
6. Quotes at Jordan, *Tumult and Silence at Second Creek*, 273. See 126–27 for mention of "Brandon's teamster." After a close reading of the notes taken by a planter, historian Winthrop Jordan concluded that an insurrectionary plot was in fact developing near Second Creek. I favor the more recent interpretation of historian Justin Behrend who, drawing on the testimonies of the accused as well as other sources, concludes that slaves in the area were "struggling to come to grips with the implications of war and trying to determine the intentions of President Lincoln," though not necessarily conspiring to revolt. "The uncertainty of emancipation, Lincoln's plans, and the course of war prompted local white leaders to interpret slave rumors as the makings of a massive slave insurrection." Behrend also persuasively argues that many more hangings occurred as part of a wave of Confederate repression than the number counted by Jordan. See Behrend, *Reconstructing Democracy*, 22–25.
7. Littleton Barber, "Testimony by a Mississippi Freedman before the Southern Claims Commission," in Ira Berlin, Thavolia Glymph, Steven F. Miller, et al.,

Freedom: A Documentary History of Emancipation, 1861–1867, series 1, vol. 3: *The Wartime Genesis of Free Labor: The Lower South* (New York: Cambridge University Press, 1990), 723.

8. Chandra Manning, *Troubled Refuge: Struggling for Freedom in the Civil War* (New York: Alfred A. Knopf, 2016), 109. On slaves near Frankfort, see Howard, *Black Liberation in Kentucky*, 4. For the interactions between enslaved freedom-seekers and Union military policy, see Oakes, *Freedom National*.

9. George Connelly to Gerard Brandon, October 5, 1861, Forrest Flinn Collection, HNF. See also other letters regarding cotton sales from Brandon's merchants dated from January, March, August, and October in the same collection.

10. Date of death from Agnes Brandon tombstone near Brandon Hall; on the appearance of Union boats near Natchez, see Ronald L. F. Davis, *The Black Experience in Natchez, 1720–1880* (Natchez, MS: Natchez National Historical Park, 1993), 145; Kaye, *Joining Places*, 177. On Union advances in 1862, see McPherson, *Battle Cry of Freedom*, 392–422.

11. Davis, *The Black Experience in Natchez, 1720–1880*, 145.

12. McPherson, *Crossroads of Freedom*, 27. See also Phillips, *The Rivers Ran Backward*, 169–99. On the infant twins who died, see "Hon. Zeb Ward of Kentucky," *Wilkes' Spirit of the Times*, May 17, 1862.

13. "The Races," *Philadelphia Inquirer*, June 24, 1862, and June 26, 1862; "The Turf," *New York Times*, July 8, 1862. See Wall, *How Kentucky Became Southern*, chap. 1.

14. "The Turf," *New York Times*, July 8, 1862, and July 12, 1862.

15. "The Bygone Week," *New York Times*, July 6, 1862; "The News from Richmond," *New York Times*, July 3, 1862. See also McPherson, *Battle Cry of Freedom*, 491.

16. On Morgan and other raiders, see McPherson, *Battle Cry of Freedom*, 513–14; Phillips, *The Rivers Ran Backward*, 202–4; Rockenbach, *War Upon Our Border*, 80; Astor, *Rebels on the Border*, 56–57.

17. "Morgan at Versailles," *Philadelphia Inquirer*, July 24, 1862; "Exploits of a Land Pirate," *New York Evening Post*, August 1, 1862; "Morgan's Raid in the Bluegrass Region," *Gallipolis (OH) Journal*, August 7, 1862. See also Astor, *Rebels on the Border*, 113.

18. Oakes, *Freedom National*, 289–90, 301–39; McPherson, *Battle Cry of Freedom*, 503.

19. Astor, *Rebels on the Border*, 110; Phillips, *The Rivers Ran Backward*, 211–35; Rockenbach, *War Upon Our Border*, 76–118.

20. Gun scene from Howard, *Black Liberation in Kentucky*, 14. See also William M. Fliss, "Wisconsin's Abolition Regiment: The Twenty-second Volunteer Infantry in Kentucky, 1862–1863," *Wisconsin Magazine of History* 86, no. 2 (2002–2003): 3–17.

21. George B. Kinkead, Lexington, to W. S. Bodley, Louisville, December 18, 1862, Bodley Family Papers, Mss. A/B668e, Folder 69, Filson Club Historical Society.

22. "By the Orange Train," *Houston Tri-Weekly Telegraph*, March 6, 1863; "Kentucky Legislature," *Maysville (KY) Weekly Bulletin*, February 5, 1863. See also "Kentucky Legislature," *St. Louis Daily Missouri Democrat*, January 31, 1863; *Journal of the House of Representatives*, 1275.

23. Date of death from tombstone in Brandon Family cemetery near Brandon Hall. On the cotton famine, McPherson, *Battle Cry of Freedom*, 546–50; Beckert, *Empire of Cotton*, 242–73.

24. John Q. Anderson, ed., *Brokenburn: The Journal of Kate Stone, 1861–1868* (Baton Rouge: Louisiana State University Press, 1995), 127.

25. T. C. Holmes to Gerard Brandon, May 7, 1863, Forrest Flinn Collection, HNF. Holmes, who was born in Massachusetts, appears in the 1850 Census as a steamboat captain in Natchez and the owner of one slave; by 1860, he is listed as a "planter" living in New Orleans with $50,000 worth of real estate.

26. Behrend, *Reconstructing Democracy*, 30; Laura S. Haviland, *A Woman's Life-Work: Labors and Experiences of Laura S. Haviland* (Chicago: C. V. Waite, 1887), 304.

27. "Interesting Letter from Natchez," *Chicago Journal,* reprinted in *Janesville (WI) Weekly Gazette*, August 7, 1863; "Letter from Natchez," *Milwaukee Sentinel*, February 17, 1864.

28. "Letter from Natchez."

29. RB-1879.

CHAPTER FIFTEEN

1. The estimate of three hundred is based on county tax records in Texas; five hundred was Wood's estimate in RB-1879 of the number on the march. For the July 1 departure date, see affidavit of Gerard Brandon dated April 25, 1866, "Estate of Margaret Smith," New No. 163, Probate Court, Adams County, Mississippi, also cited in Gerard B. Rickey and Alan C. Rayne, eds., *"I Will Write if I Have to Use a Stick": Letters from Home—Cornelia Jane Shields' Letters to Her Children, 1864–1865* (University Park, TX: Estate of Sara Brandon Rickey, 2000), 63, n. 6.

2. Gerard Brandon kept a small journal of his trip to Texas, a photocopy of which can be found at the Historic Natchez Foundation. My own transcriptions from the photocopies are hereafter cited as Brandon Diary. Brandon also mentions the diary in a letter to his daughter Ella Brandon, October 21, 1863, in the Vonkersburg Family Collection, HNF. Because the photocopies are not bound or numbered, nor is it clear whether they represent the original page order, I have not included page numbers when citing. Gerard B. Rickey and Alan C. Rayne made their own self-published transcription of the journal in 2016, and I am grateful to Mr. Rickey for sharing it with me for comparison. An incomplete and sometimes inaccurate transcription of part of the journal, completed by Helen Rayne in 1999, can be found in the Dolph Briscoe Center at the University of Texas at Austin.

3. LH-1876; RB-1879. The estimate of four hundred miles is closer to the distance from Brandon Hall to their final stopping point in Texas, rather than from Alexandria.

4. W. Caleb McDaniel, "Involuntary Removals: 'Refugeed Slaves' in Confederate Texas," in *Lone Star Unionism, Dissent, and Resistance: Other Sides of Civil War Texas*, ed. Jesús F. de la Teja (Norman: University of Oklahoma Press, 2016), 60–83.

5. Bell Irvin Wiley, ed., *Fourteen Hundred and 91 Days in the Confederate Army: A Journal Kept by W. W. Heartsill for Four Years, One Month and One Day* (Jackson, TN: McCowat-Mercer, 1954), 84; George Hepworth, *The Whip, Hoe, and Sword: or, the Gulf-Department in '63* (Boston: Walker, Wise, 1864), 126–27.

6. Robert L. Kerby, *Kirby Smith's Confederacy: The Trans-Mississippi South, 1863–1865* (New York: Columbia University Press, 1972), 106–9.

7. Ira Berlin, Barbara J. Fields, Thavolia Glymph, et al., eds., *Freedom: A Documentary History of Emancipation, 1861–1867*, series 1, vol. 1: *The Destruction of Slavery* (New York: Cambridge University Press, 1985), 772–73. On controversies over the impressment policy in Texas, see R. H. Ward to Pendleton Murrah, January 4, 1864, Records of the Governor Pendleton Murrah, Box 301–44, Folder 10; J. Bankhead Magruder to Pendleton Murrah, January 13, 1864, Records of the Governor Pendleton Murrah, Box 301–44, Folder 12, both at Texas State Library and Archives Commission.

8. Quotes taken from Allen Manning interview in George P. Rawick, ed., *The American Slave: A Composite Autobiography*, vol. 7: *Oklahoma and Mississippi Narratives* (Westport, CT: Greenwood, 1972), 215–222A; Arthur J. Fremantle, *Three Months in the Southern States, April–June 1864* (Edinburgh: William Blackwood, 1863), 78–80, 85. For varying estimates of the numbers of refugeed slaves to Texas, compare Yael A. Sternhell, *Routes of War: The World of Movement in the Confederate South* (Cambridge, MA: Harvard University Press, 2012), 99; Berlin et al., *The Destruction of Slavery*, 676; Dale Baum, "Slaves Taken to Texas for Safekeeping During the Civil War," in *The Fate of Texas: The Civil War and the Lone Star State*, ed. Charles D. Grear (Fayetteville: University of Arkansas Press, 2008), 83–103; Randolph B. Campbell, *An Empire for Slavery: The Peculiar Institution in Texas* (Baton Rouge: Louisiana State University Press, 1989), 245.

9. Pass for Gerard Brandon, July 8, 1863, by Command of Major Franklin H. Clack, Forrest Flinn Collection, HNF. On the wartime reversals that made fleeing masters have to get "passes," see Sternhell, *Routes of War*, 153.

10. RB-1879; Brandon Diary.

11. *Marshall Texas Republican*, October 7, 1864. On the roads' condition, see Kerby, *Kirby Smith's Confederacy*, 84.

12. Robertson County Tax Rolls (1864), microfilm, Texas A&M University, College Station. According to the same rolls, "J. S. Able" owned land in

Robertson County on the John Welch and Joseph Welch grants. The number of assessed slaves is not a perfect measure of how many Brandon had brought to Texas; by 1864, he had hired many out to other counties, and some had died. On counties where refugee planters were concentrated, see Baum, "Slaves Taken to Texas for Safekeeping During the Civil War." On the Brazos Bottomlands, Robertson County, and growth of cotton in Texas, see Dale Baum, *Counterfeit Justice: The Judicial Odyssey of Texas Freedwoman Azeline Hearne* (Baton Rouge: Louisiana State University Press, 2009); Campbell, *An Empire for Slavery*; Richard Denny Parker, *Historical Recollections of Robertson County, Texas*, ed. Nona Clement Parker (Salado, TX: Anson Jones, 1955); B. P. Gallaway, ed., *Texas, the Dark Corner of the Confederacy: Contemporary Accounts of the Long Star State in the Civil War* (Lincoln: University of Nebraska Press, 1994), 69.

13. LH-1876.

14. Brandon Diary.

15. Ibid.; RB-1879. On sickness in the Civil War and immediate postwar period, see Jim Downs, *Sick from Freedom: African-American Illness and Suffering During the Civil War and Reconstruction* (New York: Oxford University Press, 2012). Brandon's journal listed eighteen "Deaths on Trip to Texas," but there is no way of knowing whether it was a comprehensive accounting. The last death listed was on February 2, 1864, when Brandon returned to Natchez for a visit, and his journal did not count deaths thereafter.

16. RB-1879.

CHAPTER SIXTEEN

1. LH-1876.

2. Dennis Murray, "Smile of Time Finds Lawyer Active Tho 92," *Chicago Tribune*, August 8, 1948, part 3, 4S.

3. "Smile of Time." In addition to Simms's death certificate, mentioned below, census records for Simms from 1870, 1880, 1900, and 1910, all available on FamilySearch, also connect him to Wood.

4. "Smile of Time"; Arthur H. Simms Medical Certificate of Death no. 73178, State of Illinois, downloaded from Cook County genealogy website.

5. On practices surrounding the birth of enslaved children in the antebellum United States, see Schwartz, *Born in Bondage*, chaps. 1–2; Marie Jenkins Schwartz, *Birthing a Slave: Motherhood and Medicine in the Antebellum South* (Cambridge, MA: Harvard University Press, 2006).

6. The 1900 Census gives his father's birthplace as Maryland, while the 1910 and 1920 Censuses give his father's birthplace as Kentucky. The 1930 Census says it was Mississippi. On naming practices, Schwartz, *Born in Bondage*, 168–70. For examples of keeping information about fathers secret, see Schwartz, *Born in Bondage*, 45. On sexual assaults inside slave jails, see Pargas, *Slavery and Forced Migration in the Antebellum South*, 103.

7. In a discussion of sex within slavery, Hortense J. Spillers questions "whether or not 'pleasure' is possible at all under conditions that I would aver as non-freedom for both or either of the parties." Spillers, "Mama's Baby, Papa's Maybe: An American Grammar Book," *Diacritics* 17, no. 2 (Summer 1987): 64–81. But see also the efforts to recover a history of enslaved women's sexuality as a site of both politics and pleasure in Stephanie M. H. Camp, *Closer to Freedom: Enslaved Women and Everyday Resistance in the Plantation South* (Chapel Hill: University of North Carolina Press, 2004), 60–92; Hartman, *Scenes of Subjection*, chap. 2; Treva B. Lindsey and Jessica Marie Johnson, "Searching for Climax: Black Erotic Lives in Slavery and Freedom," *Meridians* 12, no. 2 (2014): 169–95. In Lexington, Wood had seen at least one enslaved or formerly enslaved woman, "Beck," who had managed, probably through a sexual relationship with Lewis Robards, to obtain some degree of power not otherwise available to her. But the archive provides no basis for speculation that Wood willingly chose a sexual partner for any reason while imprisoned in a slave jail, and other records of life in the slave jails provide extensive evidence of sexual exploitation. Ultimately, slavery's violence and the archive it left behind make it difficult, if not impossible, to recover fully the lived sexual experiences of enslaved women; see Marisa J. Fuentes, *Dispossessed Lives: Enslaved Women, Violence, and the Archive* (Philadelphia: University of Pennsylvania Press, 2016); Wendy Warren, "'The Cause of Her Grief': The Rape of a Slave in Early New England," *Journal of American History* 93, no. 4 (March 2007): 1031–49.

8. LH-1876. On wet nursing by enslaved women, see Jones-Rogers, "[S]he Could…Spare One Ample Breast for the Profit of Her Owner." Wet nurses were sometimes purchased or hired because a white mother was unable, for some reason, to breastfeed her children. If this was the case with Wood, her retort to Zebulon Ward that Mary could not quiet her own child may have intensified the offense that the Wards took to her perceived impudence. Note that the 1880 Census gives 1854 as the year of Simms's birth, though other records unite around 1856.

9. William Wells Brown quoted in Buchanan, *Black Life on the Mississippi*, 87. On sexual assault on steamboats, see also Gudmestad, *Steamboats and the Rise of the Cotton Kingdom*, 39. On rape by traders, Baptist, "'Cuffy,' 'Fancy Maids,' and 'One-Eyed Men'"; Deyle, *Carry Me Back*, 126–27. On sexual violence as a means of control, see Hannah Rosen, *Terror in the Heart of Freedom: Citizenship, Sexual Violence, and the Meaning of Race in the Postemancipation South* (Chapel Hill: University of North Carolina Press, 2009).

10. LH-1876. For a persuasive discussion of the potential meanings of silence surrounding the rape of an enslaved woman, see Taylor, *Driven Toward Madness*, 92–109. See also Cathy McDaniels-Wilson, "The Psychological Aftereffects of Racialized Sexual Violence," in *Gendered Resistance: Women, Slavery, and the Legacy of Margaret Garner*, ed. Mary E. Frederickson and Delores M. Walters

(Urbana: University of Illinois Press, 2013), 191–205; Nell Painter, "Soul Murder and Slavery: Toward a Fully Loaded Cost Accounting," in *Southern History Across the Color Line* (Chapel Hill: University of North Carolina Press, 2002), 15–39.

11. Henry Bibb, *Narrative of the Life and Adventures of Henry Bibb, the American Slave, Written by Himself* (New York: Author, 1849), 14, http://docsouth.unc.edu/neh/bibb/bibb.html.

12. Schwartz notes the difficult choices that enslaved people made about what to tell the children of interracial unions about their ancestry; see Schwartz, *Born in Bondage*, 44. In the 1910 Census, Simms and his family are called "mulatto," though other records refer to him as "black." See "Simms, Arthur H.," US Census, 1910, Chicago, Ward 7, Enumeration District 406, Cook County, Illinois, NARA microfilm T624, FamilySearch. On the instability of racial ascriptions, see Martha Hodes, "The Mercurial Nature and Abiding Power of Race: A Transnational Family Story," *American Historical Review* 108, no. 1 (February 2003): 84–118.

13. Aron, *How the West Was Lost*, 146; Amy Dru Stanley, "Slave Breeding and Free Love: An Antebellum Argument over Slavery, Capitalism, and Personhood," in *Capitalism Takes Command: The Social Transformation of Nineteenth-Century America*, ed. by Michael Zakim and Gary J. Kornblith (Chicago: University of Chicago Press, 2012), 137–38. On the sexual economy of slavery and rules governing reproduction of slaves, see Berry, *The Price for Their Pound of Flesh*, chap. 1; Hunter, *Bound in Wedlock*, 9–10, 65–67; Morris, *Southern Slavery and the Law*, 43–49; Johnson, *River of Dark Dreams*, 192–99; Adrienne Davis, "'Don't Let Nobody Bother Yo' Principle': The Sexual Economy of American Slavery," in *Sister Circle: Black Women and Work*, ed. Sharon Harley (New Brunswick, NJ: Rutgers University Press, 2002), 103–27; White, *Ar'n't I a Woman?*, 99–104. On laws concerning the status of interracial children, see Morris, *Southern Slavery and the Law*, 21–29.

14. Bibb, *Narrative*, 40, 199; Stanley, "Slave Breeding and Free Love," 137–38. See also Hunter, *Bound in Wedlock*, 29–52.

15. Davis, "'Don't Let Nobody Bother Yo' Principle,'" 112–17, quoted on 112; Hartman, *Scenes of Subjection*, 95–96; Rosen, *Terror in the Heart of Freedom*, 9–11; Morris, *Southern Slavery and the Law*, 306. On the trope of black women's lasciviousness and powers of seduction, see Hartman, *Scenes of Subjection*, 86–90; White, *Ar'n't I a Woman?*, 27–43; Jennifer Morgan, *Laboring Women: Reproduction and Gender in New World Slavery* (Philadelphia: University of Pennsylvania Press, 2004).

16. Harriet Jacobs, *Incidents in the Life of a Slave Girl*, 207, 208. See also Thelma Jennings, "'Us Colored Women Had to Go Through A Plenty': Sexual Exploitation of African-American Slave Women," *Journal of Women's History* 1, no. 3 (Winter 1990): 45–74.

17. See Deborah Clark Hine, "Rape and the Inner Lives of Black Women in the Middle West," *Signs* 14, no. 4 (Summer 1989): 912–20; Dorothy Roberts,

"The Paradox of Silence and Display: Sexual Violation of Enslaved Women and Contemporary Contradictions in Black Female Sexuality," in Bernadette J. Brooten, ed., *Beyond Slavery: Overcoming its Religious and Sexual Legacies* (New York: Palgrave Macmillan, 2010), 41–60. Cf. Brenda E. Stevenson, *Life in Black and White: Family and Community in the Slave South* (New York: Oxford University Press, 1996), 236–37.

18. Cincinnati city directories between 1875 and 1880 list Wood as a widow, though it is unclear whether she provided the term or it was assigned to her on the basis of her age and singlehood. She might have answered Simms's questions about his father by saying that he had died. See also her entry in the 1910 Census under Simms's household and Wood's death certificate.

19. On child care practices on plantations, see Schwartz, *Born in Bondage*.

20. "Smile of Time."

CHAPTER SEVENTEEN

1. LH-1876.
2. Brandon Diary.
3. Ibid.
4. Ibid.
5. RB-1879. On enslaved women as caregivers, see Sharla M. Fett, *Working Cures: Healing, Health, and Power on Southern Slave Plantations* (Chapel Hill: University of North Carolina Press, 2002). For more on references to "Henrietta" in the journal, see my appendix.
6. Brandon Diary. On planters' calculations about feeding slaves, see Johnson, *River of Dark Dreams*, 176–208.
7. Brandon Diary.
8. Ibid.
9. Ibid. On opposition to refugees, see Baum, "Slaves Taken to Texas for Safekeeping During the Civil War," 91–93; Mary Elizabeth Massey, *Refugee Life in the Confederacy* (Baton Rouge: Louisiana State University Press, 1964), chap. 8; Campbell, *An Empire for Slavery*, 245. On class tensions within the Confederacy, see McCurry, *Confederate Reckoning*.
10. Brandon Diary.
11. Ibid.
12. Ibid.
13. Ibid.
14. Ibid.
15. Ibid.
16. Ibid. The man who fled west as far as Menard County was Matthew Gaines, who later became a black state legislator in Reconstruction Texas. See Ann Patton Malone, "Matt Gaines: Reconstruction Politician," in *Black Leaders: Texans for Their Times*, ed. Alwyn Barr and Robert A. Calvert (Austin: Texas State

Historical Association, 1981), 53. On Mexico as a destination for runaways, see Sean Kelley, "'Mexico in His Head': Slavery and the Texas-Mexico Border, 1810–1860," *Journal of Social History* 37, no. 3 (Spring 2004): 709–23.

17. Brandon Diary.

CHAPTER EIGHTEEN

1. RB-1879. On the continuation of wartime beyond Confederate surrender, see Gregory P. Downs, *After Appomattox: Military Occupation and the Ends of War* (Cambridge, MA: Harvard University Press, 2015).

2. For varying estimates of people still enslaved at war's end, see Downs, *After Appomattox*, 41–42; Oakes, *Freedom National*, 421. See also Susan Eva O'Donovan, *Becoming Free in the Cotton South* (Cambridge, MA: Harvard University Press, 2007), 111: "The end of the Civil War must not be confused with the end of slavery."

3. On Texas as "the last stronghold of de facto slavery," see Steven Hahn, Steven F. Miller, Susan E. O'Donovan, et al., eds., *Freedom: A Documentary History of Emancipation, 1861–1867*, series 3, vol. 1: *Land and Labor, 1865* (Chapel Hill: University of North Carolina Press, 2008), 77.

4. See statement of Brandon's account with Ranger and Company, dated June 15, 1866, in "Receipts from Cities other than Natchez and New Orleans," Forrest Flinn Collection, HNF. On the absence of troops and major military actions in the Texas cotton county, see Campbell, *An Empire for Slavery*, 231–33. Brandon even purchased Confederate bonds in Monroe, Louisiana, in May 1864, suggesting some optimism about the war. See receipt dated May 23, 1864, Forrest Flinn Collection, HNF.

5. On the bureau in Texas, see William L. Richter, *Overreached on All Sides: The Freedmen's Bureau Administrators in Texas, 1865–1868* (College Station: Texas A&M University Press, 1991).

6. George P. Rawick, ed., *The American Slave: a Composite Autobiography; Supplement Series 2*, vol. 3: *Texas Narratives, part 2* (Westport, CT: Greenwood, 1979), 779.

7. Ibid.; RB-1879. See also Baum, *Counterfeit Justice*, 40–45, 49.

8. Letter from Gerard Brandon to Ella Brandon, September 10, 1865, Vonkersburg Family Collection, HNF. Some of Brandon's planter friends who had "refugeed slaves" in Texas were already trying in September 1865 to bring them back to Mississippi. See letter from G. C. Covington to Gerard Brandon, September 17, 1865, Forrest Flinn Collection, HNF.

9. *Constitution of the State of Mississippi, as Amended, with the Ordinances and Resolutions adopted by the Constitutional Convention, August, 1865* (Jackson, MS: E. M. Yerger, 1865), 28. See also Oakes, *Freedom National*, 484–85; Foner, *Reconstruction*, 193–94. While observing that slavery was effectively at an end, the framers of Mississippi's 1865 constitution did not approve of the

change: the state would not formally ratify the Thirteenth Amendment to the Constitution until 2013.

10. Gerard Brandon to Ella Brandon, September 10, 1865. The bridal gift amount is referenced in another letter, dated June 10, 1866, also in the Vonkersburg Family Collection, HNF.

11. Hahn et al., *Land and Labor, 1865*, 60–61, 82–83. On land distribution rumors, see Hahn, *A Nation Under Our Feet*, 116–59.

12. Hahn et al., *Land and Labor, 1865*, 167; James Smallwood, *Time of Hope, Time of Despair: Black Texans During Reconstruction* (Port Washington, NY: National University Publications, 1981), 25–42, "right after freedom" quote on 34. See John Gorman, "Reconstruction Violence in the Lower Brazos River Valley," in Kenneth W. Howell, ed., *Still the Arena of Civil War: Violence and Turmoil in Texas, 1865–1874* (Denton: University of North Texas Press, 2012), 387–420; Barry A. Crouch, "A Spirit of Lawlessness: White Violence; Texas Blacks, 1865–1868," *Journal of Social History* 18, no. 2 (Winter 1984): 217–32.

13. "From Middle Texas," *Flake's Daily Bulletin*, August 2, 1865, 1. See also Smallwood, *Time of Hope, Time of Despair*, 34.

14. RB-1879; Letter from Gerard Brandon to Ella Brandon, October 29, 1865, Vonkersburg Family Collection, HNF.

15. Gerard Brandon to Ella Brandon, September 10, 1865. On the disappointing crop, Carl H. Moneyhon, *Texas After the Civil War: The Struggle of Reconstruction* (College Station: Texas A&M University Press, 2004), 35–36.

16. Nancy Cohen-Lack, "A Struggle for Sovereignty: National Consolidation, Emancipation, and Free Labor in Texas, 1865," *Journal of Southern History* 58, no. 1 (February 1992): 57–89; Grant quoted on 87.

17. "From Texas; Important Orders by General Granger," *New York Times*, July 7, 1865; Andrews quoted in Cohen-Lack, "A Struggle for Sovereignty," 67. See also Richter, *Overreached on All Sides*, 3–16.

18. Senate Executive Document 27, 39th Cong., 1st sess., 78–79. See also Gregg Cantrell, "Racial Violence and Reconstruction Politics in Texas, 1867–1868," *Southwestern Historical Quarterly* 93, no. 3 (January 1990): 333–34.

19. Senate Executive Document 27, 78–79.

20. Ibid., 82. See also Richter, *Overreached on All Sides*, 23.

21. Baum, *Counterfeit Justice*, 53.

22. Ibid., 53–55.

23. Ibid., 55.

24. Champe Carter Jr., Sub-Asst. Commissioner, to Maj. General J. B. Kiddoo, Galveston, June 21, 1866, "Texas, Freedmen's Bureau Field Office Records, 1865–1870," Sterling, NARA microfilm M1912, roll 26, FamilySearch.

25. On the government as a distant ally, see Gregory P. Downs, *Declarations of Dependence: The Long Reconstruction of Popular Politics in the South, 1861–1908* (Chapel Hill: University of North Carolina Press, 2011).

26. Downs, *After Appomattox*; Hamilton quoted on 43.
27. On Johnson's encouragements to states to ratify the Thirteenth Amendment, Oakes, *Freedom National*, 483–84.
28. For a full narrative of these political struggles between Johnson and Congress, see Eric Foner, *Reconstruction: America's Unfinished Revolution* (New York: Harper & Row, 1989).
29. Phillips, *The Rivers Ran Backward*, 306; Rockenbach, *War Upon Our Border*, 176; Foner, *Reconstruction*, 262–64.
30. Barry A. Crouch, "'All the Vile Passions': The Texas Black Code of 1866," in *Dance of Freedom: Texas African Americans During Reconstruction*, ed. Larry Madaras (Austin: University of Texas Press, 2007), 134–58; Throckmorton quoted on 140.
31. Gerard Brandon to Aaron "Tip" Stanton, June 17, 1866, Vonkersburg Family Collection, HNF.
32. Ibid.
33. Gerard Brandon to Ella Stanton, July 23, 1866, Vonkersburg Family Collection, HNF; Brandon to Aaron Stanton, June 17, 1866.
34. Gerard Brandon to Ella Stanton, July 23, 1866.
35. Brandon to Aaron Stanton, June 17, 1866; RB-1879.
36. William W. Pugh to Robert Campbell Martin Sr. [June 1865], transcription in Martin-Pugh Collection, item 677, Nicholls State University; Hahn et al., *Land and Labor, 1865*, 322. See also René Hayden, Anthony E. Kaye, Kate Masur, et al., eds., *Freedom: A Documentary History of Emancipation, 1861–1867*, ser. 3, vol. 2: *Land & Labor, 1866–1867* (Chapel Hill: University of North Carolina Press, 2013), 101.
37. For an example of refugees leaving without paying workers, see copy of November 23, 1865, letter, Records of the Assistant Commissioner for Texas, 1865–1869, "Received and Retained Reports relating to Rations, Lands, and Bureau Personnel, 1865–66," NARA microfilm M821, roll 29, FamilySearch. My thanks to Edward Valentin for calling my attention to this source.
38. RB-1879.

CHAPTER NINETEEN

1. "Hon. Zeb Ward of Kentucky," *Spirit of the Times*, November 19, 1864, 184. See also *Nashville Union*, November 8, 10, and 11, 1864, all on 3.
2. Astor, *Rebels on the Border*, 125–28; Richard D. Sears, *Camp Nelson, Kentucky: A Civil War History* (Lexington: University Press of Kentucky, 2002). On the connections among enlistment, freedom, and citizenship, see Oakes, *Freedom National*, 353–62.
3. Astor, *Rebels on the Border*, 128; Oakes, *Freedom National*, 388.
4. D. C. Humphreys to "Alie," June 24, 1864, Box 18, Folder 10, Alexander Family Papers, Kentucky Historical Society. For names and muster records of

the men enslaved by Ward, see Tim Talbott, "Zeb Ward's Slaves Run Off to Join the Union Army," *Random Thoughts on History*, November 29, 2013, http://randomthoughtsonhistory.blogspot.com, accessed February 7, 2018.

5. Humphreys to "Alie"; Astor, *Rebels on the Border*, 134, 139.

6. Anne Marshall, *Creating a Confederate Kentucky: The Lost Cause and Civil War Memory in a Border State* (Chapel Hill: University of North Carolina Press, 2010); Phillips, *The Rivers Ran Backward*, 285–325.

7. "Woodford County Farm for Sale," *Louisville Daily Courier*, August 22, 1866.

8. On Ward's loss of horses during Morgan's raid, see Humphreys to "Alie." In September 1865, an agent for the New York credit reporting firm R. G. Dun & Co. had pronounced Ward "good"—a reliable businessman who could be counted on to pay whatever debts he contracted. The same report also noted his closing up of his business in Versailles. See Kentucky, Woodford County, 1852–78, vol. 41, 263, R. G. Dun & Co. Credit Report Volumes, Baker Library, Harvard Business School. On stories that he was an aide-de-camp, and then a government purchasing agent, see "Busy Life Ended," *Arkansas Gazette*, December 29, 1894.

9. On the shift of racing northward, see Wall, *How Kentucky Became Southern*.

10. "Blessed are the Peace-Makers: Griefs of a Kentucky Peace-Maker at the Hands of Rebels," *Chicago Tribune*, April 19, 1866; "Important Decision," *Louisville Daily Courier*, October 16, 1866.

11. See Jesse Crawford Crowe, "The Origin and Development of Tennessee's Prison Problem, 1831–1871," *Tennessee Historical Quarterly* 15, no. 2 (June 1956): 111–35; Larry D. Gossett, "The Keepers and the Kept: The First Hundred Years of the Tennessee State Prison System, 1830–1930" (PhD thesis, Louisiana State University, 1992), 33–63.

12. Crowe, "The Origin and Development of Tennessee's Prison Problem," 122; Mancini, *One Dies, Get Another*, 154.

13. Although the interpretation is outdated, there are still valuable details about this period in Thomas B. Alexander, *Political Reconstruction in Tennessee* (Nashville, TN: Vanderbilt University Press, 1950).

14. "Proposals for Leasing the Convict Labor of the State Penitentiary of Tennessee," *Louisville Daily Courier*, June 11, 1866, 2. On Memphis, Rosen, *Terror in the Heart of Freedom*, 23–83; Stephen V. Ash, *A Massacre in Memphis: The Race Riot that Shook the Nation One Year After the Civil War* (New York: Hill & Wang, 2012).

15. "Tennessee State Prison," *Nashville Union and Dispatch*, November 29, 1866. On Kentucky origins of Briggs and Hyatt, see "Convict Labor," *Nashville Republican Banner*, November 29, 1866; "Nashville," *Louisville Daily Courier*, July 17, 1866, 4; letter from C. M. Briggs to Beriah Magoffin, March 26, 1861, Civil War Governors of Kentucky Digital Documentary Edition, https://civilwargovernors.org/. Another early partner named Moore was also a Kentuckian; Ward may have been his replacement. Briggs had lived in Nashville for some period prior to the lease.

16. "Nashville Agricultural Works," *Nashville Union and American*, June 18, 1867, signed by "Hyatt, Briggs & Ward"; "Proposals"; "Dissolution of Partnership," *Nashville Union and American*, August 3, 1867; "Bagging! Bagging!," *Nashville Republican Banner*, September 29, 1867, 3. See also "Cotton Planters Take Notice," *Nashville Union and American*, October 7, 1866, 1. On the fire, see Crowe, "The Origin and Development of Tennessee's Prison Problem," 127; Mancini, *One Dies, Get Another*, 154.

17. Gossett, "The Keepers and the Kept," 67; Crowe, "The Origin and Development of Tennessee's Prison Problem," 123. Conservatives swept county elections in March 1866: Alexander, *Political Reconstruction in Tennessee*, 104.

18. Crowe, "The Origin and Development of Tennessee's Prison Problem," 124.

19. Foner, *Reconstruction*, 252–61, 276–80.

20. Allen W. Trelease, *White Terror: The Ku Klux Klan Conspiracy and Southern Reconstruction* (New York: Harper & Row, 1971), 6–7.

21. Elaine Frantz Parsons, *Ku Klux: The Birth of the Klan During Reconstruction* (Chapel Hill: University of North Carolina Press, 2015), 27–71; Trelease, *White Terror*, 3–46.

22. For another Klan-like group of the period in Tennessee, see Edward John Harcourt, "Who Were the Pale Faces? New Perspectives on the Tennessee Ku Klux," *Civil War History* 51, no. 1 (2005): 23–66.

23. Trelease, *White Terror*, 29–34.

24. *Report of Evidence taken before the Military Committee in Relation to Outrages Committed by the Ku Klux Klan in Middle and West Tennessee, submitted to the Extra Session of the Thirty-Fifth General Assembly of the State of Tennessee, September 2d, 1868* (Nashville: S. C. Mercer, 1868), 15–18.

25. Trelease, *White Terror*, 43.

26. Ben H. Severance, *Tennessee's Radical Army: The State Guard and Its Role in Reconstruction, 1867–1869* (Knoxville: University of Tennessee Press, 2005), 180–91.

27. Trelease, *White Terror*, 45–46; Jack Hurst, *Nathan Bedford Forrest: A Biography* (New York: Alfred A. Knopf, 1993), 302–15.

28. "The Interview at Nashville," *Memphis Public Ledger*, August 4, 1868, 2.

29. "The Peace Movement," *Nashville Republican Banner*, August 1, 1868. See also "Reconstruction: The Law and Order Movement in Tennessee," *New York Tribune*, August 5, 1868. On the difference between federal troops and the milita, see Trelease, *White Terror*, 32. For evidence that Ward had interacted with the Confederate generals in the past, see the notice of his stay at a Memphis hotel at the same time as Gideon Pillow, in *Memphis Public Ledger*, January 28, 1868. His ties to the turf may also have brought him into contact with such men, given the ties between competitive horsemanship and the origins of the Klan: Paul Christopher Anderson, "Rituals of Horsemanship: A Speculation on the Ring Tournament and the Origins of the Ku Klux Klan," in Stephen Berry, ed., *Weirding the War: Stories from the Civil War's Ragged Edges* (Athens: University of Georgia Press, 2011), 215–33.

30. "Busy Life Ended."
31. Severance, *Tennessee's Radical Army*, 189–91.
32. *House Journal of the First Session of the Twenty-Fifth General Assembly of the State of Tennessee, for the Years 1867–68* (Nashville: S. C. Mercer, 1868), 416; Alexander, *Political Reconstruction in Tennessee*, 167–68. Much of the conflict is summarized in an open letter to the state legislature drafted by Ward and Briggs and published under "State Prison," *Nashville Union and American*, December 2, 1868, 1. See also "The New Penitentiary Bill," *Nashville Union and American*, March 10, 1868; Mancini, *One Dies, Get Another*, 154–55; Crowe, "The Origin and Development of Tennessee's Prison Problem," 127; Gossett, "The Keepers and the Kept," 74.
33. *Twenty-Fourth Annual Report of the Executive Committee of the Prison Association of New York, and Accompanying Documents, for 1868* (Albany, NY: Argus, 1869), 137–40.
34. Ibid., 138; "Prison Association of New York," *Nashville Union and American*, July 17, 1869, 4; "The Penitentiary: A Wordy War between the Lessees and Warden," *Nashville Republican Banner*, September 5, 1868, 4.
35. Alexander, *Political Reconstruction in Tennessee*, 218–19; Mancini, *One Dies, Get Another*, 154–55. The conservative victories were made possible by a judicial ruling that returned control of voter registration to local authorities, enabling ex-Confederates to obtain ballots.
36. *Covington City Directory, Also, Complete City Directories of Cynthiana, Paris, and Lexington, for 1871* (Cincinnati: T. J. Smith, 1871), 319; "Glimpses of Yesterday," *Arkansas Gazette*, June 9, 1940; "Ward, Zeb," US Census, 1870, Ward 4, Lexington, Fayette County, Kentucky, NARA microfilm M593, roll 460, FamilySearch.
37. "A Splendid Prize," *Nashville Union and American*, November 13, 1867; "The Races: Fifth Day of the Fall Meeting Over the Memphis Course," *Memphis Public Ledger*, November 16, 1867. On the Congress, see Mooney, *Race Horse Men*, 152; "Journal of the Turf Congress, Assembled at Louisville, Ky., June, 1867," *Louisville Daily Courier*, July 9, 1867, 3; "The Turf Congress—A Meeting to be Held in Nashville," *Louisville Daily Courier*, August 29, 1868, 4.
38. "The Turf: Fifth Day of the Spring Meeting of the Buckeye Club," *Cincinnati Enquirer*, June 4, 1870, 8; "The Turf," *Louisville Courier-Journal*, May 15, 1870; "The Races," *Nashville Republican Banner*, October 12, 1870.
39. For summons delivery on June 3, 1870, see Chicago Case File. There is no certain evidence tying Ward to the Buckeye Club races being held that same day, but Wood's 1879 interview in the *Ripley Bee* reported that "service was obtained" on Ward while he was "coming to Cincinnati to attend the horse races." That interview dated the summons incorrectly, however, as having occurred in 1869. See RB-1879. I nevertheless find it plausible that Ward attended the races in Cincinnati on the same day the summons was issued and

delivered; had he been elsewhere, it likely would have taken longer for the sheriff to inform him, and there is no available documentary evidence placing him somewhere else that day.

CHAPTER TWENTY

1. "'The Old Evil': A Case of Alleged Kidnapping," *Cincinnati Enquirer*, June 8, 1870, 8.
2. Ibid.
3. Kull, "Restitution in Favor of Former Slaves"; Westley, "Restitution Claims for Wrongful Enslavement and the Doctrine of the Master's Good Faith"; Sinha, *Abolition*, 107, 109, 114, 153, 173–74.
4. Roy E. Finkenbine, "'Who Will…Pay for Their Sufferings?': New York Abolitionists and the Failed Campaign to Compensate Solomon Northup," *New York History* 95, no. 4 (Fall 2014): 637–46; Ana Lucia Araujo, *Reparations for Slavery and the Slave Trade: A Transnational and Comparative History* (London: Bloomsbury, 2017), 53; Claude F. Oubre, *Forty Acres and a Mule: The Freedmen's Bureau and Black Land Ownership* (Baton Rouge: Louisiana State University Press, 1978).
5. LH-1876. According to Chicago Case File, she returned in April.
6. A copy of the handwritten contract between Gerard Brandon and Henrietta Wood, hereafter cited as "1866 Contract," was shared with me by Mr. David M. Blackman, Wood's great-great-grandson, who received it from his mother. While its exact provenance is unknown, the contract appears to have been saved by Wood and then passed down to descendants.
7. See Amy Dru Stanley, *From Bondage to Contract: Wage Labor, Marriage, and the Market in the Age of Slave Emancipation* (New York: Cambridge University Press, 1998).
8. Justin Behrend, "Black Political Mobilization and the Spatial Transformation of Natchez," in *Confederate Cities: The Urban South during the Civil War Era*, ed. Andrew L. Slap and Frank Towers (Chicago: University of Chicago Press, 2015), 190–214; Christopher M. Span, *From Cotton Field to Schoolhouse: African American Education in Mississippi, 1862–1875* (Chapel Hill: University of North Carolina Press, 2009).
9. Behrend, *Reconstructing Democracy*, 1–10.
10. 1866 Contract. Whitehurst's papers are housed at the Mississippi Department of Archives and History.
11. 1866 Contract; LH-1876. See also O'Donovan, *Becoming Free in the Cotton South*, 172–83, 199–207. On struggles over children, see Catherine A. Jones, *Intimate Reconstructions: Children in Postemancipation Virginia* (Charlottesville: University of Virginia Press, 2015), 64–75; Noralee Frankel, *Freedom's Women: Black Women and Families in Civil War Era Mississippi* (Bloomington: Indiana University Press, 1999), 123–45; Mary Niall Mitchell, *Raising Freedom's*

Child: Black Children and Visions of the Future after Slavery (New York: New York University Press, 2008), 143–87.

12. Aaron Stanton to Ella Brandon Stanton, December 25, 1868, Box 1, Dunbar Merrill Flinn Papers, HNF. On gendered dimensions of Reconstruction amendments, see Amy Dru Stanley, "Instead of Waiting for the Thirteenth Amendment: The War Power, Slave Marriage, and Inviolate Human Rights," *American Historical Review* 115, no. 3 (June 2010): 732–65. On recovery of the planter elite, see Wayne, *The Reshaping of Plantation Society*. On Christmas gifts as an index of economic security, cf. Jones, *Intimate Reconstructions*, 88.

13. See Williams, *Help Me to Find My People*; Williams, *They Left Great Marks on Me*; Glymph, *Out of the House of Bondage*; Hunter, *Bound in Wedlock*; Hunter, *To 'Joy My Freedom*; Jones, *Intimate Reconstructions*, 47–64; Rosen, *Terror in the Heart of Freedom*; Rothman, *Beyond Freedom's Reach*; Downs, *Sick from Freedom*; Behrend, *Reconstructing Democracy*, 50–51, 83, 111–12; Frankel, *Freedom's Women*; Jones, *Labor of Love, Labor of Sorrow*, 43–73; Leslie A. Schwalm, *A Hard Fight for We: Women's Transition from Slavery to Freedom in South Carolina* (Urbana: University of Illinois Press, 1997); Melissa Milewski, *Litigating Across the Color Line: Civil Cases Between Black and White Southerners from the End of Slavery to Civil Rights* (New York: Oxford University Press, 2018), 9; Elsa Barkley Brown, "Negotiating and Transforming the Public Sphere: African American Political Life in the Transition from Slavery to Freedom," *Public Culture* 7 (1994): 107–46.

14. LH-1876.

15. Lynch quoted on Foner, *Reconstruction*, 562. See also Nicholas Lemann, *Redemption: The Last Battle of the Civil War* (New York: Farrar, Straus & Giroux, 2006).

16. Joe William Trotter Jr., *River Jordan: African American Urban Life in the Ohio Valley* (Lexington: University Press of Kentucky, 1998), 59; Nancy Bertaux, "Structural Economic Change and Occupational Decline Among Black Workers in Nineteenth-Century Cincinnati," in Henry Louis Taylor Jr., ed., *Race and the City: Work, Community, and Protest in Cincinnati, 1820–1970* (Urbana: University of Illinois Press, 1993), 141–42; Phillips, *The Rivers Ran Backward*, 161–62, 332.

17. Trotter, *River Jordan*, 56; Darrel E. Bigham, *On Jordan's Banks: Emancipation and Its Aftermath in the Ohio River Valley* (Lexington: University Press of Kentucky, 2006), 107–11. Full residential segregation by race was not yet fully accomplished, however, until the twentieth century. See Henry Louis Taylor Jr., "City Building, Public Policy, the Rise of the Industrial City, and Black Ghetto-Slum Formation in Cincinnati, 1850–1940," in Taylor, *Race and the City*, 156–92.

18. Bertaux, "Structural Economic Change," 137, 144. Similar patterns could be observed in other postwar cities. On Atlanta, Georgia, for example, see Hunter, *To 'Joy My Freedom*.

19. Taylor, *Frontiers of Freedom*, 197–99; Leonard Harding, "The Cincinnati Riots of 1862," *Bulletin of the Cincinnati Historical Society* 25, no. 4 (October 1967): 239.

20. See "Smile of Time" for Simms's claim. On search for family, Williams, *Help Me to Find My People*.

21. The short, handwritten letter from Lucinda Tousey to "My Friend Henrietta" was shared with me by David M. Blackman, Wood's great-great-grandson, who found it among family keepsakes. Though it is dated only as "Mar 7," Tousey's comment that it had "been two years this month (the 28th) since the death of my husband" dates the letter to 1870. Tousey invited Wood to visit her in Lawrenceburg, but there is no record that she did.

22. "Wood, Henrietta," US Census, 1870, Ward 1, Covington, Kenton County, Kentucky, Family 610, NARA microfilm M593, roll 478, FamilySearch.

23. "Myers, Harvey," US Census, 1870, Ward 1, Covington, Kenton County, Kentucky, Family 609, NARA microfilm M593, roll 478, FamilySearch.

24. "Covington News: Sold," *Cincinnati Enquirer*, May 16, 1866; "The Renomination of Mr. Carlisle—His Letter of Acceptance," *Cincinnati Enquirer*, February 3, 1866, 1; Tom Owen, "John White Stevenson," in *Kentucky's Governors*, updated ed. (Lexington: University Press of Kentucky, 2004), 98–100. Myers was the editor of two compendiums of Kentucky laws and decisions used by fellow attorneys: Harvey Myers, ed., *The Code of Practice in Civil and Criminal Cases for the State of Kentucky: with All Amendments made prior to Jan'y 1, 1867, with Notes of the Decisions of the Court of Appeals of Kentucky, and of the Courts of Ohio and New York* (Cincinnati: R. Clarke, 1867); Myers, ed., *A Digest of the General Laws of Kentucky: Enacted by the Legislature, between the Fourth Day of December, 1859, and the Fourth Day of June, 1865* (Cincinnati: R. Clarke, 1866).

25. "The S. S. Newman Tobacco Trial," *Cincinnati Enquirer*, December 11, 1869, 7; "Declined," *Cincinnati Enquirer*, December 14, 1865, 2; "Resigned," *Cincinnati Enquirer*, November 29, 1865, 3; "The Contested Election Cases," *Cincinnati Enquirer*, August 26, 1865, 1; "Covington News," *Cincinnati Enquirer*, February 8, 1866, 1; "Mr. Harvey Myers," *Cincinnati Enquirer*, December 13, 1865, 2; "Covington News: Conservative Democratic Ticket," *Cincinnati Enquirer*, August 7, 1865, 2.

26. "Meeting of the Members of the Bar," *Cincinnati Enquirer*, November 28, 1871, 7. On the testimony debate, see Victor B. Howard, "The Black Testimony Controversy in Kentucky, 1866–1872," *Journal of Negro History* 58 (1973): 140–65.

27. RB-1879.

28. Roy E. Finkenbine, "Belinda's Petition: Reparations for Slavery in Revolutionary Massachusetts," *William and Mary Quarterly* 64, no. 1 (January 2007): 95–104. For at least a few years, Belinda received the allowance she requested. On enslaved people's thinking about remuneration and reparations, see

Lynda J. Morgan, *Known for My Work: African American Ethics from Slavery to Freedom* (Gainesville: University Press of Florida, 2016).

29. Leon F. Litwack, *Been in the Storm so Long: The Aftermath of Slavery* (New York: Alfred A. Knopf, 1979), 333–35.

30. Welch, *Black Litigants in the Antebellum American South*, 3–5, 31–33. On the circulation of legal knowledge among enslaved people, making them "savvy legal actors," see also Twitty, *Before Dred Scott*, 71–95.

31. The petition to the Cincinnati court is included within Chicago Case File.

32. Chicago Case File.

33. RB-1879; Chicago Case File.

34. William M. Wiecek, "The Reconstruction of Federal Judicial Power, 1863–1875," *American Journal of Legal History* 13, no. 4 (October 1969): 333–59. Ward's lawyers invoked that new removal rule even though they did not need it to win their motion. An older law already permitted defendants to remove to a federal court when they were nonresidents in the state of the suit, as long as damages claimed exceeded $500. Since Ward lived in Kentucky in 1870, Wood's suit for $20,000 already met both conditions. See Edward A. Purcell Jr., *Litigation and Inequality: Federal Diversity Jurisdiction in Industrial America, 1870–1958* (New York: Oxford University Press, 1992), 14–15.

35. Horace Greeley, *Mr. Greeley's Letters from Texas and the Lower Mississippi* (New York: Tribune Office, 1871), 46, 55. See also David W. Blight, *Race and Reunion: the Civil War in American Memory* (Cambridge, MA: Harvard University Press, 2001), 122–30.

36. Phillips, *The Rivers Ran Backward*, 309.

37. "The Free Trade Meeting at Steinway Hall," *Tiffin (OH) Tribune*, June 13, 1872. See also *Cincinnati Enquirer*, March 12, 1872, 4; "Impeachment," *Akron (OH) Summit Beacon*, September 7, 1853, 3; "A Humilating [*sic*] Fact," *Warren (OH) Western Reserve Chronicle*, May 28, 1856, 2; "The Campaign: Radical Meeting at the Columbia Last Evening," *Cincinnati Enquirer*, August 15, 1868, 1; "George Hoadly," s.v., *Ohio History Central*, http://www.ohiohistorycentral.org/w/George_Hoadly. Hoadly supported Samuel Tilden, the Democrat, in 1876, and became governor of Ohio as a Democrat in 1884. He recounted his political evolution in a speech reprinted under "Democratic Ratification, in Avondale Last Night," *Stark County Democrat*, July 27, 1876, 6.

38. Hereafter, all references to dates in the motions of the case through the court are drawn from Appearance and Judgment Dockets, vol. 5, 1431, US Circuit Court, Southern District of Ohio, Cincinnati, RG 21, National Archives at Chicago, hereafter cited as Chicago Docket.

39. "Zeb. Ward in Trouble," *Nashville Union and American*, January 15, 1871; "The Dregs of American Slavery," *Cincinnati Gazette*, January 16, 1871; Chicago Docket; Chicago Case File.

40. Chicago Docket; Chicago Case File.

CHAPTER TWENTY-ONE

1. Lawrence M. Friedman, *A History of American Law* (New York: Simon & Schuster, 1973), 126–34, 278–82.
2. Kellen Funk and Lincoln A. Mullen, "The Spine of American Law: Digital Text Analysis and U.S. Legal Practice," *American Historical Review* 123, no. 1 (February 2018): 132–64; Friedman, *A History of American Law*, 340–58.
3. Friedman, *A History of American Law*, 342–43, 348; Howard Schweber, *The Creation of American Common Law, 1850–1880* (New York: Cambridge University Press, 2004), 16–21.
4. For the history of "trespass" versus "case" in English common law, see D. J. Ibbetson, *A Historical Introduction to the Law of Obligations* (New York: Oxford University Press, 1999); C. H. S. Fifoot, *History and Sources of the Common Law: Tort and Contract* (1949; New York: Greenwood, 1970), 44–92, 184–213.
5. See Mitchell G. Williams, "Pleading Reform in Nineteenth-Century America: The Joinder of Actions at Common Law and Under the Codes," *Journal of Legal History* 6, no. 3 (1985): 307.
6. Wood's lawyers also departed from the standard actions chosen by attorneys in Southern wrongful enslavement suits before abolition. In most of those cases, notes Robert Westley, "plaintiffs alleged assault and battery or false imprisonment—using the archaic form of *trespass vi et armis*," though they sometimes claimed "*indebitatus assumpsit* in an action at equity," particularly when they wanted to pursue "restitution for the value of service rendered." The latter option may have seemed unavailable to Wood's lawyers, however, because of the slow disappearance of "equity" suits in the nineteenth century and because Ward had not actually exploited Wood's labor for most of the time under dispute in the case. See Westley, "Restitution Claims for Wrongful Enslavement and the Doctrine of the Master's Good Faith," 306–9; Kennington, *In the Shadow of Dred Scott*, 25–40.
7. Thanks to Kellen Funk for alerting me to the significance of the Conformity Act. For context, see Stephen B. Burbank, "The Rules Enabling Act of 1934," *University of Pennsylvania Law Review* 130, no. 5 (May 1982): 1015–197.
8. Chicago Case File.
9. Ibid.
10. "The Deadly Deringer," *Louisville Courier-Journal*, March 30, 1874, reprinted from *Cincinnati Enquirer*, March 29, 1874; "Meeting of the Grant and Wilson Club," *Cincinnati Enquirer*, September 9, 1872, 7.
11. A description of the shooting can be found in "The Deadly Deringer"; "Terrell's Trial for the Murder of Harvey Myers," *Cincinnati Enquirer*, September 23, 1879.
12. *Williams' Cincinnati Directory* (Cincinnati: Directory Office, 1875), 849, 999; Chicago Docket. The entry for "Woods Henrietta" describes her as a "widow."

She appears at the same address in every city directory through 1880. Wood and Simms do not appear in the city directories between 1870 and 1874, suggesting they remained in Covington until then.

13. Mancini, *One Dies, Get Another*, 119–20.
14. Garland E. Bayliss, "The Arkansas State Penitentiary Under Democratic Control, 1874–1896," *Arkansas Historical Quarterly* 34, no. 3 (Autumn 1975): 198–99; Arkansas, Pulaski Co., 1845–1878, vol. 11, 288, R. G. Dun & Co. Credit Report Volumes, Baker Library, Harvard Business School.
15. Chicago Docket.
16. Chicago Case File.
17. Ibid.
18. Ibid.; Chicago Docket.
19. Chicago Docket.
20. Bronner, *Lafcadio Hearn's America*, 8; Hughes, *Period of the Gruesome*; John Clubbe, "The Forging of a Writer: Lafcadio Hearn in Cincinnati," *Ohio Valley History* 7, no. 1 (Spring 2007): 1–31.
21. Cott, *Wandering Ghost*, 28–29, 38–61.
22. Taylor, *Frontiers of Freedom*, 185–202; Cott, *Wandering Ghost*, 81–109.
23. Lafcadio Hearn, *Children of the Levee*, ed. O. W. Frost (Lexington: University of Kentucky Press, 1957), 44–46. See also 62.
24. Hearn, *Children of the Levee*, 63.
25. Ibid., 33–48, quoted on 35. See also Taylor, *Frontiers of Freedom*, 187.
26. LH-1876.

CHAPTER TWENTY-TWO

1. LH-1876.
2. Ibid.; "The Terrell-Myers Tragedy," *Cincinnati Enquirer*, March 30, 1874, 4; "The Myers Murder—The Funeral Yesterday—An Impressive Demonstration," *Cincinnati Enquirer*, April 1, 1874, 7; "The Myers Murder—Bar Meeting Yesterday," *Cincinnati Enquirer*, March 31, 1874, 5.
3. LH-1876; Hearn, *Children of the Levee*, 79.
4. Summary of Hearn's interview in *Covington Journal*, April 8, 1876; Chicago Docket.
5. Chicago Docket. Kinkead died the following year, and the deposition he gave is no longer extant.
6. "A Celebrated Case," *Cincinnati Enquirer*, April 16, 1878; "Kidnaping of the Slave Times," *Louisville Courier-Journal*, April 17, 1878, reprinting report from *Cincinnati Commercial* dated April 16. See also "A Slave Case," *Cincinnati Daily Gazette*, April 16, 1878; "The Courts," *Cincinnati Daily Star*, April 16, 1878; Circuit Court Order Book S, 231, US Circuit Court, Southern District of Ohio, RG 21, Civil Records, National Archives at Chicago. Juries at the time remained all-white. See Nancy S. Marder, "The Changing Composition

of the American Jury," in *Then & Now: Stories of Law and Progress*, ed. Lori Andrews and Sarah Harding (Chicago: IIT Chicago–Kent College of Law, 2013).

7. Circuit Court Order Book S, 231.

8. *Brooklyn Daily Eagle*, April 18, 1878; "A Relic of Slavery Times," *Philadelphia Times*, April 18, 1878, reprinting "Cincinnati Dispatch to the *New York Herald*."

9. Foner, *Reconstruction*, 454–59, 553–56.

10. Ibid., 512–63. See also Heather Cox Richardson, *The Death of Reconstruction: Race, Labor, and Politics in the Post–Civil War North, 1865–1901* (Cambridge, MA: Harvard University Press, 2001).

11. Richard White, *The Republic for Which It Stands: The United States During Reconstruction and the Gilded Age, 1865–1896* (New York: Oxford University Press, 2017), 192, 203; Blight, *Race and Reunion*, 123.

12. Ames quoted in White, *Republic for Which It Stands*, 305. See also Lemann, *Redemption*. On the Freedman's Bank, Levy, *Freaks of Fortune*, 104–49; Foner, *Reconstruction*, 531–32.

13. Foner, *Reconstruction*, 557–58, 562.

14. "An Innocent Woman Lynched," *Somerset (PA) Herald*, April 24, 1878. See Williams, *They Left Great Marks on Me*.

15. Foner, *Reconstruction*, 529–31.

16. "A Slave's Claims," *Pittsburgh Daily Post*, April 17, 1878; "A Celebrated Case," *Cincinnati Enquirer*, April 16, 1878.

17. Circuit Court Order Book, Volume S, 232–33.

18. Renée Lettow Lerner, "The Rise of Directed Verdict: Jury Power in Civil Cases Before the Federal Rules of 1938," *George Washington Law Review* 81, no. 2 (2013): 448–525.

19. Roberta Sue Alexander, *A Place of Recourse: A History of the US District Court for the Southern District of Ohio, 1803–2003* (Athens: Ohio University Press, 2005), 63, 73, 276.

20. "US Circuit Court of the SD of Ohio: Henrietta Wood vs. Zeb Ward—Judge Swing's Charge," *American Law Record* (Cincinnati: Bloch, 1872–77), vol. 6, 675–81, hereafter cited as "Judge Swing's Charge."

21. Ibid., 676–77.

22. Ibid., 679. The case cited by Swing, *Collins v. America*, was one of several that showed the rise of "reversion" and "reattachment" of slave status in antebellum court decisions: see Patricia Hagler Minter, "'The State of Slavery': Somerset, the Slave, Grace, and the Rise of Pro-Slavery and Anti-Slavery Constitutionalism in the Nineteenth-Century Atlantic World," *Slavery and Abolition* 36, no. 4 (2015): 603–17; Finkelman, *An Imperfect Union*, 187–88.

23. "Judge Swing's Charge," 680.

24. Ibid., 679.

25. Ibid.

26. Ibid., 681.

27. The jury's verdict is included in Chicago Case File.

28. Chicago Case File.

29. "A Curious Case," *Paw Paw (MI) True Northerner*, April 26, 1878; "A Remarkable Suit," *Galveston Weekly News*, April 29, 1878; "Damages for Sale into Slavery," *New Orleans Daily Picayune*, April 22, 1878, reprinting "Chicago Times."

30. "An Old Wrong Righted," *New York Herald*, April 19, 1878; "A Slaves's [sic] Triumph," *York (PA) Daily*, April 19, 1878; "The Good Old Times: The Suit of Henrietta Wood, of Cincinnati—Heavy Damages Granted by the Jury," *New York Times*, April 18, 1878; "Retribution at Last," *Montpelier (VT) Green-Mountain Freeman*, April 24, 1878; *Cincinnati Daily Gazette*, April 18, 1878; "Long-Delayed Justice," *San Francisco Daily Evening Bulletin*, February 25, 1879.

31. *Worcester Daily Spy*, April 20, 1878; "The Price of Liberty," *Chicago Inter Ocean*, May 3, 1878.

32. For "trifling recompense" see *St. Albans (VT) Daily Messenger*, March 3, 1879; "Fact and Rumor," *Christian Union* (New York), April 24, 1878, 356; *Cincinnati Daily Gazette*, February 17, 1879, 4.

33. "An Old Wrong Righted."

34. *Brooklyn Daily Eagle*, April 18, 1878, 2; "A Relic of Slavery Times," *Philadelphia Times*, April 18, 1878; *New York Daily Tribune*, April 19, 1878, 5; *Cincinnati Daily Gazette*, February 17, 1879, 4. Despite the claim made by the *Tribune*, the end of slavery did lead to numerous "complications of a legal nature," particularly in Southern courts. See Joseph A. Ranney, *In the Wake of Slavery: Civil War, Civil Rights, and the Reconstruction of Southern Law* (Westport, CT: Praeger, 2006); Giuliana Perrone, "Litigating Emancipation: Legacies of Slavery in the Post-Emancipation United States," *LSE Human Rights Blog*, October 19, 2015, http://blogs.lse.ac.uk/humanrights/2015/10/19/litigating-emancipation-legacies-of-slavery-in-the-post-emancipation-united-states/. In one 1874 case in South Carolina, a plaintiff successfully won $800 in a jury trial for a wrong done to the plaintiff while he was still a slave. But the state Supreme Court overturned the decision: "To permit those who were slaves and are now free to bring actions and carry on prosecutions against persons who were or were not slaves, for wrongs and injuries committed against them during the existence of slavery, would open the door to a flood of litigation that would prove disastrous to all classes of persons in the State." See *Russell v. Cantwell*, 5 SC 477 (1874).

35. "An Unsettled Account," *New York Times*, April 21, 1878.

36. "The Ward-Woods Case," *Cincinnati Enquirer*, April 18, 1878, 4. The same article wrongly reported that it was Wood's lawyers who filed for a retrial.

37. Baxter's history is documented in Robert Tracy McKenzie, *Lincolnites and Rebels: A Divided Town in the American Civil War* (New York: Oxford

University Press, 2006); Alexander, *Political Reconstruction in Tennessee*, 147–48, 232–33; Charles A. Newell Jr., "Baxter, John," in *Dictionary of North Carolina Biography*, vol. 1 (Chapel Hill: University of North Carolina Press, 1979), 121; Oliver P. Temple, *Notable Men of Tennessee from 1833 to 1875: Their Times and Their Contemporaries* (New York: Cosmopolitan, 1912), 66–74; "Baxter, John," US Census (Slave Schedules), 1850, Henderson County, North Carolina, NARA microfilm M432, roll 653, FamilySearch.

38. "Overruled: Judge Baxter's Decision in a Famous Kidnaping Case," *Cincinnati Commercial*, February 16, 1879.

39. Ibid.

40. Ibid. On the legal fictions that made freedom suits possible, see Welch, *Black Litigants in the Antebellum American South*, 165–67; Fede, *Roadblocks to Freedom*, 139–69.

41. "Overruled."

42. Ibid.

43. Ibid.

44. "Res Adjudicata: Wood v. Ward," *St. Louis Central Law Journal* 8, no. 10 (March 7, 1879): 191.

45. RB-1879.

46. Ibid.

47. Chicago Docket.

48. Chicago Case File.

EPILOGUE

1. "Henrietta Woods" and "Arthur H. Sims," US Census, 1880, Enumeration District 9, Chicago, Cook County, Illinois, NARA microfilm T9, roll 184, FamilySearch.

2. "Smile of Time." See Christopher Robert Reed, *Black Chicago's First Century* (Columbia: University of Missouri Press, 2005), 171–227; Margaret Garb, *Freedom's Ballot: African American Political Struggles in Chicago from Abolition to the Great Migration* (Chicago: University of Chicago Press, 2014).

3. "Smile of Time"; 1880 Census; see numerous results for a search for "Simms, Arthur" in the Chicago City Directories collection, Fold3 database. These jobs were common but near the bottom of an emerging occupational hierarchy in black Chicago. See Reed, *Black Chicago's First Century*, 241–66.

4. On the marriage, see "Smile of Time" and Arthur H. Simms and Caroline Person, June 21, 1883, in "Ohio Marriages, 1800–1958," database, FamilySearch. On the birth of Arthur Simms Jr., see record of his birth certificate, No. 55310, April 10, 1884, in "Illinois, Cook County, Birth Certificates, 1871–1940," database, FamilySearch.

5. "Simms, Arthur H.," s.v., in "College of Law," *Catalogue of the Northwestern University, and the Garrett Biblical Institute, Evanston, Ill., 1887–88* (Evanston,

IL: [Northwestern University], 1888), 127. On race and Pullman's preferences for porters, see Larry Tye, *Rising from the Rails: Pullman Porters and the Making of the Black Middle Class* (New York: Henry Holt, 2004), 1–29. For history of the Union College of Law, see James A. Rahl and Kurt Schwerin, *Northwestern University School of Law: A Short History* (Chicago: Northwestern University Law School, 1960), 5–11; James E. Babb, "Union College of Law, Chicago," *The Green Bag* 1, no. 8 (August 1889): 330–38. Another famous alumnus was future governor of Illinois Frank O. Lowden, who graduated valedictorian from the college in 1887 (completing the two-year program in one) and married Florence Pullman, the daughter of the famous railroad car manufacturer, perhaps increasing the plausibility of Simms's memory that he had once met Pullman himself: see "Smile of Time." A diploma from the college admitted graduates to the Illinois Bar automatically. On the rise of law schools in this period, see Friedman, *A History of American Law*, 525–38.

6. Cook County Tract Book 356-D, 358; Document 6,44,592, Book 1603, 229, both in the office of the Cook County Recorder of Deeds (hereafter CCRD). A later, though unlikely, family story held that Pullman himself had paid for the porter's education. Perhaps a memory of the wages Simms had earned had mutated into a story about a wealthy patron.

7. Margaret Garb, *City of American Dreams: A History of Home Ownership and Housing Reform in Chicago, 1871–1919* (Chicago: University of Chicago Press, 2005), 38–39.

8. For the lawyer's suit, see *Cincinnati Daily Gazette*, December 15, 1879.

9. "Smile of Time."

10. Cook County Tract Book 356-D, 358, CCRD. See "Chicago Investments," *Indianapolis Freeman*, December 26, 1891; "Chicago Real Estate," *Indianapolis Freeman*, April 23, 1892. On lending practices, see Elaine Lewinnek, *The Working Man's Reward: Chicago's Early Suburbs and the Roots of American Sprawl* (New York: Oxford University Press, 2014). Simms was not alone in using real estate investments as a means of acquiring cash. Similar practices are documented in Garb, *City of American Dreams*, 36–59.

11. See "Union College of Law" in *Northwestern University Thirty-First Annual Commencement, Thursday, 10 a.m., June 20, 1889* (Evanston, IL: [Northwestern University], 1889); "Arthur H. Simms," Northwestern University Archives, Alumni Biographical Files, School of Law, Series 51/5, box 3, Class of 1889; "Admitted to Practice," *Chicago Daily Inter Ocean*, June 13, 1889. Simms's position at the Harrison Street Police Court, which was at a border between a black residential area and a vice district, is mentioned in "Smile of Time" and confirmed in *Journal of the Proceedings of the City Council of the City of Chicago for the Municipal Year, 1891 and 1892* (Chicago: John F. Higgins, 1892), liv, 118. At the time the Harrison Street Police Court was at the center of debates about black criminality and segregation in the city: see David

A. Joens, *From Slave to State Legislator: John W. E. Thomas, Illinois' First African American Lawmaker* (Carbondale: Southern Illinois University Press, 2012), 52–53; Garb, *City of American Dreams*, 181–82. On the rise of black lawyers in Chicago during the period, see J. Clay Smith Jr., *Emancipation: The Making of the Black Lawyer, 1844–1944* (Philadelphia: University of Pennsylvania Press, 1993), 369–86. For examples of the cases Simms took, see references to him in *Chicago Inter Ocean* from the 1910s, found on Newspapers.com.

12. "St. Mark Literary, State and 47th Streets," *Broad Ax*, February 11, 1905; "Englewood Notes," *Broad Ax*, April 22, 1905. On Simms and mercantile associations, see *Chicago Tribune*, December 10, 1891, 14; "The Empire Mercantile Association," *Indianapolis Freeman*, April 30, 1892; *Colored People's Blue Book and Business Directory of Chicago, Ill., 1905* (Chicago: Celerity, 1905), 81. The capital stock of the first of these mercantile associations was $100,000 at its incorporation. On the literary societies, see *Colored People's Blue Book*, 85; Anne Meis Knupfer, *Toward a Tenderer Humanity and a Nobler Womanhood: African American Women's Clubs in Turn-of-the-Century Chicago* (New York: New York University Press, 1996), 108–22. According to "Smile of Time," Simms eventually joined the Berean Baptist Church.

13. "In Chicago and Its Suburbs," *Chicago Defender*, March 30, 1912; "Deaths of the Week," *Chicago Defender*, December 7, 1912; Wood Death Certificate. Per email from Eliza Hill of Dignity Memorial (which now manages Lincoln) on October 24, 2015, Wood's grave has no headstone, but a burial record card shows that hers was burial number 462 at the cemetery, and her grave can be found in Lot 3, Section 3, Row 1, Grave 6. The burial record card gives her age as ninety-four years.

14. Quotes are from author's interviews of Winona Adkins, great-granddaughter of Arthur Simms, by phone, February 29, 2016; and in Oakland, CA, February 18, 2017. The jazz musician was her uncle, William Adkins, who died in 2001 and recorded and toured with Count Basie. The Tuskegee airman was her father, Winston A. Adkins. Her brother, Geoffrey Adkins, was a medical doctor specializing in obstetrics and gynecology, and their mother was the librarian. See LeAnn Spencer, "Saxophonist William Adkins, Mainstay in Chicago Jazz," *Chicago Tribune*, March 6, 2001; "Tuskegee Airmen Pilot Listing," Tuskegee University website, https://www.tuskegee.edu/support-tu/tuskegee-airmen/tuskegee-airmen-pilot-listing; obituary for Dr. Geoffrey Adkins, published in *Chicago Sun-Times*, August 10, 2011; "Death Notice: Marjorie R. Adkins," *Chicago Tribune*, September 22, 2009.

15. "The Week's Census," *Jet*, November 1, 1951, 25. Date for transfer of records from email by Douglas Bicknese to author, March 6, 2018.

16. Other biographers and historians have also experienced the strange mixture of intimacy with and distance from their subjects that I also have come to feel, a position with opportunities for both better understanding and misunderstanding

a historical subject's experience. See Jill Lepore, "Historians Who Love Too Much: Reflections on Microhistory and Biography," *Journal of American History* 88, no. 1 (June 2001): 129–44; Craig Thompson Friend, "Lunsford Lane and Me: Life-Writings and Public Histories of an Enslaved Other," *Journal of the Early Republic* 39, no. 1 (Spring 2019): 1–26; Arlette Farge, *The Allure of the Archives*, trans. Thomas Scott-Railton (New Haven, CT: Yale University Press, 2013); Greg Childs, "Insanity, the Historian, and the Slave Catcher: 'Capturing' Black Voices," *Black Perspectives*, February 15, 2015, and Christopher Bonner, "Why Do History?," *Black Perspectives*, February 25, 2015, both at https://www.aaihs.org. Throughout this book, I have referred to people primarily by their full or last names, with some rare exceptions in the case of primary subjects such as Wood, Brandon, Simms, and Ward, where a first name felt better suited to the context or helped to differentiate individuals.

17. See works surveyed in Carole Emberton, "Unwriting the Freedom Narrative: A Review Essay," *Journal of Southern History* 82, no. 2 (May 2016): 377–94; Yael Sternhell, "Revisionism Reinvented? The Antiwar Turn in Civil War Scholarship," *Journal of the Civil War Era* 3, no. 2 (June 2013): 239–56. Also see Downs, *Sick from Freedom*; Gregory P. Downs and Kate Masur, eds., *The World the Civil War Made* (Chapel Hill: University of North Carolina Press, 2015); David W. Blight and Jim Downs, eds., *Beyond Freedom: Disrupting the History of Emancipation* (Athens: University of Georgia Press, 2017). Cf. Thavolia Glymph, "'Between Slavery and Freedom': Rethinking the Slaves' War," paper delivered at The Future of the African American Past conference, Washington, DC, May 19–21, 2016, online at https://futureafampast.si.edu/conference-papers.

18. Douglas A. Blackmon, *Slavery by Another Name: The Re-Enslavement of Black Americans from the Civil War to World War II* (New York: Doubleday, 2008); Michelle Alexander, *The New Jim Crow: Mass Incarceration in the Age of Colorblindness* (New York: New Press, 2010). On the Thirteenth Amendment loophole, see Dennis Childs, *Slaves of the State: Black Incarceration from the Chain Gang to the Penitentiary* (Minneapolis: University of Minnesota Press, 2015), 57–92.

19. Stephen Kantrowitz, *More Than Freedom: Fighting for Black Citizenship in a White Republic, 1829–1889* (New York: Penguin, 2012); Rosen, *Terror in the Heart of Freedom*; Neil Roberts, *Freedom as Marronage* (Chicago: University of Chicago Press, 2015). For other examples of books looking at a particular life or family as a way to gauge larger questions about slavery and emancipation, see Erica Armstrong Dunbar, *Never Caught: The Washingtons' Relentless Pursuit of Their Runaway Slave, Ona Judge* (New York: Atria, 2017); Rothman, *Beyond Freedom's Reach*; Sydney Nathans, *To Free a Family: The Journey of Mary Walker* (Cambridge, MA: Harvard University Press, 2012); Nathans, *A Mind to Stay: White Plantation, Black Homeland* (Cambridge, MA: Harvard University Press, 2017); Rebecca J. Scott and Jean M. Hebrard, *Freedom*

Papers: An Atlantic Odyssey in the Age of Emancipation (Cambridge, MA: Harvard University Press, 2012). See also Sue Peabody, "Microhistory, Biography, Fiction: The Politics of Narrating the Lives of People Under Slavery," *Transatlantica* 2 (2012), http://transatlantica.revues.org/6184; Emberton, "Unwriting the Freedom Narrative," 394.

20. Coates's article, which first appeared in 2014, is reprinted in his *We Were Eight Years in Power: An American Tragedy* (New York: One World, 2017), 163–208. On the resurgence of reparations debates in the first decade of this century, see Araujo, *Reparations for Slavery and the Slave Trade*, 179–84; Salamishah Tillet, *Sites of Slavery: Citizenship and Racial Democracy in the Post-Civil Rights Imagination* (Durham, NC: Duke University Press, 2012), 133–67; Alfred L. Brophy, *Reparations: Pro & Con* (New York: Oxford University Press, 2006); Martha Biondi, "The Rise of the Reparations Movement," *Radical History Review* no. 87 (Fall 2003): 5–18.

21. For Ward's story about the check, see the prologue. I first learned of that story in an email from Katherine Mooney, dated April 28, 2015.

22. William Darity argues for a legislative approach to reparations partly because, unlike reparations by judicial fiat, any successful legislation would require "public recognition of a grievous injustice." He notes that the greatest obstacle to such a law is "the depth of opposition to such a program." See William Darity Jr., "Forty Acres and a Mule in the 21st Century," *Social Science Quarterly* 89, no. 3 (September 2008): 656–64, quotes on 656 and 659. For a critique of a "litigation" model of reparations on similar grounds, see Roy L. Brooks, *Atonement and Forgiveness: A New Model for Black Reparations* (Berkeley: University of California Press, 2004), 98–100. For a survey of the historical arguments used both by advocates and critics of redress for slavery, see Ariela Gross, "When Is the Time of Slavery? The History of Slavery in Contemporary Legal and Political Argument," *California Law Review* 96 (2008): 203–321. For examples of some of the antireparations arguments I in turn summarize here, see Brophy, *Reparations*, 75–94; George Lipsitz, *The Possessive Investment in Whiteness: How White People Profit from Identity Politics* (Philadelphia: Temple University Press, 1998), 20.

23. Berry, *My Face Is Black Is True*; Benjamin William Arnett, *The Black Laws: Speech of Hon. B. W. Arnett of Greene County . . . in the Ohio House of Representatives, March 10, 1886* (Columbus: Ohio State Journal, 1886), 16–17. On the 1916 case of *Johnson v. MacAdoo* as the "first known reparations lawsuit," see Tillet, *Sites of Slavery*, 141; Brooks, *Atonement and Forgiveness*, 119. Robert Westley notes that when we "ask the post-emancipation question of when was the proper time to seek reparations for slavery, the resounding response that comes down through ages of resistance to racial oppression is not yet, perhaps never." See Westley, "Restitution Claims for Wrongful Enslavement and the Doctrine of the Master's Good Faith," 292; Westley, "The Accursed Share," 85–91.

24. Bayliss, "The Arkansas State Penitentiary Under Democratic Control, 1874–1896"; Jane Zimmerman, "The Convict Lease System in Arkansas and the Fight for Abolition," *Arkansas Historical Quarterly* 8, no. 3 (Autumn 1949): 171–88; Calvin R. Ledbetter Jr., "The Long Struggle to End Convict Leasing in Arkansas," *Arkansas Historical Quarterly* 52, no. 1 (Spring 1993): 1–27; Henry Williams Gilmore, "The Convict Lease System in Arkansas" (master's thesis, Arkansas State Teachers College, 1930); Mancini, *One Dies, Get Another*, 117–20. For a description of convict labor on Ward's cotton farm, "The New Arkansas Traveler," *Topeka (KS) Commonwealth*, October 7, 1875.

25. George Washington Cable, *The Silent South, Together with The Freedman's Case in Equity and the Convict Lease System* (1885; New York: Charles Scribner's Sons, 1907), 16, 170–73; "Southern Prison Horrors," *Chicago Inter Ocean*, February 15, 1890. Though the 1890 article was unsigned, other evidence points to Tourgée's authorship. See Carolyn L. Karcher, A *Refugee from His Race: Albion W. Tourgée and His Fight Against White Supremacy* (Chapel Hill: University of North Carolina Press, 2016), 103–4; "Sheol! The Terrible Convict System of the South," *Cleveland Gazette*, April 12, 1890, 1; "Worse Than Death: The Ills Which Afro-American Convicts Endure in the South," *Detroit Plain Dealer*, March 14, 1890. On Ward's unwillingness to share information while lessee, see his letters in Cable, *Silent South*, 125 (quote); "Infamies of the Southern Convict Lease System," *New York Globe*, February 2, 1884.

26. *Report of the Board of Commissioners for the Leasing, Management, and Regulation of the Arkansas State Penitentiary* ... (Little Rock, AR: W. E. Woodruff Jr., 1875), quoted on 2; Mancini, *One Dies, Get Another*, 119–20. See also Senate Executive Document 13, 44th Cong., 1st sess., 11–14; "Arkansas Letter," *Cincinnati Enquirer*, March 13, 1877; "The Whipping Post," *Arkansas Gazette*, February 9, 1879; *Fort Smith New Era*, March 5, 1879, 2, and December 17, 1879, 3.

27. Opie Read, *I Remember* (New York: R. R. Smith, 1930), 146. For other versions of the story, see "A Story of Col. Zeb Ward," *Little Rock Arkansas Gazette*, October 3, 1888; *Nashville Tennessean*, September 5, 1888; *Independence (KS) Daily Reporter*, June 26, 1886, with slight variation; "Took Gen. Grant's Place," *Washington Evening Star*, October 29, 1888.

28. "Col. Zeb Ward," *Louisville Courier-Journal*, December 14, 1887; *Cincinnati Enquirer*, May 23, 1889, 8. See also Wall, *How Kentucky Became Southern*, 1.

29. *Arkansas Gazette*, March 23, 1880, 8; "Col. Ward Interviewed," *Arkansas Gazette*, June 29, 1889, 5, reprinting *Memphis Ledger*. See also "Out-of-Town People," *St. Louis Republic*, January 4, 1894, 5; "Louisville Gives Up the Lucre," *Arkansas Gazette*, February 24, 1895; "Little Rock Notes," *Memphis Public Ledger*, June 6, 1879, 2; "Men of Means," *Arkansas Gazette*, April 22, 1890, 8; Dallas T. Herndon, *The Highlights of Arkansas History* (Little Rock: Arkansas History Commission, 1922), 131.

30. *Little Rock Daily Arkansas Gazette*, June 25, 1886. See also March 9 issue; "Local Paragraphs," *Arkansas Gazette*, January 6, 1885.

31. "The Negro Exodus," *Anderson (SC) Intelligencer*, December 11, 1884; *Memphis Appeal*, February 5, 1885, 4. See also *Arkansas Democrat*, December 5, 1884, which reports Williams passing through Atlanta with a "party of 250 negro laborers bound for Morrilton, Ark. They will be employed on Zeb Ward's farm in place of convict labor." On Peg Leg Williams and labor recruiters, see also Kenneth C. Barnes, *Journey of Hope: The Back-to-Africa Movement in Arkansas in the Late 1800s* (Chapel Hill: University of North Carolina Press, 2004), 37; William F. Holmes, "Labor Agents and the Georgia Exodus, 1899–1900," *South Atlantic Quarterly* 79 (Autumn 1980): 436–48; Karl Jacoby, *The Strange Career of William Ellis: The Texas Slave Who Became a Mexican Millionaire* (New York: W. W. Norton, 2016), 91–93.

32. The value of Ward's estate, consisting "largely of improved property in Little Rock, and of valuable plantations," is estimated in "Busy Life Ended." One calculation compares the relative value of $600,000 from 1894 to $17.6 million in 2017. See Samuel H. Williamson, "Seven Ways to Compute the Relative Value of a U.S. Dollar Amount, 1774 to present," *MeasuringWorth*, https://www.measuringworth.com/uscompare/. On convict leasing in the New South, see Mancini, *One Dies, Get Another*; Alex Lichtenstein, *Twice the Work of Free Labor: The Political Economy of Convict Labor in the New South* (London: Verso, 1996); David M. Oshinsky, *"Worse Than Slavery": Parchman Farm and the Ordeal of Jim Crow Justice* (New York: Free Press, 1996); Talitha L. LeFlouria, *Chained in Silence: Black Women and Convict Labor in the New South* (Chapel Hill: University of North Carolina Press, 2015); Sarah Haley, *No Mercy Here: Gender, Punishment, and the Making of Jim Crow Modernity* (Chapel Hill: University of North Carolina Press, 2016).

33. On the Great Migration, see Isabel Wilkerson, *The Warmth of Other Suns: The Epic Story of America's Great Migration* (New York: Random House, 2010); James R. Grossman, *Land of Hope: Chicago, Black Southerners, and the Great Migration* (Chicago: University of Chicago Press, 1989). On the riot, see Lewinnek, *Working Man's Reward*, 151–77.

34. "Acquit Seven of Riot Murders," *Chicago Defender*, September 27, 1919; "Attorney F. A. McDonnell Speaks at Movement," *Chicago Defender*, October 4, 1919; "In the Grip of the Law," *Chicago Defender*, February 7 and February 28, 1920. See also Chicago Commission on Race Relations, *The Negro in Chicago: A Study of Race Relations and a Race Riot* (Chicago: University of Chicago Press, 1922), 26–28; Khalil Gibran Muhammad, *The Condemnation of Blackness: Race, Crime, and the Making of Modern Urban America* (Cambridge, MA: Harvard University Press, 2010).

35. Home Owner's Loan Corporation map description from Robert K. Nelson, LaDale Winling, Richard Marciano, Nathan Connolly, et al., "Mapping Inequality," *American Panorama*, ed. Robert K. Nelson and Edward L. Ayers,

accessed March 14, 2018, https://dsl.richmond.edu/panorama/redlining/
#loc=15/41.7910/-87.6222&opacity=0.8&sort=295&area=D74&city
=chicago-il. See also Garb, *City of American Dreams*, 177–207; Richard
Rothstein, *The Color of Law: A Forgotten History of How Our Government
Segregated America* (New York: Liveright, 2017), 59–75; Thomas Lee Philpott,
*The Slum and the Ghetto: Neighborhood Deterioration and Middle-Class
Reform, Chicago, 1880–1930* (New York: Oxford University Press, 1978),
146–200.

36. "Address by Dr. Martin Luther King Jr. to the Chicago Freedom Movement
Rally, Soldier Field, Chicago, Illinois, Sunday, July 10, 1966," available at The
King Center website, www.thekingcenter.org. See also Beryl Satter, *Family
Properties: How the Struggle over Race and Real Estate Transformed Chicago
and Urban America* (New York: Metropolitan, 2009). On the racial wealth
gap, see William Darity Jr., Darrick Hamilton, Mark Paul, et al., *What We Get
Wrong About Closing the Racial Wealth Gap* (Durham, NC: Samuel DuBois
Cook Center on Social Equity, 2018).

37. My thanks to Douglas Bicknese and his dedicated staff for all their help, and
for his permission to quote him below.

38. Chicago Case File.

APPENDIX: AN ESSAY ON SOURCES

1. Deborah Gray White, "Mining the Forgotten: Manuscript Sources for Black
Women's History," *Journal of American History* 74, no. 1 (June 1987), 237–42.

2. See Fuentes, *Dispossessed Lives*; Brian Connolly and Marisa Fuentes, eds.,
"From Archives of Slavery to Liberated Futures?," special issue of *History of
the Present* 6, no. 2 (Fall 2016); Laura Helton, Justin Leroy, Max A. Mishler,
et al., eds., "The Question of Recovery: Slavery, Freedom, and the Archive,"
special issue of *Social Text* 33, no. 4 (December 2015); Saidiya Hartman,
"Venus in Two Acts," *Small Axe* 12, no. 2 (June 2008): 1–14; Maria R. Montalvo,
"The Slavers' Archive: Enslaved People, Power, and the Production of the Past
in the Antebellum Courtroom" (PhD diss., Rice University, 2018).

3. On the ways enslaved people marshaled memories of physical markings and
other information to locate loved ones after emancipation, see Williams, *Help
Me to Find My People*, 153–88. In seeing Wood as a theorist of her own
attempted erasure from the archive, I am informed by Mia Bay, Farah J. Griffin,
Martha S. Jones, et al., eds., *Toward an Intellectual History of Black Women*
(Chapel Hill: University of North Carolina Press, 2015); David Kazanjian,
"Freedom's Surprise: Two Paths Through Slavery's Archives," *History of the
Present* 6, no. 2 (Fall 2016): 133–45.

4. "Franklin County, 1856," 2, Kentucky Birth, Marriage and Death Records
(1852–1910), Microfilm #994027–994058, KDLA, Ancestry.com. The entry
discussed here is fourth from the bottom.

5. On the ambiguity in records of racial identity, see Hodes, "The Mercurial Nature and Abiding Power of Race."
6. *Bullittsburg Baptist Church Ledger Books*, images digitized from microfilm by Boone County Public Library. Transcriptions of some of the books are available on the Baptist History Homepage, http://baptisthistoryhomepage.com/bullittsbrg.minutes.index.html. For Terrill and the baptisms, see June 4, 1809; January 5, 1811; January 20, 1811; and April 5, 1812. See John Boles, ed., *Masters and Slaves in the House of the Lord: Race and Religion in the American South, 1740–1870* (Lexington: University Press of Kentucky, 1988); Ellen Eslinger, "The Beginnings of Afro-American Christianity Among Kentucky Baptists," in Friend, *The Buzzel About Kentuck*, 198–215.
7. *Bullittsburg Baptist Church Ledger Books*, entries for January 20, 1811; November 7, 1812; and February 4, 1817. See also Friend, *Kentucke's Frontiers*, 201.
8. *Bullittsburg Baptist Church Ledger Books*, entries for November 7, 1812; February 5, 1814; and August 1825. On the possibilities and limits of using a church to win public recognition of familial ties, see Hunter, *Bound in Wedlock*, 54–59; Stevenson, *Life in Black and White*, 244–45.
9. *Bullittsburg Church Ledger Books*, entries for August 1826; February 5, 1814; May 3, 1817; and June 5, 1819.
10. *Bullittsburg Baptist Church Ledger Books*, entries for July 1819.
11. Another "Daphne" owned by Michael Glore was also mentioned in the church minutes. For evidence of Terrill's move, see *Bullittsburg Baptist Church Ledger Books*, entry for June 1827; "John Terrill," US Census, 1820, Burlington, Boone County, Kentucky, NARA microfilm M33, roll 18, FamilySearch. Terrill appears only four lines below Moses Tousey in that census. See also "Terrill Family," *Chronicles of Boone County*, BCPL, https://www.bcpl.org/cbc/doku.php/terrill_family.
12. I thank Gerard Rickey for pointing out to me that there was another black woman named "Henrietta" associated with the extended Brandon family, as noted in Brandon, *The Brandon Family*, 72. In that memoir, Gerard Brandon's nephew speaks of a "faithful colored servant Henrietta" who had worked for the James C. Brandon family for a long time and was still living in 1932 at age eighty-five. She would have been a teenager at the time of Gerard Brandon's flight to Texas, and Brandon did take Phoebe, another woman owned by his brother James, to Texas, where he made special arrangements to hire her out. No such arrangements are mentioned for Henrietta, however, and a contemporary family letter that mentioned Brandon's arrangements for Phoebe made no mention of Henrietta. Nor does the mention of "Henrietta" in 1932 say decisively that she had worked for the family as a slave. See Rickey and Rayne, eds., "*I Will Write if I Have to Use a Stick*," 79. These facts, combined with evidence (such as the 1866 contract) that ties Henrietta Wood to Gerard Brandon at the time of the flight, lead me to identify the "Henrietta" in his journal as Wood.

13. Brandon Diary.

14. Entry for "Henrietta" under "Arthur Sims," US Census, 1900, Enumeration District 1080, Hyde Park Township, Chicago, Cook County, Illinois, NARA microfilm T623, FamilySearch. The woman quoted is Elvira Boles: see Litwack, *Been in the Storm so Long*, 33; Elvira Boles, El Paso, Texas, in "Born in Slavery: Slave Narratives from the Federal Writers' Project, 1936 to 1938," Library of Congress, https://www.loc.gov/resource/mesn.161/?sp=112.

15. Saidiya Hartman, "Venus in Two Acts," 2; Fuentes, *Dispossessed Lives*, 64.

16. Census records throughout this book were found on FamilySearch, as indicated in the notes. Digital databases of newspapers on Newspapers.com, GenealogyBank.com, and America's Historical Newspapers from Readex were also used to find most newspapers cited, with the exception of papers that were not digitized for the needed years, such as the *Cincinnati Commercial*, the *Cincinnati Gazette*, and the *Ripley Bee*. Except for newspapers, any record that does not have a digital source cited was found through archival research or requests from archives. On the need to combine digital search with archival search, see Lara Putnam, "The Transnational and the Text-Searchable: Digitized Sources and the Shadows They Cast," *American Historical Review* 121, no. 2 (April 2016): 377–402. For two contrasting perspectives on the use of convict labor in genealogical research, see Shane Bauer, "Your Family's Genealogical Records May Have Been Digitized by a Prisoner," *Mother Jones*, August 13, 2015; Megan Smolenyak, "Inmates Indexing Genealogy Records," *Huffington Post*, August 13, 2015.

17. It is useful to compare Wood's recollections with those of Bob Maynard, who was interviewed by the WPA at age seventy-nine, and remembered being enslaved near Falls County, Texas, by Gerard Brandon ("Gerard Branum," according to the transcript) of Natchez. Though Maynard's narrative includes the core story of Brandon's flight to Texas from Mississippi, his recollection of events is not as accurate as Wood's, not surprisingly given Maynard's young age at the time of the Civil War. My thanks to Justin Behrend for alerting me to Maynard's interview. See George P. Rawick, ed., *The American Slave: A Composite Autobiography*, vol. 7: *Oklahoma and Mississippi Narratives* (Westport, CT: Greenwood, 1972), 223–26.

18. Instead of removing the n-word from quotations from the nineteenth-century sources used in this book, which serve as evidence of what Wood was up against in her struggle for liberty and justice, I opted instead to spell out the other phrases that these sources tried to abbreviate or elide, like "G–d d–n." The decision was not an easy one, however; for an alternative approach, see Berry, *The Price for Their Pound of Flesh*.

19. Cott, *Wandering Ghost*, 60–69.

20. Hearn, *Children of the Levee*, 33, 47–48.

21. LH-1876. Hearn wrote about Cincinnati Jews in several articles, including "Haceldama," his article about the kosher butcher, and "A Hebrew College,"

Cincinnati Enquirer, July 9, 1873; Hughes, ed., *Period of the Gruesome*, 293. See also Hearn, "The Hebrews of Cincinnati," in *Barbarous Barbers*, 127–34.

22. LH-1876.

23. Hearn, *Children of the Levee*, 92.

24. Ibid., 54–60; "Mr. Handy's Life," *Cincinnati Enquirer*, January 25, 1874.

25. See "Life among the Lowly, No. 1," *Pike County Republican* (Ohio), March 17, 1873. On the Hemings family, see Annette Gordon-Reed, *The Hemingses of Monticello: An American Family* (New York: W. W. Norton, 2008). On newspaper narratives in the period, see Blassingame, *Slave Testimony*.

26. Cott, *Wandering Ghost*, 83–90.

27. Hearn, *Children of the Levee*, 66–67; Cott, *Wandering Ghost*, 84–88; Taylor, *Frontiers of Freedom*, 188.

28. Hartman, "Venus in Two Acts," 12; Stephanie Smallwood, "The Politics of the Archive and History's Accountability to the Enslaved," *History of the Present* 6, no. 2 (Fall 2016): 117–32, quoted on 125. See also Kidada E. Williams, "Maintaining a Radical Vision of African Americans in the Age of Freedom," in "Forum: The Future of Reconstruction Studies," *The Journal of the Civil War Era* (2017), https://journalofthecivilwarera.org/forum-the-future-of-reconstruction-studies/.

29. A static version of my research notebook has also been deposited for preservation in the Rice University Digital Scholarship Archive at https://scholarship.rice.edu. In treating my notes like an open notebook, my aim has been to practice what Thavolia Glymph powerfully describes as "a kind of re-archiving." See Glymph, "Black Women and Children in the Civil War: Archive Notes," in Blight and Downs, eds., *Beyond Freedom*, 123.

INDEX